An Introduction to Berkeley UNIX

Paul S. Wang

Kent State University

Wadsworth Publishing Company
Belmont, California
A Division of Wadsworth, Inc.

Computer Science Editor: Frank Ruggirello
Editorial Assistant: Reita Kinsman
Production Editor: Stacey C. Sawyer
Designer: MaryEllen Podgorski
Print Buyer: Randy Hurst
Copy Editor: Celia Teter
Compositor: Maryland Composition
Cover: John Osborne
Signing Representative: Art Minsberg

UNIX is a registered trademark of American Telephone and Telegraph Company (AT&T).

Printed in the United States of America

2 3 4 5 6 7 8 9 10—92 91 90 89 88

Library of Congress Cataloging-in-Publication Data

Wang, Paul, 1944–
    An introduction to Berkeley UNIX.

    Bibliography: p.
    Includes index.
    1. Berkeley UNIX (Computer operating system)
I. Title.
QA76.76.063W36 1988   005.4′3   87-31801
ISBN 0-534-08862-7

ISBN 0-534-08862-7

Preface

UNIX is one of the most popular operating systems today and is fast becoming the standard for the computing world. Because wide-spread use of UNIX will continue to increase, the time and energy you invest in learning UNIX is certain to pay dividends. For computer users, application programmers, administrators, and systems programmers, familiarity with the UNIX operating system means improved efficiency and effectiveness.

Of the many versions of UNIX in use today, the systems developed and supported by the University of California, Berkeley, in the early 1980s have proved to be among the most popular. Berkeley UNIX's wide acceptance and use in education and research has broadened to government and industry as well. Yet, although there are many books on UNIX, none before this has been written specifically for Berkeley UNIX. This book covers a well-selected set of topics suitable for a number of courses on UNIX programming. And although perfectly suitable as a user's first book on UNIX, *An Introduction to Berkeley*

UNIX goes well beyond the simple "user's guide," covering many topics comprehensively and in depth.

Hands-on practice is encouraged; it is the only way to gain familiarity with an operating system. The text includes many examples and complete programs ready to enter into the computer. Exercises of varying difficulty are provided at the end of each chapter.

Right for Your System

If you use a Berkeley UNIX system, a Berkeley UNIX look-alike, or Berkeley UNIX made compatible with SYSTEM V, this book is written especially for you. The text anticipates questions and provides answers. Unlike most introductory books on UNIX, which treat the system more or less generically, discussion of important topics is thorough, comprehensive, and directly related to distinctively Berkeley UNIX features such as support for networking, interprocess communication, the *csh* shell, and many others. It avoids subjects like system management, which are not really useful for most readers, and presents the material in a style suitable for learning or teaching on a Berkeley UNIX operating system.

User Friendly and Comprehensive

There is both breadth and depth to this book's presentation. Chapter 1 contains a complete primer on Berkeley UNIX to get the new user logged on and working with the system as quickly as possible, without awkwardness or confusion. Being able to play and experiment with the system adds to the user's interest and motivation to learn further. Once introduced and comfortable, the user is guided through a well-selected set of topics covering the type of detailed material appropriate for a one-semester course at the advanced undergraduate or beginning graduate level. Such topics include:

Utilities: The principal display editor **vi** is covered in depth. A second popular display editor, **emacs**, also is covered. Comprehensive coverage of how to send, receive, and manage electronic mail on-line is discussed. Many UNIX commands are covered, and the way UNIX *filters* work and how they can be connected into useful *pipelines* are explained in detail.

Shell usage and programming: The *csh* shell is the preferred user interface in Berkeley UNIX, and its use is described thoroughly, as are ways of making the system more convenient. Shell-level programming for both the *csh* and *sh* shells and many well-constructed example programs are discussed with side-by-side comparisons of *csh* and *sh* features.

C-level system programming: The UNIX system is written in the C programming language. Being able to write programs for UNIX in C provides the ability to modify, improve, and extend existing UNIX facilities as well as add new facilities; this also provides a beneath-the-surface look at how UNIX works. Some familiarity with the C language would be helpful but is not necessary. The discussions are self-contained, and simple examples are given before more complex subjects are presented.

Networking: One of the major strengths of Berkeley UNIX is its support for interprocess communication and networking. Chapter 10 is devoted to this topic. User-level commands for remote login, file transfer, mail, and so on are explained. System-level support for the *socket* abstraction and its use to support interprocess communications across a network are explained in detail. Many examples of networking processes are given.

Program maintenance: The UNIX **make** facility for automating program maintenance is covered in depth. This topic is of practical importance, especially for those who program extensively in a UNIX environment. Ample coverage and examples are provided to enable you to start using the **make** facility for your own software projects.

Document formatting: One of the most used features of UNIX is document formatting. This includes the **nroff/troff** formatting language, the *ms* macro package, and the table and equation layout routines. Chapter 12 is devoted to this topic. Coverage is oriented toward practical use of the formatting facility to prepare documents. Popular *templates* for letter and paper writing are provided.

Flexible Usage

For a system programming-oriented course, Chapter 2 on text editing and Chapter 12 on document formatting can be skipped and left for students to read on their own. Thus, you can concentrate on shell and C-level system programming and possibly on a term project in software writing. However, for an application-oriented course, Chapter 9 and some sections on C-level programming can be omitted, and the document formatting chapter covered instead.

For an *introduction to operating system principles* course, this book is a good supplement. Discussion of UNIX subjects such as *csh*, file system structure, concurrent process management, I/O structure, signals/interrupts, and interprocess communication provides concrete examples and adds to students' understanding of the abstract operating system principles being studied.

If you use Berkeley UNIX in school or at work, this book enables you to use the system's capabilities more effectively, increasing your productivity. For example, you will be able to edit files more efficiently, use convenient user-interface features, format documents on-line, and automate software maintenance. Ready-to-use examples provide many immediate practical applications.

On-Line Examples

Throughout the text, concepts and usages are explained thoroughly with examples. Every effort has been made to find examples with practical value and to present them as complete programs ready to be entered into the computer. There is a shell program for letter writing, a template for formatting a paper, and many other immediately useful programs. The examples and templates contained in this book also are available in machine-readable form from the author.

Easy Reference

An Introduction to Berkeley UNIX offers a smooth, readable style uncharacteristic of a book of this type. Nevertheless, it is understood that such books are used as much for reference as for concentrated study, especially once the reader gets going on the system. Therefore, information in this book is organized and presented in a way that also facilitates quick and easy reference. The text includes ample appendices, a synopsis of commands covered, and a thorough and comprehensive index. This book will be a valuable aid for anyone who uses Berkeley UNIX.

Acknowledgments

The actual writing of this book began early in 1986 when the author was on sabbatical from Kent State University to Hewlett-Packard Laboratories in Palo Alto, California. At H-P, Ira Goldstein and Martin Griss provided support and encouragement, not to mention access to their excellent computing facilities. Thanks and deep appreciation go to my colleague Michael Rothstein who read drafts, corrected mistakes, and contributed ideas and examples. Michael also wrote most of the problems for the exercises. Thanks also are due to all the students in operating system courses who helped develop the material and tried out earlier versions of the manuscript. Deep appreciation goes to John G. Michalakes, a computer science student with experience in editorial work, who helped edit many parts of the book. In addition, my thanks to the following reviewers for their suggestions and comments: David Alan Bozak, State University of New York at Oswego; Stephen W. Ching, Villanova University; Michael Clancy, University of California at Berkeley; and James Wilson, Stanford University.

I also wish to thank my wife Jennifer for her encouragement, understanding, and valuable input to the document formatting discussion in Chapter 12. Finally, my deep gratitude goes to my mother Mrs. Chang Pei Wang who has paid so much attention to my education and who is always there when times are difficult. To her I dedicate this book.

Contents

7 The FILE SYSTEM in UNIX 210

8 UNIX Programming in C 239

9 UNIX System Programming   267

10 Communications and Networking   319

Appendices

Bibliography   501
Index   504

Introduction

If computer hardware is the body, the operating system is the soul. This one piece of software orchestrates the many complicated pieces of delicate electronics and brings them to work in harmony. It glues together the central processing unit, memory, disk drives, terminals, compilers, application programs, on-line files, programmers, system administrators, and ordinary users. The operating system serves all. The same piece of hardware under a different operating system literally would be a different computer.

The name UNIX applies to a family of operating systems originally developed at Bell Laboratories, the research arm of AT&T. The beginnings of UNIX trace back to 1969 and a small, innovative group of people working to develop an improved computing environment. Today UNIX has become the *de facto* industry standard. On personal computers, workstations, minicomputers, and even the most powerful mainframes, UNIX systems provide a simple, efficient, and elegant computing environment for increased productivity.

Many versions of UNIX exist, but they are all basically the same system adapted to run on different computers. In fact, major computer makers now offer supported UNIX systems with their own enhancements: ULTRIX from Digital Equipment Corporation (DEC), HP-UX from Hewlett-Packard, and AIX from International Business Machines (IBM). But the two most widely used versions continue to be the AT&T–supported UNIX systems and Berkeley UNIX, from the University of California, Berkeley (UCB).

There has been a fair amount of give and take between the AT&T and Berkeley systems. Berkeley UNIX grew out of AT&T's seventh edition UNIX (1979). UCB added a new display editor, a new user interface, and most importantly, *virtual memory management*, which made UNIX ideal for the 32-bit VAX computers introduced by DEC in the late 1970s. The added power of virtual memory and a policy of discounting UNIX licenses for educational purposes caused a UNIX explosion at colleges and universities, beginning with the 4.1 bsd (Berkeley software distribution) in 1981 and continuing through the most recent release, 4.3 bsd. AT&T, in turn, drew on and incorporated many of Berkeley's best features in its 1983 release of UNIX SYSTEM V. This book is oriented primarily toward Berkeley UNIX, although many aspects of AT&T SYSTEM V are covered as well.

UNIX Features

In all its versions, UNIX has become an industry standard for operating systems, because it offers a range of features that makes it powerful, versatile, and generally easy to use. Many of these features will become clear as you go through the chapters.

Hierarchical File System

The entire file system is tree structured and is anchored at a single directory called the *root*. The root directory contains files and other directories that, in turn, contain more files and directories. The file system tree is divided into *volumes*, which can be *mounted* or *dismounted* by attaching them to a node in the file tree. A physical storage device can contain one or several file system volumes.

File Access Control

Each file in the file system is protected by a sequence of bits specified by the owner of the file. Access to files is controlled by the operating system. Systemwide access is granted to so-called *super users*, usually the system administrators.

Compatible File, Device, and Interprocess I/O

UNIX arranges for I/O to physical devices and I/O to a file to look the same to a user program. Further, UNIX provides a mechanism for the user to *redirect* a program's I/O so that with no change to the program itself, input or output can be directed to a terminal, a file, or even to another program's I/O. The ability to combine and connect existing programs in this *pipeline* fashion provides great power and flexibility.

Compactness and Efficiency

The UNIX system *kernel*, the central part of the operating system, is relatively small as compared to other time-sharing systems. Beside this central kernel, many commands provide different functionalities. The syntax of the commands is generally terse, so that once the user gets accustomed to it, UNIX becomes quite convenient.

Concurrent Processes

UNIX provides a set of system commands to initiate and manipulate asynchronous concurrent processes. A user can maintain several jobs at once and switch between them. Concurrent processes can be connected by *pipes* to form a *pipeline* that performs functions useful to a user. Furthermore, concurrent processing is used heavily in the operation of UNIX itself, reflecting modern operating system methods.

Utilities

Each UNIX system comes with many utility programs including text editors, language compilers, document processors, electronic mail, file manipulation, database, software engineering, networking, and other system facilities.

Redefinable User Interface

The UNIX user-interface program is called the *shell*. It receives commands from the user and manages command execution for the UNIX system. Because the shell is defined by each user, tailor-made user interfaces for particular applications, such as word processing, can coexist with other shells.

Portability

UNIX can be ported, or moved, to different computers easily. Because UNIX is almost entirely written in the high-level language C, all that is required is a C compiler for the computer you are porting UNIX to. The C language is designed to be portable as well, making the job of porting UNIX relatively easy.

The UNIX Environment

The UNIX system is a multiuser time-sharing system. You interact with the system by issuing commands and receiving results through a terminal. Within the overall file system, you have your own private file directory known as your *home directory*. The word "private" requires some qualification: System security was not really a major consideration when UNIX was designed, and although there is access control for individual files, you can browse through the entire file system and access any file not specifically protected.

If you are new to UNIX, an on-line interactive *learn* facility is available to help you. You also can communicate with other users by electronic mail, which lets you make announcements, ask questions, and give answers. Expensive paper-based communication is greatly reduced.

UNIX allows a high degree of *customization* on a per-user basis. The shell, as well as important utilities such as *mail* and the editors, refers to *initialization* files. You can tailor these files to make the utilities run according to your needs and preferences.

The UNIX programmer's manual is the official documentation for the UNIX system. The Berkeley UNIX programmer's manual consists of several volumes, and a large percentage of it is on-line for easy reference.

Evolution of UNIX

The UNIX operating system began in 1969 as a file system project on a DEC PDP-7, following Bell's withdrawal from Multics, a joint operating system research project between Bell Laboratories, General Electric, and the Massachusetts Institute of Technology. Several members of the Bell research group including Rudd Canaday, Ken Thompson, and Dennis Ritchie went looking for a new computing environment; they dubbed their new system UNIX. The first version had a new file system Thompson had developed and was a single-user system.

Work continued, the system grew in size and power, and as it grew so did the close relationship that still exists between UNIX and the C programming language. Early versions of UNIX and its utilities were being written in assembly language, which had neither the convenience nor the portability envisioned for UNIX. Thompson and Ritchie had been working on an early version of C, which they improved and expanded, enabling UNIX to be rewritten in a high-level computer language in 1973. Their last major collaboration was on AT&T's seventh edition UNIX in 1979.

During the early 1970s, UNIX ran mainly on DEC-manufactured computers where it blossomed on the PDP-11/70, gaining acceptance within Bell Labs and in a good number of universities. Subsequently, a group led by Professor R. S. Fabry at UCB added a number of new features to the seventh edition UNIX and released Berkeley UNIX 4.1 bsd in June 1981. A rapid success, the 4.1 bsd offered the new **vi** display editor, the *csh* shell, and most important, virtual memory management. The popularity of Berkeley UNIX systems grew with the release of 4.2 bsd in 1983, which added a new file system and full net-working and interprocess communication support. The most recent Berkeley system, the 4.3 bsd, was released in 1986. Berkeley UNIX now runs on many different computers from various manufacturers including the popular DEC VAX and the Sun Microsystems SUN workstations.

Bell Labs, meanwhile, has kept pace with UNIX's growing popularity with periodic updates and enhancements: UNIX/32V, SYSTEM III, and SYSTEM V UNIX. Major new facilities in these versions include virtual memory manage-ment, job control, interprocess communication, and networking. As UNIX has become an operating system standard, hardware and software vendors have been busy adapting it to different computers, sometimes adding proprietary enhancements and giving their systems such names as HP-UX (Hewlett-Pack-ard), ULTRIX (DEC), AIX (IBM), and XENIX (Microsoft). From a user's point of view, little difference exists between these systems. Having learned the material contained in this book, you can use any of these UNIX systems with ease.

Berkeley UNIX

Although this text covers many aspects of SYSTEM V, it concentrates on Berke-ley UNIX, which is widely used in colleges and universities both in this country and abroad. One major advantage of Berkeley UNIX for computer science teaching and research is that it comes with source code at no additional cost, which makes modifications to the system possible at all levels, allowing easy experimentation with improvements and new features. Industrial and government research laboratories also use Berkeley UNIX heavily, and because of certain features in Berkeley UNIX, many prefer it over SYSTEM V. Such features include the *csh* shell, which makes the user interface easier to use and program, and *job control*, which means you can maintain several jobs at once and switch between them. Another advantage of Berkeley UNIX is its support for TCP/IP, a popular networking protocol.

This book introduces Berkeley UNIX applications and programming and explores such aspects as:

- display text editing

- electronic mail

- commands, filters, and pipelines

- shell usage and programming

- UNIX system programming in C

- networking facilities

- document preparation

Because UNIX is best learned with frequent experimentation and practice, Chapter 1 is a "primer" that gets the new user started quickly. In later chapters many important features of Berkeley UNIX are described in more detail. Throughout the book examples and practical ways to use the UNIX system are discussed. Also included are many complete programs ready to be entered into the computer. The material is presented to be easily read as a textbook or conveniently consulted as a reference.

Note: Throughout the book, "zero" is set as 0 or □, lowercase "oh" is set as o or o, uppercase "oh" is set as O or O, lowercase "ell" is set as l or l, and one is set as 1 or 1.

A UNIX Primer

1

T o learn UNIX you must use it, and, of course, to use it you must learn it. Such a paradox is rather common—you probably learned to drive a car this way, and UNIX is not much more formidable. You just need some basic help getting started. This chapter presents some tools and "rules of the road" that make up a working knowledge of the operating system and how to use it. Once you understand the material in this chapter, you will be able to use the operating system to learn more in each successive chapter. At first you need a learner's permit to drive a car. Consider this chapter your learner's permit for UNIX; with a little practice you will be using UNIX almost right away. Here's what you need to know.

You and the computer

- Getting on and off the system—login and logout

- Telling the system what to do—the shell, command syntax, typing the command (and fixing mistakes), executing a command, aborting a command

Managing your data

- Creating files—getting started with the **vi** editor

- Accessing files and directories—the UNIX file structure, file names, your home directory, moving between directories, system directories

- Protecting files—access control, changing protection, super users

Getting the job done

- Handling I/O—standard input, standard output, redirection

- Creating and running a program—compilation, loading, execution, using interpreters, getting hard-copy output

- Job control—multiple jobs, background and foreground, suspending processes, interrupting jobs

Your community

- Other users—the **who** and **finger** commands

- Communication— the **mail**, **write**, and **talk** utilities

- On-line help—the **man** utility

Read this chapter with a terminal handy and try out the different commands and features as you come to them. In each case, you are given enough information to get you on the system and learning. The details will be covered in depth in subsequent chapters.

1.1 Getting Started: Login and Logout

To access your UNIX system, you must have a user identification, or *userid*, which your system administrator can provide, and a *password*. At most installations your userid will consist of your last name, your first initials and last name (often all lowercase), or some other character string. Your password is a safeguard against unauthorized use of your userid. You need to choose a password of at least six characters (your local system may enforce other conventions as well, such as a minimum length or that there be at least one numeral). Since you are the only one who knows your password, you must be careful with it. Forgetting your password means the system administrator must create a new one for you. Giving out your password to the wrong person could have even more dire consequences; you could be blamed for whatever damage they caused, intentionally or otherwise. The best rule is: Do not tell anybody your password, but keep it written down somewhere safe. Once you have a userid and password, you can begin your first UNIX session.

The first step is the login procedure. This sequence protects the system against unauthorized use and authenticates the identity of the user. To log in, press RETURN, and you will see the message:

```
login:
```

Type in your userid and press RETURN. Although UNIX ordinarily distinguishes between uppercase and lowercase characters, it makes no difference for user-ids. Even so, if you type your userid in all uppercase characters, UNIX will assume that your terminal has no lower case. It is always best to type in your userid exactly as it was given. Once you've entered your userid, the system will ask for your password by displaying:

```
password:
```

Enter your correct password carefully and press RETURN. What you type will not appear on your terminal—this is to protect your password from roving eyes around you. If you mistype either your userid or your password, the message:

```
login incorrect
```

will be displayed, and you are allowed to try again. If you are a new user and, after several careful tries, you are unable to log in, it may be that the system administrator has not yet established your userid on the computer. Wait a reasonable length of time and try again. If you still have a problem, contact your system administrator.

Once you have logged in, the system will record your login in a system log, display a message showing the time and terminal used for your last login, and initiate a command interpreter program to take your commands. This command interpreter, or *shell*, displays a *prompt* on the far left side of a new screen line indicating that it is ready to take your commands. The prompt is usually either the character %, >, or $. In this book we will assume the prompt is %. Once you see the prompt, you are ready to begin computing.

But first let us discuss the *logout* procedure. To log out, make sure that you have exited from any program that you have been running and that you have returned to the shell level (you will see the shell prompt). Then, type the command:

```
logout
```

When logout is successful, a login message will be displayed on the terminal to indicate that it is free for the next person. It is usually not necessary to turn off the power to the terminal unless you know it won't be used for a while.

It can happen that in the course of a session you leave some loose ends, so that if you try to initiate a logout the system politely will refuse and remind you to tie up the loose ends. These situations usually involve stopped jobs, which we will explain later in this chapter. If the system objects to a logout request and you really want to log out, simply issue a second consecutive logout command, and it will succeed. The character CONTROL-D (the character d or D typed while holding down CONTROL) typed alone on a command line often can be used in place of the **logout** command. We shall use the notation:

^X

to denote a control character, where **X** is some character. Note also that although the convention is to show an uppercase character, you do not need to hold down SHIFT when typing a control character. Logout with **^D** is convenient but dangerous, because one typing error can log you out. Many experienced UNIX users choose to disable this "logout on **^D**" feature (see Section 1.10).

1.2 Talking to UNIX: The User Interface

After login, you communicate with UNIX through a user interface program called the *shell*, and the shell program invoked after login is called your *login shell*. The shell displays a prompt signaling that it is ready for your next command, which it then interprets and executes. On completion, the shell resignals readiness by displaying another prompt. There are two popular shells: the original shell written by S. R. Bourne known as the *Bourne shell* or *sh* and the C-shell or *csh* developed later at UCB by William Joy. For the Bourne shell, the prompt is usually the character $ on a line by itself. For *csh* the prompt is usually the character %. Most people prefer *csh* because it offers more features than *sh*, but this text will refer to either as the shell and make a distinction only when necessary.

Entering Commands

Virtually anything you want done in UNIX is accomplished by issuing a command. UNIX offers many different commands, but some general rules apply to all of them. One set of rules relates to *command syntax*—the way the shell expects to see your commands. A command consists of one or more words separated by blanks. A *blank* consists of one or more spaces and/or tabs. The first word is the *command name* (in this book the name of a command will appear in **boldface**); the remaining words of a command line are *arguments* to the command. A command line is terminated by pressing RETURN. This key generates a NEWLINE character, the actual character that terminates a command line. Multiple commands can be typed on the same line if they are separated by a semicolon (;). Sometimes a *flag* is inserted between the command name and the arguments to specify an *option* for that command. For example: **ls** is the name of the command that lists the names of files in a directory. If a space and then –l is added to **ls**, the *long form* option is activated, which calls up a more detailed report for each file than just **ls**. The general form for a command looks like this:

`command-name` [*–flag*] ... [*arg*] ...

The brackets are used to indicate *optional* parts of a command. An optional part can be given or omitted. The ellipses (...) are used to indicate possible repetition. These conventions are followed throughout the text. The brackets or elipses themselves are not to be entered when you give the command.

After receiving a command, the shell processes it and then executes it. After execution is finished, the shell will type a prompt to let you know that it is ready to receive the next command. Figure 1.1 illustrates the shell command interpretation loop. *Type ahead* is allowed, which means you can type your next command without waiting for the prompt, and that command will be there when the shell is ready to receive it.

Trying a Few Commands

When you see the shell prompt, you are at the shell level. Now type:

`echo Here I am`

Figure 1.1 ▪ Command Interpretation Loop

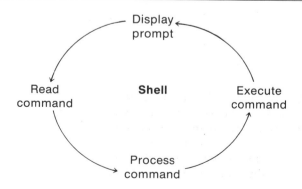

You'll see that the **echo** command echos what you type. Next, enter:

```
echo -n Hello there; echo user
```

This command line contains two commands. (If you make a mistake typing these commands, glance ahead to the next subheading on correcting typing mistakes.) The flag −n causes **echo** to omit a NEWLINE character at the end of its output, so the word *user* appears on the same line as *Hello there*.

One use of **echo** is to examine the value of a *shell variable*. For example, if you type:

```
echo $TERM
```

you'll see the value of the shell variable TERM, which indicates what type of terminal you are using. Note that the *value* of a shell variable is obtained by prefixing the variable name with a dollar sign ($) (more on shell variables in Chapter 5).

A UNIX installation is usually identified by a *hostname*. To find out what is your system's hostname, you can try the command:

```
hostname
```

which displays your system's hostname, if there is one. Another command is **who**. Type:

```
who
```

to list current users on the system. A list of people who are on the system will be displayed together with their login times and terminal lines. **who** gives you an idea of how many people are sharing the computing facility and which terminals they are using. If you wish to communicate with someone on the system, you can use **who** to find out if this person is currently logged in.

With access to UNIX comes the ability to keep *files* on-line. Some standard files are supplied for each new user. The command:

```
Is -a
```

lists the names of all your files, including the standard ones. A standard filename usually begins with a period. The −a is another flag or option to **ls**. An option is usually given as a single character preceded by −. (Ordinarily you use **ls** without the −a option to avoid sifting through the standard files every time.)

If you are using *csh*, one standard file is .login, which contains such initializations for individual users as terminal type, modem speed, and so on. The initialization file for *sh* is .profile.

If you are curious about what's in the file .login, type the command:

```
cat .login
```

to display the contents of the file on your terminal. Don't be discouraged by what you don't understand in this file. When you have progressed further in this book, the contents will become clear. Be careful when applying **cat**, because some executable files and those containing object code will send nonprintable characters to your terminal. If you are unsure about the type of file, use **cat** with the −v option to prevent nonprintables from being sent to the terminal.

The UNIX system keeps track of time and date precisely, as you would expect any computer to do. The command:

```
date
```

displays the current date and time as given by the following typical output showing Eastern Daylight Time:

```
Mon May 11 19:43:49 EDT 1987
```

The UNIX system has an on-line dictionary. To look for words, you can use:

```
look prefix
```

All words in the dictionary with the given prefix are displayed on your terminal.

Another useful command is **passwd.** Type:

```
passwd
```

to change your password. This command will prompt as follows:

```
Changing password for your userid
Old password:
New password:
Retype new password:
```

pausing after each prompt to wait for input. Many UNIX installations give out new userids with a standard password, and the new user is expected to use the **passwd** command to change to a personal password as soon as possible.

The command **man** consults the on-line manual pages for all available commands. Thus:

```
man command
```

will display the on-line documentation for the given command. Try:

```
man passwd
```

just to see what you get. Details on the **man** command can be found in Section 1.12.

Correcting Typing Mistakes

As you entered the preceding commands, you probably made at least one keystroke error. UNIX provides three *erase characters* for correcting typing errors before RETURN has been pressed:

character erase   deletes one previous character on the input line

word erase   deletes one previous word on the input line, also known as *word kill*

line erase   deletes the whole line, also referred to as *line kill*

These three characters allow simple corrections of typing errors, *input editing*. You need to find out exactly which three characters are used for input editing on your system, but the following erase characters commonly are used for CRT terminals:

^H   (BACKSPACE) character erase

^W   word erase

^U   line erase

These characters may or may not be exactly what your system uses. For example, on some UNIX systems, the defaults are:

character erase

@   line erase

An example of character erasing is the following key sequence:

`la a^H^H^Hs -a`

which results in:

`ls -a`

The user also can redefine the system-supplied default erase characters.

Aborting a Command

Apart from correcting typing mistakes, you also can exercise other controls over your interaction with UNIX. For instance, you may abort a command before it is finished. Or you may wish to halt, resume, and discard output to the terminal.

Sometimes, you may issue a command and then realize that you have made a mistake. Perhaps you give a command and nothing happens. These are occasions when you want to abort execution of the command. To abort, simply type the *interrupt character*, which is usually DELETE (or ^C); this interrupts (terminates) execution and returns you to the shell level. It is important for you to identify which character is your interrupt character. Try the following:

1. Type part of a command.

2. Before you terminate the command, press DELETE or ^C.

3. The character that cancels the command and gives you a prompt is your interrupt character.

You also can control the output that you receive on the terminal. If the information is scrolling by too fast for you to read:

^S

will halt output until you press:

^Q

to resume output. If there is too much output, and you don't want to see it at all, type:

^O

and the rest of the output will be discarded.

1.3 Editing: The Visual Editor vi

You now know commands to do such things as list file names and display their contents. You still need to be able to create files—which is the job of a *text editor*. A text editor is a program that helps you enter or modify text in a file. There are several editors in UNIX, but **vi** (pronounced vee-eye) is still the standard full-screen editor. The **vi** editor is especially suited for use with a CRT terminal, and although less efficient, **vi** also can be used with a hard-copy terminal over low-speed lines.

Full-screen editors such as **vi** make use of special protocols for addressing and moving the cursor—protocols available on most CRT terminals. Since these protocols differ from terminal to terminal, the operating system must know the type of terminal you are using. This will be no problem for terminals connected directly to your system; the system already knows the type. Informing the system to accommodate a different terminal type is possible (see Chapter 2), but it is recommended that you use a direct-connect CRT terminal for the time being.

To invoke the editor **vi** from the shell level, type:

vi *file*

to edit the file named *file*. If the file exists, your screen will display the beginning of the file. Otherwise, you are creating a new file by that name. Once inside **vi**, you are working in an environment different from the shell. In **vi** you can create text, make changes, move text about, and so on. To exit from **vi** and save the file with the changes, type the **vi** command:

ZZ   (save *file* and exit **vi**)

which makes the changes permanent on the disk, terminates **vi**, and returns to the shell level. If you want to quit **vi** without saving the changes, type the **vi** command:

`:q!`   (exit **vi**, no save)

followed by RETURN.

Let us go through a quick editing session. Type:

`vi myprog`

to call up a file named myprog. Because myprog does not exist, it will be created. The screen will clear except for a column of tilde characters ($\sim$), a cursor, and perhaps a brief message on the last line. The **vi** editor has two modes: the *command* mode and the *insert* mode. The command mode moves the cursor with the arrow keys, deletes text, moves text, and so on; the insert mode enters and changes text. The **vi** editor always begins in the command mode. Enter the insert mode by pressing **i** (you do not need to hit RETURN) and enter the following text:

```
echo    It is time for all
echo    good men to come to
echo    the aid of their country.
```

We are done inserting text, so exit the insert mode by pressing ESC.

If you want to change *It is time* to *Now is the time*, the procedure is simple. Recall that we are in the command mode after pressing ESC, so we may use the arrow keys to move the cursor to the *I* of *It*, the beginning of the first word we want to change. Now press **dw**, and *It* is deleted (**dw** will be explained shortly). Note how the word disappears and the rest of the line slides over so that the *i* in *is* is now at the cursor. Next, press **i** to return to the insert mode and type the word *Now*, a space, and then ESC to exit the insert mode. We want to insert the word *the* before the word *time*, so position the cursor at the *t* in *time*. Now, press **i** for the insert mode and type *the* and a space. Hit ESC to return to the command mode. The correction is finished.

New users of **vi** sometimes find it difficult to remember which mode they are using. You can find out which mode you are in quickly by tapping SPACEBAR a couple of times. If the cursor moves to the right without changing the text, you are in the command mode; if the text after the cursor is pushed further right (or if characters disappear), you are inserting space and you must be in the insert mode. Backspace a couple of times to delete the spaces, and you're back to where you started. There is another method: Press ESC a couple of times; if you hear your terminal "beep" as you type ESC, you are in command mode.

As you use **vi**, any changes you make are only to a buffer. To leave the editor and save myprog to disk, type **ZZ** (without hitting RETURN). The editor will report that it has saved the buffer in a new file named myprog and then return you to the shell. You have just created and edited a file named myprog containing the following three lines:

```
echo    Now is the time for all
echo    good men to come to
echo    the aid of their country.
```

This file is an actual program consisting of shell-level commands. Such programs are called *shell scripts*. Shell-level programming is the subject of Chapter 6. Now type:

```
chmod +x myprog
```

to make the file myprog executable. Then type:

```
myprog
```

to execute the simple shell script. The **chmod** command is discussed further in Section 1.5.

The **vi** editor is very powerful, and many different commands are available to handle all sorts of needs, many of which you may never use. The following is a list of basic **vi** commands that will serve most practical purposes:

Cursor Movement

h	(or LEFT ARROW) moves the cursor one position to the left (Figure 1.2)
j	(or DOWN ARROW) moves the cursor down one position
k	(or UP ARROW) moves the cursor up one position
l	(or RIGHT ARROW) moves the cursor right one position
+	moves the cursor to the beginning of the next line (same as RETURN)
—	(minus sign) moves the cursor to the beginning of the previous line
^	moves the cursor to the beginning of the current line
$	moves the cursor to the end of the current line

Figure 1.2 ▪ Cursor Movement

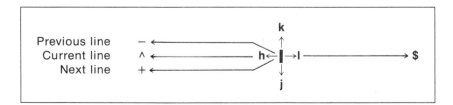

G	moves the cursor to the end of the file
*i***G**	moves the cursor to the beginning of the *i*th line of the file

Deletion

x	erases the character at the cursor; *n***x** erases *n* characters from the cursor. The positive integer *n* is called a *repeat number* or *count*. Many of the commands given here can take a repeat number.
*n***dw**	deletes *n* words. As noted previously, the *n* is a repeat number and may be omitted if the repeat number is one.
*n***dd**	deletes *n* lines; **dd** for deleting one line. Where a line is deleted, an @ is sometimes shown in its place to indicate its absence.

Insertion

i	enters the insert mode. Subsequent keystrokes will be inserted immediately to the left of the cursor. When the insertion is completed, press ESC to mark the end of the insertion and to return to the command mode. An insertion may consist of more than one line. The given text is inserted to the left of the cursor.
a	enters the insert mode. **a** is identical to **i**, except that the insertion occurs to the immediate right of the cursor.

Other

*/pattern*ESC	searches from the current cursor position down to the first occurrence of *pattern*. For example, /whileESC searches for the text pattern *while*. The cursor will be left at the beginning of the pattern found. Some special characters can be used to specify patterns. The RETURN key can be used instead of ESC to terminate a search pattern.
ZZ	saves the file being edited and exits from **vi**
:q!	quits; exits **vi** without saving the file

The UNIX *interrupt character* (usually ˆ**C**) is used to send an interrupt to **vi**. The interrupt causes **vi** to abort the current command and return to the command mode.

Although this section is only an introduction, it should provide enough material for you to get started editing your files. For a more complete description and advanced usage of **vi** as well as another popular editor called *emacs*, see Chapter 2.

1.4 Accessing Files and Directories

Like other modern operating systems, UNIX allows users to keep their programs and data on-line in files that are immediately accessible. The structure used to store and manage on-line files is called a *file system*. UNIX's files are put in a tree structure with a root named by the single character /. If a file contains a program or data, it is known as a *regular file*. If it contains the names and addresses of other files, it is called a *directory*, and it, in turn, may contain other files and directories. Internal nodes on the UNIX file tree represent directories; leaf nodes represent files. This *hierarchical* file structure is one of UNIX's outstanding features. A sample UNIX file tree is shown in Figure 1.3.

Current Working Directory and File Names

When you get a userid and account on your UNIX system, you are given a file directory known as your *home directory*. Your home directory will have your userid as its name, and it will usually be a child of another directory, such as user. Your files are kept in your home directory, and since some of these files can be directories, you also may have subdirectories connected as children to your home directory. These subdirectories may themselves have files and directories. In fact, it is a good idea to have your files organized by category into different subdirectories, especially once your collection of files becomes too large to handle conveniently within a single directory.

To access a file or directory in the file system you must call it up by its name, and there are several methods to do this. The most general, and also the most cumbersome, way to specify a file name is to list all the nodes in the path from the root to the node of the file or directory you want. This path, which is specified as a character string, is known as the *absolute pathname*,

Figure 1.3 ▪ A Sample File Tree

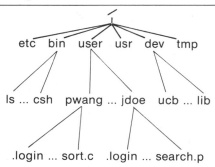

or *full pathname*, of the file. After the initial /, all components in a pathname are separated by the character /. For example, the file sort.c in Figure 1.3 has the absolute pathname:

/user/pwang/sort.c

The full pathname is the complete name of a file. As you can imagine, however, this name often can be lengthy. Fortunately, a file name also can be specified relative to the *current working directory* (also known as the *working directory* or *current directory*). Thus for the file /user/pwang/sort.c, if the current working directory is /user then the name pwang/sort.c suffices. A *relative pathname* gives the path on the file tree leading from the working directory to the desired file. The third and simplest way to access a file can be used when the working directory is the same as the directory in which the file is stored. In this case, you simply use the file name. Thus, a UNIX file has three names:

- A full pathname (for example, /user/pwang/sort.c)
- A relative pathname (for example, pwang/sort.c)
- A (simple) file name (for example, sort.c)

The ability to use relative pathnames and simple file names depends on the ability to change your current working directory. If, for example, your working directory is jdoe and you wish to access the file sort.c, you may specify the absolute pathname /user/pwang/sort.c, or you could change your working directory to pwang and simply refer to the file by name, sort.c. When you log in, your working directory is automatically set to your home directory. The command:

pwd   (print working directory)

prints the absolute pathname of your current working directory. The command:

cd *directory*   (change working directory)

changes your working directory to the specified directory (given by a simple name, an absolute pathname, or a relative pathname).

Two *irregular files* are kept in every directory, and they serve as pointers:

file **.**   is a pointer to the directory in which this file resides

file **..**   is a pointer to the *parent* directory of the directory in which this file resides

These pointers provide a standard abbreviation for the current directory and its parent directory, no matter where you are in the file tree. You also can use these pointers as a shorthand when you want to refer to a directory without having to use, or even know, its name. For example, the command:

cd .

has no effect, and the command:

```
cd ..
```

changes to the parent directory of the current directory. For example, if your working directory is jdoe, and you want to access the file sort.c in the pwang directory, you may use ../pwang/sort.c. Why does this work?

Your home directory already comes with a name, your userid. But you name your files and subdirectories when you create them. UNIX is lenient when it comes to restrictions on file names. In UNIX you may name your file with any string alphanumeric (letter and/or digit) characters except the character /. Note that on many systems, if a file name begins with the character #, it is intended as a *scratch file* and is liable to be deleted automatically by the system in a few days.

Handling Files and Directories

We already have seen how a file can be created using a text editor such as **vi**. In addition, files may be copied, renamed, moved, and destroyed; similar operations are provided for directories. The command **cp** will copy a file and has the form:

```
cp filename1 filename2
```

The first argument is the file to be copied, and the second is the destination. If the destination file does not exist, it will be created; if it already exists, its contents will be overwritten. The **mv** (move) command:

```
mv filename1 filename2
```

is used to change the name of *filename1* to *filename2*. No copying of the file content is involved. The new name may be in a different directory—hence the name "move." If *filename2* already exists, its original content is lost.

Once a file or subdirectory has outlived its usefulness, you will want to remove it from your files. UNIX provides the **rm** command for files and **rmdir** for directories:

```
rm filename1 filename2 ...
rmdir directoryname1 directoryname2 ...
```

The argument **rm** is a list of one or more file names to be removed. **rmdir** takes as its argument a list of one or more directory names; but note, **rmdir** only will delete an empty directory. Generally, to remove a directory, you must first clean it out using **rm**.

A file usually is created with an editor, but this won't work for directories; there is nothing really there to edit. Instead, UNIX provides the **mkdir** command, which takes as its argument the name of the directory to be created:

```
mkdir name
```

When specifying a file or directory name as an argument for a command, you may use any of the forms outlined. That is, you may use either the full pathname, the relative pathname, or the simple name of a file, whichever you prefer.

System Directories

The file system is such a useful structure that UNIX itself keeps much of its program and data there. Directories used by the system are called *system directories*, and they contain such things as executable commands, source code for programs, documentation, system management data, and so on. The concept of files is so universal in UNIX that devices such as terminals, printers, and tape drives are considered files by the operating system and are kept in the file system under an appropriate system directory. The following are a few of the major system directories:

/bin and /usr/bin	contain executable (binary) files for UNIX commands
/etc	contains system data files such as the password file, terminal capabilities, and so on
/dev	contains special files representing I/O devices
/usr/man	contains on-line manual pages for UNIX commands and system calls
/tmp	provides a directory where temporary *scratch* files can be written to. All users may read and write in this directory. Files in this directory will be removed by the system from time to time.

You may browse through the system directories. Try:

```
cd /bin
pwd
ls
```

or you can input:

```
ls /bin
```

1.5 Protecting Files: Access Control

Security was never a major concern for the designers and implementers of UNIX. In fact, elaborate schemes to protect files and directories were considered impediments to the main goal of UNIX—to create an efficient computing environment where teams of people could work together and share information on a project. The result: Any user may browse through the entire system looking at and using any file that is not specifically protected by its owner. UNIX stands in contrast to other operating systems in which access to and knowledge of the file system is limited solely to files in a user's own directory and subdirectories.

UNIX uses a 9-bit code to control access to each file. These bits, called *protection bits*, specify access permission to a file for three classes of users. A user may be the owner of a file, a member of a group with access to a file, a member of the user community, or a *super user*:

u	the owner or creator of the file
g	members of a group with access to the file
o	(others) all users except the owner
root	the super users

The first three protection bits pertain to *u* access, the next three to *g* access, and the final three to *o* access. The *g* type of user will be discussed further in Chapter 7.

Each of the three bits specifying access for a user class has a different meaning. Possible access permissions for a file are as follow:

r	read permission (first bit set)
w	write permission (second bit set)
x	execute permission (third bit set)

The Super User

Root refers to a class of super users to whom no file access restrictions apply. The *root* status is gained by logging in under the userid root or through the **su** command. A *super user* has read and write permission on all files in the system regardless of the protection bits. In addition, the super user has execute permission on all files for which anybody has execute permission. Typically, only system administrators and a few other selected users ("gurus" as they're sometimes called) have access to the super user password, which for obvious reasons, is considered top secret.

Examining the Permission Settings

The nine protection bits can be represented by a 3-digit octal number, which is referred to as the *protection mode* of a file. Only the owner of a file or a super user can set or change a file's protection mode; but anyone can see it. The **ls** –l listing of a file displays the file type and access permissions. For example:

```
-rw-rw-rw- 1 smith 127 Jan 20 1:24 primer
-rw-r--r-- 1 smith  58 Jan 24 3:04 update
```

is output from **ls** –l for the two files primer and update. The owner of primer is smith, followed by the date (January 20) and time (1:24 A.M.) of the last change to the file. The number 127 is the number of characters contained in the file. The *file type, access permissions*, and *number of links* precede the file owner's userid (Figure 1.4).

The protection setting of the file primer:

```
-rw-rw-rw-
```

gives read and write permission to u, g, and o. The file update allows read and write to u but only read to g and o. Neither file gives execution permissions. There are 10 positions in the preceding mode display (of **ls**). The first position specifies the file type, the next three positions specify the r, w, and x permissions of u; and so on. Try viewing the access permissions for some real files on your system. Issue the command:

```
ls -l /bin
```

to see listings for files in the directory /bin.

Setting Permissions

Usually a file is created with the default protection:

```
-rw-r--r--
```

Figure 1.4 ▪ File Attributes

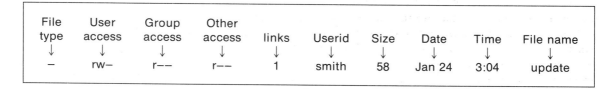

File type	User access	Group access	Other access	links	Userid	Size	Date	Time	File name
↓	↓	↓	↓	↓	↓	↓	↓	↓	↓
–	rw–	r––	r––	1	smith	58	Jan 24	3:04	update

To change the protection mode on a file, use the command:

`chmod` *mode filename*

where mode can be an octal (base 8) number (for example, 644 for rw–r––r––) to set all 9 bits specifically. Or the mode can specify modifications to the file's existing permissions, in which case, the mode is given in the form:

who op permission op2 permission2 ...

Who represents the user class(es) affected by the change; it may be a combination of the letters u, g, and o, or it may be the letter a for all three. *Op* (operation) represents the change to be made; it can be + to add permission, – to take away permission, and = to reset permission. *Permission* represents the type(s) of permission being assigned or removed; it can be any combination of the letters r, w, and x. For example:

`chmod` o – w *filename*
`chmod` a + x *filename*
`chmod` u – w + x *filename*
`chmod` a = rw *filename*

The first example denies write permission to others. The second makes the file executable by all. The third example takes away write and grants execute permission for the owner. The fourth example sets read and write permission only for all classes of user (regardless of what permissions had been assigned before).

A detailed discussion on the UNIX file system can be found in Chapter 7.

1.6 Redirecting Input and Output

Until now, our use of UNIX has been limited to issuing commands and observing their output on the terminal. However, you certainly will want results in a more useful form, either as hard copy or stored in a file. Furthermore, many instances will arise when you want input to come from a device other than the keyboard, a file, or perhaps even from another command or program running concurrently. UNIX provides an elegant solution: *input/output redirection*.

Many UNIX commands receive input from the keyboard and produce output on the terminal display. We refer to the keyboard as the *standard input* and the display as the *standard output*. There is also a *standard error* output, which the system uses to send error messages to the terminal. A command or program will use the standard input/output when no alternative is specified. Specifying an alterate input or output is called *redirecting*. The following shell notations are used for this purpose:

> *file*   (send standard output to *file*)

< *file*   (take standard input from *file*)

Even when standard output is redirected, error messages still will be sent to the terminal unless an & (ampersand) follows the > character, in which case *csh* redirects *both* standard output and standard error together.

For example:

```
ls > myfiles
```

sends the standard output of the command **ls** to the file myfiles. Try this on the computer: (1) type:

```
cat > notes
```

(2) type a few lines of input followed by ^D (with no other characters) on the last line, (3) input the command:

```
more notes
```

You'll see that **cat** has taken what you typed on the keyboard (its standard input) and produced output that was sent to the file notes.

Redirecting output is a powerful operation. For instance, the command:

```
cat file1 file2 > file3
```

creates *file3*, if it does not already exist, by appending *file2* to the end of *file1*. Watch out: If *file3* already existed, its contents would have been overwritten. It is incorrect to use either input file name as the output file name. In this example, using the name of either *file1* or *file2* for *file3* would have been an error. In *sh* this will result in your losing one of the two input files, because the shell first creates an empty *file3* to receive the redirected output *before* **cat** is even invoked.

The standard output of a command does not have to be sent to a file. It also can be redirected to another command as the second command's standard input. This is done by placing a *pipe* between the two commands. A pipe is obtained by using a vertical bar (surrounded by blanks) between two commands. For example:

```
ls | more
```

redirects the standard output of **ls** as standard input of **more**. The resulting construct is called a *pipeline*. The pipeline here makes lengthy output from **ls** easy to view on a CRT. Section 4.1 describes **more** in detail.

Pipes allow you to build new tools by combining existing commands; many of the more advanced UNIX commands are built from more primitive ones in precisely this manner. The pipe is an example of a hallmark principle of UNIX philosophy, "don't reinvent the wheel," because it allows programmers to build programs from pieces that already have been written and tested, instead of having to rewrite all the pieces from scratch. More examples on pipeline building are found in Chapter 4. The full syntax and semantics of I/O redirection for both *csh* and *sh* are described in Chapter 5.

1.7 Creating and Running Your Own Program

The UNIX system offers many languages: C, Pascal, f77 (FORTRAN 77), and LISP, just to name a few. A program written in any of these languages is kept in a *source code* file. UNIX uses a set of conventions for naming different kinds of regular files. Figure 1.5 illustrates some commonly used suffixes. A source code file cannot be executed directly. The program usually must be compiled into machine code before execution can take place. An alterative to compilation is to interpret a high-level language program directly using an *interpreter*.

We shall follow an example of creating and running a simple C language program. The **vi** editor can be used to enter the following C program under the name try.c:

```
main ( )
{ printf("running my first program\n");
}
```

This is a simple source program in C that displays the phrase "running my first program."

Compiling

Before try.c can be run, it must be compiled. *Compiling* is the process of translating a program written in a high-level language such as C or Pascal into a low-level language for execution on a particular computer. On many systems

Figure 1.5 ▪ File Name Suffixes

.c	for C source file
.f	for f77 source file
.p	for Pascal source file
.l	for LISP source file
.o	for object code file

the compiler will output a file of *object code*, which must be *linked* (combined with routines supplied by the system library) by a separate program called a linker. Once linkage is complete, the file is considered executable and is ready to be loaded into memory and executed.

UNIX-based compilers can handle both the compiling and linking of a program unless you specifically tell them not to, and their output will be an executable file. The following UNIX commands transform source code files and produce executable ones:

cc *file*.c   compiles a C program

f77 *file*.f   compiles a FORTRAN 77 program

pc *file*.p   compiles a Pascal program

In each case, if the compilation is successful, an executable file named a.out is produced in the working directory. To load and run an executable file, simply type the name of the file as if it were a command:

a.out

and the program will execute.

Let's try compiling the sample program in the file try.c:

cc try.c
a.out

Note that in UNIX the command to run a program is simply the name of the executable file. For all practical purposes, an executable file *is* a command and, as such, can have its output redirected. If you type:

a.out > foo   (to send output into file foo)

cat foo   (to view what is in foo)

A file named foo will be created, if it does not exist already, and the output of **a.out** will be written into it.

At some point you probably will want to name your executable file something other than a.out, especially since a.out will be overwritten the next time you invoke a compiler in this working directory. The **mv** command can be used to rename the file:

mv a.out *filename*

Interpreting

An alternative to compilation is to *interpret* a high-level language program. Instead of translating the source code into machine code, a program called an *interpreter* is used to execute the source code directly. An interpreter understands the source code statements and can carry them out. LISP is an interpretive language, and a LISP source program can be run using an interpreter.

There are also a few LISP dialects. If you have Berkeley UNIX, you may have Franz LISP; although Common LISP also is available on many systems. Assuming you have Franz LISP, the command:

```
lisp
```

invokes the LISP interpreter. The Franz LISP command to quit and return to the shell level is

```
(exit)
```

On Berkeley UNIX, Pascal can be run interpretively as well; the command:

pix *file*.p

is used to run the Pascal source *file*.p directly.

Getting Hard Copy Output

To get a printed copy of a file use

lpr *filename*

This command sends *filename* to a line printer. Your printing request joins a *queue* of such requests that are processed in order.

No matter which language program you run, you probably will want hard copy output for your results. One way to do this, as described earlier, is to redirect output of your program to a file and then send the file to the printer. Another, sometimes better, method is to use the **script** command:

script *file*

to record your terminal session into a file named *file*. While **script** is active, all I/O to and from your terminal is written to the file you specified (or to a file named typescript if you entered **script** without an argument). Recording stops when you type ^D at the beginning of a command line. The file then can be printed on a printer. For example, to run a C program with **script**, the following sequence of commands may be used:

```
script hardcopy
cc myprogram.c
a.out
^D
```

The **script** command requests that all subsequent I/O be recorded in the file hard copy. The ^D on the last line stops the recording and gets you out of **script** and back to the shell level.

An advantage of using **script** over simply redirecting output is that the file produced by **script** will contain both input to *and* output from the program. The file created by redirecting output will contain only output. A printout made from the file created by **script** is the same as from a hard copy terminal.

Further discussion on printing of files can be found in Section 4.9.

1.8 Communicating with Other Users

When you become a user on a UNIX system, you join a community of users who share the same computing resources, facilities, and services provided by the operating system. A principle aim in the design of UNIX was to provide a friendly, helpful, and convenient environment for its users. The success of UNIX is due in large part to the ease with which users can interact as members of this community and thus work more efficiently together. Commands such as **who** and **finger** help to identify members of your user community; **mail**, an electronic post office, allows the sending and receiving of files and messages; and **talk** allows direct, two-way communication between users.

Who Is Logged In

You couldn't write a letter to someone or call them on the telephone if you didn't have their address or telephone number. The **who**, **finger**, and related commands serve in ways similar to your phone directory. On a UNIX system, varying numbers of users can be logged in at different times. The users who are currently logged in are the ones you can have immediate interactions with on the computer. The command:

```
who
```

can be used to find out who are the users currently logged in on the system. It lists the login name, terminal name, and login time for each current UNIX user. The **who** command examines the /etc/utmp file to obtain its information. The UNIX system uses the /etc/utmp file to record such information when each user logs in. When a user logs out, the corresponding entry in /etc/utmp is deleted. Two lines from a typical **who** output are:

```
smith  ttyd1  May 26 23:47
jones  ttyh1  May 23 10:34
```

The command **w** is similar to **who**, but it gives more detailed information about the current status of each user and the system. The command:

```
w
```

displays a summary of current activities, including what each user is doing. The header line shows the time of day, how long the system has been up, the total number of users logged in, and the load averages. The load average numbers give the number of jobs in the run queue averaged over one, five, and 15 minutes. The first four lines of a **w** output are shown in Figure 1.6. Each field represents a different piece of information about the user:

`User`	userid
`tty`	terminal line used
`login@`	time of day when logged in
`idle`	number of minutes since last key stroke
`JCPU`	CPU time used by all processes controlled by that terminal
`PCPU`	CPU time used by the currently active processes
`what`	name and arguments of the current process

If a user name is given as an argument to **w**, the output will be restricted to information on that user.

Who's Who on the System: finger

If you are a new user, you may not know many people on the system, and although the information provided by **who** and **w** is useful, you don't know who these users are. You only know their userids, which may not resemble their actual names even faintly. The command **finger** will give you such data as full name, office, address, and phone number for each user; this is sometimes referred to as the *finger database*, because **finger** is used to look up information from this database. The general form is:

`finger` *name* ...

This command will display all entries in the finger database that contain a userid and first, middle, or last name matching any of the given arguments.

Figure 1.6 ▪ **Output of w**

```
12:21 am up 4 days, 2:17, 2 users, load average:
1.31, 1.15, 0.93
User   tty    login@   idle  JCPU  PCPU  what
smith  ttyd1  11:47pm  38    24    vi    report
jones  ttyh1  10:31am  85:39 1:08  5     -csh
```

For example, either **finger** smith or **finger** clyde will result in the entry shown in Figure 1.7.

This multiline output includes a *project* field, which is the first line in the .project file in the user's home directory. The *plan* field is the entire .plan file in the home directory. Individual users may use these two files to supply additional information about themselves for the finger database. The *no plan* line in the example indicates that csmith has no .plan file.

Used with an argument, **finger** will access information on any user known to the system, whether that user is logged on or not. If **finger** is used without an argument, an abbreviated finger entry is displayed for each user currently logged in. The **f** command is a shorthand for **finger**.

Electronic Mail

Electronic mail gives you the ability to send a message to one or more recipients quickly, conveniently, and without wasting paper. A message sent via *e-mail* is delivered to the recipient(s) immediately if they are logged in or first thing when they do log in. Chapter 3 discusses the full advantages of the **mail** facility; but because you may want to use e-mail to ask questions, we provide a few pointers here.

The command **mail** is used both for sending and for receiving mail on-line. To send mail, type as follows:

mail *userid*
any number of
lines of text
constituting the body of
the letter
^D

You can type one or more userids as recipients. After you input **^D** on the last line, the message will be sent to each recipient. Mail is kept in a private mailbox

---

Figure 1.7 ▪ **A Sample finger Output**

```
Login name: csmith              In real life: Clyde Smith
(803) 555-5432
Directory: /user/grad/csmith              Shell: /bin/csh
Last login Tue May 27 14:49 on ttyhd
Project: Automation Technology Research
No Plan.
```

for each user until such mail is delivered to and processed by the user. To receive mail (to check your mailbox) type **mail** with no argument.

To experiment, send a mail message to yourself:

```
mail your-userid
~s Trying mail out
Testing mail by sending myself
this piece of electronic
mail.
^D
```

The line:

```
~s Trying mail out
```

specifies a *subject field* that states the purpose of a message. Although a subject field is optional, it helps the recipient. It's a good idea to include a subject field.

You'll be notified when new mail arrives; the shell will give you a message:

```
you have new mail
```

If mail arrives while you are logged out, it will be stored in your mailbox so that the next time you log in you will get a message:

```
you have mail
```

immediately before your first prompt is displayed.

To receive your mail, type:

```
mail
```

This displays one line for each message in your mailbox preceded by an integer index. At this point you are in *mail-receiving mode* and can issue commands to the mail program to receive and manipulate messages. Typing the index of a message followed by RETURN causes that message to be displayed on your terminal. In this case, you would see the message you just mailed to yourself.

Mail messages can be saved or discarded. Typing:

```
d index
```

discards the indexed mail message. Typing:

```
s index filename
```

appends it to the end of the given file. After all messages are processed, you can type:

```
q
```

to exit **mail** and return to the shell.

Direct Terminal-to-Terminal Communication:
talk, write

In addition to **mail**, which provides one-way communication with other users, you may use **talk** to establish a direct, two-way communication link with another user. Both of you must be logged in and using CRT terminals. When two terminals are connected by **talk**, the screen on each terminal is split into upper and lower portions. On each screen, lines you type are displayed in the upper part, and lines the other person types appear in the lower part. You can "talk" to each other simultaneously.

If you wish to initiate a **talk** session, let's say with someone whose userid is smith, simply use the command:

```
talk smith
```

The **talk** command then attempts to establish direct communication with smith by displaying the following message:

```
Message from TalkDaemon
talk: connection requested by your-userid
talk: respond with: talk your-userid
```

on smith's terminal. At this point, the recipient of the message (smith) should get to the shell level and reply by typing the command:

```
talk your-userid
```

This establishes the two-way link and the talk session can begin. While in **talk**, typing ^**L** will cause the screen to be *refreshed*, in other words, erased and redrawn. Typing mistakes can be corrected using the same characters as those used for input editing (see Section 1.2). As with some face-to-face conversations, the ability of both parties to talk at once can be a mixed blessing. One convention that facilitates "polite" use of **talk** is to hit an extra RETURN when you're done talking; this produces a blank line and signals that it's the other user's turn to type. When the talk session is over, press the interrupt character (usually ^**C** or DELETE) for your system to exit from **talk**. The **talk** command then moves the cursor to the bottom of the screen and restores the terminal to normal.

If you want to talk to a user who has logged on in more than one place, you may use *ttyname* as a second argument to **talk** to indicate the appropriate terminal name. Also, your computer may be on a local area network (LAN), which is a communications network consisting of independent computer systems (hosts) fairly close to one another (for example, on the same campus). On a LAN of UNIX systems, you can **talk** with someone on another computer. This is done simply by using *userid@host* in place of the simple *userid*.

The command **write** is similar to **talk** but is less powerful. The **write** command copies what you type onto the target user's terminal. It is useful for communicating with hard-copy terminals. The command syntax of **write** is the same as **talk**, although **write** only works for terminals on the same computer. Since **write** is a one-way channel, each of the two users must issue a:

```
write target-userid
```

to set up two-way communication. The characters typed by the two users are not separated on the screen, so only one user can type at any given time.

Sometimes a **talk** or **write** message can be a rude interruption. Perhaps you have spent 10 minutes making your screen look exactly the way you want it for a picture, and someone initiates a talk request. You have reason to be upset. Fortunately, UNIX lets you deny such intrusions. The commands:

```
mesg y
mesg n
mesg
```

respectively, grant, deny, or display the status of permission to **talk** or **write**. If you usually do not wish to be disturbed by such messages, put:

```
mesg n
```

in the .login file in your home directory, but keep in mind that by doing so you are defeating one of the advantages of being on a UNIX system.

Another source of unwanted interruption is the system program **comsat**, which constantly runs in the background and notifies current users when mail arrives by printing the first few lines of the new mail on the user's terminal. The commands:

```
biff y
biff n
```

enable and disable such notification.

1.9 Controlling Multiple Jobs

Until this point, we have used the computer in strict accordance with the command interpretation loop described in Figure 1.1. We've entered commands at the prompt, waited while the shell interpreted and executed our "job," and considered the output while the shell displayed another prompt for our next command. Our work pattern is strictly sequential, and the amount of work we can do is bound by the length of this cycle. UNIX, however, is much more powerful than this and can be used far more efficiently. It is not necessary to wait for one job to finish before issuing the command to start another; instead, jobs may be run *concurrently*.

When a job is run in the ordinary fashion, in accordance with the command interpretation loop, it is said to be running in the *foreground*. If, however, you terminate a command with an & (ampersand) character, the job will be run in the *background*, and the shell is allowed to display a new prompt and process your next command without waiting for the background job to finish. It is as if the background job does not even exist, provided it makes no demands for terminal I/O. Long-running jobs that do not need terminal I/O run nicely in the background. If a background job does generate output it will appear (often annoyingly) on the terminal, unless you take care to redirect the output to a file.

An excellent candidate for a background job is a compilation of a lengthy source program. When you issue the command for the compilation, redirect the output—any error messages—to a file and place the entire job in the background:

```
cc bigjob.c >& file &
```

Note that the first & deals with redirection (see Section 1.6) and has nothing to do with putting the job in the background. The trailing & is the significant one from the standpoint of job control. This is an example of an unfortunate UNIX trait, overloaded operators.

The *csh* provides another major convenience, the ability to *suspend* the current executing job temporarily so that another job can be started. The *csh* allows you to type a special *suspend character* (usually ^Z) while a program is running, which will cause it to stop immediately until you signal it to resume. When you type ^Z to suspend a job, the message:

```
Stopped
```

and a new shell prompt will appear on your terminal to provide confirmation that the current job has been stopped. Now you can issue any shell-level command, including one to start another job (which may itself be suspended this same way). It is possible to start then suspend or put in the background quite a few jobs, and it is easy to see how this can become unmanageable quickly. Fortunately, the command:

```
jobs
```

can be used to display a list of all unfinished jobs on the terminal. A typical output from **jobs** might look like the following:

```
[1] +    Stopped    vi factor.l
[2] -    Stopped    mail smith
[3]      Running    lisp
```

In this case, there are two suspended jobs, [1] and [2], and one job running in the background, [3]. From this state, *csh* allows you to restart a stopped job, pull a background job into the foreground, or kill a job entirely. The *jobid* is used to specify the job you wish to change and can be typed in a number of ways:

%job-number,
%name-prefix,
% +
% −

For example, the jobids %1, % +, and %v all refer to job [1] in the preceding example. The job % + is always the most recently suspended (the current job), and % − is always the next most recently suspended (the previous job). The % − is useful when you are going back and forth between two jobs. When using the name-prefix form, you need just enough prefix of the command name to disambiguate it from other jobs. For example, %mail, %ma, or %m all refer to job [2]. Note that the name-prefix form cannot distinguish between two jobs with the same command name.

A job can be resumed (brought to the foreground) by the shell level command:

fg *jobid*

If you wish, you can abbreviate the command to just *jobid*. For example, %1 will put job [1] into the foreground, % + (or simply **fg** by itself) resumes the current job, and % − resumes the previous job.

Suspending a job using ^Z is not the same as exiting or terminating it, and if you try to log out while your shell still has suspended jobs, you will get a message telling you, "there are stopped jobs." A second consecutive logout command will cause logout regardless of stopped jobs. This is not considered a good practice; one reason is that some jobs left hanging in this way will save their buffers before they die, a waste of valuable disk space.

Jobs should be exited properly, or at the very least killed, before logout. Each job provides its own way for exiting (quitting). For example, in **vi**, :q! or **ZZ** is used, in **mail q** is used, and in Franz LISP **(exit)** is used.

Sometimes you will need to terminate a program that you are running (in the foreground). This can be done by typing the interrupt character, usually DELETE or ^C, which aborts the executing job and returns you to the shell level. If the interrupt character does not stop your program for some reason, try using ^\ (CONTROL backslash). If that does not abort the job, your last resort is the **kill** command. Use ^Z to suspend the job and get to the shell level, then type:

kill −9 *jobid*

This will surely terminate the job. The −9 is optional, but it makes the termination mandatory.

To sum up, a job may be in one of three states: running in the foreground, running in the background, or stopped (suspended). No more than one job can run in the foreground at any time, but many jobs can run concurrently in the background. Many also may be stopped. To see the states of the jobs under control of your *csh*, use the command **jobs**. Use **fg** along with the jobid to bring a particular job from suspension or from the background into the foreground. Use the suspend character (usually ^**Z**) to suspend a foreground job. Use the interrupt character (usually DELETE or ^**C**) to kill a foreground job. If a job is stopped or running in the background, it can be killed by issuing the command **kill** [−9] *jobid*.

1.10 Rounding Up Useful Commands

In our discussion of how to issue commands, correct mistakes, access files, compile programs, and control jobs, we have run into only a small number of the hundreds of UNIX commands. The richness and variety of UNIX commands are major strengths of the system. It is doubtful, however, that many users know all of them; you learn the commands that accomplish what you need. This section collects the commands that should be in a new user's basic repertoire.

Recall that in UNIX both uppercase and lowercase characters are used and that they are not interchangeable. All system-defined UNIX commands are entered in lowercase. Also, there are two kinds of commands: (1) built-in shell commands that are subroutines in the shell and (2) regular commands that are initiated as jobs controlled by the shell. The importance of this distinction will become clear. In the following listing of commands, user-supplied arguments are shown in *italics*. Optional arguments are enclosed in square brackets [ ]. Possibly repeated arguments are indicated by ellipses (...). These conventions will be followed throughout the book. Only the most common usages of these commands are given. The information here is intended to get you started and is by no means complete. Details are provided in later chapters, and you should consult the on-line manual for full descriptions of each of these commands.

Login and Logout

`login` *userid*	initiates a new login. The current user is automatically logged out.
^**D**	logs you out when given as a command to your login shell. Logout by ^**D** can be disabled by placing the line "**set** ignoreeof" in your .login file.

logout	logs you out
passwd	changes your password

File-Related Commands

cat *file* ...	displays on the terminal the contents of the file(s) specified in the order they are specified
cp *file1 file2*	makes a copy of file1 in file2. File2 is overwritten if it exists and is otherwise created.
cp *file* ... *dir*	makes a copy of the file(s) using the same name in the given directory
more *file* ...	displays the file on your terminal, pausing after each complete screenful and displaying "-more-" at which point you can press SPACEBAR for another screenful, RETURN for another line, or **q** to quit. The **more** program is useful for output to a CRT. Otherwise, **more** is the same as **cat**.
mv *file1 file2*	renames file1 as file2. If file2 already exists, it is removed first.
mv *file* ... *dir*	moves the file(s) to the given directory
rm *file* ...	deletes the files specified

Directory-Related Commands

cd *dir*	changes the current working directory to the given directory. Initially after login, the current working directory is the user's home directory. This is a built-in *csh* command.
pwd	prints the absolute pathname of the current working directory
mkdir *dir*	creates a new directory
rmdir *dir*	deletes the directory. A directory should be empty of files before it is deleted.
ls [−l] [−a] [−d] [−F] [*file* ...]	lists the file names in the current working directory if no file argument is given. For each *file* given: if *file* is a directory, then the files in that directory are listed; if *file* is a regular file, then that file is listed. The −l option causes

the listing to be in "long form." Other options include: −a, which lists all files including those files whose names begin with the period character (.); −d, which lists the directory entry itself, instead of the files in it; and −F, which indicates executable files with a trailing asterisk (*) and directories with a trailing slash (/). Options for **ls** can be juxtaposed, as in −ld.

Informational Commands

`date`	displays the date and time of day
`f` *name* ... or `finger` *name* ...	consults the user database for anyone with the userid or name given
`learn`	invokes the learn program. Follow the instructions printed.
`look` *prefix*	displays all words from the on-line dictionary that have the given prefix
`man` *command*	consults the on-line manual pages dealing with the specified command
`who`	displays a list of current users on the system. The command **w** is the same but gives more information on each user.

Communications Commands

`mail` *userid* ...	sends electronic mail to the named users
`talk` *userid*	initiates an interactive **talk** session with the target user
`write` *userid*	copies what you type on your terminal to the target user's terminal

Compiling and Running Programs

`pix` *program*	invokes the Pascal interpreter on the program whose name must end in .p
`pc` *program*	compiles the given Pascal program and creates an executable a.out file
`cc` *program*	invokes the C compiler on the program (name ending in .c), producing an executable file a.out

f77 *program*	compiles the given FORTRAN 77 program and creates an executable a.out file
lisp	invokes the LISP interpreter
a.out	runs the executable file a.out. In general, the file name of an executable file is also the command to execute that file

Hard-Copy Commands

lpr *file*	prints the file on a line printer. UNIX puts this printing request in a spooling queue. Your file will be printed when it gets to the front of the queue. To examine the printer queue or learn the job number for your print request, use the command **lpq**. To remove your printing request from the queue, use the command **lprm** together with the job number of your print request. To conserve paper, you should avoid unnecessary printing and *never* try to print an executable, object code or other nontext file.
script *filename*	records terminal I/O in the given file. The **script** command creates a subshell to accomplish this task. To stop recording and exit **script**, use ^D.

Job Control Commands

jobs [-l]	lists all your jobs. If the −l option is given, the process number of each job is also listed. This is a built-in *csh* command.
kill [-9] *job-or-process*	terminates the given job or process specified by a jobid or process number. The −9 option makes the termination mandatory (otherwise, a job may refuse to be killed under certain circumstances).

1.11 Overviewing UNIX Utilities

As mentioned earlier, an abundant store of utility programs is a major strength of UNIX, and it is important to have at least an overview of what's available before going into details in any one direction. This section lists and describes briefly those utilities commonly found on UNIX systems. Your UNIX system may or may not have all of the facilities listed here:

1. *Text editors*—There are several text editors available on UNIX systems. The basic line editor **ed** is simple but inconvenient. The **ex** line-oriented editor is an extension of **ed** providing additional features and capabilities. The full-screen editor **vi** is based on **ex** and is the standard interactive editor on UNIX systems. The popular **emacs** editor was developed independently but is often provided on UNIX systems.

2. *Programming languages*—The C programming language is part of any UNIX system; UNIX itself is written largely in C. Other languages usually include FORTRAN 77 (the standardized FORTRAN of 1977), RATFOR (rational FORTRAN or FORTRAN with C-like syntax), Pascal, and LISP (List Processing Language for Symbolic Computing). In newer versions of UNIX, you may have C++, Objective C (both are C with object-oriented features), and LISP with Objects. You also may find OPS5, an expert system language.

3. *Document preparation and formatting*—A collection of programs, including **nroff/troff** (document formatting) and **spell** (spelling checking) helps prepare and format a document for output to a printer. Text is processed and transformed into a paginated, adjusted document having a user-designed style. Associated with **nroff/troff** are the mathematical equation formatting program **eqn** and the table formatting routine **tbl**.

4. *Communications and networking*—Electronic mail lets you send and receive messages on-line. Direct interactive communication also is possible for on-line users. If your computer is on a network such as LAN, you should be able to send and receive mail (**mail**), copy files (**rcp** and **ftp**), remote login to another computer across the network (**rlogin**), and even share file systems across the network. Even if your system is not on a network, there are facilities that allow you to access other computer systems through regular phone lines: for instance, **tip** for remote login and **uucp** for *unix-to-unix* communication.

5. *Compiler construction aids*—UNIX offers a set of facilities to automate the writing of parsers (a program that understands the syntax of a high-level language) and compilers. The utility **lex** can generate lexical scan programs. The program **yacc** helps generate programs that parse and produce intermediate code for higher-level languages.

6. *Debugging aids*—UNIX offers facilities for debugging programs. Available are the basic **adb** debugger, the **sdb** symbolic debugger, and the more recent **dbx** interactive debugging system.

7. *Database management*—The *Ingres relational database system* is a part of Berkeley UNIX.

8. *Software engineering tools*—Utilities such as the *source code control system* and the **make** facility help manage software projects. Source code

control helps by keeping track of source code versions, managing access to source code modules, and so on. The **make** facility is useful for program maintenance and is used extensively to maintain programs for UNIX itself.

1.12 Consulting UNIX Documentation

Your UNIX system provides complete documentation that can be consulted on-line or in hard-copy form. The documents are kept on-line in a form suitable for processing by the UNIX document formatting facilities. There are two kinds of documents: tutorial and system description articles and *manual pages*. The manual pages can be consulted interactively using the **man** command.

Each manual page provides a concise description of a UNIX command. The manual pages are divided into sections. Within each section, commands are ordered alphabetically for easy retrieval. Although the exact organization of the sections may vary with the particular UNIX system, the following is a typical organization:

1. User-level commands

2. UNIX system calls in the C language

3. System library functions for C, f77, and other languages

4. Special files, related driver functions, and networking support

5. Formats for executable and system database files

6. Games

7. Miscellaneous useful information

8. UNIX maintenance and operation

Consulting the On-Line Manual

Although printed manuals work well, they are also bulky and expensive. An on-line manual is much more convenient for taking a quick look at a command or other detail. The description for each command is put in a standard manual page format. Manual pages in each section are sorted alphabetically by command name.

The **man** command is used to consult the on-line manual pages. For example:

```
man ls
```

displays on your terminal the manual page for the **ls** command. A typical manual page contains the following information: command name and principal purpose, usage synopsis, description, files, see also, and bugs.

If the manual page is too large to fit on one screen, the program will display one page at a time until the entire entry has been shown (see **more** in Chapter 4). The synopsis part of the manual page gives a concise description of the command syntax. In the synopsis, certain characters are to be typed literally when using the command; other characters or strings are to be replaced by appropriate words or file names supplied by the user. Portions enclosed in brackets are optional, and the brackets themselves are not part of the command. Ellipses (...) are used in the synopsis to indicate possible repetitions. Most UNIX commands receive as arguments *options* or *flags* that modify the behavior of the command. As mentioned earlier, an option is usually given as a single character preceded by a dash (–).

The "files" section of the manual page gives the locations of files related to the particular command. The "see also" section gives related commands that may be of interest. The "bugs" section lists some known problems with the command.

A simplified synopsis for the command **man** is:

`man` [*section*] *title* ...

If a section number is given, **man** searches for the specified command or system routine title in that section only. A section can be a numeral or a numeral followed by a character *classifier*. For example, 3F is the part of section 3 containing FORTRAN library subroutines. If the section is not given, **man** searches all sections sequentially and outputs the first manual page it finds, if any.

The command **man** also can perform a keyword search through the name and purpose part of the manual pages, displaying each line containing any of the given keywords. This is done by using the –k option:

`man` –k *keyword* ...

Finding Information on Built-In Shell Commands

As indicated, two kinds of commands are used interactively at the shell level, those that are independent programs invoked through the shell and those that are built into the shell. Most commands are independent programs. But, both the *csh* and the *sh* shells have their own built-in commands. Examples of *csh* built-in commands are: **cd**, **echo**, **jobs**, **fg**, and **bg**.

Documentation of built-in commands is a part of the shell's description. Thus:

`man cd`

will not give you what you want. You need:

```
man csh
```

and then find the description for **cd** as a *csh* built-in command.

1.13 Summary

After login you interact with UNIX through a user interface program called the shell, which interprets your commands and allows you to initiate and control jobs. Typing errors can be corrected through input editing. Both the system and the user store data in files managed by the UNIX file system, which has a tree structure. Each file can be referred to by a full (absolute) pathname, a relative pathname, or a simple file name. Each user has a home directory in which personal files and directories can be kept. Files and directories can be created, moved, copied, listed, and destroyed. Read, write, and execute permissions are used to control file access by u (owner), g (group member), and o (others). The owner can set and change the access permissions of a file.

The shell allows redirection of I/O and connection of commands into pipelines. The *csh* shell also allows you to maintain several jobs at once. The **vi** editor is the standard full-screen text editor for creating new files or modifying old ones. Source code programs are compiled or interpreted.

You can communicate directly with other users as well as send and receive mail messages electronically. UNIX offers many facilities and a complete set of manuals. The **man** command can be used to consult the on-line manual pages.

Exercises

1. Get an account on your local system and log in using the procedure shown in this chapter. As soon as you are logged in, log out. What happened after you logged out? Why does this occur?

2. Log in on your system, then try to log out using (1) **logout** and (2) ^D. Log in again and try the following: type **vi**, press RETURN, then type ^Z. Now try to log out. What happens? Issue a second **logout**. Does it work?

3. Log in again and get a listing of all your files. Who put those files there?

4. Try changing your password to the string 123. Why doesn't it work? Make up a longer password and change your password to it. Why did you have to type your password twice this time?

5. Determine what three characters for input editing have been set up for you. Type in the command:

`1x −z foo`

then edit it to:

`1x −a bar`

by deleting "foo" with your word erase character. Finally, retype the entire command as:

`1s bar`

What does the execution of this command tell you about "bar"?

6. Type `man man` and then try starting and stopping the output using ˆ**S** and ˆ**Q**. Try `man man` again, and this time discard the output using ˆ**O**.

7. What is the full pathname of your home directory? What is the full name of your .login file.

8. If a user named "bob" is in his home directory and types:

`cd ../bob`

what happens? What happens if somebody else types the same command?

9. Execute the files stored in the directories /bin and /usr/bin by specifying them as commands. Make a listing of those commands.

10. Using **vi** insert the text:

`The quick frown fox jumped over the hazy dog.`

with two words per line. Then go back to the beginning of the text, change the uppercase "T" to a lowercase "t," change the word "hazy" on line 4 to "lazy," add an "s" to "dog," search backward for the word "frown" and change it to "brown," and save the whole thing as a file print.test.

11. Type in a simple program (in your favorite programming language) to type out the message:

`UNIX is nice once you know it.`

Compile it and run it. Use **script** to get a file containing the program's execution.

12. Send yourself an electronic mail message (many people use this technique to remind themselves of chores to be done). Receive the message you just sent yourself and file it (or discard it) according to its importance to you.

13. Try **talk**ing to yourself. What happens? Check out who is using the system. If you find a friend, try **talk**ing to him or her.

14. Joey Hacker was busy debugging his program in LISP. He typed in his program using the **vi** editor, then he invoked the LISP interpreter, tested his program, exited with ^Z (the system told him his job had been "stopped"), edited his program some more, reinvoked the LISP interpreter, ran it through, and repeated this procedure about six or seven times before deciding that his program ran and that he wanted to log off. However, when he tried logging off, the system responded, There are stopped jobs and gave him a prompt instead of logging him out.

    a. Why did this happen?

    b. What would be the correct way to exit the LISP interpreter?

    c. How can Joey log off now? Describe two procedures.

15. Find the on-line documentation for the **kill** command. What bugs does it warn you about?

Text Editing

2

A text editor is used to enter programs, data, or text into new files, as well as modify existing files. There are as many different text editors as there are computer systems. The standard editors on Berkeley UNIX are **vi** and **ex**. The **vi** editor is a screen-oriented extension of **ex**, which is a line-oriented editor. The **ex** editor is itself an extension of **ed**, the original UNIX editor, which is simple but inconvenient and generally outmoded. Another full-screen editor, **emacs**, was developed independently at MIT for the ITS operating system but is nevertheless becoming quite popular on UNIX systems. In this chapter we describe the usage of **vi** and **emacs**.

Display Text-Editing Concepts

When you edit a file, the editor creates a text *buffer* for the temporary storage of the file that you are editing. The CRT screen acts as a *window* through which the contents of the buffer can be seen. The basic unit of a text file is the character. Consecutive characters form *words, lines, paragraphs*, and so on. A file can contain any number of lines. The window can be moved forward and backward to view any part of the file depending on the commands you give the editor through the keyboard. Since both text and editor commands are entered on the keyboard, every text editor must have some convention for distinguishing between keystrokes that are meant to be commands and keystrokes that are meant to be entered into the buffer as text. As you will see in this chapter, the **vi** convention involves defining different editor modes; **emacs** takes a different approach and uses CONTROL and ESCAPE characters to distinguish between commands and text.

Both editors display a *cursor* on the screen to indicate the position where editing will take place in the buffer. This is called the *current position*. If you give the command to delete a character, then the character at the current position, known as the *current character*, is deleted from the buffer. All insertions, deletions, and other modifications are performed within the buffer. No changes are made to the actual file unless and until you specifically request that the buffer be *saved* to the disk where the file is stored.

Screen editors provide commands to:

- Move the window and move the cursor within the text file

- Insert text

- Delete text

- Substitute specified text with other text

- Search for a given string or pattern

- Cut and paste

- Perform file input and output

Terminal Setup

The procedure used by a display, or *full-screen*, editor to present and edit a window of text is actually quite complicated. It would not be possible at all except for cursor addressing capabilities and protocols that are built into modern CRT terminals and that differ from terminal type to terminal type. The fact that terminals differ in this manner makes it important for the operating system to know which type of terminal you are using and all the details of its capabilities. The UNIX system has a built-in database containing this information for most terminals in use today, so in most cases you need only set the shell *environment variable* TERM to the correct terminal code. For example, if you are using an HP2621 terminal with the *csh* shell, give the command:

setenv TERM 2621   (or, **set** term = 2621)

or, for the *sh* shell:

TERM = 2621
export TERM

It is bothersome to have to set your terminal type each time you log in, and you should include the appropriate command in your .login (for *csh*) or .profile (for *sh*). Many people use hardwired terminals at work or on campus and occasionally dial in from home through a modem. Let us assume your home terminal is a Hewlett-Packard hp2622. Then the following lines can be included in your .login file for *csh* users:

setenv TERM `tset – –m dialup:hp2622`

or the lines:

TERM = `tset – –m dialup:hp2622`
export TERM

in the .profile file for *sh* users. Note that backward quotation characters (`) are used here, which are different from the forward quotation characters ('). The backward quotations activate *command substitution*, which is explained in detail in Chapter 5. The **tset** command returns a code representing the hardwired terminal if you are on such a terminal or hp2622 if you are on a dial-in line. For more information on **tset**, enter **man tset**.

To find the correct terminal code for your terminal, consult the file /etc/termcap or obtain help from local system programmers. If the TERM setting is incorrect, neither **vi** nor **emacs** will work well, if at all. If you use a home computer, you can use the home computer's terminal emulation capability to access a UNIX system. In this case, the variable TERM should be set to the terminal your home computer emulates.

2.1 Getting Started with vi

To edit a file with **vi**, issue the shell-level command:

vi *file*

If the file exists, a copy of it will be read into the buffer, and the screen will display the beginning of the file. If the file does not exist, **vi** will create an empty buffer for you to insert and edit new text into. For a new file, the screen will display all empty lines, each of which is indicated by a tilde (~) character in the first colum. The **vi** editor uses the tildes to indicate "lines beyond the end of the buffer." The tildes are merely a convention; the ~ characters are not contained in the buffer.

Initially, **vi** is in the *command mode*. In this mode, **vi** considers all keystrokes as editing commands. To put text into the buffer, issue a command (for example, **i** or **o**) to change to the *insert mode* (see Section 2.4), then begin typing the text to be inserted. Text insertion is terminated by hitting ESC, which returns **vi** to the command mode. In other words, when you are not inserting text into the buffer, **vi** is always in command mode.

In the command mode, **vi** stands ready to receive and carry out your next command. The **vi** commands are short and easy to type: They are single-, double-, and multiple-character commands, which are carried out as soon as they are typed. Some **vi** commands are terminated by the special characters ESC or RETURN, and most **vi** commands can be preceded by an integer value, called a *repeat count*. The repeat count specifies the number of times a command is to be performed. We use the variable n to indicate this repeat count when presenting these commands. If n is omitted it is assumed to be 1. Typing errors in a **vi** command can be corrected using input editing (see Section 1.2).

The **vi** buffer window is always at least one line less than the total number of lines on your screen. The bottom line is called the *status line* and is used by **vi** to echo certain commands and to display messages. Any command beginning with a colon (:) as well as any search command beginning with a slash (/) (or **?**) is echoed on the status line. However, most other commands are not. Not being able to see what you type in the command mode can take some getting used to.

When you are finished with the editing session, you need to save the buffer and get out of **vi**. You type:

ZZ   (save buffer and exit)

If you wish to discard the buffer without updating the disk file, type:

:q! RETURN   (quit without saving buffer on disk)

instead of **ZZ**. Be careful: It's not difficult to miss **q** and hit **w** instead. Unfortunately, the **vi** command:

:w! RETURN   (write buffer over file)

writes the file out even if there is a file by the same name on the disk; so instead of abandoning the unwanted buffer, **vi** wipes out a file!!!

2.2 Moving the Screen

In **vi** and other display editors, the *screen* is a window through which a portion of the editor buffer is visible. To edit a file, first you must move the screen to that part of the file where editing will take place. There are a few ways to do this: by line number, by search, or by *browsing*.

The buffer consists of lines of text numbered sequentially beginning with line 1. The command:

*k*G   (goto line *k*)

will position the screen over the buffer so that the *k*th line is centered on the screen with the cursor placed at the beginning of the line. **G** provides a way to move the screen to any absolute position within the buffer; it also is possible to move the screen in a relative manner. To move forward and backward *n* lines from the *current line* (line with cursor), *n*RETURN and *n*– are used, respectively. The cursor is positioned over the first nonwhite character (a space, a tab, and so on) of the target line. Sometimes, pressing RETURN or – repeatedly is a convenient way to move a few lines forward or backward.

In many cases the line number of the target is not at your fingertips, but if you know an unambiguous substring of the text, a search command can be used to locate the target. The **vi** commands:

/ *text* RETURN   (forward search)

? *text* RETURN   (backward search)

search the buffer for the given *text* (these commands will be echoed on the status line). The forward search begins at the *current character* (at the cursor) and proceeds forward toward the end of buffer. If the pattern is found, the cursor will be positioned at the pattern's first character. If the search reaches the end of buffer, it will *wrap around* to the beginning of the buffer until the pattern is found or until the search returns to where it started. A backward search moves in the opposite direction, starting toward the beginning of the buffer and then wrapping around through the end until it returns to its starting point. If the pattern is not found, a message "Fail" will appear on the status line. You can locate multiple occurrences of a pattern after the first occurrence is found by typing:

n   (search for the next match)

which searches in the direction of the previous search command, or by typing:

N   (search for the next match)

which searches in the reverse direction of the previous search command.

The third way to position the screen is by browsing around until you find the section of the buffer you want. The commands:

^D	(scroll down)
^U	(scroll up)

scroll the screen forward and backward, respectively. Smooth scroll is used if your terminal has this feature, so that you can read the lines as they are scrolling by. The commands:

^F	(forward)
^B	(backward)

refresh the screen and give the next and previous screen, respectively. Two lines of text overlap the last screen to provide reading continuity.

2.3 Cursor Motion Commands

Once the screen has been positioned over the buffer location you wish to edit, the cursor must be positioned to the exact line, word, or character you wish to change. The **vi** editor has a full complement of commands to move the cursor. The following commands move the cursor to the first nonwhite character at the beginning of the target line:

H	first line on the current screen
L	last line on the screen
M	middle line on the screen

In addition:

h	moves the cursor left one character on the current line
j	moves the cursor down one line onto the same column position or the last character if the next line is not long enough
k	moves the cursor up one line onto the same column position or the last character if the previous line is not long enough
l	moves the cursor right one character on the current line
SPACEBAR	works the same as **l**
^	moves the cursor to the beginning of the current line
$	moves the cursor to the end of the current line
w	moves the cursor forward one word to the first character of the next word

e	moves the cursor to the end of the current word
b	moves the cursor backward one word to the first character that begins a word
t*char*	moves the cursor to the character just before the next occurrence of *char*acter in the current line (**T** for just after the previous occurrence of *char*acter)
f*char*	moves the cursor to the next (**F** for previous) occurrence of *char*acter in the current line
; (semicolon)	repeats the previous **f** or **F** command
, (comma)	repeats the previous **f** or **F** command in the other direction

The **f**, **;**, **F**, and **,** combinations are fast ways of moving the cursor in the current line. If your terminal has arrow keys, they will work the same as **h**, **j**, **k**, and **l**, although many prefer the letter keys because they are convenient for touch typing. Many people find it even easier to use SPACEBAR for **l**. To move the cursor to a specific column in the current line use:

*k***|**   (cursor to column *k*)

The command **|** without a preceding number is equivalent to **^**.

The **vi** editing commands also can move the cursor to sentences, paragraphs, and sections. To move the cursor backward or forward over a sentence, paragraph or section, use:

(	moves the cursor left to the beginning of a sentence
)	moves the cursor right to the beginning of a sentence
{	moves the cursor left to the beginning of a paragraph
}	moves the cursor right to the beginning of a paragraph
[[	moves the cursor left to the beginning of a section
]]	moves the cursor right to the beginning of a section

These commands can be combined with commands such as delete to specify editing actions on words, sentences, and paragraphs. For example:

d)

deletes everything from the current position up to the beginning of the next sentence.

2.4 Typing or Inserting Text

The **vi** editor uses mode to distinguish between keystrokes meant as commands and keystrokes meant as text. While the editor is in the insert mode, all keystrokes are considered text and are inserted into the buffer until you press ESC. Several commands put **vi** into the insert mode. The most frequently used command is:

i any number of
lines of text to be inserted
terminated by the first escape character **ESC**

This command inserts the text just before the cursor (if you use **a** instead of **i**, the text will be inserted to the right of the cursor). After you press **i**, **vi** goes into the insert mode. From that point on, characters typed go into the buffer and are not considered to be commands. If, for example, you were to type **i** and then ZZ, the editor would insert ZZ into the buffer. If you type **ZZ** in the command mode, you would leave the editor.

Text can be inserted more than one line at a time, and lines can be separated by pressing RETURN. As you type, **vi** displays either what you type over the existing text on the screen or pushes the existing characters to the right as you type in new text. The exact method depends on your terminal. If the inserted text overwrites existing characters on the screen, do not be alarmed. These characters are still in the buffer. When you end your insertion by pressing ESC, the screen will display the inserted text correctly. Typing mistakes can be corrected in the usual manner, although you may choose to ignore the error and correct it later after returning to the command mode.

To insert one or more lines of text after the current line, type:

o*anytext* **ESC**

This sequence opens up a blank line below the current line for the insertion. If an uppercase **O** is used, the lines are inserted above the current line. Also:

I*anytext* **ESC**

and

A*anytext* **ESC**

insert text at the beginning (before first nonwhite character) and the end of the current line, respectively.

2.5 Inserting Special Characters

Many special characters cannot be entered into the buffer directly. For example, ESC terminates the insert mode, ^H erases the previous character typed, and the interrupt character (usually DELETE or ^C) terminates insertion as well. RETURN separates lines but is not entered into the buffer as a character. To enter any of these characters into the buffer, you must precede them with

^V. **^V** takes away the special meaning of the next character typed and forces **vi** to insert the character(s) literally: **^V** *escapes* or *quotes* the next character. Thus:

```
i^V^H^VESCESC
```

inserts the two characters ^H and ESC. One instance where special characters are needed is in the .login file, where you may wish to redefine the UNIX shell-level erase and interrupt characters.

2.6 Erasing or Deleting Text

The **vi** editor provides many convenient ways to delete text from the buffer. To delete a few characters, the commands:

*n***x**   (delete next *n* characters)

*n***X**   (delete previous *n* characters)

can be used. The value of *n* can be arbitrarily large, and an omitted *n* is assumed to be 1. The command:

D   (delete to end of line)

deletes from the cursor to the end of the line.

Joining two lines together is actually a deletion. To join the lines, you must delete the character at the end of the first line that marks the separation between it and the following line. To delete the line separation and join two lines in this manner, use:

J   (join next line)

The **vi** editor will not let two words run together; it will include a space between the last character of the first line and the first character of the second line.

One or several words can be deleted easily by:

*n***dw**   (delete next *n* words)

*n***db**   (delete previous *n* words)

These commands erase the next and previous *n* words, respectively. Again, if *n* is omitted, it is assumed to be 1. Use:

*n***dd**   (delete *n* lines)

to delete the next *n* lines starting with the current line. If *n* is omitted (*n* = 1), the current line is deleted. Depending on your terminal, **vi** may remove the deleted lines and close the gap by moving lines up from below, or it may use an @ in front of an empty line to indicate a line deleted. These @s are just markers and are not in the buffer. They will disappear when the screen is redrawn.

Sometimes a whole range of lines must be deleted. The command:

: *i,j***d**   (delete lines *i* to *j*)

deletes all lines from *i* to *j*, inclusive. The **vi** commands that begin with a colon (:) are actually **ex** commands being accessed by **vi**. Most of these commands use a range *i,j* where *i* and *j* are line numbers (addresses). The address *j* must not be less than *i*. In specifying line addresses, you may use:

$ for the line at the end of the file

.   for the current line

Also allowed are such expressions as:

+4   for current line plus 4

−3   for current line minus 3

$−10   for last line minus 10

and so on. For example, you would use:

:.,$d

to delete from the current line to the end of the buffer. To delete the four previous lines and the current line (five lines all together), type:

:−4,.d

2.7 Undo and Repeat

What if you make a mistake and delete something you didn't mean to? The **vi** command:

u   (undo)

undoes the latest change made to the file. This command is very convenient and often lifesaving. (For example, what happens if you press **uu**?) The cut-and-paste discussion (Section 2.10) has more on recovering deleted text.

Another convenience is the:

.   (repeat)

command, which repeats the latest change made to the buffer. For example, after giving the command 3**x**, you can move the cursor and press **.** to delete another three characters. To illustrate the use of this feature, let us consider *commenting out* code in a FORTRAN program. Suppose you want to insert the four characters CC## at the beginning of a number of consecutive lines. You position the cursor at the beginning of the first line, then press:

I**CC##ESC**

From this point on, type the two characters:

RETURN.

to comment out each successive line. RETURN moves the cursor to the beginning of the next line, and the period (.) repeats the last change, which is the desired insertion.

2.8 Making Small Changes

The **vi** editor includes several provisions for making small changes easily and efficiently:

r *char*	replaces the current character by the given character
~ (tilde)	changes the case (upper to lower or lower to upper) of the current character
*n*c w *text***ESC**	replaces the next *n* words by the given text. The extent of the text being replaced is marked on the screen by the cursor and a $ as soon as *n*c**w** is typed.
*n*cb *text***ESC**	is the same as *n*c**w** but replaces the previous *n* words
*n*s *text***ESC**	substitutes the next *n* characters by the given text

The following are some useful combinations of commands:

xp	transposes the current character and the next character. This is really the command **x** followed by the command **p**.
easESC	pluralizes the current word. A combination of **e** and **a**.
ddp	interchanges the current line and the next line. A combination of **dd** and **p**.
dwwP	interchanges the current word and the next word
dwbP	interchanges the current word and the previous word

2.9 Text Objects and Operators

A text object is the portion of text defined by the current position in the buffer and by a cursor motion command. It is either a continuous *stream* of characters or a section of consecutive lines that is bounded at one end by the current position and at the other by the place on which the cursor would appear after a cursor motion command were executed. For example, if the cursor is on the *m* of the word "men" in the following text:

```
Now is the time for
all good men to come
to the aid of their country.
```

then **2w** specifies "men to," **tm** specifies "men to co," **b** specifies "good," − the first two lines, and + the last two lines. You might think of this concept in terms of standing at one spot (the current position or current line) and tossing a stone (a cursor motion command). The area between where you are standing and where the stone lands is the text object you are interested in.

An *operator* is a **vi** command that operates on a text object, which is given to the operator as an argument. Two important operators are **d** (delete) and **c** (replace or change away). For example:

dG   deletes the current line through end of file

The **d** is the operator and the **G** is the cursor motion command that specifies how far and in what direction to go from the current position to the other boundary of the text object. Here are a few more examples:

d$	deletes the current character through end of line
d)	deletes the current character to end of sentence
dt*char*	deletes the current character up to *char* in current line
c5w	changes away five words (use **b** in place of **w** for five words backward)
d/*text*ESC	deletes the current character up to text pattern

Another useful operator is the yank command **y**, which will be discussed in the next section.

2.10 Cut and Paste

One of the most useful operations an editor can provide is *cut and paste*. It reduces the task of rearranging major portions of a file to a matter of a few keystrokes. The **vi** editor provides auxiliary buffers that can be used for different kinds of cut-and-paste operations:

named buffers	a set of 26 buffers a–z
dtb	a single, unnamed, "deleted text buffer" (*dtb*), which always holds a copy of the latest deleted or changed away (**cw**, for instance) text
numbered buffers	the last nine blocks of deleted text are saved in a set of numbered buffers 1–9

The **vi** editor also provides commands to save a part of the main buffer in an auxiliary buffer and to copy the contents of an auxiliary buffer into the main buffer. This mechanism allows you to move text around easily in your file or between files.

Let's say you want to cut five lines from one place and move them to another place in the file. First move the cursor to the first of the five lines to be cut, then issue the command:

5dd   (delete five lines into *dtb*)

These deleted lines are held in the *dtb*. You then move the cursor to where you want to paste these five lines and use the *put* command:

p or **P**   (put *dtb* into buffer)

To insert a copy of the *dtb* into the main buffer. The exact position where the insertion takes place depends on the location of the cursor and whether the *dtb* contains whole lines or characters. If the *dtb* contains a number of whole lines (for example, our five lines saved by 5**dd**), the insert position is after (**p**) or before (**P**) the current line. If the *dtb* contains a sequence of characters (for example, text saved by 200**x**), the insertion is after or before the current character.

Copy into an Auxiliary Buffer: yank

To save text in a named buffer, you use the *yank* command **y**:

"*xy text-object*   (copy object into buffer *x*)

where the first character is a double quotation mark. The *x* is any single-character buffer name (a–z). If the command **y** is not preceded by a buffer name, the *dtb* is used. Again, the *text object* to be yanked is specified by an appropriate cursor motion key sequence as explained in the last section. For example, to save the current line and the next nine lines in buffer v, you would type:

"vy9RETURN

The **vi** editor will display the message:

```
10 lines yanked
```

on the status line to confirm completion of the command. Note that the cursor and the lines of text stay exactly the way they were. Of course, you could use any cursor motion key sequence instead of 9RETURN to specify a text object. Similar to **y**, the command:

"x**d** text-object

deletes the specified text object into the named buffer *x*.

Paste: put

To copy text from a named buffer *x* into the main buffer, type:

"x**p**

or

"x**P**

With numbered buffers:

"n**p**

or

"n**P**

will replace the *n*th previously deleted text.

Direct Text Relocation: move

There is also a command to move lines of text directly from one place in the main buffer to another location:

:*i,j*m*k*   (move lines *i* through *j* to *k*)

The range of lines *i* through *j*, inclusive, is moved after line *k*. For example:

```
:3,8m.
```

moves lines 3–8 after the current line. And:

```
:.,.+5m$
```

moves the current line and the next five lines to the end of the file.

It is often useful to mark certain lines with symbolic names when rearranging text and to refer to these names instead of absolute line numbers.

The command:

m*x*   (mark currrent position)

marks the current position with the single character name *x*. Any lowercase character can be used as a mark. To move the cursor to this line from anywhere in the buffer, you type:

'*x*   (go to line marked *x*)
`*x*   (go to character marked *x*)

Marked line addresses can be used in the same places as line numbers. For example:

: '*x***,.m $**

move the text between the mark *x* and the current line (inclusive) to the end of file.

2.11 File-Related Commands

In simple applications of **vi**, the only necessary file manipulations are reading the file into the buffer initially and writing the buffer back out onto the disk at the end of the editing session. Files may, however, be accessed more flexibly than this. The main buffer can be written out to the file in mid-session. In fact, it is advisable to check your work occasionally by writing out the modified file as you progress. Otherwise, if the system crashed or you committed some dire error that erased the main buffer, you would lose whatever changes you had made and a great deal of time. The forms of the *write* command are:

:w   writes back changes on disk
:w *file*   writes the buffer to *file*
:w! *file*   writes even if *file* exists
:*i,j***w** *file*   writes lines *i–j* to *file*

    If *file* exists, **vi** will not overwrite it with the **:w** command, unless **!** is added. It means "please carry out command as requested, I know what I am doing." The usage is a carryover from the >! type shell-level commands.

    It is often useful to read another file into the file being edited and combine the two files. You can use:

:r *file*   (read in *file*)

to read in the specified file and insert it after the current line.

If you wish to discard the current buffer and edit another file, you can type:

:vi *file*   (edit new *file*)

to replace the buffer by *file*. Whatever you have yanked from the old file will not be affected by this action and will remain in the auxiliary buffers. This command provides a way to cut and paste between files.

2.12 Text Substitution and Global Changes

Many times a file will require the same revision many times. For example, if you have written a letter about a man named John and discover that he spells his name "Jon," you will not relish having to fix each reference to his name individually. One of the most time-saving features provided by an editor such as **vi** is the ability to make *global* changes—to change each occurrence of a certain text pattern—with a single command. The more instances there are of the pattern, the greater will be the savings in time and effort. In this section we discuss several such global change commands. Complete, detailed descriptions of the global commands can be found in the **ex** reference manual. (Remember: The **vi** editor is an extension of the **ex** editor.)

Substitute

The command:

: *s/pattern/text/*

is used to substitute *text* for the *first occurrence* of *pattern* in the current line. For example:

:s/summer/winter/

substitutes the first occurrence of summer with winter on the current line. The character & when used in the replacement text represents the pattern text. Thus:

:s/summer/each &/

substitutes summer with each summer. The substitute text can be empty, in which case the effect is deletion. If the substitute command is followed by **g**, that is:

`:`s/*pattern*/*text*/g

then all occurrences in the current line are replaced.

The search and substitute operations can be combined into:

`:`/*pattern1*/s/*pattern2*/*text*/g

which first searches for a line containing *pattern1* and then substitutes *text* for *pattern2* in that line. Note: *pattern2* can be omitted if it is the same as *pattern1*. Furthermore, the character & can be used in *text* to interpolate the pattern. For example:

`:/UNIX/s//Berkeley &/`

replaces the first occurrence of UNIX with Berkeley UNIX.

The search patterns used can be more than simple strings. The way search patterns are specified is discussed in Section 2.13.

Global Substitute

The global command **:g** allows you to specify a range of lines over which other **ex** commands, such as **s**, are executed. The format is:

`:` *range* g/*pattern*/**ex**-*commands*

This means the *commands* are applied to all lines in the given *range* that contain the specified *pattern*. (If *range* is not given, the default range is all lines in the buffer.)

For example, to change the pattern LISP to Common LISP throughout the file, you would use:

`:g/LISP/s//Common LISP/g`

Note: If the trailing **g** is omitted, only the first occurrence on all lines will be replaced. Global substitute is powerful but dangerous. It does not give you a visual confirmation of each change. To remedy this, you may use an additional character **p** (after the trailing **g**); then each affected line is displayed on your terminal as the replacements are made. *Also beware:* Global changes, when issued incorrectly, can severely scramble the buffer. To guard against this, always write out the buffer to the file before doing a global replacement.

The **:g** can be applied to commands other than the substitute command. For example, to delete all lines containing the string *obsolete*, you would use:

`:g/obsolete/d`

Indentation

Another useful global change is the indentation of text. The commands:

n<<
n>>

indent and push out *n* lines starting at the current line. Each line is shifted by an amount set by the *shift width* option sw (normally eight spaces). Similarly, the commands:

<text-object
>text-object

shift the entire text object, which must consist of whole lines. In other words, text objects of individual characters or words cannot be shifted in this way. For example:

>G

right-shifts from the current line to the last line in the buffer, whereas:

>L

right-shifts from the current line to the last line on the screen.

2.13 Search Patterns

We have discussed the **vi** search command as a convenient way to move the cursor to specific locations in the file. The search command looks for a text string that matches a given pattern. The simplest pattern to find is a literal string of characters. For example:

`/four score`

searches forward for the literal pattern *four score*. If ? is used instead of /, then a backward search is performed. A pattern extending beyond the end of one line into the next line cannot be specified in **vi**. This is a shortcoming of **vi** having evolved from the line-oriented **ex**.

Special Characters in Search Patterns

Special arrangements have been made for locating patterns at the beginning or end of lines. The character ^ ($) when used as the first (last) character of a pattern matches the beginning (end) of the line. Thus the string *four score* matches the pattern:

```
^four score
```

only if it begins in column one on some line. Similarly, it matches:

```
four score$
```

only when it is at the end of a line. If some blank space or nondisplaying characters follow, the match will fail, even though it may appear to you to be at the end of the line.

So far we have considered search patterns in which each character is specified exactly. In many situations, however, it is neither necessary nor desirable to specify the pattern literally and exactly. Let us look at a practical example: Consider editing a report that contains many items labeled sequentially by (1), (2), and so on. In revising the document, you need to add a few new items and renumber the labels. A search pattern can be specified as:

```
/([1-9]
```

where the notation [1-9] matches any single character 1–9. With this notation, you can search using /([1-9] the first time and then make the appropriate modification to the number. You then can repeat the search using the search repeat command **n**, change another number, search, and so on until all the changes have been made.

The **vi** editor offers a rich set of pattern notations (Figure 2.1). They are referred to as *regular expressions*. To show the power of regular expressions, let us look at some specific matches:

[A-Z]	matches any capitalized character
\<[A-Z]	matches any word that begins with a capital
^##*	matches one or more #s starting in column one
;;*$	matches one or more ;s at the end of a line
ing\>	matches any word ending in *ing*

Quoting in Search Patterns

The use of special characters in any searching scheme inevitably leads to the question of how to search for a pattern that contains a special character. Let us say that you are editing a report and you want to search for [9], which is a bibliographical reference used in the report. Because the pattern [9] matches the single character 9, you need to *quote* the [and] so that they represent themselves rather than taking on special meanings.

In **vi** the *quote character* \ (backslash) removes the special function of the character immediately following, forcing it to stand for itself. For example:

```
/\[9\]
```

Figure 2.1 ▪ **vi Pattern Notations**

Pattern	Meaning
^	matches the beginning of a line
$	matches the end of a line
.	matches any single character
[*string*]	matches any single character in *string*
[^*string*]	matches any single character not in *string*
[*x–y*]	matches any single character between *x* and *y*
*pattern**	matches any repetition of the pattern (including zero)
\<	matches the beginning of a word
\>	matches the end of a word

searches for the literal [9]. Here are some other examples:

/\.\.\.	searches for ...
?\?!	searches backward for ?!
/\/*	searches for /*
/\\	searches for \

An unnecessary quote character will cause no harm.

2.14 Setting vi Options

The **vi** editor includes a set of options that the user can set to affect **vi** operation. These options help *customize* the editor for an individual user. There are three kinds of options:

- numeric options
- string options
- toggle (binary) options

Numeric and string options are set by:

`:set` *option*=*value*

and toggle options are set by:

`:set` *option*

or

`:set` no*option*

For example, magic is an option that normally is set. It allows for the special characters [, ., and * in search patterns. If you:

`:set` `nomagic`

these characters no longer will be special characters in search patterns. To list options and their values for examination in **vi**, use the following commands:

:set	lists option values different from the default
:set *option?*	shows the option value
:set all	lists all option settings

Several of the most useful options are discussed here:

ai The autoindent option controls the automatic indentation of lines when text is inserted. When autoindent is set, a new line is started at the same indentation as the previous line. This is especially useful when typing in programs. However, it is often the case that the supplied indentations are needed on some lines and not on others. To reject a supplied indentation, immediately after receiving it type:

^**D** cancels one shift width (default eight spaces) of indentation

Suppose, for example, that after typing RETURN while inserting, autoindent supplies you with 16 spaces (or two tabs), and you only need eight spaces. You should type ^**D** to move the cursor left eight spaces. The amount of left shift for each ^**D** is itself an sw option. The default is noai.

lisp Setting the lisp option (default value is nolisp) facilitates editing LISP programs. The **vi** editor then reads LISP S-expressions as text objects. The commands (and) move the cursor to an S-expression. The commands { and } move over a balanced set of parentheses. The command % takes the cursor to the opposite balancing parenthesis. When lisp is set, the autoindent works differently; it supplies a consistent indentation level to align LISP expressions. One useful operation is positioning the cursor at the beginning of a LISP function and typing:

= %

This *pretty prints* the LISP structure by realigning the statements.

ic   The ignorecase option forces **vi** to ignore the difference between upper and lower case during searches. The default is noic.

nu   The nu option displays line numbers in front of the lines of text. The default value is nonu.

sm   The showmatch option bounces the cursor back momentarily to show you the opening bracket when the closing bracket is typed in the insert mode. This works for) and }. If the matching bracket can't be found, **vi** beeps (if your terminal has the capability).

When a new **vi** job is initiated, all options have their default values. It often is desirable to set certain options whenever you use **vi** or **ex**. You can save options permanently by changing the shell environment variable EXINIT. Including the following line:

setenv EXINIT 'set lisp ai sm ic'

in the .login file for *csh*, or the lines:

EXINIT= 'set ai lisp sm ic'
export EXINIT

in the .profile file for *sh* users, saves the indicated options. The settings shown here are useful for editing LISP programs.

2.15 vi **Macros**

Occasionally, a sequence of editing commands is used repeatedly to make similar changes at different places in a file. If the sequence is long enough or used often enough, it may be convenient to assign a keystroke to save the sequence, which can then be used in its place. In **vi**, such named key sequences are called *macros*.

The map command establishes a named macro. The general form is:

:map *key cmd-seq*

where *cmd-seq* is a string representing one or more **vi** commands. For example:

:map v /UNIX^VESC

establishes the character v as a macro to search for UNIX in the buffer. When v is typed, it is as though the entire key sequence /UNIX **ESC** is typed. Note the use of **^V** to quote **ESC**, so that it is not taken as terminating the entire map command.

Consider editing a file where the word UNIX is used frequently, sometimes boldface and other times not. Let us say that you have decided to go through the file and make UNIX boldface in certain places. For *troff* documents, boldface UNIX is represented by:

`\fBUNIX\fP`

in the text. Thus the editing task consists of searching for the pattern UNIX and then for each occurrence, changing it to boldface if necessary. The map command is used to establish the macro:

`:map g i\fB^VESCea\fP^VESC`

Now the macro g changes any word to `\fB`*word*`\fP`, assuming the cursor has been positioned on the first letter of *word*. With the preceding macros, an otherwise tedious editing task is reduced to typing v's and g's.

Mapped macro names are restricted to a single keystroke, which may include a terminal function key. The command:

`:map #n cmd-seq`

defines function key F*n* as a macro. Because g, v, and V are not already defined as **vi** commands, they are good choices for macro names. However, **vi** also allows for saving a command key sequence in a named buffer (a–z). Once the key sequence is stored in a named buffer, then the command:

`@x`   (invoke macro in buffer *x*)

where *x* stands for the buffer name, will invoke the stored key sequence.

2.16 Invoking the vi Editor

The routine usage of **vi** simply involves the command:

`vi file`

However, this is not the only way to invoke **vi**. The usage synopsis is:

`vi [−t tag] [−r] [+ command] [−l] [−wn] file ...`

The options and their meaning are explained:

Option	Meaning
-l	This option is used to set up **vi** for editing a LISP source code file. When invoked with the −l option, **vi** automatically sets the options showmatch and lisp.
-r	This option is used to recover after an editor or system crash, or to recover from failing to exit the editor before logging out. The command:

vi −r

gives a complete listing of files saved that can be recovered. A typical output is:

```
On Sun Jun 1 at 17:10 saved 4 lines of file
".exrc"
On Mon May 26 at 22:01 saved 28 lines of file
"community"
On Tue May 27 at 23:52 saved 67 lines of file
"finger"
```

to recover any of these saved files simply use:

vi −r *name*

-w*n*	This option sets the *window size* to *n* lines. The default size at high speeds is 24, the size of most display terminals. On dial-up lines, the default size is either 16 or eight lines, depending on the speed of the line. At slow baud rates, a smaller window takes appreciably less time to redraw when screens change.
-t *tag*	This option is useful in maintaining a group of related source code or other text files. A *tag* is searched for in a file bearing the name tags in the current directory. The tags file is normally created by a command such as **ctags**. A tags file follows a simple format. It contains a number of lines, each with three fields separated by blanks or tabs:

tag-name filename **ex**−*cursor-position-command*

The lines in a tags file are sorted. The effect of the command:

vi −t *tag*

is to search for a line in the tags file with *tag* in the first field. When found, the file name in the second field is loaded into **vi** for editing, and the cursor is moved to an initial position specified by the search command in the third field. For example, the file /usr/lib/tags contains systemwide tags information for UNIX source code. The **vi** option tags contains the names of all tags files. The default setting is:

```
tags=tags /usr/lib/tags
```

A tag is searched for in sequence in the files given in the tags option.

+ *command* This indicates that **vi** should begin by executing the specified *command*. For example, the argument +50 places the cursor on line 50.

2.17 vi **Initialization: EXINIT and .exrc**

The shell environment variable EXINIT is used to initialize **vi** and **ex**, so that commands and option settings contained in EXINIT will be executed any time **vi** or **ex** is invoked. For example, the following can be put in your .login file:

```
setenv EXINIT 'se ai terse nowarn sm ic slow\
        map g i\fIESCea\fPESC'
```

In addition to this initialization mechanism, **vi** and **ex** also use the initialization file:

```
.exrc
```

in a user's home directory. Commands contained in this file are processed as though they are typed interactively every time **vi** or **ex** is invoked. Option settings and often-used macros can be put in a .exrc file, an example of which is shown in Figure 2.2.

The .exrc file in Figure 2.2 sets function key 1 (#1) to italicize a word, function key 2 to boldface a word, and g to break a line for input. The symbols ˆ**M** and ˆ[are the display representations of the nondisplayable characters RETURN and ESC, respectively.

Figure 2.2 ▪ Example .exrc file

```
map    #1 i\fIˆ[ea\fPˆ[
map    #2 i\fBˆ[ea\fPˆ[
map    g iˆMˆ[\kA
```

2.18 The emacs Editor

The **vi** editor is available on almost all UNIX systems and is a good full-screen editor. However, other text editors exist, and **emacs** is another popular editor. The **emacs** editor originally was developed at the MIT Laboratory for Computer Science. As **emacs** gained popularity, it was ported to UNIX so that today, many UNIX systems offer some version(s) of **emacs** in addition to the standard **vi** editor. The **emacs** editor is highly customizable. It also means that any general description of **emacs** is likely to be inadequate since commands you enter for the same operations can vary from version to version. The following is only a brief introduction to **emacs**. If you feel comfortable with **vi** and do not wish to study another text editor at this time, you may skip this section.

Several notable features of **emacs** are listed here:

1. Rather than operating in distinct modes like **vi**, **emacs** operates in only one mode: most characters are typed and inserted at the cursor position. Commands are given as control characters or are prefixed by ESC or `^X`. ESC or `^X`.

2. The **emacs** editor can manage multiple display windows by dividing a CRT screen into two or more horizontal sections. You can cut and paste between windows.

3. The **emacs** editor allows for user definition of editing functions and command keystrokes. Any built-in or user-defined editing function can be bound to any keystroke. For example, if you bind the function *delete-character* to the keystroke `^D`, then `^D` invokes that function. A command also can be invoked by its full name.

4. Some versions of **emacs** have built-in features that help in editing LISP, C, Pascal, and other languages.

emacs Commands

Each **emacs** command has a full name and a one- or two-character *key sequence* used to invoke the command. A key sequence is either a single control character or a two-character combination whose first character is `^X` or ESC. The key sequence for any **emacs** command can be changed to a different key sequence to suit the preference of an individual user. Following conventional **emacs** notations, a two-character key sequence will be denoted in this section as two characters separated by a hyphen. Thus:

ESC–*char*   stands for ESCape followed by any character

`^X`–*char*   stands for `^X` followed by any character

In our **emacs** presentation, a key sequence usually is followed by the full **emacs** function name normally associated with it. A full function name in **emacs** often consists of several words connected by hyphens (**exit-emacs**, for example). The full name usually gives a pretty good idea of what a command does.

There are two ways to invoke the same **emacs** command:

1. Typing the key sequence of the command
2. Typing ESC-**X** followed by the full command name

Entering and Exiting emacs

To invoke **emacs,** you simply type:

`emacs` *filename*

where *filename* is either an existing file or a new file. You can exit **emacs** by:

`^X-^C`   (exit-emacs, no write)

Because this command does not write out the edited file(s), you have to issue:

`^X-^S`   (save-buffer)

which will save the current buffer. On some versions of **emacs**, the following also will work:

`^X-^F`   (write-file-exit)

emacs Windows

The CRT screen may be divided into one or more *windows*. A buffer is associated with each window, and a part of the buffer is visible through the window. At the bottom of a window is a *mode line*. Below the mode line is a *message line*. The message line is used for two purposes: to display messages to the user and to prompt for necessary input from the user.

The mode line, which varies from version to version, contains information about the editing activity in the window. Here is a sample mode line:

`Buffer:file.c File:/user/fac/pwang/file.c 27%`

On most terminals, the mode line is displayed in reverse video (black characters on white) or some other highlight mode. The word Buffer: is followed by a buffer name that is normally the last part of a UNIX file pathname. The 27% shows the position of the window relative to the whole buffer. In this example, the cursor is 27 percent of the way down from the beginning of the buffer. Sometimes, **emacs** will set up a *help window* that has no file associated with it.

Panic Stop in emacs

Sometimes you may want to stop the currently executing command, either because it is taking too long, because you suspect it is in an infinite loop, because it is taking the wrong action, because you typed something wrong, or any other reason. In this circumstance in **emacs**, use:

^G   (abort)

which immediately stops all activity and returns you to the **emacs** top (command) level.

emacs **Cursor Movement**

In **emacs**, the editing position is always relative to the current position, which is known as the *point*. The point is not shown on the screen, but it is between the cursor and the character before the cursor. Moving the cursor, and therefore the point, allows you to view the file and move to the location where modifications are needed. The following table shows important **emacs** commands for cursor motion. In the table, the key sequences are followed by the full command names.

Key Sequence	Command Name	Key Sequence	Command Name
ESC-<	beginning-of-file	ESC->	end-of-file
^N	next-line	^P	previous-line
^A	beginning-of-line	^E	end-of-line
^F	forward-character	^B	backward-character
ESC-f	forward-word	ESC-b	backward-word
^V	next-page	ESC-v	previous-page
^S	search-forward	^R	search-reverse

For the search commands ^S and ^R, **emacs** prompts you with:

Search for:

in the message line and waits for you to type in a character string. (In some versions, **emacs** will search for the next string as you type the search string). To terminate the search string, press ESC. When responding to a prompt, you may correct typing mistakes with UNIX input editing. To repeat a previous search, enter ^S or ^R with an empty search string.

The emacs **Region**

The **emacs** editor can maintain a *mark*, which is simply a remembered cursor position. The command:

`^@`   (set-mark)

erases the old mark (if any) and defines the current position as the mark. The mark not only remembers a position in the file but also delimits one end of the *region*, which is the object of several commands to be discussed later. The other end of the region is the point. You can move back and forth between the point and the mark with:

`^X-^X`   (exchange-point-and-mark)

Note that `^X-^X` does not change the region.

Many other commands manipulate the region. For example, some commands can set the region in upper case or lower case, write out the region, and so on. Consult your **emacs** manual for details when you need these commands.

Insert and Delete in emacs

There is no need for an *insert* command in **emacs**. Characters insert themselves at the point as you type them. The following table lists some frequently used **emacs** commands for insertion and deletion.

Key Sequence	Command Name	Key Sequence	Command Name
`^I`	inserts TAB	`^Q`	quote-character
`^J`	newline-and-indent	`^O`	newline-and-backup
`^D`	delete-next-character	DELETE	delete-previous-character
ESC-**d**	delete-next-word	ESC-DELETE	delete-previous-word

To insert a control character or the character ESC, you must precede the character with `^Q` (the quote-character command). Two control characters are exceptions to this rule, and they insert themselves: `^I` inserts a TAB, `^M` a RETURN. The command `^O` inserts a new line after the point. The command `^J` inserts a new line and tabs it appropriately. The delete commands are self-explanatory. For the delete word commands, the word deleted is from the point (cursor) to the end of the word. Thus, if the point is in the middle of a word and one of the delete word commands is typed, only a portion of the word will be deleted.

Cut and Paste in emacs

The **emacs** editor maintains a *kill buffer*, which is similar in function to the *dtb* in **vi**. The kill buffer contains the text most recently *killed*, using any kill command. ˆ**Y** can be used to insert the contents of the kill buffer at the current position. The kill buffer is not deleted by ˆ**Y**, so it can be inserted repeatedly. There are many ways to place text into the kill buffer; and they are listed in the following table.

Key Sequence	Command Name
ˆ**Y**	yank-from-kill-buffer
ˆ**W**	delete-to-kill-buffer (from mark to point)
ESC-**w**	copy-region-as-kill
ˆ**K**	kill-line

The command ˆ**W** is used to delete the **emacs** region and place that text in the kill buffer. The command ESC-**w** places the region into the kill buffer but does not delete the region itself. ESC-**w** is convenient when you do not want to alter the buffer but want to copy a portion of it. The command ˆ**K** is most often used to cut and paste: It kills the text between the point and the end of the line, or if there is no such text, it joins the line to the next line. The deleted text, or line separator, goes into the kill buffer. However, if the last command executed was also ˆ**K**, the kill buffer is *appended* with the new text rather than overwritten. In this way, a lot of text can be accumulated in the kill buffer easily. You may cut and paste between windows by killing (cutting) in one window and yanking (**emacs** term for **put**ting) to another window. Window switching commands are discussed later in this section.

Global Replacement in emacs

The command **ESC-r** (replace-string) replaces all occurrences of an old string with a new string from the point to the end of the buffer. The **emacs** editor will first prompt:

`Old string:`

on the message line. And then prompt:

`New string:`

When **emacs** is finished, you will see a message like:

`Replaced 7 occurrences`

to confirm the command's completion.

Being able to make global replacements in this manner is useful, but sometimes you may want to check the context before you replace text. The command **ESC-Q** (query-replace-string) works the same as **ESC-r**, except it will position the cursor on each old string and ask you whether or not you want to make the change. The **emacs** editor prompts:

`Query-Replace mode`

and waits for you to hit any of the following keys:

SPACEBAR	makes the replacement and goes on to the next occurrence of the string
n	does not make the change and goes on to the next occurrence of the string
.	makes the change, stops searching, and returns to where the search began
=	does not make the change, stops searching, and leaves you right where you are now. This is handy when you are replacing something and you spot something else you want to work on first.
!	makes the changes throughout the rest of the file without asking, then returns you to where you began

You may stop the entire query-replace process by pressing **^G** to abort.

Dealing with emacs Windows

One of the chief advantages of **emacs** is that you can work on two files at once or on two parts of the same file at once, using two windows. The **^X-2** command splits the current window into two windows, both of which are associated with the same buffer. The cursor position in each window can be moved independently. **^X-2** is useful for viewing separate parts of a file and for cut and paste.

The **^X-^V** (visit-file) command can be used to open another file in a second window, thus allowing you to work on two files at once. Although you may have multiple windows on your terminal, you can only work in one window at a time. The window you are working in is called your *current window*. Only the current window displays a cursor. To switch your current window to another window, use ^**X-n** or ^**X-p**. To delete all other windows use ^**X-1**. You also can enlarge or contract your window size by using ^**X-z** or ^**X-^Z**. The following table summarizes the window commands.

Key Sequence	Command Name	Key Sequence	Command Name
^**X-1**	delete-other-windows	^**X-2**	split-current-window
^**X-n**	next-window	^**X-p**	previous-window
^**X-z**	enlarge-window	^**X-^Z**	shrink-window

emacs **Macros**

The **emacs** editor allows you to define a *keyboard macro*—a sequence of commands remembered by **emacs** for your later use. To define a keyboard macro, you enter ^**X-(** (start-keyboard-macro) followed by the sequence of commands to be remembered. The **emacs** editor executes the commands as they are typed in to provide feedback on what the macro actually will do when invoked. When satisfied, you type ^**X-)** (end-keyboard-macro) to complete the macro definition. ^**X-e** (execute-keyboard-macro) is used to invoke the keyboard macro. The following table summarizes the macro commands.

Key Sequence	Command Name
^**X-(**	start-keyboard-macro
^**X-)**	end-keyboard-macro
^**X-e**	execute-keyboard-macro

Some Other Important emacs **Commands**

The table here lists some other **emacs** commands; several of these are discussed further in the following paragraphs.

Key Sequence	Command Name	Key Sequence	Command Name
ˆL	redraw-display	ˆG	abort-command
ESC-x	issue-full-command-name	ˆX-ˆU	undo
ESC-?	apropos	ˆZ	pause-emacs
ˆU	argument-prefix	ESC-*number*	provides repeat

Because **emacs** allows its editing functions to be bound to user-defined keystrokes, it is likely that you will find some key sequences that work one way on one **emacs** and work another way on a different version. Also, there are more **emacs** functions than there are conveniently available key sequences. Thus, as mentioned before, **emacs** provides **ESC-x** as a way to invoke any command by its full name.

For Berkeley UNIX, suspension of an **emacs** job is possible with ˆZ (pause-emacs). As mentioned before, during the execution of any **emacs** command, you can press ˆG to abort and return to the top level of **emacs**.

A help facility uses keywords to obtain information on commands. This is the *apropos* function. To get help, enter **ESC-?**, and **emacs** will prompt you for a keyword. Type in something you think may describe the command you are looking for. A window will display all the commands containing the keyword. This feature is especially useful for beginners.

Most commands accept a *prefix argument* that usually (but not always) specifies a repeat count for the command. A repeat count can be specified for the cursor motion commands, the character- and word-delete commands, ˆX-e, and all the displayable characters. To specify a repeat count *n*, use the prefix argument ˆU-*n*. For example:

ˆU-20*

inserts 20 *s into the buffer.

File I/O in emacs

The following file I/O commands are self-explanatory.

Key Sequence	Command Name	Key Sequence	Command Name
^X-^R	read-file	^X-^I	insert-file
^X-^S	write-current-file	^X-^V	visit-file
^X-^W	write-named-file		

For More Information

This section is meant only as a brief introduction to a second text editor. Please refer to the **emacs** manual on your system for further information.

2.19 Summary

The **vi** and **emacs** text editors are both modern, full-screen display editors that take advantage of CRT terminal capabilities. A buffer is used to hold the text being edited. Changes made in the buffer are not made in the disk file until specifically requested by the user.

The **vi** editor provides editing commands such as insert, delete, search, cut, paste, global replacement, and so on. It has two modes: the command mode and the insert mode. You issue a command to insert text. While inserting text, you are in the insert mode. A sequence of editing commands, called a *macro*, can be assigned to a key, which is used to invoke the macro from there on.

The **emacs** editor is another popular editor. In **emacs**, a character is inserted directly into the buffer unless it is a control character or is preceded by ^X or ESC. It also provides multiple windows that enable you, for example, to work on two files or two different sections of the same file at once. Furthermore, **emacs** allows the user to redefine editing functions for all key sequences, allowing for a high degree of customization.

Exercises

Problems 1–5 are to be done using vi.

1. Edit the file /etc/passwd and look for an entry with your password in it. What happened? You may be surprised to find that you can look at the

password file in UNIX. Now look for an entry with your name on it. Do you know what the information refers to? (By the way, your password is encrypted between the first and second : on this line.) How can you exit the editor?

2. Edit your .login file. Choose some characters you would feel comfortable using for input editing and interrupt. Set them up in the login file using the **stty** command. Save the file without exiting the editor, log in through another terminal, and test the settings. Repeat until satisfactory.

    It is recommended that you never exit the editor until login has been tested; and most importantly, do not log out until it works to your satisfaction. Why is this a good idea? When is it feasible?

3. To create a schedule table using **vi**, edit a file (call it schedule) and form a 60-character line with 60 __ characters in it. Insert a | at regular intervals (every 11 characters), and add one more at each end, for a total of 67 characters in the line. Make two copies of this line and then change all the | on the top line to __ and all the __ on the second line to spaces to obtain six rectangles side by side. Now, make several copies of lines two and three down the file. With how few keystrokes can you make this schedule format?

4. Suppose you want to search for ^D or ^U at the beginning of any line. How would you tell **vi** to seach for this? How would you delete all such patterns in your **vi** buffer with one global replace command?

5. Examining some text typed in by someone else, you find several irregularities. Which commands would you use to fix the following problems?
    a. The text has several blanks at the end of a line. Delete them.
    b. There are many instances of multiple consecutive spaces in the file. Change them to single spaces.
    c. Find the next instance of a punctuation character immediately followed by an alphanumeric character. Define a macro to insert a space in this instance.
    d. Find the next instance of a line containing a double quotation mark (").

6. Are the **lisp** settings used in **vi** appropriate for other languages? Explain.

7. (For **emacs** users) How can keys be redefined to change their associated actions? Investigate the availability of a replace mode on your version of **emacs**. Is there any way to search for a regular expression, as in **vi**? Investigate how commands can be written for your version of **emacs**.

8. (For **emacs** users) Complete Exercises 1–5 using **emacs**. You may need to consult your **emacs** manual for features not mentioned in the text.

You may use either **vi** *or* **emacs** *to complete the following exercises.*

9. How do you delete all trailing blanks from all lines?

10. How do you delete all empty lines from a file? How do you delete all blank lines from a file?

11. How do you search for a word without regard to upper or lower case?

12. Find out **vi** definitions for sentence, paragraph, and section, as related to the commands (,), {, }, and [[,]].

Electronic Mail

3

The driving concept behind the UNIX computing environment is that good communication within the user community will mean more sharing of information, less duplication of effort, and, as a result, significantly boosted productivity. UNIX provides users with a number of ways to communicate, but the principal facility is electronic mail, through which the UNIX user can send and receive messages electronically. The mail system performs the following functions:

- Prepares outgoing mail

- Accepts posted mail

- Delivers and forwards mail

- Returns undelivered mail

- Processes received mail

You call up the mail system through the **mail** command. You can send a *message* to one or several recipients and can send copies to others (including yourself). Your message is deposited into the recipient's *system mailbox*, where all pieces of mail yet to be delivered to a specific user are kept. If the message recipient is logged in and has mail notification enabled (through **biff** y), a message:

New mail for *userid* has arrived:
first few lines of the message

appears on the recipient's terminal. This notification informs the recipient of the newly arrived message. The recipient may elect to process the message right away or may wait until a later time. Users also are notified of new mail when they first log in:

You have mail

Once you receive mail, the mail system provides facilities to read, save, reply, forward, ignore, or discard any message.

In addition to mail communication on one computer, the mail system also will handle any *network mail*. A computer network connects computers so they can communicate with each other. There are two main types of computer networks: a local area network (LAN) (Ethernet, for instance, which connects nearby computers) and a remote network (ARPANET or CSNet, for example, which connects computers nationwide or even worldwide). If your UNIX system is on a network, you can exchange mail with users on other computers in the network. Depending on your UNIX system setup, you may have the ability to reach additional UNIX-based computers not on your network using the uucp (UNIX-to-UNIX Communications Package) facility. Whether the mail system is used to send local mail or to send network and uucp mail, there is little difference from the user's point of view, although remote messages require somewhat longer addresses.

Electronic mail is fast. Local mail is delivered immediately, and network mail can arrive in minutes, a few hours, or infrequently, a day or so, depending on the type of remote network connection and how often outgoing network mail is processed. Mail by uucp may take a little longer, since it may have to go through many machines to reach its destination.

The mail system is so convenient that many people log in regularly simply to check their mail. Electronic mail is increasingly being favored over time-consuming, paper-based communication. In some ways electronic mail is even more convenient than the telephone: There's never a busy signal, and if the receiver is not there an electronic message is left. If you have a question, a memo, or a proposal, sending a message via **mail** may be the most convenient way to illicit a response. Many scientific conferences now rely heavily on electronic mail for communication between members of the organizing and program committees. Electronic mail not only speeds up the communication process but also saves on long-distance telephone charges. Within your working environment, there are surely many ways electronic mail can be used to improve communication and increase productivity.

3.1 Sending Messages

We already have talked a little about **mail** in Chapter 1. We begin here by continuing that discussion.

An Example

Suppose you, John Doe (userid jdoe), want to know how to use the laser printer to print a paper. You know that Mr. Smith (userid csmith) is a seasoned user and may be able to help you. So you send him a message (Figure 3.1).

The first line is typed at the shell level and invokes **mail**, naming csmith as the message recipient. At this point you enter the **mail** program, and it begins to read and process what you type. When sending mail, the **mail** program assumes that what you type is the content of the message—with one exception, which allows you to give commands. If at the beginning of a line you type a ˜ (tilde), then every keystroke thereafter until you press RETURN is considered a command. The ˜**s** at the beginning of the second line of the message in Figure 3.1 is a command that specifies the *subject field* of your message. In this case, the subject field is "question on laser printer." A subject field is recommended but not required. The subject field is one of several fields contained in the *message header*, which the recipient will see when reading your message.

Following the subject line in the figure are several lines that form the

---

Figure 3.1 ▪ Message Sent to Mr. Smith

```
mail csmith
~s question on laser printer
I know we have a laser printer on the system. Can you tell
me how to use it for printing my paper?
Thanks.

John Doe
^D
```

body of the message. Wording is informal and to the point. Keeping each line to a reasonable length (say, less than 70 characters) makes it easier to read. In the preceding example, the sender's full name is given at the end of the message; this is a nice touch but is not necessary. The message body is ended by a line consisting of the single character ^D, which sends the message to csmith. At this point, the **mail** program terminates and returns you to the shell level. Figure 3.2 illustrates the message delivered to csmith.

The Message Header Fields

The message header may contain several fields. Some fields are created automatically by the **mail** program:

from field   contains the name (address) and userid of the sender

date field   contains the time and date the message was sent

For security reasons, these fields cannot be specified or modified by the sender. The sender can specify the subject, to, cc, and bcc fields. We have seen the subject field already. The to field is a list of recipients; cc is a list of *carbon copy* recipients, and bcc is a list of *blind* (secret) *copy* recipients. Unlike the other lists, the bcc list is not part of the delivered message. Therefore, none of the other message recipients will know to whom—or even if—a secret copy was sent. The to field initially contains the recipients specified on the **mail** command line. The cc and bcc fields initially are empty.

Figure 3.2 ▪ Sample mail Message

```
From jdoe Wed Feb 18 23:43:41 1987
Date: Wed, 18 Feb 87 23:43:35 est
From: jdoe (John Doe)
Message-Id: <8702190443.AA01878@kentvax.CSNET>
To: csmith
Subject: question on laser printer
Status: R

I know we have a laser printer on the system. Can you tell
me how to use it for printing my paper?
Thanks.

John Doe
```

To specify or change the subject field, you type:

~s *desired subject line*

as a separate line any time before you send the message. As mentioned, the ~ is used at the beginning of a line to signify to **mail** that a command is being given, that the line does not belong to the message body. Such a feature allows the sender to "escape" temporarily from the message to, for example, specify a header field. Therefore, **mail** commands such as the ~s are called *tilde escapes*. The tilde escape ~c is used to add recipients to the cc list:

~c *name1 name2* ...

Similarly ~b is used to add recipients to the blind copy list bcc:

~b *name1 name2* ...

A tilde escape ends with a RETURN.

These tilde escapes make sending mail to more than one person and copies to others simple and convenient. Because it is so easy to send a cc, sometimes copying is done unnecessarily. Make sure you send only necessary copies.

Composing the Message Body

Short messages normally are typed directly from the terminal to the mail program. To view your message header and body so far, the command:

~p   (display the message on the terminal)

is used. To edit the message body, the tilde escape:

~v   (invoke a visual editor)

can be used to call up a screen-oriented editor (default **vi**). When you are finished editing, write out the buffer and exit the editor (use **ZZ** for **vi**). You will be returned automatically to the **mail** program, which displays:

(continue)

to signify that you have left the editor. From this point, whatever you type is appended to the end of your current message body. You may specify another editor instead of **vi**. This and other options are discussed in Section 3.5.

For longer messages, it is sometimes more convenient to compose the message beforehand using a text editor and put it into a file. The command:

~r *filename*   (read file into message)

will append the specified file to the end of the current message body. Occasionally it is useful to write the message body into a file for later use; this can be done with:

~**w** *filename*   (write message into file)

The number of lines and characters written into the file is reported, and you are allowed to continue with the message.

The ~**v** command only allows you to edit the message body. To edit the message header fields, use:

~**h**   (edit header fields)

which allows you to edit each header field in turn using simple shell input bediting.

Shell Escape

You may use ˆZ to suspend **mail** and return to the shell level for a while before finishing your message. The **mail** program also provides a temporary escape to a subshell:

~**! shell-command-line**   (shell command within mail)

The ~**!** allows the line to be executed by the subshell while you remain in the **mail** program. This option is particularly useful if the ˆZ job control feature is not available on your UNIX.

The **mail** program also allows you to reformat your message body conveniently. The command:

~**|** *shell-command*

feeds (pipes) the message body text as input to the given UNIX command (a filter), and the output becomes the new message body. For example:

~**| fmt**

often is used after the message body is typed. The command **fmt** is designed to format outgoing mail. A complete list of tilde escapes is shown in Figure 3.3.

Other Things to Know

Although making an occasional typing mistake is human, review your work carefully! Remember, everybody will know that you personally typed the contents of your mail messages. In particular, be careful with ˆ**D**. It sends out the mail, and as with nonelectronic mail, once it is sent it is gone. If for any reason you wish to quit the **mail** program without sending the message, you can use:

~**q**   (quit without sending message)

Figure 3.3 ▪ mail Send Mode Commands

Tilde Escapes	
Send Mode Command	Function
~~	quotes a single tilde
~c *users*	adds *users* to cc list
~d	reads in dead.letter
~e	edits the message buffer
~h	enters or modifies message header fields
~r *file*	reads a *file* into the message buffer
~p	displays the message buffer
~m *messages*	reads in messages, right shifted by a TAB
~s *subject*	sets subject
~t *users*	adds *users* to list
~v	invokes display editor on message
~w *file*	writes message into *file*
~?	displays a list of tilde escapes
~!*command*	invokes a shell to execute *command*
~| *command*	pipes the message through the shell *command*

Another way to get out of the **mail** program is to type the UNIX interrupt character (usually DELETE or ^C) to abort. Following the interrupt, the **mail** program displays:

(Interrupt--one more to kill letter)

Here, **mail** protects you by insisting on seeing two consecutive abort requests before quitting.

Once the message is terminated by ^D, **mail** will attempt to deliver the mail to all the recipients. If any recipient has an incorrect address or userid, the **mail** program will generate a piece of mail to the sender to that effect. Delivery to people with correct addresses is not affected.

3.2 Receiving Mail

What do you usually do when you receive nonelectronic mail? Most people start by flipping through the letters to see which ones need to be read first. Then after reading a letter, you may reply or take some other action. You may want to make a note on the calendar, file the message somewhere, forward it to someone else, save it for later action, or discard it. The **mail** program allows you to do all of these things with your electronic mail, too.

Although activated by the single command **mail**, sending mail and receiving mail are two distinct functions. When sending a message, your keystrokes are assumed to be part of the text of your message, unless a tilde escape is used. On the other hand, when receiving mail, your keystrokes are presumed to be commands telling the utility how to handle the messages you are reading. Processing of incoming messages is easy, but you must keep in mind the difference between the *send mode* and the *receive mode*.

Reading Incoming Messages

When you login, you'll see:

```
You have mail.
```

displayed on your terminal if you have mail waiting for you in your system mailbox. Each user has an individual system mailbox represented by a file in the mail spool directory (usually, /usr/spool/mail). Your mailbox has your userid as its file name. Simply type

```
mail
```

at the shell level to read your mail. Note that the difference between using mail to send messages and using it to receive them is merely whether or not you specify arguments when you call up **mail**. Including arguments, the userid(s) of your intended recipient(s), means you are sending mail; no arguments means you want to receive and read incoming messages. In the latter case, **mail** will respond by displaying a listing of your messages. Figure 3.4 shows a sample listing.

The first line in Figure 3.4 is self-explanatory. The second line gives the mailbox location and the total number of incoming messages. The remaining lines list a summary of the messages. Each line in the list represents a different

Figure 3.4 ▪ A Sample Listing of Incoming Mail

```
Mail version 2.18 5/19/83. Type ? for help.
"/usr/spool/mail/pwang": 3 messages 1 new 2 unread
U 1 csmith Sat Jun 7 11:18 11/227 "meeting"
U 2 djones Sat Jun 7 12:10 11/235 "AAAI conference"
N 3 brown Sat Jun 7 14:39 10/227 "graduate students"
```

message and contains several entries, the first of which is the message status:

N	*a new message*	(one received after you last read your mail)
U	*an unread message*	(one you left unread the last time you read your mail)

The second entry is the message number. You use this number to identify which message you wish to process in some way. Next are listed the date and time of mailing. The **mail** program then lists the size of the message in lines and in characters, separated by a /. The final entry is the subject field of the message.

After displaying the listing, **mail** signifies its readiness to receive commands by displaying the prompt:

&   (**mail** *receive mode* prompt)

To read a message, you type:

p*n*   (display message number *n*)

When reading mail, remember you are in the receive mode. Here the command **p** (for print) is followed by the desired message number. The message then will be displayed on your terminal. The header fields will be listed, followed by the body of the message. For example, Figure 3.5 illustrates a typical message.

If the message is more than one screenful, you may have to use ^**S** and ^**Q** to stop and resume the display, respectively. Otherwise, the text may scroll by too quickly. All **mail** processing commands are single letters, which is a little difficult for beginners but a welcome feature for those who process mail daily. In fact, **p***n* can be shortened to just the index of the message you wish to read; the **p** can be omitted.

When mail is being read, the message being read is designated as the *current message*. Initially, your current message is message 0 (which, of course, is nonexistent). The command **p** displays the current message if it exists, otherwise it displays the next message. After displaying the new message, that message becomes your current message. To display the following message, press RETURN. RETURN can be used to read through all the messages in se-

Figure 3.5 ▪ An Electronic Message

```
Date: 18 Mar 1986 0857-PST
From: kim
Subject: presentation tomorrow
To: yourname
Status: R

Your presentation is all set for tomorrow at 3:00 room
315 building 21. Refreshments have been ordered, and an
overhead projector as well as a 35mm slide projector are
available.

If you come about 15 min. before 3:00, I'll show you how
to set up and use the equipment.

Looking forward to your presentation.
```

quence. When there are no more messages to read, you'll see:

no more messages

At this point, you may press:

q

to exit mail processing and return to the shell level.

3.3 Processing Mail

You can do much more than just read your mail messages. There are also message handling commands for printing, filing, replying, forwarding, and discarding. The general form of a command is:

command messages [arguments as required]

Messages refers to a message number, message sequence, or a range. A message sequence consists of several message numbers separated by spaces or tabs. A range is specified by a message number followed by a – (dash) and another message number. If no messages are specified, then the command acts on the current message if it exists or, if the current message has been discarded, on the next message. Many **mail** commands can be abbreviated to their leading character.

You use the **mail** command:

d *messages*

to discard messages. If no argument is given, the current message is deleted. After deleting a message, you can change your mind and "undelete" it by using the command:

u *messages*   (restore deleted messages)

A frequently useful command is:

dp   (delete current and display next message)

which deletes the message you just read and displays the next one. If at any time you wish to review the message listing, simply type:

h *messages*

which relists the messages. When given no argument, **h** displays a summary listing of all messages not yet discarded. Note, if you have many messages, this may display only the nearest screenful of entries.

To file messages for safe keeping or later reference, type:

s *messages file*

The messages will be appended to the end of the given file. The file will be created if it does not exist already.

Forwarding and Replying

One of the more gratifying things about **mail** is its ability to reply to an incoming message simply and easily. After reading a message, you can reply immediately without exiting to the shell level and restarting **mail** in the sending mode. The command:

R *message*

Indicates that you wish to send a reply message to the sender of *message* (the current message if no argument is given). Certain header fields for the reply message are created for you as **mail** temporarily enters the sending mode. Type in the mail body (all tilde escapes in the mail-sending mode are available at this point) and send mail as discussed earlier. Once you have replied to a message, **mail** returns itself to the mail-receiving mode.

For example, after reading the message from Kim (Figure 3.5), you type **R**, and **mail** displays:

```
To: kim
From: yourname
Subject: Re: presentation tomorrow
```

and goes into the mail-sending mode. Complete the reply by typing something like:

```
Thank you very much. See you tomorrow at 2:45.
^D
```

This message is polite and confirms your arrival at 2:45. After the **^D**, **mail** returns you to the mail-receiving mode prompt &.

The **r** command is similar to **R** except, in addition to the sender, the reply is sent to all recipients of the original message. In some cases you may wish to include the incoming message in your reply for easy reference. This is done by using the tilde command:

~**m**   (interpolate current message)

while constructing the body of the reply. The **mail** program responds by displaying:

```
Interpolating: message
```

```
(continue)
```

which means the incoming message has been inserted into your outgoing message with an indentation of one TAB stop to set it apart from your new message. You can resume typing your message and if you wish, you may make annotations to the interpolated message by invoking an editor using ~**v**.

After reading a message you may wish to forward it to another person. To forward a message, type:

m *userid*

You'll see:

```
To: userid
```

and **mail** will enter the sending mode. The command **m** is short for **mail**. At this point, you can type in:

~**m** *messages*

to include the desired incoming messages. Any additional text you type also will be sent. Use **^D** to send the message and return to the & prompt.

In sum, to reply by annotating the incoming message you use:

R	(enters the send mode and replies to the sender of the current incoming message, use **r** to include all recipients)
~**m**	(interpolates the current message)
~**v**	(invokes a visual editor to make your annotations)
zz	(exits **vi** and returns to the send mode)
^D	(sends message, returns to the receive mode)

To foward a message you use:

m *userid*	(mails to *userid*, entering send mode)
~**m**	(interpolates current message)
~**v**	(invokes visual editor to make your annotations)
ZZ	(exits **vi** and returns to the send mode)
^D	(sends message, returns to the receive mode)

When You Are Finished

Once you have processed your incoming messages, you will be ready to quit the **mail** program. As mentioned, the command:

```
q
```

exits you from **mail** and returns you to the shell level. When you quit **mail**, any discarded or saved messages will be removed from your system mailbox. Any unread messages will be kept in the system mailbox for later processing. Any messages you read but did not delete are transferred to the file mbox in your home directory. If you wish to quit **mail** without updating the various mailboxes involved, you can use:

```
exit
```

In this case, undeleted messages will *not* be appended to the mbox file.

You may peruse mbox and other files of saved messages with the command:

```
mail −f file
```

If *file* is omitted, it is presumed to be your mbox file. Figure 3.6 lists the most frequently used **mail** receive mode commands.

3.4 Network Mail

If your computer is connected to a computer network, you may be able to send and receive electronic mail across the network. There are two kinds of computer networks: local area networks (LAN) and remote networks.

The computer you are using could be on a divisionwide or department-wide LAN. The LAN can be linked to a remote network through a *gateway*

Figure 3.6 ▪ The mail Receive Mode Commands

Message Processing Commands	
Receive Mode Command	Function
–	displays previous message
RETURN	displays next message
p	displays current message
n	displays message *n*
dp	discards current message and displays next message
R	replys to sender of current message
r	replys to sender and all recipients of current message
h	displays message summary listing (one screenful)
m	sends mail
s *messages file*	appends *messages* to file
w *messages file*	appends body (no header) of *messages* to file
d *messages*	deletes *messages*
u *messages*	undeletes *messages*

computer—one with access to both the LAN and the remote network. Two major, government-sponsored remote networks available in the United States are ARPANET and CSNet. ARPANET is a wide-ranging network linking major universities, industries, government laboratories, and military commands. The network has been developed under the sponsorship of the Advanced Research Projects Agency of the Department of Defense (DOD). The CSNet is sponsored by the National Science Foundation to connect major computer science research groups in universities and industry.

The UNIX systems form a network of their own through UUCP (UNIX-to-UNIX Communications Package). Any two UNIX systems can communicate over a regular telephone line. If such a connection is established, the UUCP facility can be used to transfer mail between the two computers. For more information on UUCP and networking, refer to Chapter 10.

Sending network mail is as simple as sending local mail: You use the same **mail** command. However, instead of using a simple userid to designate the recipient, you must use the network address of the recipient. The network address identifies the user as well as the destination *host* computer on the network. If you are using a LAN, you will probably use an address such as:

userid@host

(check your LAN documentation for the precise form and names to use). To send mail through a UUCP network, you use an address of the form:

host1! host2! host3! . . . ! target-machine! userid

where *host1*, *host2*, and so on form a *UUCP path* from your machine to the destination machine. If you are using the *csh* shell, you will need to quote the **!** with a \, because *csh* uses the exclamation point as an escape character. On many machines, a program with a name like **uucpmap** will create these addresses for you. Also, note that some of these addresses can become quite lengthy, and the messages then can take many days to reach their destinations.

If you are sending mail through Internet, CSNet, ARPANET, Bitnet, and so on, you will use an address of the form:

userid% subdomain.subdomain. ... @org. top

where each *subdomain* in the sequence identifies the machine within the organization (*org* is an abbreviation for organization) and *top* categorizes the organization as either a commercial organization (com), educational organization (edu), government organization (gov), country outside the United States (like uk), and so on. Some typical addresses might be:

```
pwang%hp4@kent.edu
```

and

```
brown%vm@kent.edu
```

Even though these two individuals may belong to the same organization, the two machines may belong to different networks and messages to them are routed accordingly.

In this manner, mail can be sent through any of these networks in a near-optimal fashion: In most cases, mail first will go to an Internet site, which will decide which *physical* network should be used and will route the message accordingly. In some instances an address based on the network can be used, such as:

```
userid@host.network
```

but these addresses are complicated, unstandardized, and trouble-prone; they are being dropped in favor of the other address schemes discussed.

You receive network mail in the same way as you receive local mail. However, the reply command **R** within **mail** may not work well with incoming network messages—a problem on many UNIX systems.

3.5 Customized Mail Processing

The **mail** utility provides options to customize the program according to your needs and preferences. There are two types of options: binary options and valued options. The option names are either all lower or all upper case. A binary option is either *set* or *unset*. A valued option can be set to a character string supplied by you or unset to its initial default value.

The **mail** commands **set** and **unset** are used to set options. For example,

```
set ask
```

sets the binary option *ask* instructing **mail** to prompt you with:

```
Subject:
```

each time you send a message. Many people find this convenient. Furthermore, if you type:

```
set askcc
```

it instructs **mail** to prompt you for names to put onto the cc list just before you send out a message (that is, after you have typed the final ^**D**):

```
cc: current cc list
```

At this point you may add or delete names from the cc list with input editing. When you are satisfied with the cc list, simply type RETURN, and the message will be sent.

Another binary option is *autoprint*, which when set, will cause **d** to behave exactly as **dp**. Autoprint makes going through your mail faster.

VISUAL is a valued option; it is initially set to a standard display editor (most likely **vi**). You can change the default to your favorite display editor by typing, for example:

```
set VISUAL=emacs
```

to cause ~**v** to invoke the **emacs** editor.

The valued option *folder* gives **mail** the name of the directory to use for storing groups of messages in files known as *folders*. The value is a file name (relative to your home directory) or pathname. For example:

```
set folder=letters
```

tells **mail** to use letters as your directory for storing mail folders. Anywhere that **mail** expects a file name, a simple folder file name preceded by + can be used. The folder facility makes it easy to store incoming messages in different folder files for safe keeping as well as for later disposition. To save a message into a folder you can type:

`s +`*foldername*

where the argument is a file in your folder directory.

To process messages stored in a folder, you can use:

`mail −f +`*foldername*

To keep an automatic record of all messages that you send out, you can set the valued option:

`set record=`*filename*

Then, each message you send will be appended to the end of the given file. If you do this, make sure you clean up this file from time to time to save disk space.

The valued *crt* option is used to control the displaying of messages while reading mail. It should be set to the number of lines your display terminal can handle. If the number of lines in a message is greater than the number you set, **mail** automatically will use **more** to display the message. A typical setting would be:

`set crt=24`

The command **ignore** is used to add specified header fields to the mail *ignore list*, which is a list of header fields not to be displayed when you read your mail. This command often is used to avoid reading machine-generated header fields. There can be many such header fields if the message is a piece of network mail.

Since it isn't convenient to set your chosen options each time you send a message, you may put these settings in a file named .mailrc in your home directory. The **mail** program will then refer to this file each time the program is invoked. Figure 3.7 contains a sample .mailrc file.

Many other options are described in the mail reference manual. Although, they are not used as frequently as those listed in this section.

Figure 3.7 ▪ A Sample .mailrc File

```
set ask askcc autoprint
set VISUAL/bin/emacs
set crt=24
set folder=IN
set record=OUT
ignore Received Message-ID Status
alias tennis bob carl smith john
```

Per-User Forwarding

It is possible to *forward* your own incoming mail automatically to another address using the .forward file in your home directory. This feature is handy if, for example, you are on assignment to a different part of your company for a period of time. The .forward file contains lines with correct mail addresses, as discussed previously. Any of the network mail forms discussed (UUCP, LAN, and so on) may be used. The mail delivery program will check this file and redirect all your mail to the address specified in .forward.

Aliases

It is possible to establish *mail aliases* for a group of people. A mail alias is a single name that stands for a group of mail recipients. Sending mail to an alias results in the message going to all members in the alias group. Systemwide mail aliases usually are established in the file /usr/lib/aliases. For example, the alias *faculty* can stand for all faculty users on a particular UNIX system. Personal mail aliases are established in individual .mailrc files. A line of the form:

`alias` *aliasname recipient ...*

in your .mailrc file establishes *aliasname* as the mail alias for the specified recipient(s). This feature can be especially useful for network mail or for frequently used mailing lists.

3.6 What Can Go Wrong

The most frequent error that occurs in sending mail is using an incorrect address: The userid can be wrong or mistyped, or the remote host name, in the case of network mail, can be misspelled. In any case, an incorrect address will result in a nondeliverable message. Such messages are returned to the sender by electronic mail with an indication of the reason why delivery was not possible. If the same piece of mail is sent to several recipients, an incorrect address for one will not affect the successful delivery of the message to the other receivers.

Once a message is sent, it is gone. Unless you ask your system super user to help quickly, there is no way to get it back. For important communications, you are well advised to construct the message in a file using a text editor and to check spelling using **spell** (Chapter 12). You also may want to format your message with ~ | **fmt** before sending it out.

When receiving and processing mail, you sometimes can delete a message inadvertently. In case this happens, don't panic. Just use the mail undelete command **u** to get it back. Before giving the **q** command to quit, any deleted messages can be undeleted.

3.7 Secret Mail

Messages sent via the mail system are protected by the UNIX file protection scheme. You are the owner of your system mailbox file (usually, /usr/spool/mail/*userid*) and the mailbox only allows owner access. However, super users can read anyone's mail and sometimes do.

On some UNIX systems, there is a mechanism for sending and receiving *secret* mail using an encoding and decoding technique known as a *public-key cryptosystem*. Under such a system, users must *enroll* by registering with the system before encoded messages can be received.

Use the command:

```
enroll
```

to register yourself for secret mail. The system will ask you for a password that you must remember and use to receive encoded messages. The command:

```
xsend userid
```

sends secret mail. The command:

```
xget
```

receives secret mail. Usage of these commands is similar to regular mail. The **xget** command asks for your password, then gives you the messages. The **xsend** command takes only one target recipient and uses the recipient's *encoding key* to encode your message before sending it out. A messsage announcing incoming secret mail also is sent to the recipient by ordinary mail.

3.8 Summary

The **mail** command is used both for sending and for receiving mail on the computer. The **mail** program provides two different sets of commands for sending and receiving mail. When sending mail, what you type is presumed to be the text of the message; any command you wish to issue must be preceded by a tilde (~). Therefore, when sending mail, commands you use are tilde commands. On the other hand, when receiving mail, your keystrokes are presumed to be commands for processing incoming mail. Such commands enable you to read, delete, save, forward, and reply to messages received. Mail can be sent and received over computer networks.

A separate set of commands, **xsend** and **xget**, are used to send and receive encoded mail messages.

Exercises

1. What are the advantages and disadvantages of electronic mail over other means of informal communications?

2. The mail receiving system has been compared to a "message-level editor." Which commands are similar to those used in the **vi** editor? Which commands are different?

3. You would like to send mail to the userid bill, whose owner is on machine "prism." Both your machine and his machine have UUCP mail exchange only with another machine "chaos." How would you address the mail?

4. Bill left for a job with a company called Widgets, Inc. (wi, for short), and he sent you mail saying that he can receive mail as bill on a machine called "minivax." How would you address mail to him now?

5. Joe, a student at Arizona State University, wants to send a file to another machine on campus, called "VM." He decides that the best way to send the file (anyfile.x) is by Internet mail. How would he do this?

6. If you use an editor other than **vi**, say **emacs**, how would you customize **mail** to use **emacs** through the ~**v** escape?

7. Is it possible to have **mail** display long messages with "more processing"? If so how?

Commands and Filters

4

U NIX is much more than text editing, sending mail, and a few basic commands. In fact, one of UNIX's strengths is the richness of its command set. This richness, in turn, derives from the ease with which new commands can be crafted from combinations of existing commands. Learning UNIX involves learning existing commands, learning how to develop new commands, and learning how to select the right commands for your applications. Chapter 4 introduces a collection of useful UNIX commands and demonstrates how they can be applied individually and in combination.

UNIX system commands are located in a few system directories where executable *binary* files are kept. Typically, the directories /bin, /usr/bin, and /usr/ucb contain systemwide commands accessible to all users. Many UNIX installations also have a directory such as /usr/local/bin where locally written commands can be stored for systemwide access.

The output of a command often results from a simple and well-defined transformation on the input. Commands of this type are called *filters*, and they can be strung together using pipes to perform complex functions on data. For example, the command **sort** is a filter that orders the lines of its input. The command **tr** translates specific characters of a file into other characters. You also could combine these two filters with others, if you wish, to create and maintain a simple database of addresses, for example.

This chapter presents a number of important filters along with examples of how they can be used to build pipelines. In addition, we describe an important collection of miscellaneous facilities—commands such as **lpr** are simple but indispensable; others such as **find** are powerful but complicated to use; still others, like **calendar**, can help you manage your time. To begin, we consider three filters that display files on a CRT terminal.

4.1 File Perusal on a CRT: more, head, tail

Reading a long file as it scrolls on the screen can be nearly impossible. Fortunately, the **more** command lets you pause the display after each screenful, so you can read the display and then continue. Commands to **more** are usually a single letter and can instruct **more** to display a few more lines, show the next screenful, skip forward or backward, or quit this type of output. Perusal is called *more processing*. For example, the **man** command uses more processing to display manual pages.

The simplest way to use **more** is:

more *file*   (output *file* to your terminal with more processing)

The general form is:

more [*option* ...] [*file* ...]

When no file argument is given, **more** processes its standard input. When several files are given, they are displayed sequentially with each identified by a header supplied by **more**. Some useful **more** options are explained in a list at the end of this section. For now, turn your attention to the interactive commands used during **more** pauses.

The **more** command considers a screenful to be two lines less than the number of display lines on your terminal, unless you instruct it otherwise. After displaying a screenful, **more** pauses and displays the prompt:

`--More--`

at the bottom of the screen. This prompt usually is followed by a number that indicates the percentage of the file (in characters) displayed thus far. When processing multiple files, **more** displays the name of the next file along with the prompt. At the prompt, you can issue any one of the following commands to continue the perusal. Some commands are preceded by an integer k that, when omitted, is presumed to be 1:

q or **Q**   exits (quits) from **more** without displaying the rest of the file

h   (help) displays a summary of all **more** commands

*k*RETURN   displays k more lines ($k = 1$ if not given)

SPACEBAR   displays another screenful

d or **^D**   scrolls down half a screenful

*k***s**   skips k lines first, then displays a screenful

*k***f**   skips forward k screenfuls, then displays a screenful. The **more** command shows the number of lines being skipped.

=   displays the current line number

v   calls up the **vi** editor on the file being read at the current line. When you exit **vi**, you return to **more** and continue from where you left off.

k/*pattern*   searches for the kth occurrence of the **vi** search *pattern*. If a pattern is found, a screenful is displayed, starting two lines before the line containing the pattern. *Erase* and *kill* characters may be used for editing when typing in the search pattern. Erasing forward of the first column cancels the search command.

*k***n**   searches for the kth occurrence of the previously given search pattern

'   (a single quote) returns to the point from which the last search began. If no search has been performed in the current file, ' returns you to the beginning of the file.

!*command*   issues a shell-level *command*

*k***:n**   skips forward k files (skips to the last file if k is too large)

*k***:p**   skips backward k files. If k is omitted, **more** returns to the previous file. If $k = 1$, it returns to the beginning of the current file. If k does not make sense, it returns to the first file.

:f   displays the current file name and line number

.   (dot) repeats the previous command

These commands are similar to those used by the **vi** editor, which will help you remember them. Any time output is being sent to the terminal, you can press the quit key (normally ^\) to cause **more** to stop sending output and to display the - -More- - prompt.

As mentioned, **more** can be controlled by options specified on the command line. Some command line options are as follow:

$-k$	sets screen size to k
$-s$	*squeeze* option; when set, only one blank line is displayed for any set of consecutive blank lines. This option maximizes useful information present on the screen.
$+n$	starts at line number n
$+/pattern$	locates the search *pattern* at start up time

In addition to **more**, the commands **head** and **tail** are available for displaying a file on the screen. They display the beginning and the end of a file, respectively. The command:

```
head [- k] [file ...]
```

outputs the first k (default 10) lines of each given *file* to the standard output. If no file argument is given, the standard input is used. The **head** command is a quick way to examine the first few lines of a file, which are often all that is needed.

The command **tail** is the opposite, displaying the last part of a file on the screen:

```
tail [starting-point] [file]
```

outputs the last part (from *starting-point* to the end or, by default, the last 10 lines) of the given *file*. If no file is specified, the standard input is used. The starting point is specified as:

$+k$	(line k from the beginning)
$-k$	(line k from the end)

If the integer k is followed immediately by the characters b or c, **tail** will count blocks or characters, respectively, instead of lines. The **tail** command has two other options: r and f, either of which can follow the starting point specification. The –r option instructs **tail** to display lines from the end of the file in *reverse order*. For example:

```
tail –5r file
```

displays the last five lines of *file* in reverse order; on the other hand:

```
tail –r file
```

displays the entire file in reverse order.

The --f option instructs **tail** to continue, even after the end of the file has been displayed, repeatedly probing the file in case more lines are appended.

This option provides a way of monitoring a file as it is being written by another program. A typical use is:

```
tail -f file
```

Let us say that you have written a program and compiled it into **a.out**. When run, this program will produce a *log file* that records its progress and other useful information. The commands:

```
a.out &
tail -f logfile
```

allow you to monitor logfile as output from **a.out** is produced.

In pipelines, **head** and **tail** are useful for selecting some lines from the input and excluding others. The **more** filter is used at the end of a pipeline to manage output to a CRT.

4.2 Character Translation: tr

Another useful filter is **tr**, which copies standard input to standard output, substituting or deleting specified characters. For example:

```
tr A-Z a-z < file1 > file2
```

creates *file2* as a copy of *file1*, with all uppercase letters translated to the corresponding lowercase ones. Another use is:

```
tr → % < file1 > file2
```

where → stands for TAB. This method allows you to see each tab in *file1* as a % character in *file2* (assuming *file1* does not contain any % characters). Generally:

```
tr string1 string2
```

translates *string1* characters to the corresponding *string2* characters, assuming the two strings are of the same length. If *string2* is shorter, it is treated as if it were padded with enough repetitions of its last character to make it the same length as *string1*. A range of characters can be given, as in $x-y$. A character also can be given by its ASCII code in octal (for example, \040 for SPACEBAR, \011 for TAB, and \012 for NEWLINE). For example, to replace a string of blanks with a NEWLINE, use:

```
tr -s '\040\011' '\012'
```

The −s (squeeze) option shortens all strings of consecutive repeated characters to just one character. The −c (complement) option is used to specify *string1* by naming characters *not* in it. Thus:

```
tr -cs A-Za-z '\012'
```

creates a list of all words (one per line) in the input. In this example, *string1* is all characters except uppercase or lowercase letters. When option −d (delete) is given, characters in *string1* are deleted from the output, and there is no need for *string2*.

Tab Expansion

Tabs often need to be expanded into an equivalent string of spaces or vice versa. However, this character transformation is not performed by **tr**. Since tabs must be replaced with enough spaces to move the output column position to the next TAB stop, tab expansion and its inverse transformation are slightly more complicated than simple character transformations. The filters **expand** *file* and **unexpand** *file* are used for these purposes. For example, **expand −6** *file* replaces each TAB in *file* by spaces, assuming that TAB stops are 6 (default 8) spaces apart.

4.3 Using Sorted Files

On-line data often is sorted in some kind of order for easy access and manipulation: You may want to alphabetize a list of names and addresses, combine several such lists into one, look an entry up in a list, or compare two lists already in order. Facilities are provided for these tasks. We begin with one of the most important filters: the **sort** command.

The **sort** command orders its input lines and writes them to the standard output. The units being sorted are entire lines. Each line may contain one or more fields, which are separated by one or more blanks (spaces or tabs). For example, a file called students may contain the following lines:

```
F. Smith 21 3.75 Physics
J. Baker 20 3.20 Chemical Engineering
P. Wang 22 4.00 Computer Science
```

The first line contains five fields; the next two lines contain six fields each. The **sort** command allows you to use field positions to specify *sort keys*. A sort key is defined by a starting and an ending field position. The sort keys are compared to order the lines.

Thus, if you specify the sort key as the second field to sort the file students, then the lines will be ordered by last name using, by default, the ASCII collating sequence. The result is:

```
J. Baker 20 3.20 Chemical Engineering
F. Smith 21 3.75 Physics
P. Wang 22 4.00 Computer Science
```

In the absence of any specification, the sort key is the entire line. Multiple sort keys are given in order of importance. In comparing any two lines, **sort** uses the next sort key only if all previous sort keys are found to be equal.

The command has the general form:

sort [*options*] [*key ...*] [*file ...*]

All lines in the given files are sorted together. A file named " – " is the standard input. If no file is given, **sort** uses the standard input. It writes to the standard output by default. Keys are given in order of significance. A key is given by two field positions:

+ pos1 [*– pos2*]

which specify a sort key consisting of all characters between the starting *pos1* and the ending *pos2*. When omitted, *pos2* is the end of line. Each *pos1* and *pos2* has the form:

f [*. c*]

where *f* and *c* are integers (the brackets are *not* part of the specification). The form represents a position reached by skipping *f* fields and *c* characters from the beginning of the line. If omitted, *c* is zero. The following list illustrates same examples of sort key specifications:

	Sort Keys
Specification	Key
+1 −2	Second field
+4	Fifth field to end of line
+2.3 −3.7	Fourth character of third field to seventh character of fourth field, inclusive

Therefore:

sort +1 −2 students

sorts the file students by last name. In this and many other cases, the ending field can be omitted without affecting the search.

Sort keys are compared using ASCII ordering, unless one of several options is used. A few important options are listed:

f   treats all uppercase letters as lowercase letters

n   sorts by magnitude using an initial numerical string in the sort key. The numerical string has possible leading blanks and/or a sign followed by zero or more digits, with an optional decimal point.

r   reverses the sense of comparisons and sorts the lines in reverse order

These option characters can be given globally, affecting all sort keys, or immediately after a key specification to affect only that sort key. Note some examples:

ls –l | sort –n +3   (sort by increasing byte count)

who | sort +4nr   (sort by login time, most recent first)

For multiple sort keys, consider:

sort +2nr –3 +1 –2 students

which sorts by grade point average, highest first, then by last name within each grade-point-average group.

Some other useful **sort** options are as follows:

t*x*   uses the character *x* as field separator. A frequent field separation character is the colon (:). Examples are found in /etc/passwd (password file) and /etc/termcap (terminal capabilities file).

c   checks to see if an input file is already sorted in the specified order. If the file is in order, no output is given. Otherwise, the first out-of-order line is written to the standard output along with a message.

m   assumes that all files given are in order already. Only merging is needed to create the final sorted output.

u   outputs only one line in a group of equal lines. Two lines are equal if the specified sort keys are equal. This is a convenient way of avoiding duplicate entries.

o *filename*   writes output to the specified *filename*

Using some of these options, you can merge two address lists into a master list without duplication:

sort –um addr1 addr2 –o masterlist

Consider another example:

sort +0f +0 *file1* –o *file2*

Here, the first sort key (+ 0f) sorts lines in the given *file1* into alphabetical order (ignoring case differences). The second sort key (+ 0) is used to order consecutive lines whose first sort keys are equal. Thus, *file2* lines will be in alphabetical order with capitalized words preceding corresponding uncapitalized ones.

Other commands are available to manipulate files containing lines that are sorted in ASCII collating sequence (with the entire line used as the sort key). The command:

look *string file*

displays all lines in the given *file* that have *string* as a prefix. A binary search algorithm is used for locating any lines with the given *string* prefix. The option –f instructs **look** to ignore case differences (the given *file* must be sorted with **sort** –f as well). If no file argument is given, the UNIX dictionary file /usr/dict/words is assumed. For example:

look disci

displays the following output:

```
disciple
disciplinary
discipline
```

For sorted files *file1* and *file2*, the command:

comm [–[1][2][3]] *file1 file2*

outputs three columns: lines only in *file1*, lines only in *file2*, and lines in both. The options 1, 2, and 3 suppress the displaying of corresponding columns. A file named "–" is the standard input. Common uses of this command include comparing file names in two directories, comparing registered user names (/etc/passwd) on different UNIX systems, and so on.

4.4 The grep **Commands**

The **grep** family of commands consists of three filters: **grep**, **fgrep**, and **egrep**. These commands provide the ability to search and identify files containing specific phrases or text patterns or to find all lines in given files that contain a certain pattern. These commands have many possible applications. You may search for the name of a procedure about which you are trying to learn more. You may search for something contained in a file whose name you have forgotten. Or you can extract text lines from files that pertain to a particular subject. The **grep** filters also are useful in pipelines.

Command Synopsis

The name **grep** comes from *generalized regular expression*. Generalized regular expressions are what the **grep** family of commands uses to specify search patterns. The three commands listed are similar; they differ only in what text patterns are allowed and which search algorithms are used to locate a pattern:

fgrep [*options*] [*string*] [*files*]   searches for patterns that are fixed strings. It is fast and compact.

egrep [*options*] [*pattern*] [*files*]   searches for patterns that are full regular expressions. It uses an algorithm that is slower and requires more space.

grep [*options*] *pattern* [*files*]   searches for patterns that are limited regular expressions in the style of the **vi** editor. It uses a fairly efficient algorithm.

The commands search the specified *files* or standard input for lines that match the given *pattern*. A line matches a pattern if it contains the pattern. Each matched line is copied to the standard output unless specified otherwise by an option (Figure 4.1). The output lines are prefixed with the file name if multiple files are given as arguments. Generally speaking, the **grep** commands are used either to obtain lines containing a specific pattern or to obtain the names of files with such lines.

An example: Let's say you have a file of phone numbers and addresses. Each line in the file contains the name of the person, a phone number, and an address. Let us name this file teldir (telephone directory); a few typical entries follow:

```
(216) 555-1242 Michael Smith Physics Dept. Union State Univ. Union OH 44246
(415) 555-7865 Martin Goldsmith EGT Labs P.O. Box 21951 Palo Alto CA 94303
(415) 555-3217 Bert Lin 248 Hedge Rd Menlo Park CA 94025
(617) 555-4326 Ira Goodman 77 Mass. Ave. Camb. MA 02139
```

Consider the command:

fgrep *string* teldir

If *string* is a name, then any line containing the given name is displayed. If *string* is an area code, then all entries with the same area code are displayed. If *string* is a ZIP code, then all lines with the same ZIP code are displayed. Also:

fgrep -v Mass teldir

displays all addresses except those in Massachusetts.

Here is an application dealing with multiple files: Let's say you have a

Figure 4.1 ▪ Options for the grep Family

grep Options	
Option	Description
−b	displays in front of each output line the disk block number of the line. This is useful in locating disk block numbers by content.
−c	displays only a count of the matching lines
−f *file*	takes a pattern for **egrep** from *file*; or takes one or more strings (on separate lines) for **fgrep** from *file*
−i	ignores the case of letters in making comparisons (**grep** and **fgrep** only)
−l	lists only the names of files that contain matching patterns. The file names are displayed on separate lines.
−n	precedes each matching line by its relative line number in the file.
−s	(silent mode) displays nothing (except error messages). This is used to obtain the status returned.
−v	displays all nonmatching lines
−w	searches for whole words matching the pattern. It is equivalent to surrounding the pattern by \< and \> (**grep** only).
−x	(exact) displays lines matched in their entirety (**fgrep** only)

directory named letters that you use to file away electronic mail for safe keeping and later reference. Suppose you need to find a letter in this directory, but you don't remember the letter's file name. All you recall is that the letter deals with the subject salary. To find the letter, use:

```
cd letters
fgrep −i −l salary *
```

By itself, the asterisk (*) is recognized by the shell to mean, roughly speaking, all files in the current directory. This is a convenient shorthand. The * can be used in other ways, and there are other shorthand notations for file names (see the discussion on file name expansion in Section 5.5 for more details). The **fgrep** command here searches all files under the current directory for

Figure 4.2 ▪ Extended Regular Expressions

egrep Patterns	
Pattern	Description
x	a single character x that is not endowed with special meaning matches that character
\x	any character x other than NEWLINE, when quoted by a backslash, matches that character
^	a caret matches the beginning of a line
$	a dollar sign matches the end of a line
.	a period matches any single character
[str]	a string str enclosed in brackets ([]) matches any single character in the string. A range of ASCII character codes may be abbreviated. For example, [a–z] matches any lowercase character and [0–9] matches any digit. A] may occur only as the first character of the string. A hyphen (–) must be placed where it cannot be mistaken as a range indicator.
re*	a re followed by an asterisk (*) matches a sequence of 0 or more matches of the regular expression
re+	a re followed by a plus sign (+) matches a sequence of one or more matches of the regular expression
re?	a re followed by a question mark (?) matches a sequence of zero or one matches of the regular expression
$re_1 re_2$	two concatenated re's match a match of the first followed by a match of the second. For example, cb* matches c, cb, cbb, and so on.
$re_1 \mid re_2$	two res separated by a vertical bar (|) match either a match for the first or a match for the second. For example, a+ | b+ matches a, b, aa, bb, but not ab. A NEWLINE may be used instead of a | when the pattern is given in a file with the –f option.
(re)	a re enclosed in parentheses matches a match for the regular expression. Parentheses are used to delineate patterns. For example, (cb)* matches cbcb, but cb* does not.

lines containing the salary string (ignoring case differences) and displays only the name of any file with matching lines.

The shell variable *status* records the *exit status* of any nonbuilt-in command (see Section 6.10). The **grep** commands set status to 0 if any matches are found, 1 if none, 2 if error.

Specifying Search Patterns

The **grep** search patterns are specified in the same way as **vi** search patterns (see Section 2.13). The **fgrep** search patterns, on the other hand, are restricted to literal strings. The **egrep** search patterns are extended regular expressions described in Figure 4.2. In Figure 4.2 *re* denotes any regular expression. The precedence of operators used for **egrep** patterns is ( ), [ ], *, +, ?, concatenation, and |. Care should be taken when using the characters $, *, [, ^, |, (,), and \ in the pattern; they are also meaningful to the shell. It is always safest to enclose the entire pattern in a pair of single quotation marks.

Example Patterns

It pays to be familiar with regular expressions. The **grep** command uses the same patterns as the **vi** editor; **egrep** patterns also are used by **awk** (see Section 4.6). Figure 4.3 lists some examples of how patterns are specified and used.

The **grep** commands can be used in a pipeline with other commands to filter output, for example:

```
ls -l | fgrep '.c'
```

More examples of **grep** within pipelines are discussed in Section 4.7.

4.5 A Stream Editor: sed

The **sed** program is a filter that uses line-editing commands to transform the lines of its input. It is a noninteractive, line-oriented editor derived from the editor **ed**, whose commands form a strict subset of those for **ex**. The **sed** program is used for such chores as deleting selected lines, double-spacing a program listing, and modifying all occurrences of some pattern. In fact, **sed** and **grep** perform many of the same functions. However, **sed** is more powerful than **grep**, and thus **sed** is more complicated to use.

The **sed** program buffers one input line at a time, repeating the following steps until there are no more input lines:

1. Read the next input line into the buffer, replacing its old content, and increment the line count (initially 0) by 1.

2. Apply all given editing commands to the buffer.

Figure 4.3 ▪ Some Example Patterns

Example Patterns	
Command	Description
grep ' if*'	matches the character "i" followed by zero or more f's, for example, it, if, iff
grep '\−s'	matches the string −s. The \ prevents **grep** from interpreting −s as an option.
grep '\<ex'	matches any word beginning with the characters ex
grep −i '^mcc'	matches any three characters mcc at the beginning of a line, in upper case or lower case. Thus, it also matches McC.
grep 'chapter[0−9]*'	matches a string with the prefix chapter followed by any number of digits. Thus, it matches chapter, chapter1, chapter10, and so on.
egrep '(ab)+'	matches a sequence of one or more strings ab, for instance, abab
egrep 'ab+|cd*'	matches any string that matches the pattern ab+ or the pattern cd*, for example, abb or c

3. Write the buffer out to the standard output.

4. Goto step (1).

This processing cycle is shown in Figure 4.4.

Each editing command may be applicable to all lines or to just a few. Therefore, it is possible for some lines to pass through **sed** unchanged, at the same time, others can be modified or deleted entirely. Frequently, **sed** is used in the simple form:

sed *script* [*file*] ...

where *script* consists of one or several editing commands separated by semicolons. For example:

sed 's/Unix/UNIX/g' chapter1

reads the input file chapter1, substitutes all occurrences of the string Unix

Figure 4.4 ▪ The Editing Cycle of sed

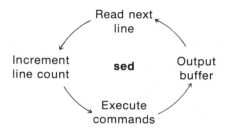

with the string UNIX, and outputs to the standard output. If no file is specified, **sed** takes its input from the standard input. The single quotation marks around the script prevent the shell from interpreting any special characters the script may contain. To further the example:

```
sed 's/Unix/UNIX/g ; s/ucb/UCB/g' chapter1
```

applies two string replacement commands to each line of chapter1. The search patterns used in **sed** commands are limited regular expressions, as recognized by **vi** and **ed**. The command:

```
sed 's/$/\
' file
```

adds an empty line after each line in *file*, producing a double-spaced output. As in **vi**, the pattern $ means the end of line.

When you specify each editing command, you can also specify its range of lines. An editing command is given in the form:

[*address1*] [*, address2*] *function* [*args*]

where *address* specifies on which input lines the *function* is applied:

- *No address* The function applies to every line.

- *One address* The function applies to every line matching that address.

- *Two addresses* The function is applied repeatedly to the next set of lines beginning with a line that matches the first address, up to and including the first line that matches the second address (but not the first address). Neither address need match any line.

For example:

```
sed '/^$/d' file
```

applies the function d (delete line) to each line matching the single address /^$/ (empty line). The output will be the same as *file* but with all empty lines deleted. Another version of this example deletes all blank lines:

```
sed '/^[⊘→]*$/d' file
```

We use the symbols ⊘ and → to stand for a space and a TAB, respectively. The address matches a line containing zero or more spaces and tabs and nothing else.

Let us look at an example involving a two-address command. In a file to be processed by the document preparation facilities of UNIX (see Chapter 12), tables are sandwiched between a leading line .TS and a trailing line .TE. Suppose you want to extract all the tables from a document. You may use:

```
sed '/^\.TS/,/^\.TE/\!d' docment > tables
```

The output file named tables will contain only the tables. The exclamation point (!) (preceded by a backslash to prevent *csh* interpretation) reverses the sense of the specified addresses: It applies the specified function to every line except the lines matching the given address.

Simple scripts are easy to give on the command line. For more complicated scripts, the –f option can be used to specify a file containing the **sed** script. Another useful option is –n, which skips step 3 of the **sed** cycle. Hence, the command:

```
sed -n '/pattern/p'
```

where p, the output line function, is equivalent to **grep** *'pattern'*. And:

```
sed -n '12,20p' file
```

outputs only lines 12–20 of the given *file*.

The function:

```
y / string1 / string2 /
```

when given two equal-length character strings, performs character translations. Thus:

```
sed 'y/abc/ABC/' file
```

functions the same as:

```
tr 'abc' 'ABC' file
```

The **sed** command offers a number of other features and options. Please refer to the UNIX manual pages for additional information.

4.6 Pattern Processing: awk

The **awk** program is another filter. It processes its input one line at a time applying user-specified **awk** *pattern commands* to each line. The **awk** program is similar to the **sed** program, but **awk** is more powerful. The **awk** mechanisms are based more on the C programming language than on a text editor, allowing for variables, arrays, conditionals, expressions, iteration controls, formatted output, and so on. The **awk** program can perform operations not possible with **sed**, such as joining adjacent lines and comparing parts of different lines.

The **awk** general command form is:

awk [–F*c*] *prog* [*file*] ...

If no files are given, **awk** uses standard input, otherwise files are processed in the order given. If a dash (–) is given as a file name, it is taken to mean standard input. The argument *prog* is an **awk** program given on the command line or in a file with the –f *file* convention.

The **awk** processing cycle is as follows:

1. Read next input line.

2. Apply all **awk** pattern commands sequentially as specified in *prog* to the current line.

3. Goto step (1).

Note: unlike **sed**, **awk** does not write lines to the standard output automatically.

An **awk** program consists of one or more pattern commands given on different lines or separated by semicolons. Each pattern command takes the form:

pattern {*action*}

If the current line matches the *pattern*, the *action* is taken. A missing pattern matches every line, and a missing action outputs the line. Thus:

ls –l | awk '/UNIX/'

is the same as:

ls –l | sed –n '/UNIX/p'

Pattern and *action* are described more fully in the following subsections.

The concept of a field here is the same as that used for **sort**: **awk** delineates each of its input lines into fields separated by white space or by a field separator character specified with the –F option. The fields are denoted $1, $2, and so on. The entire line is denoted by $0.

It is impossible to rearrange the order of fields using **sed**; it is easy using **awk**. For instance, the output of **ls** –l has eight fields:

```
-rw-rw---- 2 jsmith  512 Apr 23 21:44 report.ms
-rw-rw---- 1 jsmith   79 Feb  9 15:13 Makefile
-rw-rw---- 2 jsmith 1024 Feb 25 00:13 pipe.c
```

When the preceding lines are piped through **awk**:

```
ls -l | awk '{print $8,$4,$5,$6}'
```

The following output is produced:

```
report.ms      512 Apr 23
Makefile        79 Feb  9
pipe.c        1024 Feb 25
```

Note: In this example, the pattern command contains only the action statement, which always is enclosed between braces ({ and }).

awk **Patterns**

Let us describe the *pattern* portion of a pattern command in a little more depth. As with **sed**, the *pattern* determines whether or not **awk** takes action on the current line. In fact, a **sed** address, specified with one or two match expressions, also will work as an **awk** pattern. If you are familiar with **sed**, you already know many useful patterns. For instance:

`/^first/`	(first at the beginning of a line)
`/last$/`	(last at the end of a line)
`/^$/`	(an empty line)
`/[⊘→][⊘→]*/`	(a line with a string of one or more blanks)
`/BEGIN/,/END/`	(all lines between a line matching /BEGIN/ and another matching /END/)

are valid patterns in both **sed** and **awk**.

In **awk**, a pattern is an arbitrary Boolean expression involving *regular expressions* and *relational expressions*. Boolean expressions are formed with && (and), ‖ (or), ! (not), and parentheses. A regular expression in **awk** must begin and end with a slash (/) and otherwise is defined the same as that for **egrep** (Figure 4.2). A relational expression can be any relational expression in C formed with the operators >, > =, <, < =, = = (equal), and != (not equal). In addition, a relational expression can be any pattern matching expression:

expression ~ re
expression ! ~ re

where ~ means "contains" and !~ means "does not contain." For example, the pattern:

```
$1 ~ /Berkeley/ && $2 ~ /UNIX/
```

is true if the first field contains the string Berkeley and the second field contains the string UNIX.

A pattern may contain two patterns separated by a comma, in which case the action is applied to all lines beginning with a line matching the first pattern up to and including the line matching the second pattern (the same as in **sed**). Thus:

```
awk 'NR==14, NR==30' file
```

outputs lines 14–30 of *file*, because **awk** keeps a running line count in the built-in variable NR. Other useful built-in variables are listed in Figure 4.5.

The special commands:

```
BEGIN {action}
END {action}
```

are executed before the first input line and after the last input line, respectively. They are used for initialization and postprocessing when needed.

awk Actions

Now let us turn to the question of how *actions* are specified. An *action* contains a sequence of statements given on different lines or separated by semicolons. Possible statements are as follows:

assignment:

```
var = expression
```

output:

```
print expression [, expression] ...
printf(...)      (as in C)
```

flow control (as in C):

```
if ( conditional ) statement [else statement]
for (expression ; conditional ; expression) statement
while ( conditional ) statement
break
continue
```

additional flow control:

```
next        (skip remaining commands in prog, start next cycle)
exit        (exit awk)
```

In the preceding definitions, a *statement* can be a compound statement in the form:

```
{statement, statement, ...}
```

Figure 4.5 ▪ Built-in awk Variables and Functions

Built-In *awk* Functions	
cos(*e*)	cosine
sin(*e*)	sine
log(*e*)	natural logarithm
exp(*e*)	exponent (inverse of log)
int(*e*)	integer
length(*s*)	length of string
index(*s1,s2*)	position of string *s2* in string *s1*, value is zero if *s2* is not in *s1*
sprintf(...)	format conversion, same as in C
substr(*s,i,j*)	substring of *s* of length *j* from position *i*
split(*s,a,c*)	split *s* into substrings *a*[1] to *a*[*i*] on character *c*; return *i*
getline()	read next input line, return 0 on end of file, otherwise 1
Built-in *awk* Variables	
NF	total number of fields on current line
NR	sequence number of current line
FS	input field separator character (default blanks)
RS	input record separator (default NEWLINE)
OFS	output field separator string (default space)
ORS	output record separator string (default NEWLINE)
OFMT	output format for numbers (default %g as in printf)

The output statements use the standard output. However, they can be followed by:

> "*filename*"

to redirect the output into a file.

awk Expressions

Expressions in **awk** statements can be constants, variables, arrays, fields, or any combinations of these using the following C operators:

```
+ , - , * , / , % , + + , - - , + = , - = , * = , % =
```

Numerical constants in **awk** statements are the same as in C. String constants are placed in double quotation marks (**"string"**), and variables are initialized to the null string. An array element is denoted as a[*i*], where *i* can be an integer or any string. A blank between two expressions concatenates them into a string. Thus, for example:

```
awk '{print $2 ":" $1}' file
```

outputs field2:field1. Built-in functions (Figure 4.5) also can be used in expressions. A conditional expression in **awk** is the same as in C, except it also may involve **awk** relational expressions.

Index Preparation: An Example

The **awk** pattern processing program is powerful and involved. The best way to learn it is through use and experimentation. In this section we present an example of **awk** usage to prepare an index (for a document).

Suppose you have several index files each containing entries like:

```
csh           99
vi            155
csh           123
pipe          101
emacs         163
socket        415
pipe          23
```

where each line has two fields: an index item and a page number. Your goal is to produce an overall index file in alphabetical order with lines like:

```
csh           99,123
emacs         163
pipe          23,101
socket        415
vi            155
```

The first step is to order the entries alphabetically and by page number, which can be done with:

```
sort +0f -1 +0 -1 +1n file1 ... > index.temp
```

in which the following sort keys are used:

+0f −1   (first key, field one with case folding)

+0 −1   (second key, field one with no case folding)

+1n   (third key, field two with numerical comparison)

It then remains to collect repeated index items to form lines with multiple page numbers. Since repeated items will be on consecutive lines, an **awk** program called index.awk (Figure 4.6) can be used. To call up the program, type in:

```
awk −f index.awk index.temp > index.final
```

There are four pattern commands in index.awk. The first command sets the variable i (used for initialization) to zero. The second command compares $1 with the variable pre, which stands for the previous index item and is initially null. If $1 is equal to pre (field one is the same as the previous index item), then output the page number ($2), preceded by a comma. If $1 is not equal to pre (a new index item), then output NEWLINE, $1, TAB, and $2 except for the very first line where the leading NEWLINE is not needed. The conditional output is performed in the **if** of the third command which also records the index item ($1) in the variable pre. At the end of the input file, a final NEWLINE is output.

To practice writing **awk** programs, you may start by entering the index. awk program into a file and experiment with it. You may then try to write the same program in a different way.

Figure 4.6 ▪ Program index.awk for Index Processing

```
BEGIN {i = 0}

$1 = = pre {printf(",%s",$2)}

$1 != pre { if (i > 0) {
        printf("\n%s\t%s",$1,$2)}
    else {
        printf("%s\t%s",$1,$2); i = 1};
    pre = $1}

END {printf("\n")}
```

Built-In Functions and Variables

Refer to Figure 4.5 to review a summary of built-in **awk** variables and functions. These can be used in any expression. In the figure, e is an expression, c is a character, s is a string, and i and j are integers.

4.7 Building Pipelines with Filters

A variety of filters has been discussed; it is now time to describe how new tools can be built by connecting these filters. First, you must understand what features in UNIX make this possible and how: The answer lies in the UNIX conventions for filters, file format, I/O redirection and pipe mechanisms.

A filter is distinguished from other programs by the following characteristics:

1. A filter takes input from the standard input, so it does not require that an input file be specified as a command line argument when the filter is invoked.

2. A filter does not require specification of an output file, since it uses standard output.

3. A filter performs a well-defined transformation on the input and produces the output with no header, trailer, label, or other formatting.

4. A filter does not attempt to interpret its input data in any way. Thus, the input is never treated as an instruction or a command to the filter.

5. With few exceptions, a filter does not interact with the user for additional parameters other than those supplied on the command line.

6. Any error or diagnostic output produced by a filter is sent to the standard error output, so error messages do not disappear or alter the output from this filter for the next filter down the pipe.

All of these characteristics are necessary for a filter to fit into a pipeline. The overall purpose is to make a program produce output that can be fed into another program as input and that can be processed directly. Typically, such input contains lines of text with no decorative labels, comments, or extra formatting. A separate line is used for each data entry. If the data entries are words, then the file should follow the form of one word per line. For more complicated data entries (for example, those produced by **ls** –l), the line may consist of several fields separated by spaces, TABs or colons (for example, /etc/passwd).

Consider several examples of pipelines. One is a pipeline used to look up the correct spellings of words:

```
look prefix | fgrep string
```

All words in the dictionary /usr/dict/words with the specified *prefix* are produced by **look** and fed to **fgrep**, which selects only those words that contain the given *string*. For example:

```
look dis | fgrep sion
```

gives the following output:

```
discussion
dispersion
dissension
```

Another example is a pipeline that saves to a file those commands that you have given to your shell. The *csh* command **history** displays a numbered list of your most recent commands. To enter the last eight commands into a file, you can use the following pipeline:

```
history | tail -8 | sed 's/.*→//' > file
```

The sed command removes the leading sequence numbers ($\rightarrow$ is a tab).

A third example collects a list of directory names from the current working directory:

```
ls -l | grep ^d | sed 's/^d.*○//'
```

Here the **sed** editing command deletes a *maximal* (longest) string starting with the letter d at the beginning of a line and ending with a space ($\oslash$) for each line. Another way to accomplish the same task is:

```
ls -F | grep '/$' | sed 's/\/$//'
```

A final example has to do with maintaining an address list. Let us assume you have a file of addresses, myaddr, in human-readable form. Its entries are multiline addresses, and a single empty line follows each entry. A typical address entry would look like the following:

```
Dr. John F. Doe
Great Eastern Co.
40 North Rd.
Cambridge, MA 02139
```

This form is easy for a user to read but is hard to maintain using filters. But, you can transform this address file with the following pipeline:

```
sed 's/^$/@/' myaddr | tr '/012@' ':\012' \
  | sed 's/^:// ; s/:$//' | sort -u -t: +0 -1 > addr
```

The first **sed** substitutes the character @ for each empty line. The **tr** command translates every NEWLINE character into a colon and every @ into a NEWLINE.

At this point, each address entry is on a separate line with a colon separating the fields within each address. The second **sed** removes any colon at the beginning or the end of a line. The final **sort** command orders the address entries using the first field and removes any duplicate entries.

Now your address file addr is sorted and contains one address per line in the following form:

```
Dr. John F. Doe:Great Eastern Co.:40 North Rd.:Cambridge, MA 02139
```

You can extract an address by using:

```
grep 'John F. Doe' addr | tr ':' '\012'
```

You can delete any address by using:

```
sed '/John F. Doe/d' addr > temp.file
mv temp.file addr
```

You can insert one or more addresses by using:

```
sort -u -t: +0 -1 addr - > temp.file
```

which allows you to type in the entries from the standard input. You may insert another address file, addr2, by using:

```
sort -mu -t: +0 -1 addr addr2 > temp.file
mv temp.file addr
```

In the preceding example, the first field contains the title and name of a person. The sorted address file is not in alphabetical order with respect to names, unless everyone has the same title. To avoid this problem, you may want to modify the record format to:

```
Doe:John:F:Dr.:Great Eastern Co.:40 North Rd.:Cambridge, MA 02139
```

and sort the address file using the first, second, and third fields as keys. Then the following can be used to display an entry:

```
look 'Doe' addr | \
awk -F: '{ print $4,$2,$3 ".",$1; print $5; print $6; print $7 }'
```

For large files, the **look** command, which uses a binary search method, is much faster than the **grep** command.

4.8 Encoding and Decoding

Examples of sensitive or confidential files abound. In the college environment, it may be a completed homework assignment, an examination yet to be given, a list of grades, or a resumé. In the corporate environment, it may be salary information, personnel evaluations, project codenames, and so on. Although UNIX provides file access control through the setting of permission bits (see Chapter 1), it still is possible for an unauthorized person to gain access to a file containing confidential information. For example, a super user can access anything on the system. Also, UNIX security is not quite perfect yet.

If you have a file that must be kept confidential, UNIX provides a facility to encode it. The encoding algorithm transforms the *clear text* in your file into *cipher text*, which, unless decoded, is a meaningless assortment of characters (both displaying and nondisplaying). Thus, even if someone manages to access such a file, its contents are still protected.

The filter **crypt** provides an easy way to encrypt and decode a file:

crypt < *cleartext* > *ciphertext*

It transforms a file containing clear text and encodes it into a new file *ciphertext*. After the command is given, the user is prompted by:

Enter key:

At this point, you must type in a string of characters of your choice (followed by RETURN). These characters represent your private *key* to encrypt the clear text as well as to decode the cipher text. It is important to commit your key to memory—otherwise you will not be able to decode the cipher text later. One strategy is to use your own login password as the key. Another is to keep a small list of words that are easy to remember but cannot be linked to you too easily. This way, even if you cannot recall exactly which key you used for a file, you could try each key in the set. After you **rm** the clear text file, the encoding is done.

To decode a file use:

crypt < *cyphertext* > *cleartext*

Note that the command sequence is exactly the same as for encrypting a file, except that the order of *cyphertext* and *cleartext* has been reversed. Now all you have to do is respond to the **crypt** prompt with your key, and the file will then be decoded into clear text and saved in the new file *cleartext*. The **crypt** command uses an algorithm that involves the key as its only parameter. In other words, the algorithm implements a function that is the inverse of itself. The **crypt** command is useful at the beginning or the end of a pipeline to handle encoding/decoding.

The **vi** editor also can be used with encoded files through the −x option. To create a new, encoded file, use:

vi −x *file*

Again, you will be prompted for a key that will be used as the password to the file. To edit an existing file that has been encoded, you use the same **vi** −x command and provide the proper password. Within **vi**, you even may read other clear text into the cipher text file, which, when you finish, will be saved along with the file as cipher text.

To print an encrypted file on a printer, the following can be used:

`crypt` < *file* | `lpr`

Be careful, though: The clear text file will be vulnerable for a few minutes while the file is being printed.

4.9 Printing Files

Working with files interactively on a CRT is fast and convenient, but you still need printed copies for some of your files. On a hard-copy terminal you can type in:

`cat` *file*

to print a text *file*, but this is slow and no substitute for printing through a line printer or a laser printer. A group of related commands:

`lpr`   (request spooled printing)

`lpq`   (examine printer spooling queue)

`lprm`   (remove tasks from spooling queue)

are supplied for printing hard copies on these printers.

Printing requests are initiated by using the **lpr** command. Files to be printed on a specific printer are copied to a predefined *spool* directory to be processed sequentially. Each printer has its own *spooling queue* of files waiting to be printed. The command **lpq** displays the spooling queue. A printing request can be removed from the queue by using **lprm**. A printer spool directory is typically named /usr/spool/*printername*, whose access is restricted to the three commands: **lpr**, **lpq**, and **lprm**.

The simple command:

`lpr` *file*

spools the named *file* for printing on the default printer on your system. The general form of **lpr** is:

`lpr` [*option* ...] [*file* ...]

Several frequently used options are listed:

`-#`*n*   This option instructs **lpr** to print *n* copies of the given files.

`-P`*printerid*   This option requests that printing be done on a particular printer specified by *printerid*. The default printer on your

Figure 4.7 ▪ A Sample Printer Queue

```
Laserjet-status: Job in progress

Rank        Owner      Job  Files          Total Size
active      baker      694  homework.p     737 bytes
1st         pwang      695  chapter.4      21773 bytes
2nd         brown      696  sort.c         970 bytes
3rd         pwang      697  intro.3        2393 bytes
```

system usually has lp as its printerid. Each printer on the system is given a two-character printerid. Optionally, a printer may be given one or more aliases that are easier to remember. For example, a Hewlett-Packard Laserjet+ printer may be named lj with the alias hpjet. Your system administrator should be able to provide you with the names and locations of printers available on your system. The file /etc/printcap contains the names and capabilities of all the printers accessible through the **lpr** command.

Once a file has been spooled for printing, it joins the queue for the printer. The command:

lpq [option ...]

is used to examine the queue for the printer, which is either the default or the named –P option. A typical **lpq** display is shown in Figure 4.7. An active rank means the file is being printed.

A *userid* option restricts the displaying of jobs to only those of the specific user. A +*n* option instructs **lpq** to examine the spool area repeatedly, waiting *n* seconds between scans, until the spool area is empty.

Spooled printing requests can be canceled with the following commands:

lprm *job* ...   (cancel specific printing jobs given by job number)

lprm –   (cancel all printing jobs of user)

4.10 Time Management on UNIX

As you know, efficient use of time translates directly into increased productivity. There are many time organizers and activity planning kits available to help people manage their time. The UNIX system offers an automated reminder service, an alarm clock, and an event scheduler to help you use your time more efficiently.

On-Line Reminder Service

One of the most appreciated services on the UNIX system is its **calendar** facility. This mechanism consults user-prepared data files to provide timely reminders of important dates. To take advantage of **calendar**, put your important dates into a file named calendar in your home directory. A typical entry in the calendar file could be:

```
Mother-in-law's birthday !!! Mar. 17
```

or

```
Departmental meeting 4/7 3:30 - 4:30 gold room building 9
```

As you can see, there is no rigid format. The calendar file in each user's home directory is consulted by the system every day in the early morning hours and is invoked by the **cron** process. Each line containing today's or tomorrow's date is mailed to the user through **mail**. The **calendar** command is the heart of the reminder service:

```
calendar [-]
```

When given no argument, **calendar** consults the file called calendar in the current directory and displays lines that contain today's or tomorrow's date anywhere in the line. Most dates are recognized, such as:

```
Mar. 18
March 18
3/18
```

But 18 March and 18/3 are not considered recognizable dates. If you give the month as an asterisk (*), then it means any month. Therefore, */1 represents the first day of any month. On weekends, the logical meaning of tomorrow extends through Monday. When **calendar** is given the argument "−," it goes through all users' calendar files in their home directories and sends each user any resulting date matches by **mail**.

Note: it is not an error to have lines in the calendar file that contain no date at all. A calendar file may include any other calendar files specified with the #include syntax, as in C programs. For example, putting the line:

```
#include "seminar.schedule"
```

in your calendar file will cause all lines in the file seminar.schedule to be processed as though they are in your calendar file. For example, you may elect to put all fixed dates such as birthdays, anniversaries, license renewals, and so on in a separate file and put #include in your calendar file. Other #include calendars can be shared by all users and are maintained and documented by system administrators. Also, when reading mail on-line, messages containing dates can be appended to the end of your calendar file by using the mail **s** (save) command.

There are several shortcomings with this reminder service. Its single-line orientation means that the date and message have to fit on one line. This is not too restrictive, though, because there is no practical limit on line length. Another limitation is that reminding is done only one day before and on the same day as the date you specify, unless you include multiple dates, such as:

```
wife's birthday 3/18, order cake 3/11
```

Alarm Clock: leave

In addition to the calendar facility, UNIX has a **leave** command that serves as an alarm clock to remind you that you need to leave the terminal to take care of some other business. Its form is:

leave [*time*]

where *time* is the time to leave, which must be given in the form:

hhmm   (*hh* two-digit hour, *mm* two-digit minute)

The hour can be given in either 12- or 24-hour notation. The given time first is converted to a 12-hour clock and is assumed to be within the next 12 hours. If no time is given, **leave** will prompt you interactively for a time input.

You will be reminded by **leave** that you have to leave five minutes ahead of time and every minute thereafter until you logout.

Scheduling Commands for Later Execution

Most computations on a UNIX system are performed interactively with immediate actions and reactions between the user and the system. However, it is sometimes desirable to schedule the execution of commands at a later time when the user may not even be logged in. This capability is almost like batch processing.

The **at** command is used to schedule commands for execution at some point in the future. The commands to be executed are given to **at** either interactively from the user or from a file. Then, the **at** command schedules execution at a time specified by the user. Any output by the commands must be redirected to files.

Suppose you have written a program that computes the nth prime number when given a positive integer n, and that your program works for reasonably large values of n. This program is CPU-intensive, so you would like to run your program in the early morning hours when it cannot bother other users as much. Even so, you probably won't want to stay up late to do it. The answer is the **at** command: Before you log out and go home for the day, type:

```
at 2a
```

This invokes the **at** command, and the first argument specifies 2 A.M. as the target time. The **at** command then takes what you type next as commands to be scheduled (terminated by a **^D**). You could, for example, type:

```
prime 1000005 > prime.out
^D
```

Your program called **prime** will compute the 1000005th prime at 2 A.M., and its standard output will be redirected into the file prime.out, from which you can read the results the following morning.

You may elect to put your commands in a file instead of giving them to **at** interactively. For example:

```
at 0215p mar 4 dental
```

schedules commands contained in the file dental to run at 2:15 P.M. The file called dental may contain commands to send a reminder about a dental appointment at 2:45 P.M. on March 4. For instance, the file named dental may contain the following information:

```
mail -s 'dental appointment at 2:45 today' userid
```

The purpose of this file is to invoke the **mail** command and send a simple message.

The syntax of the **at** command is as follows:

at *time* [*day*] [*file*]

The simplest way to specify *time* is to use a four-digit, 24-hour notation (for example, 1505 is 3:05 P.M.). The **at** command also allows a four-digit, hours-and-minutes notation followed by a single character a (A.M.), p (P.M.), n (noon), m (midnight). On-the-hour specifications may use only one or two digits.

If the day specification is omitted, the time is asssumed to be the same day. The *day* option is either:

1. a month name followed by a day number

2. a day of the week name

3. a day of the week name followed by the word "week"

Standard abbreviations for months and days of the week are recognized. Item (3) specifies a day seven days (one week) later than item (2). Some examples of correctly formed times are:

```
10a jan 11      (January 11 at 10 A.M.)
1430 mon week   (Monday next week at 2:30 P.M.)
```

The **at** command performs the scheduling by making a copy of the given file (the standard input if the file is not given) to be executed by your shell (selected in your password entry) at the specified day and time. The *environment* within which the commands run is that of the user at the time when the **at** command was invoked. The scheduling is done through the **cron** program, which is the UNIX system's *clock daemon*. (A daemon is a system process that runs in the background with no attached terminal and never exits.) Each minute, **cron** examines the file /usr/lib/crontab, which contains tasks scheduled at various times, including an entry to examine activities scheduled by **at**. Typically, such **at** examinations occur every 15 minutes. If you input:

```
more /usr/lib/crontab
```

the "atrun" entry appears, among other things.

The **at** command places a copy of the commands to be executed in the directory /usr/spool/at. There, the file can be examined and altered, if you change your mind after issuing the **at** command.

4.11 Backup Files on Tape: tar

For the remainder of this chapter, let us discuss two important, more advanced, commands: **tar** and **find**. If you are a new UNIX user, you may want to skip these two sections until you have read Chapter 5.

The **tar** command is used not only to copy your files onto a tape (for safekeeping and later retrieval) but also to copy entire *directory hierarchies* within the file system. A directory hierarchy refers to all files and directories contained in a subtree of the file tree.

Let us first look at the simplest uses of **tar**. The command form is:

```
tar cvn name1 name2 ...
```

where cv*n* is followed by names of files or directories given as absolute pathnames or relative names to the current working directory. This command saves the named file hierarchies on a tape mounted on drive *n* (which is 0–9). If the digit *n* (after cv) is left out, the default drive 0 is used. The default tape density used is usually 1600 bpi.

The corresponding command:

```
tar xvn name1 name2 ...
```

extracts the given file hierarchies from a tape created by the **tar** command. The extracted files will be written into the file system under their original file names (either absolutely or relative to the current working directory).

To copy the entire file hierarchy under *dir1* to *dir2* (which should be empty) use:

`chdir` *dir1*`; tar cf -. | (chdir` *dir2*`; tar xvf -)`

The **tar** command actually works by packing the multiple files into a single *tar-format* file or by extracting files and directories from this file. A tar-format file is usually but not necessarily written to tape. For example:

`tar cvf` *tarfile name1 name2* ...

saves the named file hierarchies into the single file *tarfile*. This single file is easier to transfer from one computer to another, although it still is hard to mail, because it contains nondisplaying characters. To restore the files contained in a tar-format file, use:

`tar xvf` *tarfile*

Note that this command does not delete the *tarfile*.

The **tar** command has the following general form:

`tar` [*key*] [*name* ...]

The **tar** actions are controlled by *key* characters. Some key characters are:

c   creates a new tar-format file

x   extracts from a tar-format file all or specified files

t   displays the names of all or specified files contained in the tar-
         format file

The t can be used to verify the file names in the tar-format file after its creation or before extracting files from it. Any of the preceding primary key characters can be followed by secondary key characters:

v   indicates the verbose mode

f   specifies the name of a tar-format file/device to be used instead of
         the default tape drive. When used, it is the last character on the
         key and is followed by a file name. The file name — refers to the
         standard input/output.

0-9   a digit between 0 and 9 indicates the tape drive to be used. The
         default is drive 0 (usually /dev/rmt8).

There are other primary and secondary key letters, although the information presented here should be sufficient for most applications. Refer to the UNIX manual pages for more details about the use of **tar**.

4.12 Searching the File Tree: find

We saw in Chapter 1 how the UNIX file system is organized into a tree structure. It is sometimes necessary to search a part of this tree and visit all nodes in a subtree. This means visiting all files in a given directory and, recursively, all files contained in subdirectories of the given directory.

Say, for example, that you have a directory called project5, which contains files and subdirectories, and that you wish to protect all files on the subtree rooted at project5 by denying read and write permissions to everyone except yourself. How can this be done? One way is to execute:

chmod go-rw *file*

on each *file* in the subtree. This requires a lot of typing on your part. A better way is to use an automatic file tree searching mechanism to apply the **chmod** command to each file. The **find** command provides just such a tree searching mechanism.

The **find** command visits all files in a subtree and selects files based on given *Boolean expressions*. The selection feature allows the application of a command (like **chmod**) to a subset of files visited by the search mechanism. To apply **chmod** on all files under project5, type:

find project5 −exec **chmod** go-rw \{\} \;

which takes the subtree rooted at project5 and executes the specified **chmod** command on each file in the subtree. The exact syntax is explained shortly.

The **find** command can be used to locate (displays the pathname of) files whose names match a given pattern on the subtree. For example:

find . −name *.c −print

The **find** command searches the subtree rooted at the current directory visiting each file. The file that currently is being visited is referred to as the *current file*. If the name of the current file matches the pattern *.c (the file name ends in .c), then the next expression (−print) is evaluated. The −print expression simply displays the pathname of the current file on the standard output. Thus, the effect of the preceding example is to find all C source files under the current directory and display their pathnames.

The general form of the **find** command is:

find *filename* ... *expression* ...

The command name is followed by one or more file names, each either an ordinary file or a directory, and then by one or more expressions. The tree search is conducted on each file or directory given. Each expression is a predicate on the current file and always produces a true/false value, although the expression also may have other effects. An expression is evaluated only if all preceding expressions are true. In other words, expression evaluation for the current file terminates on the first false expression, and the search process then goes on to the next file on the subtree.

The expressions used in **find** are *primary expressions* or a Boolean combination of primary expressions. Some important primary expressions are explained here. The effect and the Boolean value of each also is described. (Since some expressions may involve concepts and features we have not covered yet, you may skip those expressions for now if you wish.) In the descriptions, the argument n is used as a decimal integer that can be specified in one of three ways: an integer, an integer preceded by $+$, or an integer preceded by $-$. Specifying $+n$ means more than n, $-n$ means less than n, and n means exactly n.

`-atime` *n*	true if the file has last been accessed in n days
`-name` *filename*	true if the *filename* argument matches the current file name. Normal shell-level file name expansion notation may be used if quoted (watch out for [, ?, and *). File name expansion and quoting are discussed in Chapter 5. It always is safe to enclose the file name in single quotation marks. For instance, `-name 'chapter.*'`.
`-exec` *cmd*	executes the given shell command *cmd* and returns a value true if the executed command returns a zero exit status. The end of the command must be punctuated by the two characters `\;`. A command argument denoted by { and } is replaced by the pathname of the current file. This form is used to apply a given command to some or all of the files visited by the tree search. For instance:

`find . -name '*.c' -exec chmod go-w {} \;`

	removes the write permission for group (g) and other (o) from all files ending in .c.
`-newer` *file*	true if the current file has been modified more recently than the argument *file*
`-print`	always true; causes the pathname of the current file to be displayed
`-type` *c*	true if the type of the file is *c*, where *c* is any of the characters b, c, d, f, and l: for block special file, character special file, directory, ordinary file, or symbolic link, respectively. File types are discussed in Section 7.1.
`-user` *userid*	true if the file belongs to the user *userid* (login name or numeric userid)

A valid expression for the **find** command is either a primary expression or a Boolean expression formed using primary expressions. The following operations (in order of decreasing precedence) can be used to combine *e1* and *e2*, which are two primary expressions:

(*e1*)   makes *e1* into a single primary expression

! *e1*   this expression is true if *e1* is not true (the Boolean *not* operation)

e1 e2   this expression is true only if both *e1* and *e2* are true (the Boolean *and* operation)

e1 −o *e2*   this expression is true if either *e1* or *e2* is true (the Boolean *or* operation)

The following are several additional examples. To remove all files named a.out or *.o that have not been accessed for at least two weeks:

```
find / \( -name a.out -o -name '*.o' \) -atime +14 -exec rm \{\} \;
```

To display the names of all files not owned by smith under the current directory, type in:

```
find . \! -user smith -print
```

Note that the characters {, }, (,), and ! are quoted in these examples to prevent shell interpretation.

4.13 Summary

This chapter describes a wide-ranging collection of useful commands. Many commands discussed are *filters*, which produce output by performing a simple, well-defined transformation on their input. Filters can be used by themselves or together as components in a *pipeline*. The **grep** commands, the stream editor **sed**, and the pattern processing program **awk** are examples of powerful filters. When filters are combined, new tools can be built. For example, several different pipelines involving **tr**, **sed**, **grep**, and **awk** can be used to create, maintain, and access an address database.

You can manage your time and activities on a UNIX system more efficiently by using of the calendar file and the commands **leave** and **at**. You can input important dates and appointments into a calendar file to obtain system-generated reminders through **mail**. You can set an on-line alarm clock with **leave** and schedule commands for future execution using **at**.

The **crypt** and **vi** −x facilities are used to encode/decode files to ensure privacy. The **tar** command stores/retrieves multiple files onto/from a single file (usually on tape). The **find** command visits all nodes in the given file hierarchies, applying user-specified **find** expressions to each file.

The following chart summarizes the commands described in this chapter.

Command	Description
at	schedules jobs to be run at some future time
awk	a powerful pattern processing language
calendar	an on-line reminder service
crypt	encodes/decodes text files
expand	expands TABs into an equivalent number of spaces
find	searches the file tree
grep	displays lines in files that match specified patterns
fgrep	a restricted **grep** with increased speed
egrep	**grep** with extended pattern matching
leave	an on-line alarm clock
lpq	displays printer spooling queue
lpr	requests spooled printing
lprm	removes jobs from spooling queue
more	displays files on a CRT
sed	a stream editor
sort	orders lines in files
tar	saves/retrieves files on tape
tr	a character translation filter
vi −x	edits an encoded file
unexpand	replaces blanks in lines by TABs

Exercises

1. Consider how **expand** works. Write an algorithm for figuring out how many spaces should be generated for a TAB.

2. You have written a program in Pascal that is in several different files, all in the same directory. You now want to edit the function "anytown," but cannot remember which file it is in. How can you locate it?

3. When compiling your PASCAL program, you notice that you should not have used the variable eof. How can you locate which files have to be edited?

4. How can you use **grep** to locate all lines that do not contain the pattern –option?

5. How would you remove all files whose names start with # and were written more than one day ago? These are usually temporary files.

6. Consider the following **sed** command:

```
sed -n '/begin/,/end/p' file
```

Discuss its effect if *file* contains many lines with begin and/or end in them.

7. Refer to Section 4.7 on building pipelines and follow the example on page 128 on managing an address file. Suppose you want to redo the address file so that it also contains telephone numbers. How could you design the record format? Write a pipeline for consulting the address file as a phone directory. Write a pipeline to add a phone number to an existing address entry.

8. Write an **awk** program to transform the file myaddr to addr so that a single **awk** command can perform a task equivalent to that defined by the pipeline (involving **sed**, **tr**, and **sort**) in Section 4.7.

9. Using **vi**, can you read a file encrypted with **crypt**? What about decoding a file encrypted with **vi**?

10. The y function of **sed** can perform most of the same translations as **tr**. Is there anything **tr** can do that **sed** cannot? If so, discuss.

11. How do you set up your calendar file to remind you of a meeting on November 23?

12. What date would you specify in your calendar file to have **calendar** remind you to order cookies for a meeting that is held on the third Wednesday of each month? The cookies should be ordered the week before the meeting.

13. Your friend Tom's birthday is October 3. How can **calendar** help you remember his birthday? How could you send him an electronic birthday card so that it arrives early morning on his birthday?

14. How could you run the same process every day at 3 A.M.

15. How could you make a listing of all file names ending in .c or .p in a file hierarchy?

16. How could you find all files under the directory /usr/src/lib that use the function "system"?

Interactive Use of the Shell

5

An important part of any operating system is its user interface. It is through this interface that computations are controlled and operating system services are obtained. The user interface of UNIX is the *shell*, a command interpreter that provides an interactive environment for the user and a medium through which other programs are invoked.

In many operating systems, the user interface is an integral feature that must be used whether or not it is suitable to the task at hand. UNIX, however, is structured so that the same underlying computer system can be accessed through a separate *user-interface module* called the shell. The shell is simply another user program. You may replace a shell with a different shell as the need arises. Further, different users may use different shells on the same UNIX system at the same time—a feature that allows a high degree of per-user customization. For example, a secretary can be using a special-purpose word processing shell; at the same time, other users on the system may prefer more general-purpose shells. You may select a shell from a set of available shell programs or you may write your own.

In UNIX, the two most widely used interfaces are the *sh* shell and the C shell. The *sh* shell is also known as the *Bourne shell*, because it was originally written by S. R. Bourne of Bell Laboratories. The C shell (*csh*) was developed later at U. C. Berkeley (largely by William Joy) as one of Berkeley's enhancements to UNIX. *Csh* and *sh* have much in common. Both are general-purpose command interpreters that interact with the user, both offer a simple programming language for defining procedures involving UNIX commands, and both can be used in a *batch mode* to process commands in a file.

Csh is often prefered, however, because it offers more features for interactive use and its syntax follows that of the C language. In this chapter, we discuss the interactive use of *csh*. Programming in *csh* and *sh* is presented in Chapter 6.

5.1 Interacting with *csh*

The shell begins work as your command interpreter immediately after you log in. It is simply a user program whose job is continually to execute the *command interpretation cycle*:

1. Display the prompt

2. Receive and parse (analyze the syntax of) the next command

3. Perform *input processing* (Section 5.5)

4. Carry out or initiate the requested operations

5. Wait for initiated operations to finish

6. Goto step (1)

Csh is the default shell on Berkeley UNIX systems. *Csh* usually uses the character % as its prompt, but it can be redefined by the user.

A shell-level command line consists of one or more *words* separated by *white space* or *blanks* (spaces and/or TABs) and terminates with a RETURN. RETURN (transmitted to UNIX as a NEWLINE character) terminates a command unless quoted by a backslash character (\\), in which case the quoted RETURN becomes a blank. (Quoting is discussed in Section 5.9.) The first word in a command is the *name* of a program to be executed; the other words are *arguments* to the program. There are two types of commands: *csh* built-in commands and *regular* commands. A built-in command invokes a routine programmed within *csh*. To execute a built-in command, the shell simply calls up the appropriate subroutine within itself. A regular command is any other executable program in UNIX that is not built in to the shell. These commands include system commands such as **ls** and **rm** as well as your own executable programs such as **a.out**. The shell spawns a separate *process* to execute a regular command. The distinction between built-in and regular commands is an important one, as you will discover.

Several commands can be given on a single command line if they are separated by semicolons (;). The shell will execute these multiple commands sequentially, from left to right. A sequence of commands separated by semicolons and enclosed within parentheses forms a single command. For example:

(**echo** first line ; **echo** second line) > *file*

creates a file containing the lines first line and second line. A sequence of simple commands separated by a vertical bar (|) forms a *pipeline*. The command separators || and && have special meanings that control the execution of commands on the command line. For example:

cmd1 || *cmd2*   (execute *cmd2* only if *cmd1* fails)

cmd1 && *cmd2*   (execute *cmd2* only if *cmd1* succeeds)

After issuing a command, it is not necessary to wait for a prompt before typing in additional input. This feature is known as *type ahead*. What you type ahead will be there for the program when it is ready to receive input. You also can instruct the shell not to wait for a command to finish by typing an ampersand (&) at the end of the command. In this case, the shell immediately returns to process your next command, while the previous command continues to run *detached* from the shell. Such detached but running processes are said to be running in the *background*. For example:

print *file* **&**

will start the print process and return you to the shell level without waiting for **print** to finish. The ampersand instructs *csh* to skip step (5) in the command interpretation cycle while the print command continues in the background. A background process can be reattached to the shell—that is, brought to the *foreground*—by the command:

fg *jobid*

as mentioned in Chapter 1.

5.2 Command Execution

Execution of a built-in command simply involves a subroutine call by the shell. Invoking a nonbuilt-in command is more complicated. The first word of the nonbuilt-in command is taken to be the name of an executable file, which can be in one of two forms: It can be the absolute or relative pathname of the executable file, or if the executable file is in one of several "important" directories, the simple file name itself will suffice. The procedure by which the shell finds the executable file for a command is as follows:

1. If the command name is an absolute or relative pathname, then the name of the executable file has been given explicitly and no search is necessary.

2. If the command name is a simple file name, the executable file is found by searching through an ordered sequence of directories specified by the *command search path*. The first such file found is used.

If the executable file cannot be found, or if it is found but the execute permission on the file is not set, then an appropriate error message is displayed on the terminal. The error message most likely will be "file not found" or "permission denied."

The *csh* variable *path* is set to a list of directories that forms the command search path, which usually includes the following directories: /bin, /usr/bin, /usr/ucb, and /usr/local/bin. These directories contain most system-supplied executable programs such as **rm**, **ls**, **mail**, **vi**, **cc**, and many others. The search path can be modified to include additional directories. For example:

set path = ($HOME/bin $path)

adds the directory bin in your home directory to the beginning of the search path. Now, regardless of your current directory, you can use a simple file name to run a program whose executable file resides in the $HOME/bin directory.

Csh creates a hash table of all executable files on the search path when you log in. This speeds up the command search, but it also means that if you create a new executable file in any of the directories on the search path, the new command won't be reflected in the hash table until you log in again or use the *csh* built-in command **rehash** to recompute the hash table for commands.

The special period symbol (.) often is placed at the end of the search path to enable you to invoke any command in the current directory with a simple file name. Since . stands for the current directory, which is not fixed, and since there is no way to include commands in . in the hash table, *csh*'s command search through . is slow. Thus, it is inefficient to put a fixed directory name after . on the command search path. In other words, it is best to put . at the end of $path.

Once an executable file has been found, the shell creates a separate process to run the program following these three steps:

1. A new (child) process is created that is a copy of the shell.

2. The child process is overlaid with the executable file, then the command name together with any arguments are passed to it.

3a. The interactive shell waits for the child process to terminate before re-turning to receive the next command, unless the command line includes a trailing ampersand (&).

3b. If the command line ends with &, the shell returns without waiting, and the command is run in the background.

A subshell is also used to process commands enclosed in parentheses.

5.3 Input/Output Redirection

Standard Input and Output

The UNIX system provides input/output (I/O) services for processes. For each process, a set of *file descriptors* numbered 0, 1, 2, and so on is used for I/O transactions between the process and the UNIX operating system. When a process opens a file or a device for I/O, a file descriptor is assigned to the process to identify the I/O *channel* between the process and the open file or device. The first three file descriptors automatically are assigned I/O channels for a new process when it is created:

1. File descriptor 0 is connected to the keyboard for input.

2. File descriptor 1 is connected to the terminal for output.

3. File descriptor 2 is connected to the terminal for output.

In UNIX terminology, file descriptor 0 is called the *standard input*, file descriptor 1 is called the *standard output*, and file descriptor 2 is called the *standard error*. Most UNIX commands receive input from the standard input, produce output to the standard output, and send error messages through the standard error. However, the standard I/O channels of a command can be redirected by the shell.

Redirection

The shell allows the user to *redirect* the standard I/O channels of any command invoked through the shell. We mentioned redirection in Chapter 1 and have seen a few instances of I/O redirection already. Let us look at another simple example:

```
ls > filelist
```

shows a command that will create in your current directory a file named filelist containing the output of the **ls** command. The symbol > instructs the shell to redirect the **ls** output away from the standard output (the terminal screen) to the newly created file filelist. If a file already exists, it will be wiped out and replaced by a new file with the same name, unless you specify otherwise. The command:

set noclobber

sets the *csh* variable *noclobber* so that attempts to redirect output to an existing file will result in an error. This feature protects against accidental loss of a file through output redirection. If you do mean to wipe out the file, add an exclamation point:

>!

Many users set the noclobber variable in their .cshrc file (see Section 5.8).

The symbol >> operates much the same as >, but it appends to the end of a file instead of overwriting an existing file. For instance:

cat f1 f2 >> f3

appends f1 and f2 to the end of f3, in that order. If the variable noclobber is set, use >>! if file f3 does *not* already exist.

The standard input of a command also can be redirected using the operator <. Thus, commands that take interactive input from the keyboard can be instructed to take input from a file instead. For example:

lisp < *file*

where *file* contains input to the lisp interpreter. Since most commands in UNIX take input from a file if it is given as an argument, as in:

sort *file*

the usage:

sort < *file*

is correct but unnecessary.

If no file is given as an argument, a command usually takes input from its standard input (the keyboard). Thus, **sort** sorts what is typed in at the keyboard. Such interactive input is terminated with **^D** at the beginning of a line. Let us look at another example:

cat > *file*

After giving this command, what you type on the keyboard is put into *file*. Once again, input is terminated by **^D** at the beginning of a line. This method allows you to create a file without using a text editor and also to transfer a file from your home computer to a UNIX system.

Csh allows you to redirect standard error and standard output of a command to the same file by using & after the > or >> symbols for output redirection. Each of the following is a valid redirection of standard error together with standard output:

>& *file*	(standard output and standard error into a new *file*)
>&! *file*	(standard output and standard error into a new *file* even if *file* exists)
>>& *file*	(standard output and standard error appended to the end of *file*)
>>&! *file*	(standard output and standard error appended to the end of *file* even if *file* does not exist)

Pipes

As mentioned in Chapter 1, in addition to being able to redirect I/O to and from files, you also can redirect the output of one program as input to another program. The vertical bar symbol (|) is used to establish a *pipe*, which connects the output of the first command to the input of the second. Thus:

```
ls -l | more
```

pipes the standard output of **ls** to the standard input of **more**. The resulting command is called a *pipeline*. Sometimes, for new UNIX users, it is hard to understand the difference between | and >. Just remember that the receiving end of a pipe | is always another program, and the receiving end of a > is always a file. You can pipe the standard error together with the standard output using |& instead of |. More elaborate examples of pipelines were described in Section 4.7.

5.4 More Job Control

Some aspects of job control were discussed in Chapter 1: the terms *foreground*, *background*, and *suspended*; the commands **jobs** and **fg**; and the use of ^Z to suspend the current job. If these are unfamiliar, take a few moments to reread Section 1.9 on job control. Note also that *job suspension* is a feature peculiar to Berkeley UNIX and the *csh* shell. Much of the material in this section will not apply to other shells such as *sh*.

Running a job in the background is the preferred way to run longer programs. Even so, whether or not a process is running in the background or in the foreground, there is no effect on the assigned I/O channels. Therefore, unless output is redirected, the output from the background process still will interfere with output from any foreground job. Further, if the background job requires input from the terminal, it will stop itself and wait to be brought to the foreground to receive the input it needs. For jobs to run efficiently in the background, redirecting standard I/O to files usually is essential.

When a background job terminates, the shell displays a message to notify the user:

[*jobnumber*] `Done` *command as given*

The message is displayed after normal completion of a background process. The following message is displayed when a background process terminates abnormally:

[*jobnumber*] `Exit 1` *command as given*

As discussed before, a new job can be run in the background by terminating the command with an ampersand (&). To reactivate a suspended job and run it in the background, use the command:

bg *jobid*

If no jobid is specified, the most recently suspended job will be activated and run in the background. The command:

`stop jobid`

suspends the specified background job. Recall from Chapter 1 that the command **jobs** will list jobids for all stopped jobs and background jobs.

To abort a foreground job or command, you can input the *interrupt* character (usually delete or **^C**). To abort a background job, input the **kill** command:

`kill jobid`

A *process number* also can be used as an argument to the **kill** command. The process number is displayed when a job is put in the background, and it also can be recalled with the command:

`jobs -l`

which gives the process numbers for all jobs. Occasionally, the **kill** command will fail to terminate a job. In this case, the command:

`kill -9 jobid`

will execute a mandatory kill on the process. The argument −9 instructs **kill** to send a specific *signal* to the process, which forces it to terminate. Signals are described further in Section 6.10.

The **kill** command discussed here is built into *csh*. There is also a regular command **kill** that can be used, for example, from the *sh* shell. Among other differences, the nonbuilt-in **kill** allows process specification only by process number.

Long-Running Programs

If a program is substantial, it may need to run for hours or perhaps even days. It is hardly practical to force a user to remain logged in for the duration of such a program. Therefore, when you log out, UNIX kills all jobs initiated from your terminal *except* those jobs running in the background. A background job will continue to run after you log out, provided it makes no attempt to perform I/O to its *control terminal*, which, since you have logged out, no longer exists. If such I/O is requested, the background job will be terminated. However, I/O redirected to files is permitted, and a combination of I/O redirection and job control can be used to keep a job running after logout.

When you prepare a job to run after logout, make sure any possible input and output (including error output) have been redirected to a file. Then all that remains is to put the job in the background and log out. For example:

command > & *file* &
```
logout
```

The *command* will keep running after you log out. The standard output and standard error are redirected to the specified file. It would be nice to be able to reattach the job the next time you log in, but this is not yet possible in UNIX. You can, however, use the **ps** command to examine the status of the background process when you log in again (assuming the process has not finished). You also can examine the output file by using a variety of commands. The –f option of the **tail** command is especially useful in this regard. Until it is aborted or killed, the command:

```
tail –f file
```

will display additions to the specified file as they are appended. Using this command, you could gauge the progress of the background process by examining its current output to the file.

5.5 Input Processing

A command undergoes a number of transformations before it is executed by the shell. These transformations are called *input processing* and occur in step (3) of the shell command execution cycle. *Csh* transforms each command by applying the following steps in sequence:

1. History substitutions

2. Alias substitutions

3. Variable substitutions

4. Command substitutions

5. File name expansions

History Substitution

The *csh history* mechanism records and allows you to reuse previous commands. Each command line issued by you, whether successful or not and whether consisting of one or more commands, is kept as an item in the *history list*, which is displayed using the built-in command **history**. Each item in the history list is known as an *event*, and each event is identified by a sequence number. The total number of events kept on the history list has a limit, which is set by:

set history = *number*

(This is another setting that can be kept in the .login file.)

The history mechanism can save you a great deal of typing by allowing you to substitute history events into the current command line with just a few keystrokes. The history mechanism also is used frequently to correct errors in the most recently given command. Admittedly, it is sometimes easier to

Figure 5.1 ▪ Frequent History Substitutions

History Substitutions	
!	a special character for history substitution
!*n*	the event with sequence number *n*
!−*n*	the *n*th previous event
!!	the last event (same as ! − 1)
!*prefix*	the most recent event with the specified *prefix*
ˆ*xx*ˆ*yy*	the last event, with the string *xx* replaced by the string *yy*
!*	all the arguments of the last event
!$	the last argument of the last event
!ˆ	the first argument of the last event
!:*n*	the *n*th argument of the last event
event:s/*xx*/*yy*/	the given *event* with the string *xx* replaced by *yy*

retype the command than to remember how to invoke the history mechanism. Nevertheless, for lengthy commands with complicated syntax, the history mechanism can save you a great deal of aggravation.

History substitution is *keyed* (activated) by the exclamation point character (!), and it works by recalling items from the history list. Items that can be recalled from the list and substituted into the current command include any history event, any word or words of any event, and parts of certain words. These items also can be modified before their inclusion into the current command. Figure 5.1 shows an incomplete but generally sufficient list of history substitution rules. Figure 5.2 contains some applications of history substitutions in commands. Each example is described here, and the numbers correspond to the numbers in the figure:

1. Reuse the name *file3*.

2. *Name* turns out to be a directory.

3. Mistyped the command name **sort**.

4. *File* is not in the current directory but in the directory *dir*.

5. *Dir* is not in the current directory but in the home directory.

Figure 5.2 ▪ **History Examples**

	Csh History Examples		
Number	Last Event	Current Command	Effect
1.	`diff` *file1 file2* > *file3*	`vi !$` or `vi !:4`	`vi` *file3*
2.	`ls −l` *name*	`^−l^−ld`	`ls −ld` *name*
3.	`srot` *file* (srot: command not found)	`^ro^or`	`sort` *file*
4.	`vi` *file* (file not found)	`cd` *dir*; `!vi` or `!−1`	`cd` *dir*; `vi` *file*
5.	`cd` *dir* (no such file or directory)	`cd; !−1`	`cd`; `cd` *dir*
6.	`mail` smith`!`ucbvax (ucbvax event not found)	`!!\!ucbvax`	`mail` smith\\!ucbvax
7.	`setenv` TERM = hp2392 (setenv: too many arguments)	`^=^`	`setenv` TERM hp2392
8.	`ls` *dir*	`^s^s −F`	`ls −F` *dir*

6. The character ! in the mail address needs to be quoted (see Section 5.9); otherwise it invokes a history substitution.

7. The equal sign is not needed for **setenv**.

8. Note that blanks are allowed in the string replacement.

Having illustrated a number of examples, you are ready to proceed to the general form of a history substitution:

event [: *word designator*] [: *modifier* ...]

The event is given in one of the following ways:

Event number	!12 gives event 12 on the history list
Relative position	!−2 gives the second most recent event. A special case is !!, which refers to the last event.
Command prefix	!vi gives the most recent event with the prefix **vi**
Matching string	!?*string* gives the most recent event containing *string* anywhere within the event

Following the event are the optional word designators. The purpose of a word designator is to choose certain words from the history event. If no word designators are used, the entire event will be selected. The following word designators can be used:

n	selects the word *n* (the command name is word 0); for example, !−3:2 gets the third word of the event !−3
$	selects the last word; !$ gives the last word of the last event
^	designates the first argument (second word); !^ gives the first argument of the last event
i−j	designates word *i–j* inclusive
−j	same as 0–*j*
i−	designates word *i* up to but not including the last word
*	designates all argument words; !* gives all arguments of the previous command
i*	same as *i–$*

An optional sequence of modifiers also can be used. One frequent usage is:

event:s/*xx*/*yy*/

to substitute the string *xx* by *yy* in *event*. If a word is a long pathname, it is sometimes convenient to use a modifier to extract a portion of it, but most modifiers are seldom used interactively. Writing programs in the shell language (shell procedures) is discussed in Chapter 6, and at that point you will be able to see why modifiers are needed. A number of modifiers are listed in Figure 5.3; refer to the *csh* manual for a complete list.

Once a command line has gone through history substitution, it too becomes part of the history list as the most recent event.

Alias Substitution

The alias facility allows you to redefine an existing command name with a string of characters of your own choosing. You can, among other things, give existing commands new names that are shorter or easier to remember. The built-in command:

`alias` *name definition*

defines the given *name* as an alias for the specified *definition*. The definition is a string of characters referred to as the *alias string*. Here are some simple but useful alias definitions:

`alias ^L clear`	`alias dir ls`
`alias h history`	`alias list cat`
`alias j jobs`	`alias remane mv`
`alias m more`	`alias appendtoend 'cat >>'`

With these aliases defined, the command **clear** can be given simply by typing ^L, the command **history** can be abbreviated to **h**, and so on. Because it is possible for an alias to contain multiple words, and because any special characters used by *csh* within the alias string need to be quoted (see Section 5.9), it may be easiest to enclose the entire alias string in single quotation marks, as in the following example:

`alias ls 'ls -F'`

The command **ls** when occurring in the command position will be replaced by the string ls –F. Thus, the **ls** command always is given with the –F option,

---

Figure 5.3 ▪ **Modifiers of the History Mechanism (if !\$ is /usr/src/ucb/prog.c)**

Modifier	Meaning	Example	Value
h	head	`!$:h`	`/usr/src/ucb`
t	tail	`!$:t`	`prog.c`
r	root	`!$:r`	`/usr/src/ucb/prog`
e	extension	`!$:e`	`.c`

which causes, among other things, directory names to be marked with a trailing /, symbolic links to be marked with a trailing @, and executable files to be marked with a trailing *

To display the alias definition, use:

alias   (display all aliases)

alias *name*   (display the alias)

To remove alias definitions, use:

unalias *name* ...

Now that you know how aliases are defined, displayed, and removed, let us look more closely at the alias substitution mechanism provided by *csh*. After a command is scanned, separated into words, and history-substituted, its first word (**alias** works only on the first word of a command) is checked to see if it has an alias. If it does and if the alias character string does not involve history substitution, then the command name is replaced by its alias. Any arguments are not affected. If, on the other hand, the alias character string does involve history substitution, the following two steps are taken:

1. The alias string is history-substituted as though the current command (the one being alias-substituted) were on the history list as the latest history event.

2. The resulting alias string replaces the *entire* command (not just the command name).

After an alias substitution, the transformed command will undergo further processing, beginning with the alias substitution step. Thus, there is a potential for *looping*. *Csh* halts obvious infinite loops such as:

alias ls 'ls -F'

where the command name and the alias name are the same, and continues on normally. Other loops cause an error.

Consider the following examples of aliases with history substitution:

alias cd 'cd \!*; pwd'
alias csmail 'mail \!:1%\!:2@relay.cs.net'

The history substitution character ! must be quoted using \ to prevent substitution from occurring at alias definition time. (See Section 5.9 for more on quoting.) The function of the **cd** alias is to transform:

cd *directory*

into

cd *directory*; **pwd**

which not only changes the working directory but also displays the name of the new working directory. Many users like this added feedback.

The **csmail** alias transforms:

csmail *user host*

into

mail *user*%*host*@`relay.cs.net`

which is the way to send a piece of mail to a *user* at *host* through the relay computer between CSNet and ARPANET.

Variable Substitution

The shell allows the use of variables, whose values can be a string of zero or more words. Some variables are reserved for controlling functions of the shell, such as noclobber for setting an option and path for command search. These are called *special shell variables*. You are allowed to use your own variables as well as set and reset values for special shell variables. *Csh* and *sh* have different sets of special variables. Those for *csh* are discussed in Section 5.6.

Generally speaking, a variable identifier can be any word whose first character is a letter and the rest of which consists of letters, digits, and underscore characters. The **set** command assigns a value to a variable. Once a variable is set, it can be used in subsequent commands. For example:

set `maildir = /usr/spool/mail`

gives the variable maildir a string value that names the mail spool area. With this variable set, you can input:

cd `$maildir`

which is a command with a variable in it. After variable substitution, this command becomes:

cd `/usr/spool/mail`

This procedure provides an easy way to remember names of frequently accessed directories.

As you can see, variable substitution is keyed by the character $. That is, a word that begins with a $ is a variable. If $ is followed by a blank, then it stands for itself. The **echo** command can be used to display the value of a variable. The command:

echo `$maildir`

will display /usr/spool/mail on your screen. You also can display all variables you have set so far by typing:

set   (display all current variable values)

with no arguments. The *extent* of a variable can be delineated by braces ({ and }). For example:

```
set x = abc
echo ${x}def
```

displays the string abcdef.

```
echo $xdef
```

results in the error message:

```
xdef: undefined variable
```

A variable is always string-valued, and a single variable may have a value consisting of more than one word. The command:

```
set path = ($home/cmd /usr/local/bin /usr/ucb /bin /usr/bin .)
```

gives the variable path a value consisting of six words. To access and set individual words in the value of a multiword variable, use subscripts enclosed in brackets ([and]). For example:

```
echo $path[3]
```

or

```
set path[2] = $home/commands
```

It is also possible to select a range of words from a multiword variable or to select a part of a single variable (see Section 6.4).

Command Substitution

It is possible to substitute the output of a command as a string of words into the text string of a command. The substitution is enclosed by backquote (`) characters. For example:

```
set dir = `pwd`
```

assigns the output of the **pwd** (print working directory) command to the user variable dir. Another example:

```
set files = `ls`
```

assigns to files words produced by the **ls** command, namely the file names in the current directory. The result of command substitution also can form part of a single word, as in:

```
set name = `pwd`/test.c
```

For command substitution, the output of the command normally is broken into separate words at blanks, tabs, and NEWLINEs, with null words being discarded. The resulting text then replaces the backquoted string.

File Name Expansion

Because most words used in a UNIX command refer to file names, the shell provides *file name expansion* to make it easier to specify files. When a *pattern* is used in place of a file name in a command, the pattern is *expanded* to represent all the file names matching the pattern. If a directory is specified, files from that directory are matched against the pattern. Otherwise, files in the current working directory are used. If a word contains any of the following characters *, [, {, or begins with ~, the word specifies a pattern. Let us look at an example:

```
ls -l *.c
```

provides a long listing of all files whose names end in .c in the current working directory. The *.c is a pattern, and it expands to match all file names in the current working directory ending with .c. The command:

```
ls -l dir/*.c
```

serves the same function as the previous command but does so in the given directory *dir*. The command:

```
ls -l book/section*/*.ms
```

gives a long listing of all files ending in .ms in all sections under the book directory.

File name patterns are matched against existing file names. Rules for patterns are as follows:

*	the "wildcard"; it matches any string of characters of length zero or more. Thus to get rid of all files in a directory, you can **cd** to that directory and input **rm** *.
?	matches any single character
[...]	matches any one of the characters contained between [and]. For instance, a[rxz]b matches arb, axb, or azb. The pattern chapter[0–9] matches chapter0, chapter1, and so on.
~	matches the home directory of the user when used alone. It can be viewed as a shorthand for $home. When prefixing a

userid as in ˜user, the word expands to the home directory of that user.

{.,.,.}   is a shorthand. The pattern x{a,b,c}y expands to the three words xay, xby, and xcy.

Exceptions: The character . at the beginning of a file name and the character / contained in a pathname must be matched explicitly. Thus, the command **ls** * does not list any files whose names begin with a dot.

A file pattern can contain more than one special character. When more than one file name matches a pattern, the pattern is expanded into a sorted list of these file names. It becomes an error if there is no file name to match a pattern, unless the variable nonomatch is set.

File name expansion is also known as *globbing*. If the special variable noglob is set, then file name expansion is inhibited. This is useful when manipulating words that are not names of files.

5.6 *csh* Special Variables

There are two kinds of special variables in *csh*, *toggle* variables and *value* variables. A toggle variable is either *set* or *unset* by:

```
set toggle
unset toggle
```

A value variable is set to a string value in the same way as a user variable. To view all special and user-defined variables that have been set, along with their values, type in the **set** command with no arguments.

Setting special variables controls the way certain *csh* operations are carried out. Those variables that affect interactive use of the shell are listed here for easy reference. Other special variables affecting the processing of *shell procedures* are discussed in Chapter 6.

Toggle Special Variables

ignoreeof   If unset, a ˆ**D** (the end-of-file character) typed at the beginning of a line instructs the login shell to log out or a nonlogin shell to terminate. If set, the shell ignores ˆ**D** from the terminal. This variable prevents shells from accidentally being killed by ˆ**D**. This variable usually is set in the .cshrc file.

noclobber   As described in Section 5.3 on I/O redirection, if noclobber is set, restrictions are placed on output redirection to ensure that files are not destroyed accidentally and that >> redirections refer to existing files.

noglob If set, file name expansion is inhibited. This variable is most useful in those shell scripts not dealing with file names or after a list of file names has been obtained and further expansions are not desirable.

nonomatch If set, it does not become an error to give a file name pattern matching no files; rather, the pattern is expanded to itself.

notify If set, the shell notifies you asynchronously of background job completions. The default provides such notices just before displaying a prompt.

Value Special Variables

cwd always contains the full pathname of the current directory

home records the home directory of the user, initialized from the environment. The file name expansion of ~ refers to this variable.

path Each word of the path variable specifies a directory in which commands are to be sought for execution. If there is no path variable, then only full pathnames will be executed. The default search path is usually (/bin /usr/bin /usr/local/bin .), but this may vary from system to system.

cdpath the value of cdpath is a list of alternate directories searched to find subdirectories in **chdir** commands

prompt is the string that your shell will use as your prompt. If a ! appears in the string, it will be replaced by the current history event number unless it is preceded by a \. The default is % (# for the super user).

time controls the automatic timing of commands. If set to *t*, any command that takes more than *t* cpu seconds will cause some timing information to be displayed when it terminates.

mail This variable specifies the frequency and file locations to check for incoming mail. For example:

    set mail = (300 /usr/spool/mail/smith)

If the first word of the value of mail is numeric, it specifies a different mail-checking interval, in seconds, than the default, which is 10 minutes. When the specified interval has elapsed, the shell checks for newly arrived mail just before displaying the next shell prompt. A shell message is displayed if new mail has arrived, "You have new mail." If multiple mail files are specified, then the shell displays the message, "New mail in *name*" when there is mail in the file *name*.

history   The value of history specifies the maximum number of history events kept. Thus, **set** history = 15 means that only the most recent 15 events will be kept. Too large a value can exceed shell memory. The last executed command always is saved on the history list.

savehist   is given a numeric value to control the number of entries from the history list that are saved in ~/.history when you log out. During start up, the shell includes the contents of ~/.history in the history list, enabling history to be saved across logins. Too large a value can slow down the shell during start up.

histchars   can be given a string value to change the characters used in history substitution. The first character of its value is used as the history substitution character, replacing the default character (!). The second character of its value replaces the character ^ in quick history substitutions.

5.7 Examples of *csh* Usage

By studying examples, you can gain a deeper understanding of how the shell works and how the various substitutions can be used. Almost all examples given here are of practical value, and you may consider adopting any or all of them for your own use. The examples will work as given on Berkeley UNIX; minor modification may be needed for System V.

Customized Prompt

The default *csh* prompt is %. This single character is nice and simple, but many UNIX users prefer a more informative prompt. In *csh*, the prompt is redefined by setting the special variable prompt:

```
set prompt = 'kentcs:pwang{\!}%'
```

This line is usually included in the user's .login file. This particular prompt shows the userid pwang, the system name kentcs, the history event number inside { }, and the shell type (% for *csh*). This type of prompt is especially helpful when your UNIX system is one node on a local area network, because it tells you at a glance which computer in the network you are currently using.

An Interesting Alias for cd

You know that **cd** changes the current working directory and is used often. Here an alias is defined for **cd**, and another alias is defined for **back**, so that after issuing a **cd** command, you can return to the previous directory using **back**:

```
alias cd 'set old=$cwd; chdir \!*; pwd'
alias back 'set back=$old; cd $back; unset back'
```

In this example, we have used history inside the alias definition for **cd**, where cwd is a special variable and old is a user-defined variable. Note that the alias strings are enclosed in single quotation marks to prevent interpretation of $, ;, and * at alias definition time and that ! is quoted by \. (Quoting is discussed in Section 5.9.) Having defined these aliases. The command:

cd *dir*

is alias-substituted into a sequence of three commands. The first:

set old=$cwd

records the value of the current working directory in the shell variable old. The second command:

chdir *dir*

is then followed by the command:

pwd

which provides feedback to the user. Any time after performing the first **cd**, the command:

back

changes the directory back to the previous directory, which is recorded in the variable old. This procedure makes it simple to return to the previous directory and to go back and forth between the two. If you like this pair of aliases, add them to your .login file.

I/O Redirection for File Transfer

UNIX users who have personal computers at home sometimes will want to transfer files between their home PC and the UNIX system. If the PC terminal-emulation software has the proper ability to send and receive a file, then I/O redirection can be used by UNIX to handle the file transfer.

Assume that you are at home using your PC, which is connected to your UNIX system through a modem. After login on UNIX, you change directory using **cd** to the directory where file transfer is to take place.

To transfer a file to UNIX:

1. Let's say that you wish to transfer the file named pcfile from your PC. Type in **cat** > *file*, which causes the standard input to go into the named file.

2. Press the escape character for your PC, followed by the send file command to your PC. Details on the escape character and the command will depend on the terminal-emulation software you are running on your PC.

3. Start transmitting pcfile from the disk on your PC. You should see the characters in pcfile being sent through to UNIX.

4. After pcfile is transmitted, press ^D to terminate the **cat** command. A copy of pcfile is made in *file*.

To transfer a file from UNIX to your PC:

1. Let's say now that you wish to transfer the file unixfile to your PC. Press the proper escape character for your PC and give the receive file command for your PC.

2. Type in **cat** *unixfile*, which outputs the specific file to the standard output, which is your PC. Since your PC has been set up to receive a file, every character it receives also goes into the file you have named.

3. When **cat** is finished, press the escape character again and give the command to save the file on your floppy or hard disk.

Terminal Initialization

The command **tset** sets up your terminal by identifying its type and then performing terminal-dependent initializations. The terminal type on each hard-wired port is specified in the /etc/ttytype database. For ports not hardwired to specific terminals, the terminal type will be a generic name such as *dialup* or *network*. The **tset** command usually is performed to set up your terminal when you log in. For example:

```
set term = `tset - -m dialup:vt200`
```

can be included in your .login file. The argument – instructs **tset** to output the terminal type (to standard output). The argument −m dialup:vt200 instructs your terminal type to be set to vt200 when you dial in.

5.8 Shell Startup and Initialization

As mentioned, the shell itself is a user program. The term *user program* refers to programs not built into the UNIX operating system kernel. Examples of kernel routines are file system routines, memory management programs, process management programs, and interrupt handlers. The commands **ls**, **vi**, **mail**, and **cat** are user programs. In fact, all UNIX commands are user programs, including both the C shell and the Bourne shell. Their executable files are usually /bin/csh and /bin/sh, respectively.

The login shell is selectable on a per-user basis and is specified in the user's *password file entry* in the password file /etc/passwd. This file contains a one-line entry for each authorized user on the system. Each passwd entry consists of the following fields:

- Login name (contains no uppercase letters)

- Encrypted password

- Numerical userid

- Numerical groupid

- User's real name, office, extension, and home phone

- User's home directory

- Program to use as the shell

The fields are separated by colons (:). For example, a passwd entry may look like the following:

```
jjsmith:qkztZqtags:20:15:Joe J. Smith,304 MLH,2949:/user/jjsmith:/bin/csh
```

Immediately after login, the system invokes the specified shell as the user's login shell. The login shell specified in the passwd entry can be changed using the command *chsh* (change shell). For example:

```
chsh jjsmith /bin/sh
```

will change jjsmith's login shell to *sh*. When a *csh* is invoked, it first executes commands in the *initialization* file .cshrc in the user's home directory. If the *csh* is a login shell, it also executes commands in the .login file in the home directory (after .cshrc). The purpose of both these files is to customize the shell for the individual user. The distinction is that .cshrc is used by every *csh*

Figure 5.4 ▪ A Sample .login File

```
alias j 'jobs -l'
alias lll logout
alias l 'ls -F'
alias cd 'set old=$cwd; chdir \!*; pwd'
alias back 'set back=$old; cd $back; unset back'
alias ^L clear
limit coredumpsize 0 #prevents csh from creating coredump files
set history=30
set noclobber
set ignoreeof
set mail = (500 /usr/spool/mail/pwang)
# tset identifies terminal type and initializes terminal
set term = `tset --m dialup:vt200`
set prompt = 'kentcs:pwang{\!}%'
set path=(/usr/ucb /bin /usr/bin /usr/local /usr/games .)
# EXINIT is environment variable used by vi and ex
setenv EXINIT 'se ai shell=/bin/csh terse nowarn sm'
# set terminal and special characters
stty crt -tabs kill ^U erase '^?' intr ^C
biff y
date
```

upon invocation, and only the login *csh* uses the .login file. Thus, .cshrc contains settings intended for all invocations of *csh*, and .login contains additional settings intended for the login *csh*.

A nonlogin *csh* is a subshell, and the execution of any *csh* script (see Chapter 6) involves a subshell *csh*. Therefore, the setting for the special variables ignoreeof, noclobber, and any aliases used also in shell procedures should be contained in .cshrc instead of in .login.

Settings that should be contained in your .login file include terminal type, all environment variables, and special, top-level aliases. Figure 5.4 illustrates a sample .login file. The number sign (#) is a *comment character*, because the shell ignores the part of a line following a #. The symbol ^? in the **stty** command represents the DELETE key not control-?. As opposed to .login, the .logout file is executed by the login *csh* before logout. Useful operations in the .logout file include removing scratch files, clearing the screen of the CRT, locking up certain files, and so on.

5.9 Shell Special Characters and Quoting

The shell uses many special characters in establishing the command language syntax and as keys for the various substitutions provided. Some familiar special characters are listed in Figure 5.5. Additional special characters related to writing programs in the shell command language are explained in Chapter 6.

Special characters help achieve many shell functionalities. But because the shell interprets a special character differently from a regular character, it is impossible for a special character to stand for itself unless additional arrangements are made. For example, if there is a file named f&g.c, how can you refer to it in a shell command? The solution to this problem is the use of more special characters, known as *quote characters*. [If you are getting the impression that there are many special characters in UNIX, you are absolutely right. In fact, any character on the keyboard that is not alphabetic or numeric is probably special in some way. Notable exceptions are the period (.) and the underscore (__). A table of all special characters for *csh* can be found in Appendix 4.]

Quoting in *csh*

Three quote characters are used in *csh* commands: the backslash (\), the single quotation mark ('), and the double quotation mark ("). The character \ quotes

Figure 5.5 ▪ Some *csh* Special Characters

Characters	Use
>, <, &, and !	I/O redirection
|	pipe
$	variable substitution
!	history substitution
[, *, and ?	file name expansion
& and ;	command termination
`	command substitution
NEWLINE	command line termination
^C or DELETE	interrupt and abort

or *escapes* the next character. For example:

```
cat f\&g.c
```

or

```
mail kentvax\!pwang
```

The special characters & and ! lose their special meaning when preceded by \. Instead, they stand for the literal characters themselves. If a space or TAB is preceded by a \, then it becomes part of a word (that is, it loses its special meaning to delineate words). If the NEWLINE character is preceded by a \, it is equivalent to a blank. Thus, using a \ at the end of a line *continues* the shell command to the next line.

Whereas the \ escapes the next character, a pair of single quotation marks (') quotes the entire string of characters enclosed:

```
echo 'a + b >= c * d'
```

When enclosed by single quotation marks, all characters except ! are escaped. The resulting string (after history substitution) forms all or part of a word. In the preceding example, the quoted string forms one word with the spaces included. The command:

```
cat /user/pwang/'my >=.c'
```

is used to type out a C program in the file /user/pwang/my> = .c. In this example, the quoted string forms part of a word. To include a single quotation mark in a string, the \ is used, as in:

```
echo It\'s a good day
```

The following rules summarize quotation with single quotation marks:

1. All characters except ! are taken literally.

2. The quoted string, after history substitution, forms part or all of one word.

3. The character combination \NEWLINE within single quotation marks gives rise to a single character NEWLINE instead of a blank.

Sometimes it is desirable to allow certain substitutions within a quoted string. Quotation with double quotation marks (") serves this purpose. A pair of double quotation marks functions the same as a pair of single quotation marks with just two differences: First, variable substitutions are allowed within double quotation marks; that is, variable substitution keyed by the $ sign always works within double quotation marks. In fact, there is no way to suppress the special meaning of $ within double quotation marks. For example:

```
echo "your current working directory is $cwd"
```

will still use the value $cwd. Furthermore:

```
echo "\$cwd shows $ is not quoted"
```

shows that within double quotation marks, variable substitution is not escaped by \. Second, command substitutions are allowed inside double quotation marks and are treated slightly differently from normal command substitutions. Normally, the output of a backquoted (`) command is broken into separate words at blanks, tabs, and NEWLINEs, with null words being discarded; this text then replaces the original backquoted string. However, when command substitution is within double quotation marks, only NEWLINEs force new words; blanks and tabs are preserved. The single, final NEWLINE in command substitution does not force a new word in any situation. For example:

```
set date = `date`
```

and

```
set datestring = "`date`"
```

are different in that $date includes multiple words, but $datestring is one word.

5.10 Summary

Csh follows a command interpretation cycle to handle user requests. A command is either a built-in shell routine or an executable program that is located directly or found by searching the file system along the command search path. Redirection of the standard input (<), redirection of the standard output (>, >>, and >>!), redirection of standard error together with standard output (>&, >&!, >>&, and >>&!), and pipes (|) are supported.

Job control allows you to run many jobs at once. The character ^Z is used to suspend an ongoing job. History, alias, variable, command, and file name substitutions are performed in sequence to transform a command line. The history and variable substitutions are keyed by the special characters ! and $, respectively. File name expansion uses the matching characters (*, [...], ~, ?, and {...}) to generate file names.

Many special characters are used in the shell, and it is important to quote a special character if it is to stand for itself. For quoting, the special characters \, ', and " are used. There are subtle differences between these quoting mechanisms.

Many special variables in *csh* are used both to keep status information (for example, cwd, user, and term) and to control how *csh* works (for instance, ignoreof, mail, and history).

The shell is a user program and is selectable on a per-user basis. You can customize your shells through initialization files. The *sh* initialization file is .profile. For *csh*, there are two initialization files: .cshrc for every shell and .login for the login shell. *Csh* also uses a .logout file.

Exercises

1. Why is the command **logout** built into the shell?

2. A favorite security trick of some people is to place an executable file called ls in their home directory. The idea here is that if somebody wants to look at what files the user has, he or she will first **cd** to the directory and then invoke **ls**, whereupon the user's **ls** file is executed rather than the system version. If the snoop follows the recommendations given in the text, will this trick work? Why or why not?

3. Using the commands **cat**, **tail**, and **from**, write a pipeline that will give you a numbered list of your messages, stating who they are from and the date and time of their arrival in reverse order. How could you produce a listing sorted by sender in alphabetical order?

4. How could you produce a listing of all your files in the current directory, sorted in decreasing order by size? Can you store this list in a file?

5. Create a pipeline that will sort together the contents of two files *a* and *b* and leave the sorted output in file *c*. How can this pipeline be modified to include a few lines typed in at the terminal?

6. You have written a program that takes input from the terminal (standard input) and writes it to the standard output. How could you run this program if you wanted input to come from a file named "in" and output to be stored at the end of a file named "out"?

7. Peter wanted to join the contents of files a and b together, so he typed:

   `cat a b >> a`

   What really happened here? How could you join these files together?

8. Peter then wanted to print out a numbered listing of file a. He typed:

   `cat -n a > lpr`

   but no printout appeared. Why? What happened here?

9. Referring to the table of *csh* history examples, experiment with and explain the meaning of each example.

10. If you mistyped your last command (and typed ka instead of ls), how could you reissue the correct command?

11. Define an alias nprint so that the command **nprint** *file* will output *file* (using **print**) with its lines numbered. Note that the header still should contain the file name.

12. What command could you type to edit all files of the form *.c that had the string getc anywhere in their text?

13. Consider the two *csh* initialization files: .cshrc and .login. Which initialization commands should be kept in .login and which in .cshrc? Why?

14. It would be nice if the current working directory were part of the *csh* prompt. Define an alias **cd** to make this happen.

Writing Shell Scripts

As you now know, the shell functions as an interactive command interpreter. But it does more; it also defines a simple programming language. A program written in this language is known as a *shell procedure* or *shell script*, which, in its simplest form, is just a sequence of commands in a file. The file, when executed, performs the tasks as if each command in the script had been entered and executed individually, but without all the typing. Shell scripts can save you a lot of time if you find yourself repeating a sequence of commands over and over. The shell language also includes variables, control structures such as if-then-else, looping, and means for input and output.

As with other UNIX commands, a shell script can be invoked through your interactive shell and can receive arguments supplied on the command line. Sometimes, scripts written by individual users also can be of general use: Such scripts can be installed in a system directory accessible to all users, frequently /usr/local/bin, which stores commands added by users at a UNIX installation.

This chapter covers shell script writing and techniques for effective shell-level programming. Both the *csh* and *sh* languages are presented with many program examples.

6.1 Invoking Shell Scripts

As mentioned, a shell script is a program written in the shell language. The program consists of string-valued variables, control-flow constructs, commands, and comments. The shell script is kept in a text file whose file name is said to be the name of the script.

There are two ways to invoke a shell script: by *direct interpretation* and by *indirect interpretation*. In direct interpretation, the command:

csh *file* [*arg* ...]

or

sh *file* [*arg* ...]

invokes the program *csh* or *sh*, respectively, to interpret the script contained in *file*, passing the script any *argument* specified.

In indirect interpretation, the script file containing the script is first made *readable* and *executable* with the **chmod** command (to turn on the appropriate protection bits). Then the script can be invoked in the same way as any other command: by giving the script name on the command line followed by any arguments.

In either direct or indirect interpretation of a shell script, *two shells* are involved: (1) the interactive shell (usually the login shell) that interacts with the user and processes the user's commands, and (2) the invoked shell that actually interprets the script. The invoked shell is a process spawned by the interactive shell. Since the spawned process is also a shell, it is referred to as a *subshell*. The effect of this can be illustrated by the following experiment.

First create a file named try that contains the simple script:

```
cd /usr/lib
pwd
```

To run this script, type:

```
csh try
```

The script called try displays the string /usr/lib, which is the output of the **pwd** contained in the script. However, once it is finished, if you type **pwd** in your interactive shell, your old working directory will appear. Obviously, the **cd** command executed in the script has not affected the current working directory of your interactive shell. This is because **cd** is executed by a subshell. Details of the relationship between the invoking shell and the invoked shell are discussed in the section entitled "Executable Text File Formats" and in Section 6.11.

A Simple Example

Let us now consider a simple *csh* script. The purpose of this script is to consult a database of telephone numbers that we will keep in a file named phone-numbers in your home directory. Each entry in this file will be one line with the name of a person, a phone number, and some other information.

The script named tel is:

```
# this csh script consults an on-line telephone database
grep -i $1 ~/phonenumbers
```

The first line, which begins with the character #, is a *comment*. In *csh* or *sh* scripts, the part of any line from the first # to the end of line is ignored by the shell. The symbol $1 is called a *positional parameter*. The value of the positional parameter $*n* is the *n*th command line argument. Thus, if the first argument is smith, then $1 has that value, and the script is equivalent to:

```
grep -i smith ~/phonenumbers
```

Recall that ~ is your home directory. Now you should issue the command:

```
chmod +rx tel
```

to make tel readable and executable. The command:

```
tel smith
```

runs the **tel** script (in the current directory). The preceding command assumes that the special period symbol (.) is included in your command search path. Otherwise, you need to use:

```
./tel smith
```

If the **tel** script is put in a directory whose name is on the command search path, then:

```
rehash
```

installs the newly created executable file tel in the *csh* command search table. Now you may use just:

```
tel smith
```

no matter what your current directory is, without having to specify the **tel** command with a pathname.

Usually, you would create a directory *bin* or *cmd* in your home directory to hold all scripts and other executable commands. By including the line:

```
set path = ($home/cmd $path)
```

in your .login file, you can invoke executable files in the directory $home/cmd in the same way as other system commands.

6.2 Shell Script Basics

In this section, some important basics are discussed that apply equally well to *csh* and *sh*. (A thorough discussion of details specific to *csh* programming begins in Section 6.3.) A shell script consists of a sequence of built-in and nonbuilt-in commands separated by NEWLINE or semicolon (;) characters. Comments are introduced by #, as previously mentioned. Script commands are executed in sequence. If the execution of a script command results in an error, script execution will be aborted if the offending command is a built-in shell command. Otherwise, for a nonbuilt-in command, the default action is to skip the offending command and continue with the next command in the script.

Executable Text File Formats

When the shell initiates execution of a nonbuilt-in command, it reads the first few characters of the executable file containing the command to determine what type of executable file it is. If the file begins with a *magic number*, a code nearly impossible to create in a text file, then it is a binary file (the default output file for UNIX compilers, a.out, is binary). Otherwise, the file is assumed to be an *executable text file*, which can be a *csh* script, a *sh* script, or some other program. To distinguish between the types of executable text files, the following rules are used:

1. If the first character of the file is not #, then it is a *sh* script.

2. If the first character of the file is a # and the second character is not a !, then the file is a *csh* script.

3. If the first two characters of the file are #! followed immediately by the full pathname of an executable file, then the executable file named is the one to be used to interpret this file.

Your interactive shell spawns an appropriate subshell to interpret a *csh* or *sh* script. The subshell inherits the *environment* of the interactive shell. To illustrate what happens with a #! executable text file, let us look at an example.

Suppose the file:

```
#! /bin/cat
now is the time
for all good men
to come to the aid of their country.
```

is made executable under the name tryme. Then, the command:

```
tryme > tryme.output
```

results in the execution of the following command line:

```
/bin/cat tryme > tryme.output
```

Note: The first line of the script, with the #! deleted, is put *in front* of the command line that invoked the script. The resulting command line is then executed.

Thus, if a *csh* script begins with:

```
#! /bin/csh −f
```

instead of a single #, it is loaded more quickly because the −f option prevents the loading of the .cshrc file. Make sure the settings in your .cshrc will not be needed in the script when you use this technique.

Positional Parameters

In scripts, the variables $0, $1, $2, and so on are known as *positional parameters*. The variable $0 refers to the name of the command. Thus, $0 has the value tel in the telephone directory example (Section 6.1). The variables $1, $2, and so on refer to the command line arguments. For example, if the executable file myecho contains the single line:

```
echo $1 $3
```

then the command:

```
myecho how are you doing
```

echos back:

```
how you
```

Other Preliminaries

In describing the shell languages, the term *commandlist* means a sequence of zero or more commands separated by NEWLINE or semicolon (;) characters. The term *wordlist* refers to zero or more blank separated words.

The presentations in this chapter are oriented toward script writing. However, most constructs discussed here can be used interactively as well. Some topics (for example, command grouping) are as relevant to interactive use as to script writing.

6.3 *csh* Scripts

In this section, we explore the *csh* language in detail and give examples of useful scripts. Try running these scripts and keep on-line those you find useful.

csh Positional Parameters

When a *csh* script is invoked, the special variable argv is set to the list of arguments given on the command line. Thus, as alternatives to the special variables $1, $2, and so on, *csh* scripts can use $argv[1], $argv[2], and so on to access command line arguments. The value of the variable $argv[*] is a wordlist of all the arguments given. The value of the variable $#argv is the number of arguments given. The name argv reflects the C-like syntax used by *csh*. The value of $0 is the command name; $argv[0] is undefined.

The foreach Command

The **foreach** command is used to execute a commandlist repeatedly. The *control variable* takes on a new value each time through the loop. The general form is:

```
foreach var (wordlist)
    commandlist
end
```

The parentheses are needed even if *wordlist* is empty. The keyword **foreach**, the variable *var*, and the parenthesized *wordlist* must appear together on one line by themselves. Similarly, the keyword **end** must appear alone on a separate line. The *commandlist* is executed once for each word in *wordlist* as, each time through, the control variable *var* takes the word for its value. As an example, let us rewrite the **tel** script given in Section 6.1 as:

```
# consult my telephone database for args given
foreach x ($argv[*])
grep -i $x $home/phonenumbers
end
```

The built-in variable $argv[*]$ is the list of all command line arguments. So programmed, **tel** can be used on one or more names, as in:

tel smith doe wang

The **foreach** command can be used to go through each file in a directory. Try the following script:

```
# example to go through all files in the current directory
foreach file (*)
echo $file
end
```

and you'll see the file names in the current directory displayed. Since the file name expansion does not match any file name that begins with a ., those file names will not be echoed. To get *all* files use:

```
foreach file (.* *)
echo $file
end
```

How would you get a list of all files except . and ..?

The if Command

This construct allows for logical branching. There are two forms of the **if** command:

if (*expr*) *simple-command*

and

if (*expr*) **then**
commandlist₁
[**else**
commandlist₂]
endif

In the first form, if the given logical *expr* is true, then the *simple command* is executed. The simple command may not be a pipeline or a commandlist, parenthesized or otherwise. In the second form, if the given logical *expr* is true, then *commandlist₁* is executed. When the optional else portion is given, *commandlist₂* is executed if *expr* is not true. The second form allows for nested **if** statements. One simple usage of **if** is to check for the correct number of arguments at the beginning of a script:

```
# check and set parameters
if ($#argv > 2 || $#argv < 1) then
  echo usage: $0 \[ from-file \] to-file
```

```
else
  if ($#argv == 2) then
      set from = $argv[1]
      set to = $argv[2]
  else
      set to = $argv[1]
  endif
endif
```

Note that the relational and logical expressions here are similar to those in C. See the following section called "Expressions" for more details.

Within the **if** statement, the **else if** construct can be used. The general form is:

```
if (expr₁) then
      commandlist₁
else if (expr₂) then
      commandlist₂
[else
      commandlist₃]
endif
```

If *expr₁* is true, *commandlist₁* is executed. If *expr₁* is not true, and if *expr₂* is true, then *commandlist₂* is executed. There can be any number of **else if** constructs. The previous example can be rewritten with the **else if** construct as:

```
# check and set parameters
if ($#argv > 2 || $#argv < 1) then
    echo usage: $0 '[from-file] to-file'
else if ($#argv == 2) then
    set from = $argv[1]
    set to = $argv[2]
else
    set to = $argv[1]
endif
```

The preceding example is only part of a script. Now let us look at a complete script using **foreach** and **if**. The script is named **findcmd** (Figure 6.1), and it locates a command on the command search path ($path) and displays its full pathname. The expression –e file is true if the file exists. The command:

exit(*arg*)

terminates the script's execution and returns a small integer *arg* to a calling program. This integer is known as the *exit status*, which the calling program

Figure 6.1 ▪ The findcmd Script

```
## this procedure finds where a given command is on the search path
## the pathname for the command
## is displayed as soon as it is found
## otherwise a message to the contrary is displayed

set cmd = $1
foreach dir ($path)
   if (-e $dir/$cmd) then
      echo FOUND: $dir/$cmd
      exit(0)
   endif
end
echo $cmd not on $path
```

can check to see whether the command terminated normally or abnormally. Samples uses of the **findcmd** script are as follows:

```
findcmd talk
findcmd cc
findcmd f77
```

The shift Command

The built-in command:

```
shift
```

shifts to the left components of the multiword variable argv, discarding argv[1]. The command:

```
shift var
```

shifts any variable *var*. If **shift** is applied to a variable whose value consists of one word, the value of the variable becomes the null string. If **shift** is applied to a variable whose value is null, an error results.

The switch Command

Although the if-then-else command provides a two-way logical branch construct, the **switch** command provides a multiple branch similar to that in C.

The general form of **switch** is:

```
switch (str)
    case pattern₁:
            commandlist₁
        breaksw
    case pattern₂:
            commandlist₂
        breaksw

    ...
    default:
            commandlist
endsw
```

The given string *str* is successively matched against the case *patterns*. Control flow is switched to where the first match occurs. As in file name expansion, a case label may be a literal string, contain variable substitution, or contain pattern-matching characters *, ?, and [...].

Thus, for instance, the **switch** string ab.c matches the case label *.c. The **breaksw** command causes execution to break out of the **switch** statement and continue after the **endsw**. The **default** is a catch-all case label that matches anything. The **case**, **breaksw**, and **default** statements are all optional. If a **breaksw** is left out, then control *falls through* to the next case. For example, if the first **breaksw** is left out and *str* matches *pattern₁*, then control will reach *commandlist₂* after *commandlist₁*, despite the fact that *str* does not match *pattern₂*.

As an example, a script for appending either the standard input or a file to the end of another file is shown in Figure 6.2. Let the name of this script

---

Figure 6.2 ▪ The append Script

```
# append $1 to $2 or standard input to $1
switch ($#argv)
    case 1:
        cat >> $argv[1]
        breaksw
    case 2:
        cat >> $argv[2] < $argv[1]
        breaksw
    default:
        echo 'usage: append [from] to'
endsw
```

be **append**. The command:

```
append file1 file2
```

appends *file1* to the end of *file2*. The command:

```
append file
first line
second line
third line
^D
```

appends the three lines to the end of *file*.

The while Command

In addition to the **foreach** command, the **while** command controls iteration with an arbitrary condition such as a test on a variable representing an integer index.

The general form of the **while** command is:

```
while  (expr)
     commandlist
end
```

The *expr* is evaluated, and if it is not zero, then *commandlist* is executed, and **expr** is retested. The iteration continues until *expr* tests zero. A simple example is the following script:

```
# while example
set i = $#argv
while ($i)
     echo $argv[$i]
     @ i--
end
```

which displays the command line arguments in reverse order. We may, if we wish, implement the **tel** script with **while**, as follows:

```
# tel script using while
while ($#argv > 0)
          grep -i $argv[1] $home/phonenumbers
          shift
end
```

Numerical Computations

Since shell variables are string-valued, it takes some effort to specify an arithmetic computation using numbers. The @ command is provided by *csh* especially for the purpose of enabling numerical computation.

The general forms of the @ command are:

@ *var* = *expr*

@ *var*[*n*] = *expr*

where *expr* is an arithmetic expression. The *expr* is evaluated, and the numerical value is assigned to *var* (or the *n*th component of *var*) in the form of a string. In the second form, the *var* and its *n*th component already must exist. Therefore, the @ command is essentially a form of the **set** command that allows arithmetic expressions on the right-hand side of =.

Based on C syntax, the following arithmetic expressions are correct *csh* usages for assigning numeric values:

```
@ x = $#argv/2
@ argv[$j] = $j + 4
@ x += 3
@ i++
```

As a convenience, if the @ command is given with no argument, it functions the same as the **set** command when given no argument—that is, it displays the values of all variables.

The goto Command

The **goto** command provides a way to branch unconditionally to a target line in the script identified by a *label*. The general form is:

goto *word*

where *word* is a label somewhere in the script in the form

word:

alone on a line, possibly preceded by blank characters. The effect of **goto** is to transfer control to the line after the label.

The break and continue Commands

The **break** command is used inside the iteration control structures **foreach** and **while**. When **break** is executed, control shifts to the first line after the end of the nearest enclosing **foreach** or **while**. This command provides a means to "break out" of an iteration loop before normal termination.

The **continue** command is used in the same manner as the **break** command, except it transfers control to the beginning of the next iteration instead of breaking out of the loop entirely. The example script **clean** (see Section 6.7) involves some typical applications of **break** and **continue**.

Expressions

Logical as well as arithmetic expressions are used in the *csh* language. As described, the **if** command takes a logical expression, and the **while** and **@** commands take arithmetic expressions. Also, the **exit** command can be given an arithmetic expression yielding an integer *status* for the caller. In this section, rules for forming expressions are discussed.

In general, logical and arithmetic expressions are similar to those of C. Logical operators are:

||	or
&&	and
!	not

and logical constants are:

0	false
1	true

Relational operators resulting in Boolean (true–false) values are:

= =	equal
!=	not equal
= ~	string match
!~	string nonmatch
< =	numerical less than or equal to
> =	numerical greater than or equal to
>	numerical greater than
<	numerical less than

The right-hand sides of the expressions with string-matching operators = ~ and !~ may contain pattern characters such as *, ?, and [...]. The matching is in the same sense as that used in file name expansion.

Binary arithmetic operators are:

*	times
/	quotient
%	remainder

+	plus
−	minus

And bitwise logical operations are:

&	bitwise and
|	bitwise or
^	bitwise exclusive-or (XOR)
<<	left-shift
>>	right-shift
~	one's complement

Thus, the following are valid, logical expressions:

`($#argv > 2 || $#argv == 0)`	(zero or more than two arguments)
`($1 =~ -*)`	(first argument begins with −)
`($name !~ *.c)`	(variable name does not end in .c)
`($char != \# && $char != @)`	($char is neither # nor @)

Note that all substitutions except file name expansion are performed inside an expression.

Strings beginning with 0 (zero) are treated as octal numbers. A null string (or a missing argument) is considered zero in an arithmetic context and is considered false in a logical context. For example:

`@ i=`	(sets i to zero)
if ($string) **then**	(if $string is not null then)

The numeric value of an expression is a string representing a decimal integer. The components of an expression always should be separated by spaces, although spaces are optional around symbols that are recognized by the parser: &, |, <, >, (, and). Parentheses are used as they are mathematically to group expressions.

Also available in expressions are file queries of the form *−x file*, where *x* is a single character. Available *csh* file queries are listed in Figure 6.3. The given *file* is command and file name expanded and then tested. If the file does not exist or if it is inaccesssible, all queries return 0 for false. For example, the following code fragment is valid:

```
if (-e $file && -f $file && -w $file) then
    cat $1 >> $file
...
endif
```

As additional expressions, there are command executions enclosed in

Figure 6.3 ▪ csh File Queries

Expression	True if *File*
−r *file*	is readable by the user
−w *file*	is writable by the user
−x *file*	is executable by the user
−e *file*	exists
−o *file*	is owned by the user
−z *file*	has a size of 0 (zero)
−f *file*	is an ordinary file
−d *file*	is a directory

braces ({ and }), as in:

if ({*command₁*} && {*command₂*} ‖ {*command₃*}) **then**

  ...

endif

It is best to include white space before and after the { and }. If a command *cmd* exits with *status* 0, then:

{*cmd*}

yields 1, the Boolean value of true. Otherwise, it returns 0 for false. A subshell is used to execute commands inside { and }. If more detailed status information is required, the command should be executed outside an expression, and the special variable status should be examined.

6.4 Using Variables

There are four kinds of variables:

1. Positional parameters such as $1 and $argv[2]

2. Special variables such as $cwd and $nonomatch

3. Environment variables such as $HOME and $EXINIT

4. Ordinary variables that are of your own choosing

Variables can have names that consist of up to 20 letters and digits that start with a letter. In variable names, the underscore character is considered a letter.

Variable Assignment and Value

Variables are set with the **set** or the **@** command:

```
set dir = $cwd
set j = 1
@ k = $j + 1
set list = (a b c d)
set x = 'u v w'
```

The value of a variable is always a string. The value of $j, for instance, is the string 1, and $k is the string 2. The variable $list is multivalued, with the first component a, the second component b, and so on. The variable $x is not multivalued; its value is the string 'u v w'. An environment variable is assigned with the command **setenv** (instead of **set**).

As mentioned previously, variables are used in expressions and commands and are keyed by the character $. Except in a few cases, it is an error to reference a variable not already set. Sometimes it is necessary to use braces ({ and }) as delimiters when referencing a variable to prevent its being confused with any other variables with the same prefix. For example:

```
set    d = x
set    dir = $home/cmd
echo ${d}ir is not $dir
```

To select a portion of a multivalued variable, use the notation:

$*var*[*selector*]

For instance, in the example above:

```
$list[1]      (is a)
$list[3]      (is c)
```

The selector specifies a word or a *range* of words. The selector is subject to variable substitution and may consist of a single number or two numbers separated by a –. Numbering of the possible indices for a variable starts at 1. If the first number of a range is omitted, it defaults to 1. If the last number of a range is omitted, it defaults to the number of components, for example:

```
$argv[1-3]
$argv[*]      (same as $argv[1-])
```

The selector * selects all words.

It is not an error for a range to be empty if the second index is omitted or if it is smaller than the first. Thus if only three positional parameters are supplied, the variable reference:

`$argv[4-]`   or   `$argv[2-1]`

will not cause an error in a script. The value returned is the empty string. The notation:

`$#var`   or   `${#var}`

gives the number of words in a multivalued variable. Thus, $#list is 4 and $#argv is the number of command line arguments.

Variable Modifiers

To make variable usage even more flexible, the value obtained from a variable (except an environment variable) can be modified before it is introduced into a command or expression. Variable *modifiers* are given after a colon (:) at the end of a variable; they modify the value returned. If braces ({ and }) are used, then the modifiers must appear between the braces. Most UNIX implementations allow only one colon modifier per variable substitution. For the variable substitutions described thus far, the modifiers :h, :t, :r, :q, :x, :gh, :gt, and :gr may be used. The meanings of the modifiers are as follows:

h   removes a trailing pathname component, leaving the head

t   removes all leading pathname components, leaving the tail

r   removes an extension .xxx component, leaving the root name

e   removes the root name, leaving the extension

g   (prefix) gh, gr, gt, and ge *globally* modify all words of a multiword variable

q   quotes the substituted words, preventing further substitutions

x   like q, but breaks into words at blanks, tabs, and NEWLINEs

For a multivalued variable such as $path, only the first word is changed by :h, :r, :t, or :e. Figure 6.4 illustrates modifier usage on simple and multivalued variables. All the modifiers listed in the figure can modify a history event in the same way. You also can refer to the *csh* manual for more details.

Special Substitutions

In addition to the regular methods of referencing variables, there are also some special variable substitutions. These substitutions may not be modified by colon modifiers. These special substitutions are described here.

Figure 6.4 ▪ Variable Modifiers

$list is (/a/b/c.f u/v/w.c)	
Modifier	Value
$list[1]:h	/a/b
$list:h	(/a/b u/v/w.c)
$list:t	(c.f u/v/w.c)
$list:r	(/a/b/c u/v/w.c)
$list:e	(f u/v/w.c)
$list:gh	(/a/b u/v)
$list:gr	(/a/b/c u/v/w)
$list:gt	(c.f w.c)
$list:ge	(f c)

A notation is provided to test whether a variable is set or not. The variable:

$?*var*   or ${?*var*}

substitutes the string 1 if *var* is set, 0 if it is not. This is most useful in logical expressions where 0 represents false and 1 represents true. For example:

```
if ( ! $?term) then
    set term = 'tset - -m dialup:hp2621'
endif
```

sets the variable term if it is not set already. The variable:

$?0

has value 1 if the $0 (the file name of the script) is set, it has the value 0 if it is not. However, it is an error to use $?1, $?2, and so on; the ? does not work with subscripted variables such as $path[2]. Thus $?path[2] will not work.

The special variable

$$

substitutes the process number of the shell executing the script. This number is unique to each process and can be used for generating unique file names.

6.5 Input and Output

The input/output mechanism used in shell scripts is quite simple and does not provide the more sophisticated control of a regular programming language. As described earlier, the command:

echo *words*

is used to display zero or more words on the standard output. Of course, arguments are subject to the usual shell substitutions. A NEWLINE is displayed after the last word. If no argument is given, nothing is displayed. A NEWLINE is displayed if **echo** is followed by a null string (two consecutive single quotation marks). The −n option prevents the NEWLINE from being displayed, as in:

echo −n type yes or no :

To read input typed in by the user, the metavariable $< is used. For example:

```
switch ($<)
    case yes:
        . . .
        breaksw
    case no:
        . . .
        breaksw
endsw
```

The metavariable $< reads a line from the standard input, and this line is returned as the value of the metavariable $< without further interpretation. Thus, if the characters * and $ are used in the input line, they will not be variable- or file-name-substituted. In some applications, the input from the user is a shell command line, which can be executed in the script using the **eval** command. For example:

```
echo −n enter command:
set cmd = $<
eval $cmd
```

As with any command, the argument $cmd is interpreted by the shell performing all substitutions. The **eval** command then treats the resulting words as a command line, which is evaluated and executed in the regular manner.

6.6 The Here Document

It is possible to include in a script input that is normally entered interactively. In shell script terminology, this type of input is known as a *here document*. For example, you may create a file named happynewyear that contains the following:

```
mail -s 'Happy New Year' friends <<ABC
The time is `date`.
May I wish you a very happy and prosperous NEW YEAR.

                    signed...
ABC
```

The purpose of this file is to invoke the **mail** command and send a message to each name on the **mail** alias list called friends, which is defined in your .mailrc file (as discussed in Section 3.5). The here document consists of all text between the first ABC and the second ABC. Having set up this file, you then can issue:

```
at 0010a Jan 1 happynewyear
```

to schedule the greeting to be sent out at 12:10 A.M. on New Year's Day.

Consider another example, the **tel** script discussed earlier. Instead of using a separate file containing the telephone numbers, the data can be included in the **tel** script as a here document:

```
foreach var ($argv[*])
    grep -i $var <<EOF
        smith 7089
        black 9976
        ...
        young 0231
EOF
```

The here document is actually a form of input redirection. After the << is an arbitrary word (in this case, EOF) followed by a NEWLINE that delimits the beginning and end of the here document. The general form of a here document is:

```
command << word
zero or more
lines of input
included here
word
```

Figure 6.5 ▪ The timestamp Script

```
# script name: timestamp
# usage: timestamp file
# this script stamps date and time on a document

cat >> $1 << here
****************************
RECEIVED by $user on `hostname`
`date`
here
```

The delimiter *word* is not variable-, file-name-, or command-substituted. The last line must contain only the same *word* and no other characters. The intervening lines are variable- and command-substituted, but blanks, tabs, and NEWLINEs are preserved. The resulting text, up to but not including the line with the end delimiter, is supplied as standard input to the command.

An example is the **timestamp** script (Figure 6.5). The here document contains a variable substitution and two command substitutions. The **hostname** command displays the name of the host computer. The **date** command displays the date and time.

Substitutions can be suppressed within a here document by quoting all or part of the delimiter word with \, ", `, or '. Thus, some quoted delimiter words are as follows:

```
\EOF
'here'
a"b"
`a`b
```

6.7 Example *csh* Scripts

Let us now consider some more substantial *csh* scripts.

Example: clean

Modern operating systems such as UNIX make it easy to create, copy, and otherwise manipulate on-line files. However, most users are hesitant about removing files, and the clutter of obsolete files becomes unworkable. One reason is the sheer tedium of looking through files and discarding those that are no longer needed. Thus, although disk storage is decreasing in cost, new supplies of additional disk space never seem to match the demand. The **clean** script provides some help.

The command:

clean *directory*

displays the name of each file in the given *directory* and allows the user to decide interactively whether or not to keep or delete specific files. The **clean** script is programmed as follows:

```
## script name: clean
## helps to remove unwanted files from a directory

if ($#argv != 1) then
        echo usage: $0 directory; exit(1)
else if (! -d $1) then
        echo $1 not a directory; exit(1)
endif

set dir = $1
chdir $dir
set files = *

# process files
foreach file ($files)
     if (! -f $file) continue
     echo ' ' ## gives a blank line
     echo "file = $file" ## identifies file being processed
     echo ' '
     head $file
     while (1)
          echo -n rm $file '?? (y, n, !, or q)' :
          set c = $<
          switch ($c)
             case y:
                if ( {rm $file} ) then
                  echo '*****' $file rm-ed
                else
                  echo cannot rm $file
                endif
                  break ## break out of while
```

```
               case n:
                 echo '*****' $file not rm-ed
                 break
               case q:
                 exit(0)
                case \!:
                   echo command:
                   eval $<
                   ## in $< the variable $file can be used
             endsw
        end ## of while
end ## of foreach
```

After checking for correct input, the script changes the current working directory to the given directory and sets the variable $files to *, which then expands to a list of all file names in the given directory. The **foreach** command is used to go through each file. On any given iteration, if $file is not an ordinary file, then it is skipped (via **continue**). For a regular file, the beginning of the file is displayed using the **head** command after identifying the file name with **echo**. The user is prompted with:

```
rm file ?? (y, n, !, or q) :
```

indicating four possible (single-character) responses (terminated by RETURN). User input is read using the $< variable substitution. Once the user has responded to the prompt, a **switch** statement is used to carry out actions depending on the user's response.

The cases for n, y, and q are clear. If the user wishes to execute a *csh* command before deciding on the disposal of the file, the user can type in the character !. In this case, the program reads a command as a string from the user and executes it as a shell command using **eval**. Note that the variable $file can be used in this input and that there is no restriction as to what command can be used. Commands the user is likely to use to decide whether or not to discard the file are as follows:

```
ls -l $file
tail $file
more $file
vi $file
```

The user could, instead, decide to use **mv** to move the file to another directory.

After the ! case is handled, control falls through and reaches the end of the **switch** statement, it then moves to the control portion of the **while** statement. If the user mistypes some character other than one of the four expected by the script, the **while** loop is restarted. Since 1 is always true, the **while** statement will be repeated unconditionally. Also, note that the **clean** script provides feedback, telling the user each action it has taken.

Example: ccp

This script creates a command that copies files from a *source* directory to a *destination* directory using the following conditions on any ordinary *file* to be copied:

1. If *file* is not in *destination*, copy.

2. If *file* is in *destination* but not as recent as that in *source*, copy.

3. Otherwise, do not copy.

The **ccp** script is as follows:

```
## script name: ccp
## conditional copy
##
## usage:
##          ccp from to [file ...]
## where:
##          'from' is the source directory
##          'to' is the destination directory
##          [file ...] is a list of optional file names to be copied, if not
##              given, all files in 'from' directory will be processed

if ($#argv < 2) then
        echo usage: $0 from-dir to-dir '[file ...]'; exit(1)

else  if ! -d $1 || ! -d $2) then
        echo usage: $0 from-dir to-dir '[file ..]'
        exit(1)
endif

set dir = $cwd; chdir $2; set to = $cwd
chdir $dir; chdir $1; ## now in from-dir

if ($#argv == 2) then
    set files = *
else
    set files = $argv[3-]
endif

foreach file ($files)
if (-d $file) continue
        # if file doesn't exist then cp
        if (! -e $to/$file) then
        echo $to/$file is a new file
```

```
        cp $file $to
        continue
    endif
    # if file in $from is more recent then cp

        find $file –newer $to/$file –exec cp $file $to \;
end
```

It's important to note the care used in handling the user-supplied directory names. Such seemingly redundant **chdir** and **pwd** operations are, in fact, quite necessary, because the user may give either relative or absolute names for these directories. The **find** command is described in Section 4.12.

Example: total

It is possible to write *recursive* shell scripts. In fact, recursion usually provides the easiest way to perform the same task over an entire directory hierarchy. Suppose we need to compute the total number of bytes used by all files and directories in a certain file hierarchy. The **du** command only provides a rough accounting in kilobytes. The script **total** recursively descends through a directory hierarchy and sums the bytes used by extracting information provided by the **ls** command. The **total** script is given as follows:

```
## script name: total
## compute total disk space used in bytes for a directory hierarchy
## a recursive script

set nonomatch ## empty directories will not cause problems
if ($#argv != 1) then
    echo usage : $0 directory
    exit(1)
endif

set count = 0
foreach file ($1/*)
    if (-f $file ) then
        set x = `/bin/ls –l $file`
    else if ( –d $file ) then
        set x = `/bin/ls –ld $file`
        set y = `$0 $file`    ## recursive call
        @ count = $count + $y
    else
        echo $file not included in the total >>! /tmp/total
        continue
```

```
      endif
      @ count = $count + $x[4]
end
echo $count
```

Note that to invoke the **ls** command, the form **/bin/ls** is used. It's a good idea to use full pathnames for commands in a script, because it eliminates the need for a command search, and thus speeds up the script. Using full pathnames also avoids the possibility of a file having the same name somewhere in the hierarchy being invoked mistakenly if the command search path has the directory . in it.

Example: mapc

The **mapc** script takes a user command entered interactively and *applies* it to files in a directory (or a hierarchy if the flag −r is given). The **mapc** script is:

```
## script name : mapc
## asks the user to input a command that is applied to each file
## contained in the given directory (or hierarchy)
## for example
##    mapc .
##    input command : ls −l $file
## will execute the given command with the variable $file
## going through each regular file in the current directory
## the −r option is used to indicate application to
## all files in the hierarchy

set nonomatch ## empty directories will not cause problems

if ($#argv < 1 || $#argv > 2) then
     echo usage: $0 '[−r]' directory; exit(1)
else if ($#argv == 1) then
     set r = 0; set dirs = ($1)
else if (f$1 == f−r) then
     set r = 1; set dirs = ($2)
else
     echo usage: $0 '[−r]' directory; exit(1)
endif
if (! −d $dirs[1]) then
     echo $dirs[1] not a directory; exit(1)
endif
## obtain interactively entered command line
echo −n input command :
set cmd = $<
```

```
## main loop
while ( $#dirs > 0 )
      set dir = $dirs[1]; shift dirs; chdir $dir
      foreach file ( $cwd/* )
       if ( -f $file ) then
           eval $cmd  ## execute user command
       else if ( $r == 1 && -d $file ) then
           set dirs = ( $file $dirs )
       endif
      end ## of foreach
end ## of while
echo done
```

The **mapc** script is the most involved script discussed so far. The conditional expression for checking the −r flag is interesting: The prefix f is an arbitrary character used to avoid the −r used for checking file readability. The ways **chdir** and $cwd are used are also important. Whenever **chdir** is used, you must consider whether or not a relative file name can cause difficulties.

The following are two examples of the **mapc** command:

mapc *dir*
    `input command:` **mv** `$file $file.old`

mapc −r *dir*
    `input command:` **ls** −l `$file ; eval $<`

6.8 Debugging Shell Scripts

Unlike a regular programming language, the *csh* language provides little in the way of debugging tools, but there are several mechanisms that can help in shell script writing. First, there are the special shell toggle variables, verbose and echo, that can be set and unset. Including the command:

set verbose

in your shell script causes the shell to display each command after it has been transformed by the history substitution. This command can be used to check the correctness of history substitutions, as well as to track the execution sequence of a script. The command:

set echo

causes the words of each command to be displayed just before execution. For nonbuilt-in commands, all substitutions occur before being displayed. For built-in commands, display takes place before command and file name substitutions. With echo **set**, the user gets a better idea of what commands actually are being executed. Echo and verbose settings can be deleted or commented out once a script has been debugged.

Another debugging mechanism is provided by the *csh* command line options. To invoke these options for running your script, you must use direct interpretation in the general form:

csh [*–options*] *script* [*arg* ...]

Options are indicated by one or more consecutive characters. Here is a list of options useful for debugging shell scripts:

e   *csh* exits if any command terminates abnormally or yields a non-zero exit status

n   *csh* parses each command without execution, which aids in syntax checking

v   *csh* sets the verbose toggle before executing the script

x   *csh* sets the echo toggle before executing the script

V   *csh* sets the verbose toggle before reading the .cshrc file

X   *csh* sets the echo toggle before reading the .cshrc file

When you run a new script for the first time, use:

csh –n**v** *script arg* ...

The –n option detects and reports incorrect syntax. When –n is combined with command echoing (the –v option), you get a good indication of any syntax problems. Make whatever corrections are necessary until your script runs without any –nv detected errors, then run your script using:

csh –**x** *script arg* ...

which displays the exact form of each command just before it is executed. Again, correct any errors uncovered by this option.

Another technique for script debugging is to put the **echo** command in front of lines that, if executed, could damage or remove files before the script has been tested sufficiently. For example:

```
        ...
        if ( ... ) then
echo rm $file
echo "cat ... > $file"
        else
        ...
        endif
        ...
```

With **echo** shielding the actual file manipulation, the script can be tested. Once the script is debugged, the **echo** text can be removed. Note that some lines following the **echo** command must be enclosed in double quotation marks.

It is advisable to test a newly created script on scratch files and directories before applying it to real files. It is also a good idea to test the final script using a different userid if the script is to be released for general use.

6.9 Advanced Use of alias

The *csh* aliasing mechanism usually is used to redefine command names and to provide shorthand for certain command usages, but it also can work in conjunction with the history mechanism. Thus, the alias specifications may contain references to the history list. Defining an alias that uses the latest history event can provide a metasyntax for defining new commands at the shell level.

In Section 5.7, a pair of aliases, **cd** and **back**, was discussed. The **cd** and **back** commands are limited to dealing with just two directories, because they work by recording the previous working directory. *Csh*, however, has two built-in commands, **pushd** and **popd**, that use a stack to record many directories. These built-in commands are not easy to use, because you need to keep a mental image of where each directory is on the stack as it is pushed, popped, and rotated automatically.

Figure 6.6 illustrates some alias-defined commands that use a *directory list* to record directories and to change interactively to any directory on the list, using an index. Removal of a directory from the list is by specific request rather than as a side effect of changing directories. This discussion presents a good example of the alias facility being used with the *csh* built-in commands. The five aliases listed in the figure work as follows:

pd   records a directory on the directory list pdl

ccd   displays pdl first and prompts the user for an index. It

Figure 6.6 ▪ The ccd Aliases

```
set pdl =
alias pd ' chdir \!:1; set pdl = ($pdl $cwd); pwd'
alias ccd 'echo $pdl; echo -n index:; set pdi = $<; chdir $pdl[$pdi]; pwd'
alias cdn 'chdir $pdl[\!:1]; pwd'
alias ud 'echo $pdl; echo -n index:; set pdi = $<; @ pdii = $pdi + 1;' \
        '@ pdi = $pdi - 1; set pdl = ($pdl[-$pdi] $pdl[$pdii-]);' \
        'echo $pdl; unset pdi pdii '
alias pdreset set pdl =
```

	then changes directories to the target directory. If the index given is 0, the effect is **chdir** $home. If the index is out of range, no operation is performed.
cdn *n*	provides a way of directly changing to the *n*th directory without interactive delay
ud	removes a directory from pdl
pdreset	resets pdl to an empty list

The two features of this group of aliases are (1) they allow you to change working directories by interactive selection, and (2) they preserve the order of directories on the directory list. Try out these aliases. If you like them, they can be included in your .login file. Or if you prefer, you can make these aliases self-loading by replacing the initialization line with:

```
set pdl = ( $cwd )
```

and putting these alias definitions in a file named pdfile. Then, include the following line in the .login file:

```
alias pd 'chdir \!*; source pdfile; pwd'
```

One restriction imposed by the alias syntax is that an alias string cannot involve multiple lines. Consequently, an alias cannot involve a control flow structure such as an **if-then**. This situation can be remedied if you have a way to alias a shell script so that it is executed by the interactive shell rather than by a subshell. The built-in **source** command allows an interactive shell to read and execute commands contained in a file. However, simply using **source** is not enough, because arguments often have to be supplied to the script. The proper way to alias a shell script that can take command line arguments is as follows:

```
alias name 'set argv = (\!*); source script'
```

where *script* is a file containing the shell procedure activated by the named alias. Note that, in this case, argv[0] will not be set. See Problem 14 at the end of the chapter for an example.

6.10 Error and Interrupt Handling

An error may occur during the processing of a shell script at several different stages. A syntax or substitution error will result in the premature termination of execution. Execution of the script also is aborted if a built-in command fails to execute properly. An example of such an error is:

```
cd $x
```

where $x is not set, nonexistent, not a directory, or has the wrong access permissions. However, if a nonbuilt-in command results in a run-time error, the interpretation of the script continues with the next command. Error messages are produced and sent to the standard error output, which also is known as *standard diagnostic* output. The diagnostic output can be redirected together with the standard output as explained in Section 5.3.

In UNIX, when a program terminates (because of either completion or error) an *exit status* is set to a small integer value to provide an indication of the circumstances under which execution was terminated. By convention, the exit status is 0 if termination is normal and greater than 0 if termination is abnormal. A *csh* built-in command gives an exit status of 0 when successful and an exit status of 1 when unsuccessful. The special shell variable $status is set by *csh* after the execution of each command. The value of $status is 0 if the last command was successful and greater than zero (usually 1) if it failed.

To test whether a command has failed, the following construct often is used:

```
if ( ! { command } ) then
        code to execute in case command fails
     endif
```

where { *command* } returns 1 (true) if *command* terminates normally and 0 (false) if *command* terminates abnormally.

Interrupt Handling

An *interrupt* is an asynchronous *signal* sent to a running program by another process or through the keyboard by the user. The user can send an interrupt signal to a shell running a script by typing in the *interrupt character*, normally ^C or DELete. There are various system-defined signals that can be sent to an executing program using the **kill** command. Signals will be discussed in detail in Section 9.6. For now, it is sufficient to state that:

```
kill –2 pid
```

sends the interrupt signal 2 to the process *pid*, which causes it to terminate. The process *pid* can be given either as a jobid or as a process number. If this does not terminate the process, use:

```
kill –9 pid
```

which sends signal 9, unconditionally terminating *pid*.

The shell's default response is to terminate if it receives any interrupt signal, but this can be modified. The *csh* built-in command **onintr** (on interrupt) controls the action of the shell on interrupts. The three **onintr** forms used in scripts are shown in Figure 6.7.

Sometimes a shell script needs to create and use temporary files, which

Figure 6.7 ▪ *csh* Interrupt Handling: The onintr Commands

Command	Effect
`onintr` *label*	goto *label* on interrupt
`onintr –`	ignore all interrupts
`onintr`	restore default interrupt actions

Figure 6.8 ▫ Interrupt Handling in a *csh* Script

```
# interrupt handling in csh script
  ...
onintr int                # now create temporary file
touch /tmp/t$$
  ...
# and proceed normally
  ...
rm /tmp/t$$               # normal termination
exit(0)
int:                      # interrupt exit
rm /tmp/t$$; exit(1)
```

are deleted before the script terminates. However, if the script terminates due to an interrupt, the temporary files may be left lying around. The **onintr** facility also can be used to solve this problem (Figure 6.8).

6.11 Environment of a Command

The exact manner in which a command works depends on the *execution environment* within which it is supposed to do the job. For example, the text editor **vi** needs to know the capabilities of the terminal it is dealing with. So does the command **more**. For file access permission purposes, any program that accesses files needs to know the userid of the user who invoked it. In UNIX, shell environment parameters are kept in a set of *environment variables*, which can be assigned values by the user. These environment variables, together with other values (for example, userid and current working directory), constitute the *environment* of the shell. This environment is *inherited* by (passed to) every nonbuilt-in command that the shell initiates.

The environment variable TERM records the terminal type. Once the terminal type is known, the *termcap* database can be consulted for details on the capabilities of a specific terminal (more on this in Chapter 9). The command search path is another environmental parameter whose value is contained in the environment variable PATH. The *csh* built-in command **printenv** displays all environment variables and their values. A sample output of **printenv** is:

```
HOME=/user/smith
SHELL=/bin/csh
PATH=/usr/ucb:/bin:/usr/bin:/usr/local/bin:.
TERM=hp2622
USER=smith
EXINIT=se ai shell=/bin/csh terse nowarn sm
```

where HOME indicates the user's home directory; SHELL, the login shell; PATH, the command search path; TERM, the terminal type; USER, the user's userid; and EXINIT, initial option settings for **vi** and **ex**. The built-in command **setenv** is used to assign values to environment variables. The usage is:

setenv *NAME value*

For instance, to set the terminal type, you can use:

setenv TERM hp2622

As a rule, environment variables use uppercase letters; they are not to be confused with regular shell variables, which are assigned using the **set** command. However, the value of an environment variable is substituted using the same $-keyed mechanism. Users may define new environment variables. The built-in command **unsetenv** removes an environment variable.

csh Predefined Variables Versus Environment Variables

The following variables have special meanings to *csh*. They are set by the shell at time of initialization (before .cshrc is read): cwd, home, path, shell, status, term, and user. The value of $cwd is changed every time the user changes the working directory. The value of $status indicates the exit status of the last command. The value of $shell is the default login shell.

The *csh* variables user, term, path, and home have a special relationship with their uppercase environment variable counterparts. At initialization time, the shell copies the environment variables as follows: USER into the variable user, TERM into term, PATH into path, and HOME into home. If the user sets the value of any of these four *csh* variables, the new value will be copied to the corresponding environment variable automatically. Thus, in *csh*:

```
set term = hp2621
```

not only changes $term but also sets the environment variable TERM. (Note that this process occurs only for the four variables user, term, path, and home.) However, if the user uses **setenv** to change the values of USER, TERM, PATH, or HOME, no automatic copying is done in the other direction. Also, when the variable path is reset, an automatic **rehash** is performed.

Environment Inheritance

Let us describe the general interaction of a process with its environment. Basically, the environment of a process *inherits* (gets a copy of) the environment of its invoking program. The process *p2* inherits its environment *e2*, which is the same as the environment *e1* of its invoking program *p1*. At the onset of *p2*, a local variable is created in *e2* for every environment variable in *e1*. The local variable has the same name and is assigned the same value. New environment variables can be introduced or existing variables can be reset in *e2* by *p2*. In *csh*, the **setenv** command is used. In *sh*, the = and **export** commands are used. The environment *e1* is never affected by the actions of *p2*. Therefore, a command invoked by *p1* inherits *e1*, and a command invoked by *p2* inherits *e2* as its initial environment.

6.12 Summary of *csh* Built-In Commands

Most of the *csh* built-in commands have been discussed in this chapter and in Chapter 5. All *csh* built-in commands are listed in Figure 6.9 for your easy reference. If you wish to consult the UNIX on-line manual for these commands, you need to refer to the manual pages on *csh*—type in

```
man csh
```

to do so.

Figure 6.9 ■ *csh* Built-In Commands

Command	Function
alias, unalias	displays, sets, and unsets aliases
alloc	displays the core allocation
bg, fg, stop, suspend, jobs, notify, wait, kill	job control commands
cd, chdir	changes the working directory
echo *args*	outputs *args* to standard output
eval *arg*	processes *arg* as a shell command
exec *command*	overlays *command* on the current shell
exit	terminates the current shell
foreach, while, break, continue, end	iteration controls
glob *text*	file name expands *text*
goto *label*	transfers control to *label*
history	displays the history list
if, then, else, endif	conditionals
limit, unlimit	sets and unsets limits on resources
login, logout	logs in, logs out
nice	modifies the priority level of a process
nohup, onintr	interrupt trapping functions
dirs, popd, pushd	directory stack manipulations
rehash, unhash, hashstat	functions for the command hash table
repeat	issues a command several times
set, unset	sets and unsets variables
setenv, unsetenv, printenv	sets, unsets, and displays environment variables

Figure 6.9 ▪ (*continued*)

shift *var*	left-shifts a multiword variable
source *file*	causes the shell to read and execute commands in *file*
switch, breaksw, case, default:, endsw	flow controls
time	displays time used
umask	displays or sets file protection mask
@	same as **set,** but allows numeric expressions

6.13 The *sh* Shell

Sh (Bourne shell) is the original UNIX shell. It is smaller and simpler than *csh*. It is a standard user-command interpreter for System V, and it also is available on all Berkeley versions. In interactive use for issuing UNIX commands, it is similar to *csh*. Thus, *sh* is not presented here in as much detail as *csh*, but the major differences between *sh* and *csh* are described. *Sh* control flow constructs are summarized and contrasted with their corresponding *csh* constructs. Several examples of *sh* scripts also are given. The materials included here should be sufficient for most purposes. The user should refer to *The UNIX System* by S. R. Bourne for a more comprehensive description of *sh*.

6.14 Differences Between *sh* and *csh*

For the purpose of issuing commands interactively, there is little difference between the two shells, although many UNIX users prefer *csh* for its job suspension, history, and aliasing capabilities. Major differences between *sh* and *csh* are listed here.

Job Suspension

Sh does not provide a job suspension and resumption mechanism. Thus, in *sh*, ^Z does not stop a job running in the foreground. This means you cannot initiate another job until the current job has been completed.

History and Alias Substitution

Sh uses the same command execution cycle as does *csh*, except that it does not support history or alias substitution. Variables and command substitutions function the same as in *csh*.

File Name Expansion

Sh file name expansion works the same way as that in *csh*. The only difference is that when a pattern does not match any file, it always expands to itself in *sh*, while it can cause an error in *csh* unless the toggle variable nonmatch is set.

Redirection of Standard Error

The I/O redirection and pipe mechanisms work the same way in both *sh* and *csh*. *Sh* uses a slightly different syntax for I/O redirection (see Section 6.15). In *csh*, standard output and standard error cannot be redirected independently; they can be redirected independently in *sh*.

Prompts

The primary prompt is usually % for *csh* and $ for *sh*. The secondary prompt (used after the first line in a multiline command) is ? for *csh* and > for *sh*. The primary prompt is defined by the *sh* variable PS1 and the *csh* variable *prompt*. The *sh* variable PS2 defines the secondary prompt. *Csh* does not provide user control over its secondary prompt.

Variable Assignment

In *sh*, the variable assignment operator is =. For example:

```
PS1=sh:
```

sets the primary prompt to sh:. Note: No spaces are allowed around the = sign. *Csh* uses the **set** *var* = ... syntax.

Environment Variable

To set an environment variable in *csh*, the command **setenv** is used. In *sh*, a variable is set in the environment using the **export** command. The value assignment is performed with the regular = syntax. For example:

```
TERM = hp2622; export TERM
```

are entirely equivalent to the *csh* command:

```
setenv TERM hp2622
```

Another example of *sh* environment variable setting is:

```
PATH = $PATH:$HOME/cmds; export PATH
```

Note: The *sh* command search path is one string with the colon (:) separating the directory names, unlike the *csh* special variable $path, which has multiple parts accessible through subscripts.

Initialization File

Unlike *csh*, which uses .cshrc, .login, and .logout files, *sh* reads the file .profile in the user's home directory for login initialization. Thus, .profile corresponds to .login for *csh*. There is no *sh* counterpart to .cshrc or .logout. A nonlogin *sh* does not read any initialization file.

Positional Parameters

Positional parameters can be accessed in both *csh* and *sh* scripts as $0, $1, and so on. In *sh*, $* refers to all the command line arguments, and the variable $# is used instead of the *csh* $#argv. The variables $argv[1] and so on are not used in *sh* scripts.

Command Grouping

Sh allows the use of { and } to group several commands into one command. This usage is not present in *csh*. Command grouping with (and) follows the same semantics in *csh* as in *sh*. However, in *csh*, all commands grouped within parentheses must be on the same line (which can be continued using the \). This restriction is not present in *sh*.

Arithmetic and Relational Operations

Sh does not provide any of the built-in arithmetic or relational operators as does *csh*. The UNIX command **expr** can be used to perform arithmetic and relational operations in *sh* scripts.

Indexed Variables

Csh provides variables that contain multiple parts that are accessed by indexing, using the notation $path[2], for example. *Sh* does not have indexed variables.

Interrupt Handling

Sh provides a command **trap** that sets up the handling of user-specified interrupts. The command allows for different signals to be handled differently. In *csh* the **onintr** command traps only signal 2.

6.15 I/O Redirection in *sh*

The I/O redirection syntax and semantics of *sh* and *csh* are similar, but they are different enough to create some confusion. With *sh*, the following names are recognized in conjunction with I/O redirection:

0	(standard input)
1	(standard output)
2	(standard error)
nulldev	(data sink)

Csh does not provide a notation to reference the standard I/O channels specifically. The file /dev/null always can be used as a *data sink*, where discarded output is sent. Unlike *csh*, *sh* does not use the character ! in I/O redirection. Figure 6.10 illustrates the I/O redirection of *sh* as compared with that of *csh*. Note the 1 in 1> can be omitted, since standard output is the default file descriptor for output redirection.

Figure 6.10 ▪ Shell I/O Redirection

sh	*csh* Equivalent	Remark
>*file* or >>*file*	same	standard output into file
<*file*	same	standard input from file
<<*word* ... *word*	same	here document
1>*file1* 2>*file2*	none	a drawback for *csh*
2>*file*	none	another drawback for *csh*
1>*file* 2>&1 1>>*file* 2>&1	>& *file* >> &*file*	standard output and error into file
2>&1 | *command*	|& *command*	standard output and error into pipe

6.16 Writing *sh* Procedures

As mentioned before, programs written in *sh* syntax can be stored in a file and made executable. If *file* contains an *sh* procedure, it can be invoked either by:

sh *file* [*args*]

or, if *file* has its execution permission also turned on, simply by:

file [*args*]

The latter form of invoking an *sh* script can be issued in a *csh* shell provided that the *sh* script *file* begins with a character other than # (which begins all *csh* procedures) or begins with the string #! /bin/sh. Conventionally, a *sh* script begins with the character :, which is the null operation command in *sh* (which means that the command : is a legal *sh* command that does nothing except evaluate any arguments given).

The special variables $0, $1, $2, ..., $*, and $# are used for positional parameters. The *sh* built-in command:

set − *

sets the positional parameters to the file name expansion of *. An unbound variable is supplied a null string value unless the command:

set −u

has been given, in which case using an unbound variable will cause an error and terminate the *sh* script.

Appendix 5 contains a table in which frequently used constructs of *csh* and *sh* are compared side-by-side for easy reference.

6.17 Examples of *sh* Scripts

This section contains three examples of *sh* scripts. To contrast *sh* with *csh* further, these examples are the *sh* versions of the *csh* examples presented in Section 6.7.

sh **Example:** clean

This *sh* script implements the **clean** command for removing unwanted files from a directory, as described earlier for *csh*. The *sh* script **clean** is as follows:

```
: ## a sh script
## sh script clean
## helps to rm unwanted files from a directory
if /bin/test ! $# -eq 1
then echo usage: $0 directory
     exit 1
fi ## end of if
dir = $1
if /bin/test -d $dir
then :
else echo $dir not a directory
     exit 1
fi

chdir $dir
files = *
for file in $files
do
```

```
echo ' ' ## gives a blank line
echo "file = $file"
if /bin/test -d $file
  then continue
fi
echo ' '
head $file
while :
do
echo "rm $file ?? (y, n, !, or q) :"
read c
case $c in
    y) if /bin/test ! -w $file
            then echo $file write-protected
            else rm $file
                if /bin/test -f $file
                then echo cannot rm $file
                else echo '*****' $file rm-ed
                fi
        fi
        break ;;
    n) echo '+++++' $file not rm-ed
        break ;;
    q) break 2 ;;
    !) echo command:
        read cmd
        eval $cmd ;; ## in $cmd $file can be used
    *) : ;;
  esac ## end of case
  done ## end of while
done ## end of for
```

sh Example: ccp

The **ccp** (conditional copy) command, has been described earlier for *csh*. The *sh* script for **ccp** is as follows:

```
: ## sh script ccp
set -u ; FROM = $1; TO = $2

/bin/test $# -eq 2 && /bin/test -d $FROM && /bin/test -d $TO ||
{ echo usage: $0 \<from directory\> \<to directory\> ; exit 1;}
```

```
wd = 'pwd'
cd $FROM
set - *
cd $wd
for i do

        if /bin/test -d $FROM/$i          # a directory
        then continue
        fi
        if /bin/test -f $TO/$i
          then find $FROM/$i -newer $TO/$i -exec cp $FROM/$i $TO\;
          else cp $FROM/$i $TO
        fi
done
```

sh **Example:** total

The **total** command computes the total number of bytes used in a directory
hierarchy, as described earlier for *csh*. The *sh* script **total** is as follows:

```
: ## sh script name: total
# compute total disk space used in bytes for a directory hierarchy
# a recursive script
if /bin/test ! $# = 1
then
    echo usage : $0 directory
    exit 1
fi

cmd = $0
count = 0
for file in $1/*
do
  if /bin/test -f $file
  then
    x = '/bin/ls -l $file'
  else
    if /bin/test -d $file
        then
            x = '/bin/ls -l -d $file'
            y = '$cmd $file' ## recursive call, obtains subtotal
            count = 'expr $count + $y'
        else
            echo $file not included in the total >&2 # to stderr
            continue
```

```
      fi
    fi
set - $x
count= `expr $count + $4`
done
echo $count
```

6.18 Summary

Both *csh* and *sh* offer simple programming languages to write shell scripts that can be invoked as commands. A shell script is a text file containing a sequence of shell-level commands. The first character of a *csh* script should be a #; the first character of a *sh* script *should not* be a #. A good convention to follow is to use a colon (:) as the first character of a *sh* script.

A shell script can be invoked in one of two ways: It can be given as an argument to an appropriate shell or invoked as an executable file. Both *csh* and *sh* provide string-valued variables, simple conditional and flow control statements, and other program writing essentials. *Csh* offers a programming syntax close to that of the C language. For *csh*, variables may be multivalued.

Positonal parameters are used in shell scripts to refer to command line arguments. The command **onintr** is used to handle interrupts in a *csh* script. Shell scripts can be recursive.

Environment variables are part of the execution environment, which is passed to subshells (a script, for instance) and to commands initiated by the interactive shell. Certain environment variables are predefined. Other environment variables can be defined and set using **setenv** in *csh* or = and **export** in *sh*. The *csh* special variables user, term, path, and home are connected with their corresponding environment variables (their uppercase counterparts) in a special way. There are many similarities and differences between *sh* and *csh*; these differences are summarized in Section 6.14.

The *csh* history and alias mechanisms can be combined to define new commands. This is a way to modify or add to *csh* built-in commands.

Exercises

1. *Csh* allows the use of $0, $1, $2, and so on to refer to positional parameters. Is it possible to use $10, $15 and so on?

2. The character * is a special character in *csh*.

a. Explain how it is used for file name expansion.

b. List at least two situations in command line usage when the character * is not quoted but does not serve the function of file name expansion.

3. Refer to the **timestamp** example (Figure 6.5). How would you put a time stamp at the beginning of a file?

4. When is the character # not a comment character in a *csh* script?

5. Consider the conditional copy script. Can you think of commands other than **cp** that could be put in a similar conditional situation? Can you modify **ccp** to take a command name as a user-supplied argument. The resulting script should be able to perform conditional **cp** if cp is the argument given and will perform a conditional command for any given command.

6. Referring to the **mapc** script:

a. Why is it necessary to set the nonmatch flag?

b. What is the difference between using $cwd/* and simply * in the **foreach** expression?

c. What is the difference between pushing a directory to the top of $dirs and to the bottom, that is, between `set dirs = ($dir $dirs)` and `set dirs = ($dirs $dir)` in the script?

d. Discuss similarities and differences between **mapc** and the **find** command.

7. Can you suggest ways to improve **clean**? What about cleaning out only "old" files? Is an "undo" feature desirable? What about also cleaning out subdirectories? How would you implement the improvements?

8. Explain what the following alias does in detail:

```
alias oops "echo '\!-1:q' >/tmp/cmd$$; vi /temp/cmd$$; "\
           "source /tmp/cmd$$; rm -f /tmp/cmd$$"
```

9. What are the major differences between *csh* and *sh*?

10. If the variable `var` is set, what is the value of `$var[-]`?

11. Write a shell script to change the names of all files of the form *.for in a directory (supplied as argument 1) so that they have the same root as before but now end in .f77. How hard would it be to generalize this script so any two extensions could be used?

12. Write a collection of shell scripts that would mimic the way **rm**, **cp**, and **mv** operate, *but* rather than erasing any files, would put them in a directory named $del in the current directory. Write an additional shell script **unrm** to make these files reappear. When would be a good time to delete the erased files permanently?

13. Write a script that will encode/decode a file and leave it in the same place as before.

14. Write a shell script **findfile** so that:

    findfile *name dir1 dir2 ...*

    searches the named file in the directories specified. If the file is found in one of the directories, the current directory is changed to it. Why does this script have to be sourced through aliasing rather than invoked as a command?

15. Consider the **mapc** script. Explain the second application of **mapc** given in this chapter (the one involving **eval $<**).

16. Consider the name . and its inclusion on the command search path ($path). What difference does it make if you do or do not include .? If you do include ., where should it be placed relative to other directory names on the search path? Why?

17. Is it possible to use different prompts depending on how many *csh* levels have been invoked? If so, how?

The File System in UNIX

7

O ne essential feature of any modern computer system is the on-line storage of user data. On-line data are stored in files immediately accessible to the users. Files are identified by their file names, which are given by the user. On-line files may contain many kinds of data. For example: A file may contain a letter, a report, a program written in a high-level language, a compiled program, an organized database, a library of mathematical routines, or one of many other forms data may take.

The operating system provides a consistent set of facilities allowing the user to create, store, retrieve, modify, delete, and otherwise manipulate files. The *physical* storage media (usually magnetic disks) are divided into many *blocks* of *logical* storage areas. A file uses one or more of these blocks, depending on the amount of data in the file. Blocks are used and freed as files are created and deleted. The software mechanism that creates, stores, retrieves, protects, and manages on-line files is called the *file system*.

In this chapter the UNIX file system is discussed in detail, including such topics as type and status of files, file system implementation, quotas, special files, and organization of system files. A clear understanding of how UNIX treats files will be helpful for topics covered in later chapters.

7.1 File Types

Chapter 1 discussed how files in the UNIX file system are organized into a *tree structure*. This tree is called the *file tree*. There are four types of files on the file tree:

1. An *ordinary file* that contains text, programs, or other data

2. A *directory* that contains names and addresses of other files

3. A *special file* that represents an I/O device

4. A *link* that is a pointer to another file

It is clear what an ordinary file is. Let us now describe each of the others in turn.

Directories

A directory is a file whose content consists of *directory entries* for the files in the directory. There is one directory entry for each file. Each directory entry contains only the name of the file and a pointer to the file itself. For Berkeley UNIX, the file name can be up to 255 characters long. The pointer is an index, called the *i-number*, to a table known as the *i-list*, which encompasses the storage space of a file system. Each entry in the i-list is an *i-node*, which contains status and address information about a file or points to free blocks yet to be used.

Special Files

By representing physical input/output (I/O) devices such as terminals, printers, tape, and disk drives as special files in the file system, UNIX achieves compatible file I/O and device I/O. This means that file I/O and device I/O use the same system calls in UNIX. Such an arrangement results in great simplicity and system flexibility in application programs. By convention, all UNIX special files are under the directory /dev. There are two kinds of special files: a *character* special file and a *block* special file. A character special file represents a character-oriented I/O device such as a terminal or a printer. A block special file represents a high-speed I/O device that transfers data in blocks (many bytes) such as a tape or disk drive. Typical block sizes are 512 bytes and 1024 bytes.

Special files usually are owned by the super user (root). The ownership of a terminal special file is set to the user of the terminal for the duration of the terminal session.

Links

UNIX allows a directory entry to be a pointer to another file. Such a file pointer is called a link. There are two kinds of links: a *hard* link, and a *symbolic* link. A regular file is an entry in a directory with a name and an address of its data blocks. A hard link, or simply a *link*, is an entry in a directory with a name and an address of some other file's data blocks. Thus, a hard link is not distinguishable from the original file. In other words, after a hard link is made to a file, you cannot tell the file from the link. The net result is that you have two different directory entries referring to the same data blocks on disk, together with all file attributes such as size, protection information, and so on. A file may have several links to it. A hard link cannot be made to a directory or to a file on another file system. The UNIX command **ln** is used to make links. Let us look at an application of file linking. Suppose you have written a program called mailmerge that helps create form letters. Now you want everyone on the system to be able to use this program by issuing a simple command. One way to achieve this is to make a link in a system directory to your program. For example, you can input the following:

```
ln mailmerge /usr/local/bin/mmerge
```

This establishes the command **mmerge** as a hard link in the system directory /usr/local/bin to your file mailmerge. Assuming the directory /usr/local/bin is on the command search path, then once this link is in place, users on your system will have a new command **mmerge**. Because of file protection, system directories such as /usr/local/bin are usually writable only by a super user.

The general forms of the **ln** command are as follow:

1. **ln** *file*—makes a link in the current directory, by the same name, to *file*

2. **ln** *file linkname*—establishes *linkname* as a link to *file*

3. **ln** *file1 ... dir*—makes links (using the same names) in the directory *dir* to the one or more files specified

By default **ln** forms hard links. It is permitted to establish a link to a file even if you are not the owner of the file. When deleting a file (with the **rm** command), the directory entry of the file is deleted (Note: to use **rm**, write permission to the directory, not the file, is needed). A file is only physically deleted from the file system when the last link of it is **rm**ed. The total number of hard links to a file is kept as part of the file status.

Symbolic Links

A symbolic link is a directory entry that contains the pathname of another file. Thus a symbolic link is a file that serves as an indirect pointer to another file. For most UNIX commands, if a symbolic link is given as an argument, the file pointed to is to be used. For example, if the file abc is a symbolic link to the file xyz, then:

`cat abc`

displays the contents of xyz. There are some exceptions:

`rm abc`

removes the directory entry abc (even if it is a symbolic link). As well,

`ls −l abc`

displays status information for abc (not xyz). If you give the command:

`rm xyz`

then the symbolic link abc points to a nonexistent file. If abc were a hard link, this situation could not occur.

A symbolic link is distinguishable from the file itself, may point to a directory, and can span file systems. The −s option causes **ln** to create symbolic links. Symbolic links are not available on all UNIX systems, although Berkeley UNIX does support symbolic links. SYSTEM V, for example, does not.

The command **ls** −F displays a symbolic link with a trailing @. The **ls** −l command displays a symbolic link in the form:

`abc@ -> xyz`

7.2 More on File Access Control

From Chapter 1, recall that **ls** −l displays the file type and its access permissions, for example:

`−rw−rw−rw− 1 smith 127 Jan 20 1:24 primer`

The mode display for the file named primer:

`−rw−rw−rw−`

shows read and write permission to u (owner), g (group), and o (other). There are 10 positions in the preceding mode display:

Position 1	file type: d for a directory, – for an ordinary file, l for a symbolic link, s for a socket, c for a character special file, and b for a block special file
Positions 2–4	r (read), w (write), and x (execute) permission for the owner (u), a – is no permission; the letter s is used instead of x for an executable file with a *set-userid* bit that is on (Section 7.3)
Positions 5–7	r, w, and x permission for g, a – is no permission; the letter s is used instead of x for an executable file with a *set-groupid* bit that is on (Section 7.3)
Positions 8–10	r, w, and x permission for o, a – is no permission

Meaning of Permissions for a Directory

The meaning of read, write, and execute permissions is obvious for a regular file that can be either text or binary. For a directory, their meanings are different. To access a directory, the execute permission is essential. No execute permission for a directory means that you can't even perform **pwd** or **cd** on the directory. It also means you have no access to any file contained in the file hierarchy rooted at that directory, independent of the permission setting of that file. The reason: You need execute permission on a directory to access the file names and addresses stored in the directory. Since a file is located by following directories on the pathname, you need execute permissions on all directories on the pathname to locate a file. After locating a file, then the file's own access mode governs whether a specific access is permitted.

To access a directory, you normally need both read and execute permissions. No read permission to a directory simply means that you cannot read the content of the directory file. Consequently, **ls**, for example, will fail, and you cannot examine the file names contained in the directory. Any file name expansion attempt also will fail for the same reason. However, files in such a directory still can be accessed using explicit names.

The write permission to a directory is needed for creating or deleting files in the directory. This permission is required because a file is created or removed by entering or erasing a directory entry. Thus, write permission on the file itself is not sufficient for deleting a file. In fact, you don't need write permission on a file to delete it from the directory! On the other hand, if you have write permission on a file but no write permission for its directory, then you can modify the file, or even make it into an empty file, but you cannot delete the file.

Default File Protection Settings : umask

When you create a new file, the system gives the file a default protection mode. For most systems, this default setting denies write permission to g and o and grants all other permissions. The default file protection setting is kept in a system quantity known as *umask*. The shell built-in command **umask** displays the umask value as an octal number. The umask bit pattern specifies which access permissions to deny. The positions of the 1 bits indicate the denied permissions. For example, the umask value 22 has a bit pattern 000010010, and it specifies denial of write permissions for g and o. The command **umask** also sets the umask value. For example:

```
umask 77
```

sets the umask to deny all permissions for g and o. If you find yourself using **chmod** go-rwx a lot, you might want to consider putting **umask** 77 into your .login file.

7.3 File Status

For each file in the UNIX file system, a set of *status* items is kept with the file and is maintained by the operating system. These items record important information about the file that is used by UNIX to access and manipulate the file. File status items include:

mode	16-bit integer quantity used to represent the mode of a file; mode contains information about file type, manner of execution, and access permissions
number of links	Total number of hard links to this file
owner	User identification of the owner of this file
group	Group identification of this file
size	Total size in bytes of the data contained in this file
last access	Time when this file was last read or written
last modify	Time when the contents of this file were last modified; this time is displayed by the **ls** −l command
last change	Time when any status item of this file was changed
device	Hardware device where the file is stored
i-number	Pointer to where to find the file

block size	Optimal block size to use for file system I/O operations
block count	Total number of file blocks allocated to this file

The command:

```
ls -l file
```

displays many status items of a given file. The *system call* **stat** (covered in Chapter 9) can be used in a C program to access all file status information.

File Mode

The file mode consists of 16 bits. The four high bits (C–F in Figure 7.1) of the file mode specify the file type. The next three bits define the manner in which an executable file is run. The lowest nine bits of the file mode specify the read, write, and execution permissions for the owner, group, and other.

The file type is fixed when a file is created. The *run* and *access* bits are made settable by the file owner. You already know how to set the nine *access* bits with the **chmod** command. The *run* bits can be set together with the *access* bits by the **chmod** command using a numerical mode setting, as in:

```
chmod mode file
```

The numerical *mode* is an octal number that is the logical-or of any number of the settable file modes (Figure 7.2). Only the owner of a file or a super user may change the mode of a file.

File User and Groupid

In UNIX, each file has a *userid* (identification) and a *groupid*. The file userid is the userid of the owner who created the file. On Berkeley UNIX systems, each user may belong to one or more (up to a reasonable limit, say, eight) *groups* of users. Each group has a name. The password file (/etc/passwd) entry of each user contains a group affiliation. If a user belongs to more than one group, then the additional group affiliations are specified in the file /etc/group.

Figure 7.1 ▪ **File Mode Bits**

				← Run →										
F	E	D	C	B	A	9	8	7	6	5	4	3	2	1	0
←	Type	→					←				Access			→

Figure 7.2 ▪ Settable File Modes

Mode	Meaning
0001	execution permission for others
0002	write permission for others
0004	read permission for others
0010	execution permission for group
0020	write permission for group
0040	read permission for group
0100	execute permission for file owner
0200	write permission for file owner
0400	read permission for file owner
1000	sticky bit
2000	set groupid on execution
4000	set userid on execution

The groupid of a file can be set to any group name that the file owner is a member of.

The group access permissions of a file control access by members of the group specified by the groupid of the file. When a file is first created, it is given by default the groupid of the directory that contains it. The command:

`chgrp` *groupid file ...*

is used to assign a specified *groupid* to the named files. For example, if research is a group name, then:

`chgrp research *`

will change the groupid of each file in the current directory to research. The userid of a file can be changed only by the super user. The command:

`chown` *ownerid file ...*

is used to change the ownership of the named files. For example, the command:

`find . –exec chown` pwang \{\}\;

changes the ownership of all files in the current directory hierarchy to pwang.

Csh provides a set of queries (within the **if** construct) to determine the file type, access permissions, and so on of a file. In addition, in both *csh* and *sh*, the command **test** can be used to obtain information about the type and mode of a file. The **test** command is a general conditional command often used in shell scripts (especially in *sh* scripts). You can refer to the UNIX manual pages for more details on **test**.

Access Control Enforcement

A file always is accessed through a process, for instance: **ls**, **cat**, **vi**, **rm**, or your shell (to **cd**, for example). To enforce access control, UNIX uses the userid and groupid of a process to grant or deny access to a file according to the file's access mode. The userid and groupid of a process are usually that of the user who invoked the process. If the user belongs to more than one group, the process also has a multiple groupid.

Specifically, if the userid of the process is the same as the userid of the file, then the access permissions for u apply. Otherwise, if the groupid of the file matches that of the process, then the g permissions apply. Otherwise, the o settings apply.

Set-userid Mode

To understand the function of the *set-userid* mode, first consider an interesting problem created by controlled access to files. To illustrate: Suppose you want to send a piece of electronic mail to another user on the system. To do so, you can use the system **mail** command. Your message will be put in a mailbox file that belongs to another user in the mail spool directory. But the other person's mailbox file is protected against your read or write access. The question is how can you be permitted access to the mailbox through **mail** but not through **vi**. The answer is in the set-userid bit.

If the set-userid bit is turned on for an executable file, the userid of any process that invokes the file will be set temporarily to the userid of the file during its execution. The effect is that the access privileges of the invoking program become that of the owner of the executable file while running the file. The **mail** program is owned by the super user root and has its set-userid bit turned on. When a user sends mail by invoking the **mail** program, the user's process assumes the userid root for the duration of the **mail** program's execution. This configuration allows you access to another user's mailbox file through **mail**. The *set-groupid* bit works exactly the same way on the groupid of a process.

Only a super user can set a sticky bit. A sticky bit is used to make large, shared executable files start faster. Speed is gained by keeping the shared program in memory, when its sticky bit is set, so another invocation of the program will not need to be reloaded from disk. Shared files are created by adding the options −n and −z to the program loader **ld**. A shared binary file does not have to have its sticky bit set. On modern, virtual-memory paging systems, the sticky bit largely is unnecessary.

Establishing a Group

As an example application of the file access control facilities, let us consider establishing a group whose members can collaborate on a project by accessing selected files of one another. To establish the group, you first decide on a name. In this example, the groupid is projectx. Next, you must decide who will be members of the group. In this example, the group members are pwang, rsmith, jdoe, sharma, and yourself. Now ask your system administrator to put projectx and its members into the group definition file /etc/group. As soon as this is done, projectx exists on your system as a valid group.

Once projectx is established, members can assign desired access permissions to selected files to allow sharing within the group. One simple way for you to do this is as follows:

1. Establish a directory, alpha, say, under your home directory. All files in alpha are to be shared with others in projectx.

2. Change the groupid of alpha to projectx by:

    `chgrp` projectx alpha

    Once this is done, any new file created in the alpha directory will be assigned the groupid projectx automatically.

3. Now set the group access permissions for the alpha directory. Depending on the access you wish to give, use one of the following:

    `chmod` g = rwx alpha
    `chmod` g = rx alpha
    `chmod` g = x alpha

    The difference between these permissions is described in Section 7.2.

4. You must make sure that each file in alpha carries the groupid projectx, especially files established through **cp** or **mv**. As mentioned, the groupid of a file is displayed with **ls** −gl. Depending on the nature of a file, you should assign appropriate group permissions. Give the group write permission only if you allow others in projectx to modify a file.

7.4 File System Implementation

As stated earlier in this chapter, a file system is a logical organization imposed on a physical data storage medium by the operating system. This organization together with the routines supplied by the operating system allow for systematic storage, retrieval, and modification of data.

A UNIX file can be viewed as a one-dimensional array of bytes. These bytes are stored in a number of data blocks located on the physical storage medium, usually a high-speed disk drive. The original UNIX block size is 512 bytes. With modern disk drives, this small block size hampers the speed of the file system. An improvement made in Berkeley UNIX is to use larger blocks (for example, 4K-byte blocks) and allow the last block of a file to be a smaller block called a *fragment*. The addresses (locations) of the data blocks and the status information of a file are stored in a data structure known as the i-node (index node). All the i-nodes of a file system are stored in a linear list called the i-list, which is stored at a known address on the physical storage medium. I-node and i-list were mentioned in Section 7.1.

The i-node of a file contains 10 direct pointers, and one each of the other three kinds of points: indirect, double indirect, and triple indirect (Figure 7.3). A direct pointer is the address of a data block containing file data. An indirect pointer points to a block of direct pointers. A double indirect pointer points to a block of indirect pointers. A triple indirect pointer points to a block of double indirect pointers. With this arrangement, very large files can be accommodated.

The i-node contains all the vital information of a file. Therefore, the implementation of the file system centers around access to the i-node. The i-number in a directory entry is used to index the i-list and access the i-node of the file. Thus, a file pathname leads, through a sequence of i-nodes, to the i-node of the file (Figure 7.4). A hard link to a file can be seen as simply another directory entry somewhere on the file tree with the same i-number. Once the i-node of a file is located, it is read into primary memory and kept on the *active i-node table* until access to the file is closed. The i-list also contains *free* i-nodes that are used to create new files. Free i-nodes point to free storage space in a file system.

Removable File Systems

In UNIX, the phrase "a file system" is used to refer to the logical storage device represented by a single i-list. The complete UNIX file storage system may contain one or more file systems. One of these systems is the *root file system*; the others are *removable file systems*. The location of the i-list of the root system always is known to the operating system. A removable file system is

Figure 7.3 ▪ The I-Node

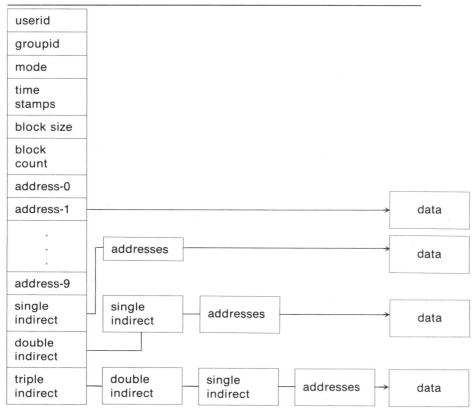

attached (mounted) to the root file system at any leaf node. UNIX allows for mounting and demounting of removable file systems.

A super user may use the command:

mount *dev directory* [−r]

to mount the file system stored on the block special file *dev* at the node specified by *directory*, which is usually an empty directory created for this purpose. This directory is called the *root directory* of the mounted file system. If the option −r is given, the file system is mounted as read only. The **mount** command without any arguments displays the names of all the file systems and the points on the file tree where they are mounted. The command **umount** is used to dismount a removable file system. The command **df** displays the space usage of all the file systems.

Figure 7.4 ▪ File Address Mapping

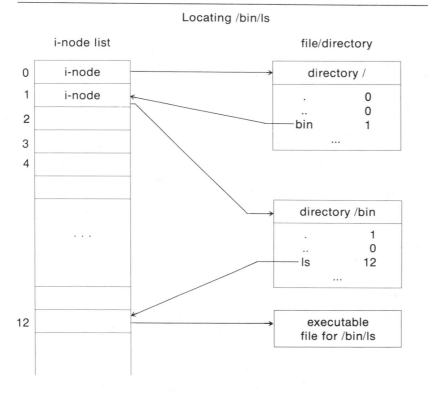

7.5 The File System Table

Each different file system on UNIX is represented by its own block-type special file. The names of the file system special files, together with other information for control and management of the entire file system, are kept in a file. This file is the *file system table*, and it usually is kept in /etc/fstab. This file contains one line for each file system. Some typical lines in fstab are as follows:

```
/dev/hp1a:/:rw:1:1
/dev/hp1b:swap:sw:0:0
/dev/hp2a:/tmp:rw:1:2
/dev/hp3a::sw:0:0
/dev/hp1g:/usr:rq:1:2
/dev/hp2h:/usr/local:rw:1:3
```

```
/dev/hp3h:/user:rq:1:3
/dev/hp3f:/user/fac:rw:1:2
```

Each line contains five fields. A colon (:) is used to separate two fields. The fields are:

1. Block special file name

2. Directory name where mounted

3. Two-character file system type indicator as follows: rw, for both read and write access; ro, for read-only access; sw, for use as a virtual-memory swap area; rq, for a read-write file system that is quota checked and quota enabled at reboot time; and xx, for an entry to be ignored

4. Frequency (in number of days) used by the **dump** program for backing up the file system

5. *Pass number* that tells the file system consistency check program **fsck** the order in which to check all the file systems

The order of the entires in fstab is significant, because programs such as **fsck**, **mount**, and **umount** work through the entires in /etc/fstab sequentially.

7.6 File System Quotas

Traditionally, the UNIX system does not restrict the use of file system space for any user. Thus, it is theoretically possible for a single user to use up all the file space available on the entire computer system. In some application environments, one may wish to have more control over file space use.

The quota mechanism on Berkeley UNIX is designed to allow restrictions on disk space usage. The code for enforcing quotas originally was implemented by Robert Elz at the University of Melbourne, Australia. A separate quota can be set for each user on each file system. Quotas can be enforced on some file systems and not on others. For example, in a computer science department, one file system for student use may have quota enforced; at the same time, another file system for professor use may have no quota enforced. The quota specifies limits on a user's number of files and number of disk blocks. There are two kinds of limits: *soft* limits and *hard* limits. If a user-initiated operation causes the soft limit to be exceeded, a warning appears on the user's terminal. The offending operation is allowed to continue if the hard limit is not exceeded. The idea is to encourage users to stay within their soft limits between login sessions. In other words, exceeding the soft limit temporarily is all right, as long as the user releases file space and returns within the soft limit before logout. At login time, a warning is provided if any soft limits still are violated. After a few such warnings, the user's soft limits can be enforced as hard limits.

The quotas for users in a file system are recorded in coded form in a file called quotas, which is located in the root directory of the file system. For a mounted file system, its root directory is its mount point on the file tree. The command:

`edquota` *userid* ...

calls up an editor that is used to set and modify the quota limits for the given users. Only a super user can invoke **edquota**. The command **quota** displays your disk usage and your quota limits. A super user can give this command an optional userid to display the information of a specific user. A super user also can turn on and off quota enforcing for an entire file system using the commands:

`quotaon` *filesys* ...
`quotaoff` *filesys* ...

7.7 Creating Special Files

As previously mentioned, the UNIX system uses special files to represent physical I/O devices—which results in uniform file I/O and device I/O. Special files normally are created exclusively under the system directory /dev. The command:

`mknod` *filename* [b or c] *major minor*

is used to establish a special file by the given file name. The character b is used if the device is a block I/O device such as a disk or tape. The character c is used for a character I/O device such as a terminal or a line printer. Each physical I/O device on UNIX is assigned a major device number according to the type of device it is and a minor device number indicating the unit number within the same type of devices. These numbers are integers. For example, a second line printer may have major device number 7 and minor device number 2. The exact device numbers are found in the system configuration file in the directory /etc/conf. Only a super user can create special files or access the system configuration file.

7.8 A Road Map to the File System in UNIX

The file system in UNIX is much more than a place where on-line user files are stored. It contains the operating system itself, executable commands, sys-

Figure 7.5 ▪ The Root Directory: /

Where	What
/vmunix	executable kernel of UNIX itself
/dev/	all special files (devices)
/bin/	basic executable commands such as **rm**, **cp**, **sh**, **csh**, and **ed**
/etc/	system data and maintenance files such as the password file (passwd), the file system table (fstab), the terminal capability database (termcap), and the system initialization scripts (rc)
/lib/	parts of the C compiler and the system call object libraries
/sys/	UNIX system source files including /sys/h/ with header files defining system data structures /sys/conf/, with site-specific configuration files, and /sys/sys/ with machine-independent system source files
/tmp/	system scratch files directory, access permission granted for all
/lost+found	directory that must exist in the root directory of every file system for the file system check program to put detached files into

tem tables, library routines, documentation, system administration log files, temporary scratch areas, and so on. In this section, we present the organization of these system files in the UNIX file system. Although there could be some differences between individual UNIX installations, the description contained here is typical, and it should provide you with a better feel of how to get around in the file system. It also should provide a global view of UNIX's constituent parts and where they are on the file tree. Figures 7.5 and 7.6 illustrate. A directory is indicated by a trailing /.

Figure 7.6 ▪ **The Directory /usr**

Where	What
/usr/bin	additional executable commands, helps to keep /bin/ small
/usr/dict/	on-line dictionary (word lists) used by **look** and **spell**
/usr/include/	more standard #include header files
/usr/lib/	more object libraries including f77 I/O, math, **troff** macros in tmac/, fonts in font/, and data for **uucp** in uucp/
/usr/local	system facilities particular to the local installation—the place where commands written locally and documentation for local usage are put
/usr/man/	on-line version of UNIX manual pages; for example, section *i* in the **troff** source form is in file man*i*, and the corresponding formatted version is in file cat*i*
/usr/doc/	articles in UNIX user's manual
/usr/src/	source code for UNIX commands
/usr/spool/	spool area for various delayed actions such as line printing, local mail, and network mail
/usr/ucb/	programs developed at the University of California, Berkeley, such as **vi**, **dbx**, and **talk**

7.9 Some File-Related Commands

Some additional commands that are useful in dealing with files and managing the file system are listed in Figure 7.7. The function of each command is indicated, but no full explanations are given. For more detailed information and options on these commands, refer to the respective manual pages.

Figure 7.7 ▪ Some File-Related Commands

Command	Function
basename	removes prefixes and suffixes from a file name
cmp	compares two files to see if they are identical
comm	selects or rejects lines common to two sorted files
ctags	creates a tags file for a group of source files written in C, Pascal, f77, and so on, which enables easy location of functions and type definitions with **vi** −t
df	displays disk space free on all file systems
diff	compares two files or directories and outputs the differences
du	displays all file sizes in kilobytes in a directory hierarchy
head	displays the beginning of a file
mount, umount	mounts and dismounts a file system
rmdir	removes (unlinks) empty directories
size	displays size of an object file
sort	sorts or merges files
split	splits a file into pieces
sum	computes a checksum of the given file and gives the number of blocks in it
tail	displays the last part of a file
touch	updates the last modified time of a file; if file does not exist, creates an empty one
uniq	reports repeated lines in a file
uuencode **uudecode**	encodes/decodes a binary file for transmission via **mail** (see **uucp** in Section 10.2)
wc	counts the numbers of words, lines in given files

7.10 Summary

The UNIX file system contains files and directories arranged in a tree structure that grows down from the root directory /. There are four types of files: directories, special files, links, and regular files. There are two kind of links: hard links and symbolic links. A symbolic link can link to a directory and can span file systems. It is a unique feature of Berkeley UNIX.

The set-userid bit for executable files is an important concept. When a process executes a set userid file, its effective userid becomes that of the file owner for the duration of the file's execution.

The file system is organized by the i-list, which is a list of i-nodes that contains status and address information for each file and all free space in the file system. File status information includes userid, groupid, mode, time stamps, and disk addresses. Part of the file mode specifies file access permissions.

A file system has its own i-list and space quota settings. The entire UNIX file system may contain several file systems: a root file system and several mounted file systems.

Exercises

1. Determine the file types of all files in /usr/include. Are any of them in other directories? Which are they? What do you find for /usr/include/sys?

2. Try the **umask** command. What does it tell you about the files you create? Try setting the umask value and then creating some files. Look at their protection bits.

3. In the command:

   find . −exec **chown** pwang \{\} \;

   explain the use of the \ characters.

4. How many mountable file systems are there in the system you use? How many are mounted at this time? How much free space is there in the file structure where most of your files are stored? How does the fstab file correspond to the actual files mounted on the system?

5. Do you have a quota imposed on your file usage? (You probably do.) What is it? What does it say about your file usage? Do other system utilities agree with what the quota command says? Why or why not?

6. Why is a hard link indistinguishable from the original file itself?

7. File manipulation commands such as **rm** and **ls** existed before symbolic links were introduced into Berkeley UNIX. In what way should these commands be modified to accommodate symbolic links?

8. How would you go about figuring out the size of the largest file a UNIX file system can accommodate with its i-node structure? Note: It is probably larger than any file structures available on the system.

9. Consider the special files . and .. . Is it correct to say that these files are system-created hard links to directories?

10. Consider the *csh* script **clean** in Chapter 6. Does the script still work correctly if there are symbolic links in the directory it is trying to clean? If there is a problem, how would you fix it?

11. The term *file system* has been used in two distinct senses. Can you clearly identify these different uses?

12. Try to **rm** a file to which you have no write permission. What message does **rm** give? How did you respond? Were you able to delete the file? Why?

13. What would happen if you perform **ls** *dir* with read permission to *dir* but no execute permission? Why?

14. When does a process not assume the userid of its invoker?

UNIX Programming in C

8

With a basic understanding of commands, structure of the file system, and shell-level programming, you now are ready to explore UNIX system programming itself, which is the subject of Chapters 8, 9, and 10. The facilities in UNIX for programming at the C-language level and the workings of some important UNIX functions including terminal I/O, piping, process control, and networking are described. The material presented will enable you to implement new commands as well as write C programs to control and utilize the system.

The UNIX system and almost all of its commands are written in the C language. The C language was developed in parallel with the UNIX system. The portability of UNIX is due, in large part, to the portability of C. In this chapter, a collection of topics that relates to the C language for UNIX system programming are explored:

- Command argument conventions
- Actions of the C compiler
- I/O library and directory access
- Use and maintenance of program libraries
- Error handling and recovery
- Debugging using the **lint** and the **dbx** debugger

8.1 Command Arguments

Commands in UNIX usually are written either as shell scripts or as C programs. Arguments given to a command written in C are passed on as character strings to the C function main, which should be declared as follows:

```
int main(argc, argv, arge)
    int argc;
    char *argv[];
    char *arge[];
```

The parameters argc, argv, and arge are described in Figure 8.1. For example, if the command name is **cmd**, and it is invoked as:

cmd *arg1 arg2*

then

argc	is 3
argv[0]	points to the command name **cmd**
argv[1]	points to the string *arg1*
argv[2]	points to the string *arg2*
argv[3]	is 0

A program may omit the parameters for the function main if they are not needed. Many programs omit the parameter arge and use other ways to obtain values for environment variables. More information on accessing environmental values is contained in Section 9.5. Thus, two simpler declarations for main are

```
int main(argc, argv)
    int argc;
    char *argv[];

int main ()
```

Figure 8.1 ▪ Command Line Parameters

`argc`	number of command line arguments, including the command name
`argv[n]`	pointer to the *n*th argument as a character string terminated by NULL
`arge`	environment variables and values

UNIX Command Argument Conventions

Generally speaking, UNIX commands use the following convention for specifying arguments:

`command` [*options*] [*files*]

An option usually is specified as:

– character

which is a hyphen followed by a single character. A command may take zero or more options. When giving more than one option, the single-letter options sometimes can be combined by preceding them with a single –. For example:

`ls -l -g`

can be given alternatively as:

`ls -lg`

Some commands such as **ps** and **tar** use options but do not require a leading hyphen. Other options may require additional characters or words to complete the specification. The –o option of the **troff** command is an example. The command:

`troff -o12,56-78 document`

instructs **troff** to print page 12 and pages 56–78 of the given *document*. Because of this convention for specifying options, it is a bad idea to use a file name with a leading hyphen.

A file argument can be any valid file name: simple, relative pathname, or full pathname, and can include the pointers **.** and **..** . It is incorrect to write a program that expects a restricted file name or makes any assumptions about which name form is supplied by the user.

Figure 8.2 ▪ Example: echo

```
/* the echo command */

int main(argc, argv)
    int argc;
    char **argv;
{
    while (argc > 0) {
        argv++;
        printf("%s%c", *argv, (1 != argc) ? ' ' :\n);
        argc--;
    }
    return(0);
}
```

A Simple Example

The **echo** command displays the command line arguments (Figure 8.2). The program increments argv, which is a pointer to the array of character-string pointers, and displays a space after each string. The last argument is followed by a NEWLINE (\n). Note that the function main returns an int, and the last statement of main is:

```
return(0)
```

for normal termination of execution, because the value returned by main becomes the exit status of the command. (See Section 9.4 for more discussion on the exit status.)

8.2 The C Compiler

In preparation for system programming in C, it is important to understand the functions of the C compiler and its usage. A compiler not only translates high-level language programs into machine code to run on a specific computer, but it also arranges for a suitable *run-time environment* for the program by providing I/O, file access, and other interfaces to the operating system. Therefore, a compiler not only is computer-specific but also operating-system-specific. On UNIX systems, the **cc** command is used to compile C programs. The **cc** compilation process consists of five phases (Figure 8.3):

1. *Preprocessing*—The first phase is performed by the **cpp** (C preprocessor) program. It handles constant definition, macro expansion, file inclusion, and conditional compilation.

2. *Compilation*—Taking the output of the previous phase as input, the **ccom** program performs syntax checking, parsing, and assembly code generation.

3. *Optimization*—This optional phase improves the efficiency of the generated code for speed.

4. *Assembly*—The assembler program **as** is used to create an object file containing binary code and relocation information that is used by the linker/loader.

5. *Loading*—The **ld** program is the linker/loader, which combines all object files and links in the necessary library subroutines to produce an executable program.

The cc Command

As mentioned, **cc** is used to compile C programs. The suggested form of the **cc** command is as follows:

cc [*option*] ... *file* ... [-l*name*] ...

Figure 8.3 ▪ Compilation Phases

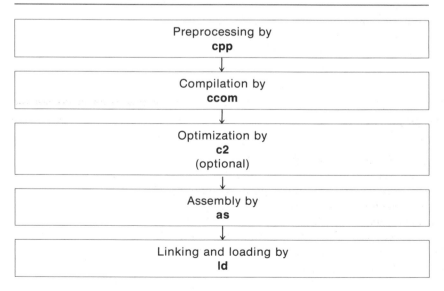

A file name ending in .c is taken to be a C source file, and a corresponding .o file is produced. A file name ending in .s is taken to be an assembly language file, and a corresponding .o object file is produced. A file name ending in .o is taken to be an object file, and it is loaded into the final executable module. When compiling a single .c file into an executable module, the .o file produced is automatically deleted.

Any −l*name* arguments given specify libraries needed. These arguments are passed to the linker/loader phase. Some often used options are listed here:

−c	suppresses the loading phases and produces .o files only. No executable module is produced.
−o *name*	names the executable module with the specified name instead of the default a.out
−O	invokes the **c2** code optimizer phase. It is used to produce faster running code and is usually used only when producing final production versions of a program.
−g	instructs the compiler to produce additional symbol table information for the symbolic debugger **dbx**. The option −lg also is passed to the loader **ld**.
−p	adds to each subroutine code that counts the number of times it is called. These counts are written to a file named mon.out, which then can be processed by the profiling program **prof** to produce a program profile that helps pinpoint routines to improve execution speed.

The C Preprocessor

The C preprocessor is the first phase of the compilation process. The preprocessor provides important facilities that are especially important for writing system programs. Directives to the C preprocessor begin with the character # in column one. The directive:

```
#include
```

is used to include other files into a source file before actual compilation begins. The included file usually contains constant, macro, and data structure definitions that usually are used in more than one source code file. The statement:

```
#include "filename"
```

instructs **cpp** to include the entire contents of the given file *filename* (note that the " marks are part of the command). If the file name is not given as a full pathname, then it is first sought in the directory where the source code containing the #include statement is located; if it is not found there, then some standard system directories are searched. The statement:

```
#include <filename>
```

has the same effect, except the given file name is only searched for in standard system directories. One such directory is /usr/include. For example, the standard header file for I/O is usually included by:

```
#include <stdio.h>
```

at the beginning of each source code file. As you will see, an important part of writing a system program is including the correct header files supplied by UNIX.

The **cpp** directive:

```
#define
```

is used to define constants and macros. For example, after the definitions:

```
#define TRUE 1
#define FALSE 0
#define TABLE_SIZE 1024
```

names can be used in subsequent source code instead of the actual numbers. The general form is:

```
#define identifier token ...
```

The preprocessor will replace the identifier with the given tokens in the source code.

Macros with parameters also can be defined using the following form:

```
#define identifier (arg1, arg2, ...) token ...
```

For example:

```
#define MIN(x,y) ((x)>(y) ? (y) : (x))
```

defines the macro MIN, which takes two arguments. The macro call:

```
MIN(a+b,c-d)
```

is expanded by the preprocessor into:

```
((a+b)>(c-d) ? (c-d) : (a+b))
```

Another example is:

```
#define ABS(a) ((a)>=0 ? (a) : -(a))
```

The right-hand side of a macro may involve symbolic constants or another macro. It is possible to remove a defined identifier, that is, make it undefined, by:

```
#undef identifier
```

The preprocessor also handles conditional compilation, which means that sections of source code can be included in or excluded from the compiling process, depending on certain conditions that the preprocessor can check. Conditional compilation is specified in the general form:

```
#if- condition
        source code lines A
[#else
     source code lines B ]
#endif
```

If the condition is satisfied, the *A* source code will be included, otherwise the *B* source code (if given) will be included. The possible conditions are listed in Figure 8.4.

Conditional compilation can be used to include debugging code with something like:

```
#ifdef DEBUG
     printf(...)
#endif
```

To activate such conditional debug statements, you either can add a line:

```
#define DEBUG
```

at the beginning of the source code file, or you can compile the source code file with:

cc −DDEBUG *file*

Another frequent use of conditional compilation is to handle source code that is different for different hardware. For example:

```
#ifdef SUN
     table_size=table_size+4
#endif
```

Here the source line is effective only when the symbol SUN (for SUN work-stations) is defined.

Figure 8.4 ▪ Conditional Compilation

If Condition	Meaning
#if constant-expression	true if *expression* is zero
#ifdef identifier	true if *identifier* is #defined
#ifndef identifier	true if *identifier* is not #defined

Compilation and Assembly

The compiling phase takes the output of the preprocessing phase and performs *parsing* and *code generation*. If the −O option is given, then the code generation invokes code optimization routines to improve the efficiency of the generated code. The output of the compilation phase is assembly code. The generated assembly code then is processed by the assembler program **as** to produce a relocatable object code file (.o).

Linking and Loading

Although linking and loading is a phase of the **cc** command, the linker/loader **ld** can be invoked independently. It is important for system programmers to have an in-depth understanding of how **ld** works.

The linker/loader produces an executable program (the a.out file) by combining user-supplied object files with system-supplied object modules contained in *libraries* (see Section 8.4). The **ld** program treats its command line arguments in the order given. If the argument is an object file, the object file is relocated and added to the end of the executable binary file under construction. The object file's symbol table is merged with that of the binary file. If the argument is the name of a library, then **ld** scans the library's symbol table in search of symbols that match undefined names in the binary file's symbol table. Any symbols found lead to object modules in the library that should be loaded. Such library object modules *resolve* undefined symbols and are added to the binary file in the same way. Therefore, it is important that a library argument be given after the names of object files that reference symbols defined in the library.

For example, the **ld** command:

```
ld /lib/crt0.o file1.o file2.o file3.o /lib/libc.a
```

loads four object files and produces an executable binary file that runs under UNIX. The object file /lib/crt0.o provides a C program with the necessary UNIX run-time environment, and /lib/libc.a is the standard C subroutine library. Since the **cc** command automatically adds these arguments when it calls **ld**, the following command has the same effect:

```
cc file1.o file2.o file3.o
```

After all object and library arguments have been processed, the **ld** program sorts the binary file's symbol table looking for any remaining unresolved references. The final executable module is produced only if no unresolved references remain.

There are a number of options that **ld** takes. A few important ones are listed:

−l*name*	this is an abbreviation for the library name /lib/lib*name*.a, where *name* is a character string. If that file does not exist, the file /usr/lib/lib*name*.a is used. This option can occur anywhere on the command line. Other options must precede file name arguments.
−n	the executable file is made to be shared by giving it an 0410 *magic number*. When the file is executed, its text portion will be read-only and shared among all users executing the same file. (See *process control* in Section 9.4 for details on executable file format.)
−s	removes the symbol table and relocation bits from the executable file to save space. This is used for code already debugged.
−o *name*	uses the given *name* for the executable file, instead of a.out

8.3 The Standard I/O Library

The C language has a set of high-level, buffered, I/O routines in a standard I/O library. These routines provide C programs with efficient I/O operations. Since the standard I/O library is available on any system that supports C, programs that limit I/O statements to these library routines can be ported to another system essentially without modification. On UNIX systems, the standard I/O library is part of /lib/libc.a, which, as mentioned, is used automatically by the linker/loader phase of the **cc** command.

However, to use the external routines in the I/O library, the header file /usr/include/stdio.h should be included in a C program to provide the necessary declarations. The program in Figure 8.5 implements a command **lowercase**, which copies all characters from standard input to standard output while mapping (a one-to-one transformation) all uppercase characters to lowercase ones. The standard I/O routines **getchar** and **putchar** are used there.

As mentioned before, when a program is started under UNIX, three I/O channels are opened automatically. These are the *standard I/O streams*: standard input connected to your keyboard (stdin), standard output connected to your terminal (stdout), and standard error also connected to your terminal (stderr). However, they may be redirected to files or pipes. The include file stdio.h contains definitions for the identifiers stdin, stdout, and stderr. Each is a pointer to a structure called FILE contained in stdio.h. This structure contains information about the open file such as the buffer location, the current character position in the buffer, the mode of access, and so on. The I/O struc-

Figure 8.5 ▪ Source Code File lowercase.c

```
#include <stdio.h>

main()
{   int c;
    while ((c = getchar())!= EOF)
        putchar(lower(c));
    return(0);
}

lower(c)
int c;
{   static int d = 'a'-'A';
    if (c >= 'A' && c <= 'Z')
        return (c + d);
    else return(c);
}
```

ture defined by FILE is referred to as an I/O *stream*. For example:

```
putc(c, stderr)
```

writes a character to the standard error. The routines **getchar** and **putchar** can be defined as:

```
#define getchar()   getc(stdin)
#define putchar(c)  putc(c, stdout)
```

I/O to Files

The standard I/O library routine **fopen** is used to open a file for subsequent I/O:

```
FILE *fopen(filename, access_mode)
    char *filename, *access_mode;
```

The function header declaration in the C language is used to describe **fopen**. This convention is adopted for describing library and system calls. For example, to open the file passed as the second command-line argument for reading you would use:

```
FILE *fp, *fopen();
fp = fopen(argv[2], "r");
```

The allowable access modes are as follows:

"r" for reading a file. If the file does not exist or is not readable, an error results.

"w" for writing a file. If the file exists, its contents are discarded. If the file does not exist, it is created.

"a" for appending to the end of a file. If the file does not exist, it is created.

In addition to the routines **getchar**, **putchar**, **getc**, and **putc**, the standard I/O library also defines higher-level functions **gets**, **fgets**, **scanf**, **fscanf**, **fread**, **puts**, **fputs**, **printf**, **fprintf**, **fwrite**, and the routines **fflush** and **fclose** to flush and close a stream, respectively. Refer to the UNIX manual for information on these library functions.

8.4 Directory Access

The library file /lib/libc.a, automatically loaded by **cc**, contains not only the standard I/O library functions but also the standard C library, which frequently contains useful functions. For example, string operations such as **strcat** (string concatenation), **strcmp** (string comparison), and so on are contained in the standard C library. You will encounter these functions as you go along. A number of directory access functions are discussed here.

To use any of the following directory access functions, include the lines:

```
#include <sys/types.h>
#include <sys/dir.h>
```

at the beginning of your source code file. The function:

```
DIR *opendir(name)
     char *name;
```

opens the directory *name* and associates a *directory stream* with it. A pointer to this directory stream is returned. This pointer then is used in subsequent operations on this directory. If the directory *name* cannot be accessed, or if there is not enough memory to hold the contents of the directory, a NULL is returned.

Once a directory stream is opened, the function **readdir** is used to access its entries sequentially:

```
struct direct *readdir(dp)
     DIR *dp;
```

The **readdir** command returns a pointer to the next directory entry. It returns NULL after reaching the end of the directory or detecting an invalid **seekdir** operation. The directory entry structure is as follows:

```
struct direct {
        u_long      d_ino;      /* inode number of entry */
        u_short     d_reclen;   /* length of this record */
        u_short     d-namlen;   /* length of string in d_name */
        char        d_name[MAXNAMLEN + 1];
                                /* name must be no longer than this */
};
```

In Berkeley UNIX, the constant MAXNAMLEN is 255. The function

```
closedir(dp)
    DIR *dp;
```

closes the given directory stream and frees the structure associated with the DIR pointer.

To illustrate the use of these library functions, let us look at a function **dirsearch** that searchs a directory for a given entry (Figure 8.6). Note that **dirsearch** uses knowledge of the *direct* structure.

Figure 8.6 ▪ Searching a Directory

```
#include <sys/types.h>
#include <sys/dir.h>
#define FOUND 1
#define NOT_FOUND 0

dirsearch(name,dir)
char *name, *dir;
{   int length;
    DIR *dp;
    struct direct *dentry;

    length = strlen(name);
    dp = opendir(dir);
    for (dentry = readdir(dp); dentry != NULL; dentry = readdir(dp))
        if (dentry->d_namlen == length
                && !strcmp(dentry->d_name, name)) {
                closedir(dp);
                return(FOUND);
        }
    closedir(dp);
    return(NOT_FOUND);
}
```

8.5 Libraries and Archives

The **ld** program uses libraries in constructing an executable binary file, as mentioned. Let us take a closer look at how a subroutine library, also known as an *archive file*, is created and maintained under the UNIX system. This discussion is oriented toward the C language and C subroutines; however, libraries for other languages under UNIX are similar.

A library is simply a collection of independent programs. A subroutine library usually contains the object code versions of subroutines that are either of general use or of importance for a specific project. Usually the purpose of a library is to establish routines that are frequently useful to many different programs, so that they can be linked into a binary file by the linker/loader **ld**.

A library of object files is actually one form of an archive file. In UNIX, an archive file is a collection of several independent files arranged into the archive file format. An archive file begins with a magic string that identifies it as an archive file and is followed by constituent files each preceded by a header. The header contains such information as file name, owner, group, access modes, last modified time, and so on.

The command **ar** is used to create and maintain libraries and archives. The general form of the **ar** command is as follows:

ar *key* [*position*] *archive_name file ...*

The effect of the **ar** command is controlled by the *key* specified. Some important keys are listed:

c	creates a new archive file, *archive_name*, by combining the given files
r	places the given files into the existing archive file, *archive_name*. If a file is already in the archive, it is replaced. New files are appended at the end of the archive
ru	functions the same as r, except that existing files in the archive are replaced only if they are not up to date as compared to the corresponding files specified on the command line
ri or ra	after ri or ra, a *position* argument must be supplied that is the name of a file in the archive file. These keys function the same as r, except new files are inserted before (ri) or after (ra) the position file in the archive.
t	displays the table of contents of the archive file
x	extracts the files in the archive to the current directory; this, of course, results in the creation of several independent files

For example, the command:

```
ar c mylib file1.o file2.o file3.o file4.o
```

creates the archive file mylib by combining the given object *files*.

For libraries with a large number of routines, searching for the modules needed to load can be time consuming. The command **ranlib** converts an archive file into a form that can be searched more rapidly. The **ranlib** command converts the file by adding a table of contents called __.SYMDEF to the beginning of the archive. The command:

```
ranlib lib ...
```

converts each *library* given.

8.6 Error Handling in C Programs

An important aspect of system programming is the foreseeing and handling of possible errors in a program. Many kinds of errors can occur at run time. For example, the program may be invoked with an incorrect number of arguments or unknown options. A program should guard against such errors and display appropriate error messages. Error messages to the user should be written to the stderr stream, so they appear on the terminal even if the stdout stream has been redirected. For example:

```
fprintf(stderr, "%s: can't open %s\n", argv[0], argv[i]);
```

alerts the user that a file cannot be opened. Note that it is customary to identify the name of the program displaying the error message. After displaying an error message, the program may continue to execute, return a particular value (for example, -1) or elect to abort. To terminate execution, the library routine:

```
exit(status);
```

is used, where *status* is of type int. For normal termination *status* should be zero. For abnormal terminal such as an error, a positive integer *status* (usually 1) is used. The routine **exit** first invokes **fclose** on each open file before executing the system call __exit, which causes immediate termination without buffer flushing. A C program may use:

```
__exit(status);
```

directly if desired. See Section 9.4 for a discussion of __**exit**.

Errors from System Calls

A possible source of error is failed system or library calls. A *system call* is an invocation of a routine supported by the UNIX system itself. UNIX contains many system calls, and understanding them is a part of learning UNIX system programming. When a call to a standard I/O library routine such as **fopen** or a direct system call such as **open** and **signal** fails, the value returned is (almost without exception) −1. It is up to your C program to check for such returned values and to take appropriate actions. To handle system call errors properly, the header file errno.h should be included:

```
#include <errno.h>
```

This error header file defines symbolic error numbers and their associated *standard error messages* (Figure 8.7). The external variable errno is set to one of these error numbers after a system call has failed, but it is not cleared after a successful call. This variable is available for your C program to examine. The system call:

```
perror(s)
char *s;
```

can be used to print the standard error message. The call **perror**(*s*) outputs the following to stderr:

1. The argument string *s*

2. The character :

Figure 8.7 ▪ System Call Errors

Number	Name	Message
1	EPERM	Not owner
2	ENOENT	No such file or directory
3	ESRCH	No such process
4	EINTR	Interrupted system call
5	EIO	I/O error
6	ENXIO	No such device or address
	...	
64	ENOTEMPTY	Directory not empty

3. The standard error message associated with the value of errno

4. A NEWLINE character (\n)

The string argument given to **perror** is usually the name of the C function or argv[0]. Sometimes it is desirable to print a variant of the standard error message. For this purpose, standard error messages are available in the external table sys__errlist as strings indexed by errno. The variable sys__nerr is the length of this table.

Error Recovery

The two standard library routines **setjmp** and **longjmp** are provided for recovery from an error or an interrupt in a C program. To use these routines, the header file setjmp.h must be included:

```
#include <setjmp.h>
```

The routine **setjmp** is declared as:

```
int setjmp(stk)
    jmp__buf stk;
```

which, when called, saves its stack environment in *stk* for possible use later by **longjmp**. The value returned by **setjmp** is 0. The routine **longjmp** uses the saved *stk* to return control flow to the **setjmp** statement:

```
void longjmp(stk, val)
    jmp__buf stk;
    int val;
```

When called with a saved *stk* and an integer *val*, **longjmp** will restore the saved stack environment *stk* and cause execution to resume as if the original **setjmp** call has returned the value *val*. For this *backtracking* to occur correctly, the function that first invoked **setjmp** must not itself have returned in the interim. After the **longjmp** operation, all accessible data have values as of the time when **longjmp** was called.

The template program in Figure 8.8 shows how to use **setjmp** and **longjmp**. In this example, the function main sets up the eventual **longjmp** called by the function recover. Since recover never returns, it is declared "void."

8.7 Program Checking: lint

Let us now turn our attention to utilities that help debug C programs. The **lint** program is a utility that checks C programs for features that are likely to be

Figure 8.8 ▪ Using longjmp

```
#include <stdio.h>
#include <errno.h>
#include <setjmp.h>
jmp_buf stk;

main()
{  /* init and set up things here */
  if (setjmp(stk) != 0)
    {/* any adjustments after recovery */
    }
  other(...);
  }

other()
{  ...
  /* when error is detected and recovery desired */
  recover(errno);
  ...
  }

void recover(e)
int e;
{/* adjust values of variables if needed */
  longjmp(stk,e);
  }
```

bugs or that may cause portability problems. The latter is especially important for system facilities, because they usually must run on different computers. The **lint** program also checks for the use of *types* in the program, more strictly than does the C compiler. Among the items **lint** checks for are:

- Automatic variables declared but not used

- Unreachable statements

- Undefined variables used

- Loops not entered at the top

- Logical expressions whose values do not change

- Consistency of values returned by a function

Figure 8.9 ▪ Sample lint Output

```
file.c:
file.c (14): warning: argument argc unused in function main
file.c (21): warning: s set but not used in function main
wait, arg. 1 used inconsistently   llib-lc (137) :: file.c (43)
write, arg. 2 used inconsistently llib-lc (139) :: file.c (45)
write returns value that is always ignored
```

- Consistency of arguments between function calls and definitions

- Functions whose values are not used

  The **lint** command is given as:

`lint` [*options*] *file* ...

A sample **lint** output is shown in Figure 8.9. Of these findings, probably only the argument inconsistencies are important. But it is always best to be careful.

8.8 Debugging with dbx

Although **lint** and the C compiler identify problems at the syntax level, you still need a good tool for debugging at run time. The **dbx** program provides a convenient facility for source-level debugging and controlled execution of programs under UNIX. It can be used to debug a program written in any source language such as C, f77, and Pascal, provided that the object file has been compiled by a compiler that generates the appropriate symbol information for use by **dbx**. The compilers **cc**, **pc**, and **f77** produce the appropriate source information for **dbx**. Here, debugging of C programs with **dbx** is discussed. The debugger can be used in the same manner for f77 and Pascal programs.

An interactive debugging environment is provided by **dbx**. The debugging features provided include:

1. Source-level tracing

2. Source-level break point

3. Source line single stepping

4. Displaying values, declarations, and other attributes of identifiers

5. Displaying and editing source files

6. Machine instruction–level execution control and printing of memory contents

To debug a C program using **dbx**, you first must compile all object files with the –g option to **cc** and the –lg option to **ld**. One simple way to achieve this sequence is to compile all source code (.c) files using the:

cc –g *source-file* ...

command, which results in an executable a.out file suitable to run under the control of **dbx**. To invoke **dbx**, simply type:

dbx [*binary-file*]

to debug the executable *binary file*. If no binary file is given, a.out is assumed. The prompt:

(dbx)

then appears, and you can begin an interactive debugging session. When you are finished, simply type the command **quit** to exit from **dbx**. The *binary file* specified also can be a *core* file that is dumped after an execution error. In that case, **dbx** is used to examine the state of the program at the point of error.

Basic dbx Commands

This section presents some basic commands provided by **dbx** for simple debugging. To begin execution, use the **dbx** command:

run [*args*] [< *file1*] [> *file2*]

where *args* are any command line arguments needed by the binary file. You may use > and < for I/O redirection. If the binary file has been written since the last time the symbolic information was read in, **dbx** will read in the new information.

To isolate a bug, you may wish to put traces on certain functions and/or source lines before running the program. The following commands are used for tracing:

trace *line*	(trace execution of the *line*)
trace *function*	(trace calls to *function*)
trace *fun1* **in** *fun2*	(trace calls to *fun1* only inside *fun2*)
trace *var*	(trace changes to *variable*)
trace *exp* **at** *line*	(display *expression* when *line* is reached)

Any valid C expression can be used, of course. Lines are specified by line number, which can be displayed by the following commands:

list	(list the next 10 lines)
list *line1,line2*	(list the range of lines)
list *function*	(list a few lines before and after *function*)

It is often desirable to suspend execution at a certain point in a program to inspect values of variables and so on and then decide whether or not to continue execution. The **dbx** commands for this purpose are:

stop at *line*	(suspend execution at *line*)
stop in *function*	(suspend execution when *function* is called)
stop *var*	(suspend execution if *variable* is changed)
print *exp*	(display the value of *expression*)
cont	(continue execution from where it was stopped)

A point where execution is to be suspended is called a *break point*. After reaching a break point, you also may single-step source lines:

step	(execute one source line)
next	(execute up to the next source line)

The difference between **step** and **next** is that if the line contains a call to a function, **step** will stop at the beginning of that function block, but **next** will not. You also may use **where** to display the current line number and the sequence of function calls that led control flow to this point.

As debugging progresses, trace and break points are put in and taken out in an attempt to localize the bug. To remove trace and break points use:

delete *number*	(remove trace or break with sequence *number*)

Trace and break points are given a sequence number when they are installed. After a trace or stop command, this number is displayed. If you do not remember the number, use **status** to display all the trace and break points in effect. Another useful command is:

whatis *name*

which displays the declared structure of the identifier *name*.

A dbx Example

The following example illustrates how **dbx** can be used to control the execution of the lowercase.c program given in Section 8.3. User input is shown after the prompt (dbx). Output from **dbx** is indented.

```
% cc -g lowercase.c
% dbx
        dbx version of 7/5/84 16:55 (kentvax).
        Type 'help' for help.
        enter object filename (default is 'a.out'):
        reading symbolic information ...
(dbx) list
        1   #include <stdio.h>
        2
        3
        4   int main()
        5   {
        6          int c;
        7          while ((c = getchar()) != EOF)
        8              putchar(lower(c));
        9          return(0);
       10   }
(dbx) trace lower
        (1) trace lower
(dbx) stop in lower
        (2) stop in lower
(dbx) run < uuu > vvv
        calling lower(c = 65) from function main
        stopped in lower at line 14
            14   {
(dbx) whatis c
        int c;
(dbx) where
        lower(c = 65), line 14 in "lowercase.c"
        main(0x1, 0x7fffeea4, 0x7fffeeac), line 8 in "lowercase.c"
(dbx) cont
        returning 97 from lower
        calling lower(c = 66) from function main
        stopped in lower at line 14
            14   {
(dbx) status
        (1) trace lower
        (2) stop in lower
(dbx) delete 2
(dbx) cont
        returning 98 from lower
        calling lower(c = 67) from function main
        returning 99 from lower
        calling lower(c = 68) from function main
```

```
        returning 100 from lower
        calling lower(c = 69) from function main
        returning 101 from lower
        calling lower(c = 82) from function main
        returning 114 from lower
        calling lower(c = 101) from function main
        returning 101 from lower
        calling lower(c = 10) from function main
        returning 10 from lower

        execution completed, exit code is 0
(dbx) quit
```

Advanced dbx Usage

Any of the previously listed **trace** commands can be followed by:

if *condition*

making the tracing actions effective only if the given C *condition* is satisfied. You also may use:

stop if *condition*

which suspends execution as soon as the given *condition* becomes true.

When dealing with bugs related to the program's treatment of interrupt signals received, the commands:

catch *int*   (trap named *interrupt* before it is sent to the program)

ignore *int*   (stop trapping named *interrupt*)

can be helpful. By default, **dbx** traps all interrupt signals except SIGCONT, SIGCHILD, SIGALRM, and SIGKILL. More information on signals and interrupts can be found in Section 9.6.

The **dbx** debugger also provides a set of commands that perform machine instruction–level debugging. Capabilities provided include tracing and breaking at an instruction address, instruction single stepping, and displaying the contents of memory using designated formats. For example:

tracei *address*

puts a trace on the instruction at the given *address*, and:

stopi *address*

puts a break point at the machine *address*.

Figure 8.10 ■ dbx Memory-Printing Formats

Letter	Print Format
i	machine instruction
s	a null-terminated character string
d,(D)	short (long) word in decimal
o, (O)	short (long) word in octal
x, (X)	short (long) word in hexadecimal
b, (c)	byte in octal (as character)
f, (g)	single- (double-) precision real number

To display the contents of memory locations, the **dbx** commands:

add, *add/* [*format*]

and

[*add*] / [*count*] [*format*]

are used. The memory contents that are displayed start at the first *address* and continue to the second *address* or until the *count* of items is reached. If no *address* is specified, the address following the one most recently displayed is used. The single-letter *format* specifies how the memory is to be displayed. If it is omitted, the previous format specified is used. The initial format is "X." The format letters are listed in Figure 8.10.

A symbolic address is specified by preceding an identifier name with an &. Registers are given as rN$, where N is the register number. An address can be an expression involving other addresses, and $+$, $-$, and indirection (unary *). Please refer to the UNIX manual pages for **dbx** for more details on instruction-level debugging commands.

8.9 Good C Programming Practices

The following list of helpful conventions and programming techniques has been found to be valuable for improved program structure and reliability. Good programming practice can result in fewer bugs and lower maintenance costs.

1. Keep structure, constants, and macro definitions in header files. Do not use more than one copy of such declarations. Establish a separate directory to collect all header files of a software package. Use the #include statement to include header files in source files.

2. Keep related routines in one source file, and keep logically-related source (and object) files in the same subdirectory. Establish a "makefile" for each subdirectory (see Chapter 11).

3. Declare any strictly local functions as *static* to restrict their scope to their own files.

4. Avoid writing lengthy functions. Break large functions into smaller routines that perform well-defined tasks. Use descriptive names for functions. Use comments before a function to document the meaning of the arguments and the purpose of the function. Use a comment after a larger function to mark its end.

5. Always declare the result type of functions that return a noninteger result. Use an explicit return statement in each function including the function main.

6. Avoid numerical constants in your source program. Constants for buffer and table sizes should be defined in header files using #define and should contain only uppercase letters.

7. Always check the returned value of system calls for possible errors.

8. Avoid complicated structure definitions. Use typedef, and keep structure definitions in header files as much as possible.

9. Avoid complicated macros, use functions instead.

10. Run the **lint** command on C sources.

11. For system-level programs, always pay attention to how signals and interrupts should be handled.

12. Design and implement your code for easy testing. Test individual modules separately. Keep test cases in files, and eventually build complete test suites.

8.10 Summary

This chapter deals with UNIX conventions and utilities for C-level programming. The standard C function main can receive arguments specified on the command line as character strings. The **cc** command goes through five phases:

preprocessing, compiling, optimizing (optional), assembling, and linking/loading. The assembler (**as**) and the linker/loader (**ld**) can be invoked independent of the C compiler.

The standard I/O library is a part of the library of routines provided by UNIX for running C programs. A library is a type of archive file created and maintained using the **ar** command. The **ranlib** command allows a library file to be searched more quickly. The **ld** program creates an executable binary file by linking object files with library routines and then loading them. The default output file of **ld** is a.out, which is executable.

The C compiler and the **lint** command can be used to spot syntax and portability problems in a C program. The **dbx** symbolic debugger is a powerful tool for run-time source-level debugging.

Exercises

1. Modify the **echo** implementation given in the text so that using the −n option will eliminate the carriage return displayed.

2. Write a version in C of the shell script **clean** given in Chapter 6. When is it a good idea to rewrite scripts in C?

3. Compile several C source files into object files. Then use **ld** to produce the file a.out.

4. Which **dbx** commands did you use most frequently when debugging the program in Problem 2?

5. Your UNIX system may have more than 64 error numbers. To find out, write a C program to access the external table sys__errlist.

6. System include files for C programs are kept in a few system directories. Find out which directories these are on your system.

7. Write four or five C source files containing small routines, and set up some header files that are used by these source files. Establish a library file of these routines using **ar** and **ranlib**. Now write, compile, and run a C program that uses a header file and calls a few of these library routines.

8. Write an efficient template C program for processing command line options. You should allow for juxtaposed as well as separately given options.

9. Write a UNIX command named **fil**. The usage synopsis is as follows:

   fil [*from*] [*to*]

   to transform text from the named file *from* to the named file *to*. If only one file argument is supplied, it is assumed to be for the *from* file. A dash (−)means standard input; a missing *to* means standard output. The **fil** command works as follows:

a. All tabs are replaced by an equivalent number of spaces.
b. All trailing blanks at the end of each line are removed.
c. All lines longer than 132 characters are folded.
d. A form feed is added for every 66 lines from the previous form feed.
e. All BACKSPACE and nonprinting characters are removed.

10. Run **lint** on your program for Problem 9. Apply **dbx** to debug it.

UNIX System Programming

9

A system program is a procedure that uses calls to the UNIX operating system itself to perform a well-defined function. These calls to UNIX are referred to as *system calls*, and they frequently provide services (such as I/O) that are reserved for the operating system alone; thus they cannot be obtained in any other way. A system call can be thought of as a direct entry into the operating system to obtain services provided by UNIX. UNIX system programs are written in C, using the collection of system calls in UNIX.

Function and usage of many important system calls are discussed in this chapter. Topics covered include low-level input and output, file access and manipulation, process control, signals and interrupts, pipes, control of I/O to terminals, and I/O multiplexing. Examples are given to illustrate actual use of the various system calls in C programs.

9.1 Low-Level I/O

High-level I/O routines such as **putc** and **fopen**, which are provided in the standard C I/O library, are adequate for most I/O needs in C programs. These standard library I/O routines use buffered I/O streams (typedef FILE). They depend on low-level I/O UNIX systems calls to perform the actual I/O. The low-level I/O routines do not provide buffering or any other services before transferring control to entries in the UNIX system kernel.

As mentioned, UNIX features uniform file I/O and device I/O. Physical devices such as terminals are represented as *special files* in the file system. As a result, UNIX uses a simple and homogeneous interface for I/O to all files and peripheral devices. In this section, file I/O is discussed; but device I/O functions in the same manner, because devices are really nothing but special files. In addition to files, UNIX supports I/O between processes through abstract structures known as *pipes* and *sockets*. Although files, pipes, and sockets are different I/O objects, they are supported by many of the same low-level I/O calls explained here.

Descriptors

Before file I/O can take place, the program must indicate its intention to UNIX. This indication is made by the **open** system call, declared as follows:

```
#include <sys/file.h>
```

```
int open(name, access, mode)
    char *name;
    int access, mode;
```

The call opens the file *name* for reading and/or writing, as specified by the *access* argument, and returns an integer *descriptor* (a nonnegative integer) for that file. If the file does not exist, **open** creates a new file with the given name first. Subsequent I/O operations will refer to this descriptor rather than to the file name. Other system calls return descriptors to I/O objects such as pipes (Section 9.7) and sockets (Section 10.6). In any case, a descriptor is actually an index to a per-process *open file table* that contains the necessary information for all open files and I/O objects of a process.

Arguments to **open** are as follows:

name   a character string that is the file name

access   an integer code for the intended access

mode   an octal number protection mode for creating a new file

The argument *name* is self-explanatory. *Access* is a little more complex, and it is discussed in detail in the following paragraph. The protection *mode* is specified in the same way as for the **chmod** system call. It is modified by the *umask* value (see Section 9.2) of the process to arrive at the protection bit pattern for the file.

The *access* specified is formed by the logical "or" of the following single-bit values:

O_RDONLY	opens file for reading only
O_WRONLY	opens file for writing only
O_RDWR	opens file for reading and writing
O_NDELAY	prevents possible *blocking* due to the **open** system call
O_APPEND	opens file for appending
O_CREAT	creates file if it does not exist
O_TRUNC	truncates size to 0
O_EXCL	produces an error if the O_CREAT bit is on and file exists

Opening a file with O_APPEND instructs each write on the file to be appended to the end. If O_TRUNC is specified and the file exists, the file is truncated to length zero. If access is:

(O_EXCL | O_CREAT)

and if the file already exists, **open** returns an error.

In a multiprogramming environment such as UNIX, if the **open** operation cannot be accomplished immediately and there is a delay in executing the **open** call, the calling process may be forced to stop execution temporarily and run another process. This type of forced delay is known as *blocking*. For example, if an **open** call must wait for a carrier on a dial-up line, the calling process can be blocked. A blocked process may resume execution after the cause of the delay has been removed. If the O_NDELAY flag is specified and the **open** call encounters a blocking condition, instead of blocking, **open** returns immediately as normal. If the delay condition is still there when the process attempts to perform I/O on the open file, the calling process then will be blocked. (This feature is not implemented on all systems.)

If the **open** call fails, a −1 is returned, otherwise a descriptor is returned. A process may have no more than OPEN_MAX (a defined constant) descriptors open simultaneously. Three descriptors automatically are opened for any user process. They are as follows:

0	standard input, for read only
1	standard output, for write only
2	standard error, for both read and write

When a descriptor *fd* is no longer needed in a program, it can be deleted from the per-process open file table using the call:

```
int close(fd)
    int fd;
```

Figure 9.1 shows a typical use of the **open** system call. Note that the third argument to **open** is unused; it is not needed for an existing file. In this case, any integer can be used as the third argument.

Reading and Writing a File Descriptor

Reading and writing normally is sequential. For each file descriptor, there is a *current position* that points to the next byte to be read or written. After *k* bytes are read or written, the current position is advanced by *k* bytes.

The system calls **read** and **write** are:

```
int read(fd, buffer, k)
```

```
int write(fd, buffer, k)
    int fd, k;
    char *buffer;
```

where *fd* is a descriptor to read from or write to, *buffer* points to a character string to receive or supply the characters, and *k* is the number of bytes to be read or written.

Figure 9.1 ▪ The open System Call

```
#include <stdio.h>
#include <sys/file.h>
#include <errno.h>

main(argc,argv)
    int argc;
    char *argv[];
    { int fp;
    /* open argv[1] for reading */
    if ((fp = open(argv[1], O_RDONLY,0)) == -1){
            fprintf(stderr,"%s: can not open %s\n", argv[0], argv[1]);
            perror("");
            }
    /* other code */}
```

The **read** call attempts to read *k* bytes from the referenced object. It returns the number of bytes actually read and deposited in the buffer or 0 if the end-of-file has been reached. If **read** returns less than *k* bytes, it means that the end-of-file has been reached. This is the case only when reading an actual file. When reading a pipe (Section 9.7), for example, this can mean an empty pipe buffer.

Write outputs *k* bytes to the referenced object from the buffer and returns the actual number of bytes written out. Both **read** and **write** return a −1 if they fail. As an example, the **lowercase** command is written with low-level I/O calls in Figure 9.2.

Moving the Read/Write Position

A file is viewed as a sequence of bytes. The **read** and **write** operations move the current position only in a sequential manner. The system call **lseek** provides a way to move the current position to any location, therefore allowing *random access* to any file bytes. Use:

```
int lseek( fd, offset, origin ) ;
    int fd, offset, origin ;
```

to move the current position associated with the descriptor *fd* to a byte position defined by *origin* plus *offset*. The *origin* is given as:

0	beginning of a file
1	current position
2	end of a file

The offset can be positive or negative. The call **lseek** returns the current position as an integer position measured from the beginning of the file. It returns a −1 if it fails. For example:

lseek(fd, 0, 0)	moves the current position to the first byte of the file
lseek(fd, 0, 2)	moves the current position to the end of the file
lseek(fd, −1, 2)	moves the current position to the last byte of the file
lseek(fd, −10, 1)	backs up the current position by 10 bytes

It is possible to issue an **lseek** call beyond the end of file and then issue a **write** call, which creates a "hole" in the file that does not occupy file space. Reading a byte from such a hole returns a 0. It is an error to **lseek** a pipe or a socket.

Figure 9.2 ▪ lowercase.c with Low-Level I/O

```
#include <stdio.h>
#include <errno.h>
#define BUFSIZ 1024

int main(argc, argv)
int argc;
char *argv[];
{
    char buffer[BUFSIZ];
    int k;
    while ((k = read(0, buffer, BUFSIZ)) > 0) {
       lower(buffer,k);
       k = write(1, buffer, k);
       if (k == -1)
            break; }
    if (k == -1) {
        perror(argv[0]);   exit(1); }
    return(0);
}

int lower(buf,k)
char *buf;
int k;
{
    static int d = 'a' - 'A';
    while (k-- > 0) {
    if (*buf >= 'A' && *buf <= 'Z')
        *buf += d;
    buf++;
    }
}
```

9.2 Operations on Files

This section discusses system calls that create and delete files, access file status information, make links, obtain and modify protection modes, and other file attributes.

Creating and Deleting a File

The **open** system call should be used to create a new file. The system call:

```
int creat( name, mode )
    char *name;
      int mode;
```

also can be used. If the named file already exists, it is truncated to zero length, ready to be rewritten. The returned value of **creat** is a file descriptor for writing that is equivalent to:

```
open( name, (O_CREAT | O_TRUNC), mode )
```

As mentioned, the lower nine bits of *mode* (for access protection) are modified by the process's file creation mode *umask* to obtain the mode actually assigned to the newly created file. The formula:

```
( ~umask ) & mode
```

is used to derive the effective file creation mode. The default *umask* of a process is octal 022, which clears the write permission bits for g (group) and o (other). The *umask* can be set by the system call:

```
int umask( newmask )
      int newmask;
```

The returned value is the previous *umask*. For example:

```
umask(077);
```

will allow file access only for the owner. The umask setting is inherited by child processes.

After a file is created, alternative names for it can be given. The call:

```
int link( file, name )
    char *file, *name;
```

establishes another (additional) *name* for the existing *file*. The new name, of course, can be anywhere on the file structure. This type of file name is known as a hard link (Section 7.1), and it becomes indistinguishable from the original file. To remove a link, use the call:

```
int unlink( name )
    char *name
```

When the last link is removed, the file is deleted.

Creating and Removing a Directory

The system call **mkdir** is used to create a new directory file:

```
mkdir( name, mode )
    char *name;
    int mode;
```

It creates a new directory file with the given *name*. The *mode* works the same way as it does in **creat**. The new directory's userid is set to the process's effective userid. The directory's groupid is set to that of the parent directory in which it is created.

To remove a directory, the system called **rmdir** is used:

```
rmdir( name )
    char *name;
```

The named directory file is removed. The directory must be empty (that is, have no entries other than . and ..). For both **mkdir** and **rmdir**, a returned value of 0 indicates success; a −1 indicates an error.

Changing File Modes

The file mode is established when a file is created. It can be changed by:

```
chmod( name, mode )
    char *name;
    int mode;
```

```
fchmod( fd, mode )
    int fd, mode;
```

where either a file name or a file descriptor is given. Only the owner of a file (or a super user) may change the mode. The mode is the logical-or of any of the basic modes shown in Figure 9.3. After a successful completion, **chmod** returns a 0; if it fails, it returns a −1.

If an executable file is set up to be shared (this is usually the default), then mode 01000 prevents the system from abandoning the swap-space image of the text portion of the file when its last user is finished with it. This bit (01000) sometimes is referred to as the *sticky bit*. The ability to set this bit is restricted to a super user. Also, for system security reasons, writing or changing the owner of a file turns off the set-userid and set-groupid bits.

Accessing File Status

As mentioned previously, UNIX maints a set of *status* information on each file, such as file type, protection modes, time when last modified, and so on. To

Figure 9.3 ▪ Basic File Modes

Octal Bit Pattern	Meaning
04000	set userid on execution
02000	set groupid on execution
01000	keeps text image after execution
00400	read permission for owner
00200	write permission for owner
00100	execute (searches on directory) permission for owner
00070	read, write, execute (search) permission for group
00007	read, write, execute (search) permission for others

access file status information from a C program, the system calls:

```
#include <sys/types.h>
#include <sys/stat.h>

stat( name, &buf )

lstat( name, &buf )
     char *name;
     struct stat buf;

fstat( fd, &buf )
     int fd;
     struct stat buf;
```

are used. For all three calls, the status information for the named file or descriptor is retrieved and placed in *buf*. The calls do not require read, write, or execute permission of the named file. But all directories listed in the pathname leading to the file must be reachable. The purpose of **lstat** is to retrieve the status of a symbolic link. When given a symbolic link, **stat** will retrieve the status of the file to which it is linked. If the descriptor *fd* is associated with a pipe, **fstat** reports an ordinary file with an i-node number, restricted permissions, and a not necessarily meaningful length. The stat structure consists of many fields, as defined in the header file <sys/stat.h>. Figure 9.4 shows the stat structure and the defined constant codes for interpreting the value of the st_mode field.

Figure 9.4 ▪ The include File <sys/stat.h>

```
struct stat {
     dev_t     st_dev;          /* device inode resides on */
     ino_t     st_ino;          /* this inode's number */
     u_short   st_mode;         /*file type and mode */
     short     st_nlink;        /* number or hard links to the file */
     short     st_uid;          /* userid of owner */
     short     st_gid;          /* groupid of owner */
     dev_t     st_rdev;         /* the device type, for inode that is device */
     off_t     st_size;         /* total size of file */
     time_t    st_atime;        /* file last access time */
     int       st_spare1;
     time_t    st_mtime;        /* file last modify time */
     int       st_spare2;
     time_t    st_ctime;        /* file last status change time */
     int       st_spare3;
     long      st_blksize;      /* optimal block size for file system i/o ops */
     long      st_blocks;       /* actual number of blocks allocated */
     long      st_spare4[2];
};

#define  S_IFMT      0170000    /* file type mask */
#define    S_IFDIR   0040000    /* directory */
#define    S_IFCHR   0020000    /* character special */
#define    S_IFBLK   0060000    /* block special */
#define    S_IFREG   0100000    /* regular */
#define    S_IFLNK   0120000    /* symbolic link */
#define    S_IFSOCK  0140000    /* socket */
#define  S_ISUID     0004000    /* set userid on execution */
#define  S_ISGID     0002000    /* set groupid on execution */
#define  S_ISVTX     0001000    /* save swapped text even after use */
#define  S_IREAD     0000400    /* read permission, owner */
#define  S_IWRITE    0000200    /* write permission, owner */
#define  S_IEXEC     0000100    /* execute/search permission, owner */
```

Three time stamps are kept for each file:

- st_atime (*last access time*)   The time when the file was last read or modified. It is affected by the system calls **mknod**, **utimes**, **read**, and **write**. For efficiency reasons, st_atime is not set when a directory is searched.

- st_mtime (*last modify time*)   The time when the file was last modified. It is not affected by changes of owner, group, link count, or mode. It is changed by **mknod**, **utimes**, and **write**.

- st_ctime (*last status change time*)   The time when the file status was last changed. It is set both by writing the file and by changing the information contained in the i-node. It is affected by **chmod**, **chown**, **link**, **mknod**, **unlink**, **utimes**, and **write**.

The time stamps are stored as integers. A larger integer value represents a more recent time. UNIX usually uses GMT time. The integer time stamp as well as the time returned by the **gettimeofday** system call represent the number of seconds since a fixed point in the past (for example, GMT (Greenwich Mean Time) 00:00:00, January 1, 1970). The library routine **ctime** converts such an integer into an ASCII string that represents date and time.

As an application, let us consider a command **newer** used in the form:

if ({**newer** *file1 file2*}) **then**

which returns exit status 0 if the last modify time of *file1* is more recent than that of *file2* and 1 otherwise. The C code for this command can be found in Figure 9.5.

The mask S_IFMT is useful for determining the file type. For example:

```
if ((buf.st_mode & S_IFMT) = = S_IFDIR)
```

determines whether the file is a directory.

The following three system calls modify the status of a file:

chmod	changes the mode of a file
chown	changes the userid and groupid of a file
utimes	sets file times

Determining Allowable File Access

It is possible to determine whether an intended read, write, or execute access to a file is permitted before initiating such an access. The access system call is defined as:

```
#include <sys/file.h>
int access( name, mode )
    char *name;
    int mode;
```

The **access** call checks the permission bits of the named file to see if the intended access given by *mode* is allowable. The intended access mode is a

Figure 9.5 ▪ The newer Command

```
#include <sys/types.h>
#include <sys/stat.h>

main(argc,argv)
int argc;
char *argv[];
{    return(!newer(argv[1],argv[2])); /* set exit status */
}

/* whether last modify time of file1 is more recent than file2 */
int newer(file1, file2)
char *file1, *file2;
{    return(mtime(file1) > mtime(file2));
}

/* obtain last modify time of file */
int mtime(file)
char *file;
{    struct stat stb;
     if (stat(file,&stb) < 0){
            perror(""); exit(1);
            }
     return(stb.st_mtime);
}
```

logical-or of the bits R_OK, W_OK, X_OK, and F_OK as defined by:

```
#define R_OK 4    /* test for read permission */
#define W_OK 2    /* test for write permission */
#define X_OK 1    /* test for execute (directory search) permission */
#define F_OK 0    /* test for presence of file */
```

If the specified access is allowable, the call returns a 0; otherwise it returns a −1. Specifying *mode* as F_OK (that is, 0) tests whether the directories leading to the file can be searched and whether the file exists.

The real (as opposed to effective) userid and the group access list (which includes the real groupid) are used in verifying permission. Thus, this call is useful in set-userid programs.

Figure 9.6 ▪ A Program to Display the Current Working
Directory

```
#include <stdio.h>
#include <sys/param.h>
/* using getwd */
main()
{    char *name, *getwd();
     char *malloc();
     name=malloc(MAXPATHLEN);
     printf("cwd=%s\n", getwd(name));
}
```

Current Working Directory

The standard C library routine:

```
char *getwd(name)
    char *name;
```

copies the full pathname of the current working directory into the argument
name and returns a pointer to it. For example, the C program in Figure 9.6
displays the current working directory.

The system call:

```
int chdir(name)
    char *name;
```

is used to change the current working directory to the directory *name*. A value
of 0 is returned if **chdir** is successful; otherwise a −1 is returned.

9.3 An Example: ccp

It is appropriate now to look at a complete example of a command written
in C. The **ccp** program copies files from one directory to another. A specific
file is copied or not copied depending on whether updating is necessary. A
version of **ccp** implemented as a *csh* script was discussed in Section 6.7.

The **ccp** command copies files from a source directory *A* to a destination
directory *B*. The usage is:

ccp *A B* [*file* ...]

The named files, or all files (but not directories), are copied from A to B subject to the following conditions:

1. If the file is not in B, copy the file.

2. If the file is already in B but the file in A is more recent, copy the file.

3. If the file is already in B and the file in A is not more recent, do not copy the file.

To compare the recentness of two files, the last modify times in the file status are used. The following is the **ccp** program in C:

```
/* ccp : the conditional copy command */

#include <sys/param.h>
#include <sys/file.h>
#include <sys/types.h>
#include <sys/stat.h>
#include <sys/dir.h>
#include <stdio.h>
#include <strings.h>

main(argc, argv)
int argc;
char *argv[];
{       short i;
        DIR *dirp1;
        struct direct *dp;

        if (argc < 3) {/* need at least two args */
                fprintf(stderr, "%s: wrong number of arguments", argv[0]);
                exit(1); }
        else if (argc > 3) {/* files specified */
                for (i = 3; i < argc; i++)
                        ccp(argv[i],argv[1],argv[2]) ;
                return(0);
        }
        /* now exactly two args */
        if ((dirp1 = opendir(argv[1])) == NULL) {
                fprintf(stderr, "%s: cannot open %s", argv[0], argv[1]);
                exit(1); }
        for (dp = readdir(dirp1); dp != NULL; dp = readdir(dirp1))
                /* do not process dot file */
                if (strncmp(dp->d_name,".", 1)) {
                ccp(dp->d_name,argv[1],argv[2]); }
}
```

```
ccp(name,d1,d2)
char *name, *d1, *d2;
{    char f1[MAXPATHLEN], f2[MAXPATHLEN];
     strcpy(f1,d1); strcpy(f2,d2); strcat(f1, "/");
     strcat(f2,"/"); strcat(f1,name); strcat(f2,name);
     if ( access(f2,F_OK) == -1 || newer(f1,f2) ) {
          printf("cp %s %s\n", f1, f2); }
}
/* if last modify time of file1 is more recent than file2 */
int newer(file1, file2)
char *file1, *file2;
{    return(mtime(file1) > mtime(file2)); }
/* obtain last modify time of file */
int mtime(file)
char *file;
{    struct stat stb;
     if (stat(file,&stb) < 0){ perror(" "); exit(1); }
     return(stb.st_mtime);
}
```

The "system" System Call

In the **ccp** example, no file copying actually was performed. The command **printf** was indicated simply to identify the copying actions needed. To carry out the file copying, it is most convenient to invoke a shell-level **cp** command from within a C program. The system call:

```
system(string)
     char *string;
```

is used to invoke the *sh* shell and to pass the command string to the shell as if it were typed on a terminal. The **system** call returns the exit status of the *sh* shell. In **ccp** the following can be used to copy files:

```
system(sprintf (buf, "cp %s %s\n", f1, f2))
```

9.4 Process Control

The UNIX system manages multiple concurrent *processes*. A process is the execution of a program. A central part of UNIX (the kernel) deals with the control of processes. Each process is represented by an entry in the *process table*, which is manipulated by the operating system to control all processes. The CPU is scheduled by the kernel to switch from running one process to the next in rapid succession. Thus, the processes appear to run concurrently. A process can go through a number of execution *states* before completion. Some of the states are as follows:

- *running* The process is executing, and it can be in either the *user mode* or the *kernel mode*. In the *user mode*, the process is executing instructions from the user's program. It goes into the *kernel mode* when a system call or interrupt transfers control to the UNIX kernel. When the system call returns, the process returns to the *user mode*.

- *asleep* A process in this state is *blocked* and waiting for an *event* to occur. Such an event could be an I/O completion by a peripheral device, the termination of another process, the availability of data or space in a buffer, the freeing of a system resource, and so on. When a running process has to wait for such an event, it goes to *sleep*, which creates an opportunity for a *context switch*, so that another process can receive CPU service. Later when the waited-for event occurs, the process awakens and becomes *ready* to run.

- *ready* A process in this state is in line for CPU service. The kernel schedules ready processes to receive CPU service based on a well-defined policy.

- *zombie* After termination of an execution, a process goes into the *zombie* state. The process no longer exists. The data structure left behind contains its exit status and any timing statistics collected.

From a programming point of view, a UNIX process is the entity created by the **fork** system call. When UNIX is booted, only one process (process 0) exists. This process uses the **fork** system call to create process 1, which is known as the *init* process. Process 0 then becomes the *swapper* process, which handles memory management. The *init* process is the ancestor of all other processes.

The ability to use multiple processes is important in both operating system and user applications. In the next sections, process creation, execution, synchronization, termination, and interrupt handling are discussed.

Executable File Format

An executable file (for example, a.out) is created by compiling and loading source programs and is composed of, in order, five sections:

1. *Header*

2. *Program text and data*

3. *Relocation information*

4. *Symbol table*

5. *String table*

The *header* section contains information about the executable file. It contains a *magic number* (a long integer), which is the entry point to the program, and the sizes of the other program sections in bytes. The *text* section is the read-only portion of a program; the *data* section is the portion of the program that changes during execution. The *relocation information* section, the *symbol table* section, and the *string table* section are useful for debugging but are not absolutely necessary for program execution, and they may be omitted if the program is loaded with the −s option of **ld** or if the executable file has been processed by the **strip** command.

When an a.out file is loaded into memory, three logical segments are established in memory:

- text segment for code

- data segment for initialized and uninitialized data

- stack for program calls and returns

The header is not loaded into memory. The text segment begins at 0 in the virtual address space. The exact layout of the text and data segments and whether the text segment is to be shared (write-protected) depend on the value of the magic number.

The stack will occupy the highest possible locations in the virtual address space: growing downward. The stack is extended dynamically as required. A stack pointer to the current top of the stack is kept. The current upper limit of the data segment is known as the *break* point. This break point remains fixed during program execution unless the **brk** system call is used to alter it. The virtual memory addresses between the break point and the stack pointer are not part of the process address space (Figure 9.7).

In addition to the process areas previously discussed, there is a per-process kernel data and kernel stack area allocated for each process. This area is known as the *u_area* of a process. Data kept in the u_area only can be accessed and manipulated by the process while running in the kernel mode. Thus, the u_area is part of the kernel address space. The UNIX kernel uses the process table entry and the u_area to control a process.

The Process Table

A systemwide *process table* is maintained by the UNIX kernel to control all processes. There is one entry for each existing process. Each process entry

Figure 9.7 ▪ Memory Layout of a Process

Text segment	
Data segment	Break point
Unused	Stack pointer
Stack	0x7ffff000

contains such information as the following:

PID	a unique integer processid (PID)
UID	real and effective ownerids and groupids
state	the process state
event	the event the process is waiting (sleeping) for
size	the size (memory requirement) for the process
locations	the pointer to the u_area, the pointer to the per-process region table that contains pointers to the text, the data, and the stack regions of the process
priority	the parameters for the scheduling of the process
signals	the signals received but not yet treated by the process
accounting	the timing information such as execution time, idle time, kernel resource utilization, and so on used for scheduling and accounting

The per-process u_area contains additional information for a specific process:

- all open file descriptors

- the internal I/O data structures

- the current directory and current file system root

- the system call parameters, returned values, and error codes

- a pointer to its process table entry

The ps Command

It is possible for a user to obtain status information on processes. The user-level command

ps

displays information about processes on your terminal. Because UNIX is a multiuser system and because there are many system processes that perform various chores to keep UNIX functioning, many processes may be running at any given time. The **ps** command attempts to display processes that are likely to be of interest to you. And you are given options to control what processes are displayed. The **ps** command displays information only for your processes unless given the option −a. The **ps** command displays in short form unless given the option −l for the long form. Thus, for example:

```
ps -al
```

displays, in long form, all "interesting" processes. The option −g is used to force the display to include certain uninteresting processes (getty processes for terminal lines, for example):

```
ps -ag
```

If you wish to include *daemon* processes (those without a control terminal such as the cron process), add the option −x. There also are quite a few other options. As well, there are quite a few other flags. Information provided for each process includes:

PID	the process identification in numerical form
STAT	the state of the process
TIME	the CPU time (in seconds) used by the process (both the user and the system time)
TT	the control terminal of the process
COMMAND	the user command

The state (STAT) is given in a sequence of four letters, for example, RWNA. The first letter indicates the ability of the process to run:

R	for processes that can run
T	for stopped processes
P	for processes in page wait, a virtual-memory operation
D	for processes in disk I/O (or other short-term) waits
S	for processes that are sleeping for less than about 20 seconds
I	for processes that are idle (sleeping longer than about 20 seconds)

The second letter indicates whether a process is *swapped out* (not resident in primary memory):

W	a process that is swapped out
(blank)	a process in memory

| > | a process that exceeds a specified soft limit on allowable memory (not swapped) |

The third letter indicates whether a process is running with lowered or raised scheduling priority:

N	a process that has a reduced priority
<	a process that has an artificially raised priority
(blank)	a process with a normal priority

The fourth letter indicates any special treatment of the process for virtual-memory replacement. This information is usually uninteresting for the user.

Process Creation: fork

A process can create another process via the **fork** system call. The process that invokes **fork** is the *parent* process, and the newly created process is the *child* process. After the **fork** call, the child process and the parent process run concurrently. The **fork** is invoked in the form:

```
pid = fork( );
     int pid;
```

The child process created is a (logical) copy of the parent process, except for the following:

1. The child process has a unique pid.

2. The child process has a different parent pid.

3. The child process has its own copy of the parent's I/O descriptors. These descriptors reference the *same* I/O objects. Therefore, for instance, pointers in file objects are shared between the child and the parent. Thus, an **lseek** on a descriptor in the child process will affect a subsequent **read** or **write** on the same descriptor by the parent and visa versa. This descriptor copying is a feature used by the shell to redirect standard input and output for newly created processes and to set up pipes as will be discussed in Section 9.7.

When **fork** returns, it returns the pid of the child process to the parent process and returns a 0 to the child process. If **fork** failed, it returns a −1. The following is a typical use of **fork**:

```
int pid;
if ((pid = fork( )) == 0) {
     /* code for child process */
```

```
            /* usually a call to exec */
    }
/* remaining code for parent process */
```

Program Execution: The exec Routines

The **exec** routines refer to a group of program execution routines that are based on the **execve** system call. These routines include the C library routines **execl**, **execv**, **exect**, and several others, which all are variations of **execve**. We shall use the common prefix **exec** when discussing general features of these routines.

When a process calls **exec**, it overlays the current program with the image of another executable file and begins execution at its entry point. The result is that the process begins to execute a new program, under the same execution environment as the old program, which is now replaced. From the point of view of the old program that calls **exec**, **exec** is a call that never returns. An **exec** call often is combined with **fork** to produce a new process that runs another program:

1. Process A (the parent process) calls **fork** to produce a child process B.

2. Process B calls **exec** to run a new program.

The **execve** system call is as follows:

```
int execve ( name, argv, envp )
    char *name, *argv[ ], *envp[ ];
```

where

name   is the full pathname of an executable file

argv   points to its arguments

envp   points to environment values passed to the new process

This system call overlays the calling process with the named file, which must be either an executable object file or a file of commands for an interpreter (an *executable text file*). The format of an executable object (a.out) has just been discussed. An executable text file begins with a line of the form:

 # ! interpreter [option ...]

When the named file is an executable text file, the system performs an **execve** call on the required *interpreter*, giving it any indicated options followed by the named file and its original arguments. For example, a *csh* script may begin with the line:

```
#! /bin/csh
```

and a *sh* script may begin with:

```
#! /bin/sh
```

as mentioned in Section 6.2.

The argument *argv* is an array of character pointers that point to null-terminated character strings. argv[0], argv[1], . . . constitute the parameter list to be made available to the new process. By convention, at least one argument must be present in this array, and the string argv[0] gives the command name of the executed program (usually the last component of *name*).

The argument *envp* is also an array of character pointers that point to null-terminated strings that represent environment values. Details concerning the process environments are presented in Section 9.5.

Descriptors that are open in the calling process remain open after **exec**, unless the *close-on-exec* flag has been set for a specific descriptor by the **ioctl** system call. Ignored signals remain ignored across an **exec**, but signals that are caught are reset to their default values. The signal stack is reset to be undefined. Signal handling is discussed in Section 9.6.

As mentioned, a process has a real userid and an effective userid. The **execve** call changes the effective userid of the process to the userid of the executed file if the file has the set-userid bit set. The real userid is not affected. The **exec** call has a similar effect on the effective groupid of a process.

The following attributes remain the same after an **exec** call:

- processid (pid)
- parent pid
- process groupid
- access groups
- working directory
- root directory
- control terminal
- resource uses
- interval timers
- resource limits
- file mode mask (*umask*)
- signal mask

Each active process is a member of a process group that is identified by a positive integer called the *process groupid*. The groupid is the pid of a process known as the *group leader*. This grouping permits the signaling of related processes (for example, via the **killpg** system call) and the *csh* job control mechanisms. (See Section 9.6 for more details on signals.)

If **execve** returns, an error has occurred. In this case, the value returned is a −1.

The **execv** routine is the same as the **execve** routine without the third argument:

```
int execv( name, argv)
    char *name, *argv[ ];
```

For example, a program that uses **exec** to pass command line arguments to a given file looks like the following:

```
main(argc,argv)
int argc;
char **argv;
{
    argv++;
    execv(argv[0],argv);
}
```

Note that argv[0] needs to be a full pathname.

When combined with **fork**, a child process can be created to execute a new file:

```
int pid;
if ((pid = fork( )) == 0) {
    /* code for child process */
    execv(...);
    _exit(1); /* execv failed */
    }
/* remaining code for parent process */
```

Since **fork** copies the parent process, it is wasteful when used in conjunction with an **exec** call to create a new execution context. In a virtual-memory system, the system call:

```
int vfork( )
```

should be used with an **exec** call instead. Unlike **fork**, **vfork** avoids much of the copying of the address space of the parent process and is therefore more efficient.

Performing the same functions as **execve**, the **execl** routine is convenient when the file name and the arguments are known and can be given specifically.

The general form is:

int **execl**(*name, arg0, arg1, arg2, ..., argn;* ▢);

For example:

execl(" /bin/ls","ls", "-l",▢);

Synchronization of Parent and Child Processes

After creating a child process using **fork**, the parent process may proceed independently, or it may elect to wait for the child process to terminate before proceeding further. The system call:

```
#include <sys/wait.h>
```

pid = **wait**(&*status*);
    union wait *status*;
    int *pid*;

searches for a terminated child (in the zombie state) of the calling process. It performs the following steps:

1. If there are no child processes, **wait** returns immediately with a −1 value (an error).

2. If there is one or more child processes in a zombie state (terminated already), **wait** selects an arbitrary zombie child, frees its process table slot for reuse, stores the child's exit status in the **wait** argument variable, and returns the child processid.

3. Otherwise, **wait** sleeps until one of the child processes terminates and then proceeds to step 2. In this case, the **wait** calling process is blocked.

When **wait** returns after termination of a child, the **wait** argument variable (*status*) is set. Basically, *status* is an unsigned short integer (16 bits). The high byte of *status* contains the low byte of the *exit status* of the child process. The low byte of *status* contains the *termination signal* of the child process. This byte is 0 if the child has finished execution on its own. If the child's termination is due to a *signal*, then the numerical ID of the signal is contained in the low-order seven bits. Bit 8 is set only if a core dump of the child has been produced. Section 9.6 discusses UNIX signals in detail.

A parent process can control the execution of a child process much more closely by using the **ptrace** (*process trace*) system call. This call is used primarily for interactive break point debugging such as that supported by the **dbx** command. When the child process is *traced* by its parent, the **wait** call also returns when the child process is stopped (suspended temporarily). In this case, the low-order byte of the variable *status* is set to the constant

WSTOPPED, which is:

```
#define WSTOPPED 0177
```

The high-order byte contains the signal that caused the suspension.

Figure 9.8 illustrates a simple example of the **fork** and **wait** system calls. The parent process calls **fork** twice and produces two child processes. Each child simply displays its own processid and terminates. The parent process calls **wait** twice to wait for the termination of the two child processes. After each **wait**, the processid and the wait status are displayed. Note that the second child in this example returns an exit status of 1, which causes the parent to display a corresponding wait status of 256 (which is consistent with how the bytes of the wait status are set). Note also that, in the example, the system call **getpid** is used to obtain the processid of a process. A similar system call, **getppid**, returns the parent processid of a process.

Figure 9.8 ▪ The fork and wait System Calls

```
#include <stdio.h>
#include <sys/wait.h>

main()
{       int pid1, pid2, pid;
        union wait status;

        if ((pid1 = fork()) == 0) {/* child one */
                printf("child pid=%d\n", getpid());
                _exit(0);
        }
        printf("forking again\n");

        if ((pid2 = fork()) == 0) {/* child two */
                printf("child pid=%d\n", getpid());
                _exit(1);
        }
        printf("first wait\n");
        pid = wait(&status);
        printf("pid=%d, status=%d\n", pid,
           status.w_status);
        printf("2nd wait\n");
        pid = wait(&status);
        printf("pid=%d, status=%d\n", pid,
           status.w_status);
}
```

Process Termination

A process may terminate execution in three different ways:

1. The process runs to completion and its main program returns.

2. The program calls the library routine **exit** or the system call **_exit**.

3. The process encounters an execution error or receives an interrupt signal that causes its termination.

The arguments to **_exit** and **exit** are part of the *termination status* of the process. Conventionally, a zero argument indicates normal termination, and a nonzero argument indicates abnormal termination. The low-order byte of this argument is put into the second byte (bits 8–15) of the *status* variable returned by a **wait** call. The low-order byte of this *status* variable contains the kernel's indication of how the process terminated (for example, by an interrupt signal, produced a core dump, and so on).

The system call:

```
_exit( status )
    int status;
```

terminates the calling process with the following consequences:

1. All the open descriptors in the calling process are closed.

2. If the parent process of the calling process is executing a **wait** or is interested in the SIGCHILD signal, then it is notified of the calling process's termination, and the low-order *status* byte is made available to it.

3. If the calling process still has unfinished child processes, the parent processid of each unfinished child is set to 1 (the *init process*).

Most C programs call the library routine **exit**, which performs cleanup actions on I/O buffers and so on before calling **_exit**. The **_exit** system call is used by a child process when it is necessary to not interfer with I/O buffers shared by parent and child processes.

9.5 The User Environment of a Process

The parameters *argc* and *argv* of a C program reference the explicit arguments given on the command line. Every time a process begins, another array of strings that represents the *user environment*, called the *environment list*, also is passed to the process. This sequence provides another way through which you can control the behavior of a process. If the function main is declared as:

```
main( argc, argv, arge )
int argc;
char *argv[ ];
char *arge[ ];
```

then *arge* is the environment list. Independent of *arge*, the environment list is always available for a process through the global variable:

```
extern char **environ
```

Each environment string arge[i] is in the form:

name = value

and is set by the user using the *csh* command **setenv** (or by the user using the *sh* assignment and the **export** commands). Environment variables and their values are contained in the environment list. Frequently used environment variables such as PATH, HOME, TERM, USER, and so on were discussed in Section 6.11.

The **execl** and **execv** system calls pass to the invoked program their current environment, which includes the user environment list. The system call:

```
execve( name, argv, envp )
    char *name;
    char *argv[ ];
    char *envp[ ];
```

can be used to pass a different user environment array *envp* to the named program. Figure 9.9 illustrates a simple C program that uses **execve**.

Figure 9.9 ▪ Passing the Environment List

```
/* passing modified environment with execve */
main(argc, argv, arge)
int argc;
char *argv[];
char *arge[];

{    char *envp[];
     envp[0]="first=foo";
     envp[1]="second=bar";
     execve("prog2",argv, envp);
     return(0);
}
```

Although direct access to **environ is possible, it is simpler to access user environment values in a C program using the library routine **getenv**:

```
char *getenv(name)
    char *name
```

This routine searches the environment list for a string of the form:

name=value

Figure 9.10

```
/*
 *      getenv(name)
 *      searches the global list **environ and
 *      returns a pointer to value associated with name, if any,
 *      else returns NULL.
 */
#define NULL 0
extern char **environ;
char *match();

char *getenv(str)
char *str;
{   char **ptr = environ;
    char *v;
    while (*ptr != NULL)
          if ((v = match(str, *ptr++)) != NULL)
                return(v);
    return(NULL);
}
/*
 *      both s1 and s2 are strings:
 *      s1 is a name, s2 is name=value.
 *      If the names match, value is returned, else NULL is returned.
 */
static char *match(s1, s2)
char *s1, *s2;
{   while (*s1 == *s2++)
          if (*s1++ == '=') return(s2);
          if (*s1 == '\0' && *(s2-1) == '=') return(s2);
    return(NULL);
}
```

and returns a pointer to *value* or zero if no match for name is found. A C version of the **getenv** routine is illustrated in Figure 9.10.

9.6 Interrupts and Signals

Events outside a process can affect process execution. The time when such an event would occur is not predictable. Thus, these events are called *asynchronous events*. Examples of such events include floating point exception (for example, overflow), illegal instruction, illegal memory reference, termination of a child process, expiration of a time slice, a message sent by another process, as well as interrupts typed by the user at the keyboard. Asynchronous events are treated in UNIX using the *signal* mechanism. UNIX sends a signal to a process to signify the occurrence of an event. After receiving a signal, a process will react to it in a well-defined manner. For example, the process may terminate execution, or it may be suspended for later resumption.

A system-defined default action is associated with each signal. A process normally reacts to a signal by performing the default action. A process has the ability to redefine its own reaction to any signal by specifying its own handling routine for the signal.

There are many different signals in UNIX. For instance, typing ^\ on the keyboard generates a signal known as *quit*. Sending the quit signal to a process forces it to terminate and produces a core image file for debugging. Each signal has a unique integer number, a symbolic name, and a default action defined by UNIX. Figure 9.11 shows some of the many signals UNIX handles. A complete list of all UNIX signals can be found in Appendix 10.

Sending Signals

You may send signals to processes connected to your terminal by typing the ^\, ^Z, and the interrupt character (usually ^C). These signals are summarized in the following table.

Csh Keyboard Interrupts		
Character	Signal	Default Effect on Foreground Process
DELETE or ^C	SIGINT	terminates execution
^\	SIGQUIT	terminates and dumps core
^Z	SIGSTOP	suspends for later resumption

The *terminal driver*, which is a program that processes I/O to the terminal, can detect these special characters and send the appropriate signal to your interactive shell. The shell in turn generates an appropriate signal to the foreground process (or process group). Note: *Sh* cannot handle ^Z.

The user can use either the *csh* built-in **kill** command or the regular UNIX **kill** command to send a specific signal to a named process. The general form of the **kill** command is:

```
kill [ -sig ] process
```

where *process* is a process number (or jobid in *csh*). The optional argument specifies a signal number *sig*. If no signal is specified, signal 15 (SIGTERM) is assumed, which instructs the target process to terminate.

In a C program, the system call:

```
kill( pid,sig_id ) ;
    int pid, sig_id;
```

is used to send a specified signal to a process identified by the given numerical pid.

Signal Delivery and Processing

When an interrupt or an event causes a signal to occur, the signal is added to a set of signals that are waiting for delivery to a process. Signals are delivered to a process in a manner similar to hardware interrupts. If the signal is not currently *blocked* by the process, it is delivered to the process following these steps:

1. The same signal is blocked from further occurrence until delivery and processing are finished.

2. The current process context is saved and a new one is built.

3. A handler function associated with the signal is called.

4. If the handler function returns, then the process resumes execution from the point of interrupt, with its saved context restored. Among other things, this means the *signal mask* is restored.

All signals have the same *priority*. A signal mask is an integer whose bits specify all signals currently being blocked from delivery to a process. The signal mask is initialized to that of its parent (normally 0, that is, nothing is blocked). It is modified when a signal is delivered, and it can be modified by the **sigblock** and **sigsetmask** system calls. A default signal handler exists for each signal. A process can replace a signal handler with a handler function of its own, which allows the process to *trap* a signal and deal with it in its own way. The SIGKILL and SIGSTOP signals cannot be trapped.

Signal Trapping

After receiving a signal, a process normally (by the default signal-handling function) either exits (terminates) or stops (is suspended). In some situations, it is desirable to react to specific signals differently. For example, a process may choose to ignore certain signals or to define its own handler functions.

The system call **signal** is used to trap signals:

```
#include <signal.h>
```

```
old_handler = signal(sig_id, handler);
    int sig_id;
    void (*handler)();
    void (*old_handler)();
```

where *sig_id* is the number or name of a signal and *handler* is the name of a C function. The handler function of the given signal is replaced by the specified *handler*, and a pointer to the old handler is returned.

If *handler* is SIG_DFL, the default action for the given signal is reinstated;

Figure 9.11 ▪ Some UNIX Signals

Symbol	Number	Default Action	Meaning
SIGHUP	1	exit	hangup (for example, lost connection to terminal)
SIGINT	2	exit	interrupt (for example, ˆC from keyboard)
SIGQUIT	3	core dump	quit (for example, ˆ\ from keyboard)
SIGILL	4	core dump	illegal instruction
SIGTRAP	5	core dump	trace trap
SIGFPE	8	core dump	floating point exception
SIGKILL	9	exit	terminate execution (cannot be caught or ignored)
SIGBUS	10	core dump	bus error
SIGSEGV	11	core dump	memory segmentation violation
SIGSYS	12	core dump	bad argument to system call
SIGVTALRM	26	exit	virtual time alarm
SIGPROF	27	exit	profiling timer alarm

default actions for some signals (in Berkeley UNIX) are indicated in Figure 9.11. If the handler is SIG_IGN, the signal is ignored, and pending instances of the signal are discarded. If the handler is a function defined in the user process, then it replaces the current handler.

A return from the handler function unblocks the handled signal and continues the process at the point it was interrupted. The handler function remains until changed by another call to **signal**.

After a **fork** (**vfork**) the child inherits all signal-handling functions set up by the parent. The **execve** system call resets all caught signals to the default action, but ignored signals remain ignored.

The C program in Figure 9.12 is a simple example that illustrates the use of the **signal** system call to trap the SIGINT (interrupt from terminal) signal and how that call adds 1 to a counter for each such signal received. Of course, counting the number of signals received is of limited application. A more practical example has to do with cleaning up any temporary files used by a process before termination caused by a user interrupt (Figure 9.13). It is important to note that trapping of SIGINT is desirable only if it is not being ignored. If a process runs with its signal environment already set to ignore certain signals, then those signals should continue to be ignored instead of trapped. For example, the *sh* shell arranges a background process to ignore SIGINT generated from the keyboard. If a process proceeds to trap SIGINT

Figure 9.12 ▪ Trapping Keyboard Interrupts

```
/* This program demonstrates the use of signal to trap interrupts from the
   terminal. To terminate the program type control-\  */

#include <signal.h>

main()
{
    void cnt();
    signal(SIGINT,cnt);
    printf("Begin counting INTERRUPTs\n");
    for(;;); /* infinite loop */
}

void cnt()
{
    static int count=0;
    printf(" interrupt received = %d\n", count++);
}
```

Figure 9.13 ■ Removal of Temporary File After an Interrupt

```c
#include <stdio.h>
#include <signal.h>
#include <strings.h>
#include <sys/file.h>
char *tempfile;

main()
{    void onintr();
     extern char *tempfile;
     char *malloc();
     int tfd;

     if (signal(SIGINT, SIG_IGN) != SIG_IGN)
          signal(SIGINT, onintr);

     /* make a unique name for the temporary file */
     tempfile=malloc(24);
     sprintf(tempfile,"/tmp/temp%d",getpid());

     /* create temporary file for read/write */
     tfd = open(tempfile, O_CREAT|O_RDWR, 0600);
      if (tfd == -1) {
           fprintf(stderr,"failed to open %s\n", tempfile);
           exit(1);
           }

     /* other code of the program   */

     unlink(tempfile); /* remove temporary file before termination */
     return(0);
}

void onintr()
{    extern char* tempfile;
     unlink(tempfile);
     exit(1);
}
```

Figure 9.14 ▪ The signal and longjmp System Calls

```
#include <signal.h>
#include <setjmp.h>
jmp_buf top;

main()
{    void onintr();

    if (signal(SIGINT, SIG_IGN) != SIG_IGN)
            signal(SIGINT, onintr);

    setjmp(top);
    /* top level loop ... */
}
void onintr()
{    printf("\n interrupt-- return to top level\n");
    longjmp(top);
}
```

without checking to see if it is being ignored, the arrangement made by the shell would be defeated.

As with interactive utilities such as the **vi** editor and the **lisp** interpreter, it often is desirable to use the keyboard interrupt for "abort to top level" within the program. This function can be performed easily by combining signal trapping with the **longjmp** mechanism (Figure 9.14).

When the signal-handler function returns, or when a process resumes after being stopped by ^Z (SIGSTOP), the process resumes at the exact point at which it was interrupted. This is true except for interrupts that occur during certain system calls or during the reading of input from the terminal. For interrupted system calls, the external errno is set to EINTR, and the system call returns a –1. For reading input from the terminal, a partially typed line just before the interrupt is lost.

9.7 The pipe System Call

A *pipe* is a direct (in memory) I/O channel between processes. A pipe can be thought of as a first-in-first-out character buffer with a read descriptor that points to one end of the pipe and a write descriptor that points to the other end of the pipe. To establish a pipe, the system call:

pipe(*fildes*)
    int *fildes*[2];

is used. This call establishes a pipe and two descriptors:

fildes[0]   for reading the pipe
fildes[1]   for writing the pipe

The **pipe** system call is used in conjunction with subsequent **fork** calls to establish multiple processes that have access to the same pipe, therefore allowing them to communicate directly through the pipe. Consider the code listed in Figure 9.15. After the **fork**, both parent and child have their copies of fildes[0] and fildes[1], which each refer to the same pipe buffer. The child closes its write descriptor, and the parent closes it read descriptor. Now the child process can read what the parent writes into the pipe buffer. Figure 9.16 shows a parent process writing the message "Hello there" to a child process through a pipe.

Now we are ready to establish a pipe between two processes to run arbitrary programs. To do this, we must combine the **pipe**, **fork**, and **exec** system calls. It is best to look at an example.

Establishing a Pipe Between Two UNIX Commands

A command **mypipe** implemented in C takes as arguments two commands that are separated by a %. It pipes the standard output of the first command

Figure 9.15 ▪ The pipe and fork System Calls

```
int fildes[2];

pipe(fildes); /* setting up the pipe */
if (fork() == 0) {
        close(fildes[1]);
        /* child reads fildes[0] */
        close(fildes[0]);   _exit(0);
        };
close(fildes[0]);
/* parent writes fildes[1] */
```

Figure 9.16 ▪ A Simple pipe Example

```c
#include <stdio.h>
#include <strings.h>
#include <sys/wait.h>

main(argc,argv)
int argc;
char **argv;
{
    int i,pid, p[2];
    wait union status;
    char *buffer[20];

    pipe(p);                              /* setting up the pipe */

    if ((pid = fork ()) == 0) {           /* child code */
       close(p[1]);                       /* child closes p[1] */
       if ((i = read(p[0], buffer, 20)) == -1) {
           perror("child failed");        /* read failed */
           _exit(1);
           }
       printf("%s: received by child\n", buffer);
       _exit(0);                          /* child terminates */
       };

    close(p[0]);                          /* parent writes p[1] */
    write(p[1], "Hello there", 11);
    wait(&status) ;                       /* waiting for pid */
    if (status.w_status == 0) printf("child finished\n");
       else printf("child failed\n");
    return(0);
    }
```

to the standard input of the second command (Figure 9.17). Thus, for instance:

mypipe /bin/ls –l % /bin/grep pwang

should work as expected (that is, as **ls** –l | **grep** pwang). The key in this example is the connecting of stdin in one process to the read end of a pipe and the connecting of stdout in another process to the write end of the pipe. This procedure is accomplished by the **dup2** system call. Let us examine the **dup**

Figure 9.17 ▪ The mypipe Command

```
#include <stdio.h>
#include <strings.h>

main(argc,argv)
int argc;
char **argv;
{     int p[2];
      int i,pid1,pid2, status;
      wait union status;

      argv++;                             /* lose command name */
      for (i = 1; i <= argc; i++)
           if (strcmp(argv[i],"%") == 0) {
                 argv[i] = NULL; break; };
      pipe(p);                            /* setting up the pipe */

      if ((pid1 = fork ()) == 0) {        /* child one */
          close(p[1]);
          dup2(p[0],0);                   /* 0 becomes a duplicate of p[0] */
          close(p[0]);
          execv(argv[i+1],&argv[i+1]);    /* this reads the pipe */
          _exit(1);                       /* bad error execv failed */
          }
      if ((pid2 = fork ()) == 0) {        /* child two */
          close(p[0]);
          dup2(p[1],1);                   /* 1 becomes a duplicate of p[1] */
          close(p[1]);
          execv(argv[0],argv);            /* this writes the pipe */
          _exit(1);                       /* bad error execv failed */
          }
      /* parent does not use pipe */
      close(p[0]);      close(p[1]);

      while (wait(&status)!=pid1);        /* while loop waiting for pid1 */

      if (status == 0) printf("%s terminated\n", argv[i+1]);
          else printf("%s failed\n", argv[i+1]);
      return(0);
}
```

and **dup2** system calls together:

```
copyfd = dup(fd)
      int copyfd, fd;

dup2(fd, copyfd)
      int copyfd, fd;
```

The **dup** system call duplicates an existing I/O descriptor *fd*. The argument *fd* is a small nonnegative integer index in the per-process descriptor table; its value must be less than the size of the table. The size of the table can be obtained by the system call **getdtablesize**. The duplicate entry is made in the descriptor table using the lowest numbered table entry not currently in use by the process. The index (which is the descriptor) of this duplicate entry is returned as the value of the **dup** call. After **dup**, two descriptors point to the same I/O object.

For the **dup2** call, the index *copyfd* of the duplicate descriptor is specified. If this descriptor is already in use, it first is released, as if a **close**(*copyfd*) had been performed.

9.8 I/O to Terminals

On UNIX systems, each terminal line is represented by a terminal special file under the directory /dev. Conventionally, a terminal special file has a name with a tty prefix (for example, tty00, tty0a, and ttyd4). When UNIX goes into the multiuser mode, the init process (process 1) establishes an *initial login process* for each hardwired and dial-in terminal line on the system. The initial login process can handle a user's login request on a particular terminal. The init process uses a database file /etc/ttys that specifies which terminal special files should be opened, what type of terminal is connected to each line, and how to invoke an initial login process for that line. There is one entry in /etc/ttys per terminal special file. Each entry specifies the tty name, whether it is connected, the command (usually /etc/getty) for the initial login process, and some other parameters.

The init Process and Terminal Lines

To begin multiuser operation, init creates (by **fork**) a child process (normally /etc/getty) for each terminal line on which a user may log in. Each of these child processes opens the appropriate terminal special file for reading and writing. The I/O descriptors (the standard input, standard output, and standard error output) thus established receive file descriptors 0, 1, and 2, respectively.

Opening the terminal may involve a delay, since the **open** system call may not be completed until a hardwired terminal is turned on or a dial-in line receives an incoming call and establishes a modem connection. After the terminal special file is opened successfully, the getty process will prompt for a login name. It then uses **exec** on the executable file /bin/login (the **login** command), passing to it the userid.

The login process prompts for a password, checks the password, initializes the user's environment (userid, groupid, home directory, and so on), displays certain messages (message of the day, time of last login, existence of mail), and then uses **exec** to call up a shell as specified in the user's **passwd** entry. Ultimately, the shell will terminate when the user logs out. The init process, which has been waiting for such an event, wakes up, performs some bookkeeping, and initiates another child getty process that opens the appropriate terminal line.

The getty Process

A getty process is invoked by the init process to open and initialize I/O to a terminal and to read a login name. It usually is invoked as:

`/etc/getty` [*arg*]

An *argument* is used as an index into the gettytab database (/etc/gettytab), which obtains parameters suitable for the terminal line. Each gettytab entry specifies terminal characteristics using the termcap format discussed later in this section. If there is no argument or there is no such gettytab entry, the default gettytab entry is used. If there is no /etc/gettytab, a set of system defaults is used. If indicated by the entry, getty will clear the terminal screen, display a banner heading, and prompt for a login name (userid). Usually either the banner or the login prompt includes the system hostname.

Getty reads the user's name one character at a time. Any time a null character is received, it is assumed to be transmitted by pressing the BREAK key. When a null character is received, it causes the line speed (baud rate) to change to the next setting as specified by the gettytab entry, and the login prompt is displayed again. Successive BREAK characters cycle through all the speed settings for the line.

The login name is terminated by a NEWLINE character or RETURN. The latter results in the terminal *device driver* being set to treat RETURNs. Since UNIX distinguishes between uppercase and lowercase characters and most UNIX commands are lower case, getty scans the user's login name to see if it contains any lowercase alphabetic characters. If not, and if the userid is nonempty, then getty assumes the user is using an all-uppercase terminal, and the system is told to change all uppercase characters (unless preceded by a \) to lower case.

Finally, getty performs **exec** on /bin/login with the userid as an argument.

The Control Terminal

When a process with no control terminal opens a terminal special file, then that terminal becomes the control terminal for the process. The control terminal is inherited by a child process. Thus, a getty process and eventually the user's shell have the same control terminal. Besides file descriptors 0, 1, and 2, the file /dev/tty is, in each process, a reference to the control terminal. The /dev/tty file is useful for programs that want to ensure a message display capability on the terminal, no matter how the output has been redirected.

Command interpreters such as *csh* arbitrates (switches) the terminal between different jobs by placing related jobs in a single process group and switching the terminal among different process groups. I/O through the control terminal is processed by a *terminal driver* program, which drives the physical I/O hardware. A terminal driver in Berkeley UNIX facilitates, among other things, job control as provided by *csh*.

The Terminal Driver

The terminal driver occurs between the terminal and the program that receives input from and sends output to the terminal (Figure 9.18). The terminal driver performs important services for the interactive use of the UNIX system. It has three major modes, which are characterized by the amount of processing on the input and output characters:

cooked   This is the normal mode. In this mode, lines of input are collected and input editing is performed. The edited line is made available when it is completed by a NEWLINE or when a ^D is entered. A RETURN usually is made synonymous with a NEWLINE in this mode and is replaced by a NEWLINE whenever it is typed. All driver functions (editing and interrupt generation for input, delay

---

Figure 9.18 ▪ The Terminal Driver

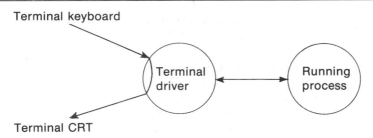

generation and tab expansion for output, and so on) are performed in this mode.

cbreak   This mode does not support the *erase character*, *kill word*, and *kill line* input editing facilities. The input character is made available to the program as it is typed. Flow control, literal-next (quoting), and interrupt processing still are performed in this mode. Full output processing also is performed.

raw   This mode provides no input processing and makes all input characters available as they are typed. No output processing is performed either.

A program usually uses the cooked mode for terminal I/O. However, if a program, for instance **vi**, needs to receive each input character as soon as it is typed in by the user, the cbreak mode should be used.

Input Processing

A UNIX terminal ordinarily operates in *full-duplex*. Characters may be typed at any time, even while output is occurring, and are only lost when the system's character input buffers become completely full, which is rare, or when the user has accumulated the maximum number of input characters allowable that have not yet been read by some program. Currently this limit is 256 characters. When this limit is reached, the terminal driver refuses to accept any further input and sounds the terminal beeper.

Input characters normally are accepted in either even or odd parity. The parity bit is stripped off before the character is given to the program. Input characters normally are echoed by putting them in an output queue as they arrive. In the cooked mode, the terminal input is processed in units of lines. A program that attempts a **read** normally will be suspended until an entire line has been received. If the requested number of characters in the **read** call is less than the number of characters in this input line, the remaining characters are available for the next **read**. Otherwise, the entire line is returned.

Input editing enables the use of the character erase, word kill, and line kill characters. On CRTs, these characters often are set to ^H, ^W, and ^U, respectively. These characters may be quoted by a \.

The driver normally treats either a RETURN or a NEWLINE character as terminating an input line. Thus, it then replaces the RETURN with a NEWLINE character and echoes a RETURN and a line feed.

The driver also has a *literal-next* (quote) character, ^V, which can be used in both the cooked and the cbreak modes. Preceding any character by ^V will prevent its special meaning. For example, typing ^V followed by the character erase is the way to enter that character. This input is preferable to the use of \. The reprint character, normally ^R, retypes the pending input (the current input line not yet terminated) beginning on a new line. Retyping occurs automatically in the cooked mode if characters that normally would be erased from the screen are fouled by program output.

Input Echoing and Redisplay

The terminal driver handles echoing of input characters, taking appropriate actions to erase characters resulting from input editing. Different actions can be selected for a CRT and a hard-copy terminal. Control characters normally are not echoed literally to the terminal. A CONTROL-X is echoed as the two-character sequence ^X. Delete is echoed as ^?.

Interrupt Generation

Several interrupt characters generate signals when typed in the cooked and cbreak modes. These signals are sent to the processes in the control group of the terminal. These interrupt characters also flush pending terminal input and output when typed in at a terminal. They are listed as follows:

^? (DELETE)	Generates a SIGINT signal. This is the normal way to abort a process that is no longer interesting or to regain control in an interactive program.
^	Generates a SIGQUIT signal. This is used to instruct a program to terminate and produce a core image, if possible, in the file named core in the current directory.
^Z	Generates a SIGTSTP signal, which is used to suspend the current process group.
^Y	Generates a SIGTSTP signal as does ^Z, but this signal is sent when a program attempts to read the ^Y, rather than when it is typed.

Output Processing

Characters output to the terminal from programs join any echoed input characters in the "output queue" of the terminal driver. Characters in the output queue are displayed on the terminal as soon as the previous character is displayed. When a process produces characters more rapidly than they can be displayed, the process will be suspended when the length of its output queue exceeds some limit and will resume when the queue has drained to some specified threshold. Even parity is used when a parity bit is needed on output (not in the raw mode). The EOT (end-of-transmission) character is not transmitted in the cooked mode to prevent terminals that respond to it from hanging up. Programs that use the raw or cbreak modes should take care of the EOT themselves.

Delay generation for certain special characters is performed in the cooked and cbreak modes. For example, delays are available after BACKSPACE (^H), form feeds (^L), RETURNs (^M), TABs (^I), and NEWLINEs (^J). The driver also will expand TABs optionally into spaces, where the TAB stops are assumed to be set every eight columns. Output mapping for all-uppercase terminals is part of output processing as well.

The terminal driver supports an *output flush character*, normally ^O. This character sets a control bit and causes subsequent output to be flushed until the control bit is cleared by a program or until more input is typed in on the terminal.

An important part of output processing is *flow control*. A *stop* character, normally ^S, and a *start* character, normally ^Q, instructs output to the terminal to be suspended and to be resumed, respectively. Extra stop characters typed when output already is stopped have no effect, unless the start and stop characters are the same character, in which case output resumes.

It is possible to put the terminal driver into the *tandem* mode. In this mode, the program outputs a stop character (default ^S) when the input queue is in danger of overflowing, and it outputs a start character (default ^Q) when the input queue has drained sufficiently. This mode is useful when the terminal is actually another computer that obeys these conventions.

Setting Terminal Options

The terminal driver allows for flexible treatment of terminal I/O. The user may set many options to make the system work well with almost any terminal. Furthermore, the system provides different device drivers, called *line disciplines*, for the control of terminal lines. For example, the following line disciplines are available on Berkeley UNIX systems:

old   The old (standard) terminal driver. This driver can be used when using the *sh* shell and for compatibility with AT&T UNIX systems.

new   A newer terminal driver, with features for job control. This driver must be used when using *csh*. This is the terminal driver described earlier in this section.

At the user level the command:

stty [*option*] ...

is used to set the many options for the terminal driver and to select line disciplines. For example:

stty crt −tabs kill^U erase ^?' intr^C

sets the following options:

crt	Uses BACKSPACE for erasing characters on a CRT terminal.
−tabs	Replaces a TAB with an equivalent number of spaces on output.
kill c	Uses the given character c as the kill line character.
erase c	Uses the character c as the erase character.
intr c	Uses the character c as the interrupt character.

Many other options are available. Refer to the UNIX manual pages for the **stty** command for details. When the command **stty** is issued with no arguments, it reports the speed and options that are different from the default settings for the control terminal. The argument *all* reports all normally used settings. The argument *everything* reports all known option settings. For example, the output in Figure 9.19 is produced by the command:

stty all

The ioctl System Call

The **ioctl** system call controls the way I/O is performed through a device driver. The exact arguments given depend on the device driver. Here, how **ioctl** is used to control terminal I/O is described. One form is:

```
#include <sgtty.h>

ioctl( fd, code, &arg);
    int fd, code;
    struct sgttyb arg;
```

Figure 9.19 ▪ Output from stty all

```
new tty, speed 1200 baud; −tabs ff1
crt
erase kill  werase rprnt flush lnext susp intr quit stop eof
^?    ^U    ^W     ^R    ^O    ^V    ^Z/^Y ^C   ^\   ^S/^Q ^D
```

where *fd* is a descriptor of the special file, *code* is specified using defined constants, and *arg* is a pointer to a structure given by:

```
struct sgttyb {
      char sg_ispeed;
      char sg_ospeed;
      char sg_erase;
      char sg_kill;
      short sg_flags;
};
```

The first two fields of this structure describe the input and output speeds. The sg_flags contains bit settings for the various options such as the cooked, c break, and raw modes for terminal I/O. For example, the TIOCGETP and TIOCSETP codes retrieve and set option parameters using the supplied structure *arg*:

```
struct sgttyb arg;
ioctl(1, TIOCGETP, &arg);
```

As another example, line discipline switching is accomplished with the TIOC-SETD **ioctl** code:

```
int ldisc = line_disc
ioctl(fd, TIOCSETD, &ldisc)
```

where *line_disc* is OTTYDISC for the standard tty driver and NTTYDISC is for the new driver. The current line discipline can be obtained with the TIOCGETD code. Pending input is discarded when the line discipline is changed.

A large number of **ioctl** calls exist for terminal I/O. Refer to the UNIX manual pages on tty for more details.

Terminal Capability Database

Programs such as **vi** and **more** work on many kinds of terminals that have different characteristics and escape codes. This device independence is achieved through the use of a database that contains descriptions of the characteristics and the capabilities of most terminals. This database is the *termcap* database, which usually is kept in the file /etc/termcap. Any program that uses terminal-dependent capabilities can obtain the name of the terminal from the environment variable TERM and retrieve a description of the terminal from termcap. A program written in this manner will work with any terminal that has a terminal description entry in termcap.

A terminal is described in termcap by specifying its capabilities and by describing how operations are performed. Each different terminal or model is described by a separate entry. An entry in termcap consists of a number of fields separated by colons (:). The first field for each entry gives one or more names for the terminal, which are separated by | characters. For historical reasons, the first name is always a two-character abbreviation, which usually is followed by commonly known names for the terminal, the last of which may contain multiple words for readability. To refer to a termcap entry, any of the specified names can be used.

After the name field are fields that specify terminal capabilities. All of these capabilities have two-character codes. For example, bs represents "can backspace with ˆH." The number of columns, co is a *numerical* capability. A numerical capability code is followed by the character # and then the value. For instance:

co#80   (80 columns)

li#24   (24 lines)

A *string* capability is specified by a = following the code and then a string that defines any associated delay and/or escape character sequence. For example:

dc=\EP   ESCape P for delete-character operation

cl=\EH\EJ   ESCape H followed by ESCape J for clear-screen operation

kl=\ED   ESCape D is transmitted by the LEFT ARROW

Each termcap entry is specified on one line that can, of course, be continued with the usual \ at the end of a line. Figure 9.20 defines a common subset of the capabilities for most popular Hewlett-Packard terminals.

Similar Terminals

Different terminals may be quite similar in their capabilities, especially if they are from the same vendor. For such terminals, one can be described as being

---

Figure 9.20 ▪ A Termcap Entry Common to Many HP Terminals

```
h0|hpsub|hp terminals -- capability subset:\
     :if=/usr/lib/tabset/stdcrt:\
     :al=\EL:am:bs:\
     :cd=\EJ:ce=\EK:ch=\E&a%dC:cl=\EH\EJ:\
     :co#80:da:db:dc=\EP:dl=\EM:do=\EB:ei=\ER:\
     :kb=ˆH:kd=\EB:kh=\Eh:kl=\ED:kr=\EC:ku=\EA:\
     :ke=\E&s0A:ks=\E&s1A:\
     :li#24:mi:nd=\EC\pt:\
     :se=\E&d@:so=\E&dB:\
     :up=\EA:xs:
```

just like another with certain additions and exceptions. These terminals can appear in the termcap database by describing the additional capabilities and exceptions first followed by the name of another termcap entry. This name is given in the form of a string capability, which must appear as the last field using the code tc. For example, the entry:

```
hh|262x|hp 262x series:\
      :bt=\Ei:\
      :tc=hp:
```

specifies that any terminal in the HP 262x series (that is, 2622, 2624, and so on) is the same as the basic HP termcap entry with the additional bt (back tab) feature. When such an entry is used, the last tc field is replaced by the full specification of the named entry (the hp entry in this example). Since an entry's fields are searched from left to right, the capabilities given at the left override the ones in the similar terminal. A capability can be canceled with *xx*@ where *xx* is the capability code.

Library routines are provided for extracting and using the termcap data base. These routines, a list of terminal capability codes and other details on termcap can be found in the UNIX manual.

9.9 A Screen-Updating Library

The *curses* package is a library of C functions that help C programs accomplish most common CRT-dependent operations such as updating the screen, cursor motion optimization, and so on with relative ease. The library provides many functions that deal with manipulating data displayed on the CRT screen. The package uses *windows*, which are logical data structures capable of representing the entire terminal screen or a portion of it. If a window is as large as the entire terminal screen, then it is referred to as a *screen*. After initialization, curses establishes two screens: *curscr* for the current state of the terminal screen and *stdscr* for the next state of the terminal screen. After modifications are made to stdscr, a function is called to refresh the terminal screen. This function performs all the necessary computations to update the terminal and the curscr screen.

The user is not limited to the curscr and the stdscr screens. In fact, any number of named screens and windows can be established to help manipulate and update the terminal screen, making it relatively easy to maintain multiple windows on a CRT screen. One program that uses multiple windows is the UNIX **talk** command.

To use the curses library, the line:

```
#include <curses.h>
```

must appear at the beginning of the C source file. To compile a file with curses function calls, use:

```
cc [flags] file ... -lcurses -ltermlib [libs]
```

Basic Usage

The curses package provides a full set of library routines for I/O to windows established on the screen and for manipulation of the windows. We present a brief overview of the basic steps involved in using the curses package. The reader is referred to the article "Screen Updating and Cursor Movement Optimization: A Library Package" in the UNIX manual for more details.

To use curses, you basically follow these steps:

- *Initialization:* In a program that uses curses, you first set the variables LINES and COLS to the number of lines and columns of the terminal, then you call **initscr( )**. This sequence properly initializes curses including the establishment of the screens curscr and stdscr.

- *Establishing windows:* After initialization, you are ready to establish additional windows if needed. The call **newwin(***line,col,y,x***)** establishes a new window at position (y,x) with the given number of lines and columns and returns a windowid (wid) for future operations to reference the window. Note curses uses (y,x) for the position line y character x in a window.

- *I/O to windows:* The basic functions that modify stdscr are **move(***y,x***)** to move the current position to location (y,x) and **addch(***c***)** to add the character c at the current position. The two operations can be combined into **mvaddch(***y,x,c***)**. A call to **refresh( )** will update the terminal screen according to stdscr. The function **getch( )** reads a character from the stdscr. For other windows, **waddch(***wid,c***)** adds a character, and **wgetch(***wid***)** gets a character.

- *Finishing:* Because **initscr( )** usually sets tty modes, the routine **endwin( )** should be called to restore the default modes before exiting.

9.10 I/O Multiplexing

In some applications, the need arises to multiplex I/O requests among a number of descriptors that maybe files and/or sockets (see Section 10.6). For example, the **talk** command uses I/O multiplexing among different terminals.

Figure 9.21 ▪ I/O Multiplexing

```
#include <sys/time.h>

    struct timeval wait;
    int fd1, fd2, read_mask, nready;
    wait.tv_sec = 2
    wait.tv_usec = 0;
    ...
    read_mask = (1 << fd1) | (1 << fd2)
    ...
    nready = select(32, &read_mask, 0, 0, &wait);
```

The **select** system call provides a synchronous multiplexing scheme:

```
#include <sys/time.h>
```

```
nfound = select(nfds, readfds, writefds, exceptfds, timeout)
    int nfound, nfds, *readfds, *writefds, *exceptfds;
    struct timeval *timeout;
```

The **select** call examines the I/O descriptors specified by the bit masks *readfds*, *writefds*, and *exceptfds* to see if any of them are ready for reading, writing, or have an exceptional condition pending, respectively. Bits 0 through *nfds*-1 of each mask are examined. The *n*th bit of a mask represents the I/O descriptor *n*. That is, if bit *n* of a mask is 1, then file descriptor *n* is examined. For example, if *readfds* is 1, then I/O descriptor 0 is examined for data available for reading. When **select** returns, the bit masks are modified to indicate (in the same manner) the I/O descriptors that are ready. The integer value *nfound* returned by **select** is the total number of ready descriptors. The parameter *timeout* is a nonzero pointer that specifies a maximum time interval the call is to wait before **select** is to return. To affect a poll (an instantaneous survey of I/O readiness), the *timeout* argument should be nonzero and point to a zero-valued timeval structure. If *timeout* is a zero pointer, **select** blocks indefinitely. The code fragment in Figure 9.21 is an example of the **select** system call.

9.11 Summary

This chapter describes the UNIX system facilities for I/O, file manipulation, and process management. I/O descriptors are used to refer to I/O channels established by calls such as **open** and **pipe**. The commands **read** and **write** can be used for I/O on any descriptors. Every process is initiated with the three descriptors 0, 1, and 2 for stdin, stdout, and stderr, respectively.

UNIX provides a full complement of calls for access to and manipulation of files and directories. For example:

`creat`	creates a file	`chmod`	changes the file mode
`unlink`	deletes a directory entry	`chown`	changes the file owner
`mkdir`	creates a new directory	`stat`	obtains file status information
`rmdir`	deletes an empty directory		

The **fork** and **exec** calls are used to create concurrent processes and to initiate different tasks. The executing environment of the parent process is passed on to a child process. The operating system maintains vital information about each process in the *process table*. The **pipe** call is used to establish a first-in-first-out I/O channel between two processes (related through **fork**). The **pipe** call can be used to establish a pipe between any two commands.

When a process receives an interrupt, its usual response is to terminate execution. The **signal** call is used to trap an interrupt and replace the default action with other program-defined operations.

UNIX provides extensive processing for I/O to the terminal. The terminal driver provides three service modes: cooked for the normal mode with full I/O processing, cbreak for no input line editing or line buffering for input, and raw for no transformation or buffering whatsoever.

Terminal independent operations are supported by the termcap data base, library routines, and the curses package. Synchronous I/O multiplexing is performed with the **select** call.

Exercises

1. Use **open** on files to implement exclusive program execution in which only one invocation of the program is allowed to exist at any time. This situation occurs when you are using a device that should be given exclusively to one user (like a printer).

2. Write your own version of a simple **cp** program (file to file) using low-level I/O.

3. Write a program that will display the information given by the **stat** system call for each file given as its argument.

4. Rewrite the script **mapc** given in Chapter 6 in the C language.

5. Write a program **quiet** that will **fork** off a process, executing its arguments. The process should return immediately so that nothing appears to happen. The net effect is that if:

   `quiet` *command arguments*

   is typed on the terminal, the *command* will be applied to the *arguments* in the background. Check your command with:

   `quiet sleep 300`

   Also try running **ps** with **quiet**.

6. Write your own version of the **system** subroutine. You may use a *csh* or *sh* shell to parse the arguments if you wish. Remember to wait for the process to end.

7. Write a program that displays the value of the environment variables PATH, HOME, USER, TERM, and other variables specified as arguments in the command line.

8. Write a program that will display a regular *csh* prompt and will echo each line typed after the prompt with the message: "Syntax error." Any interrupt characters should elicit the answer: "You cannot get rid of me THAT way!" and provide the user with another prompt. How can you exit this program? For added effect, the terminal can be set to the raw no-echo mode.

9. Write a program A that produces two child processes B and C. Establish a pipeline A to B to C back to A, so that a character written by A into the pipe will be read back by A in a circular fashion.

10. Write a program **nls** that is similar to the **ls** command but that, by default, displays regular files and directories separately.

11. Write a program **vcl** (visual clean) that performs functions of the **clean** script as given in Chapter 6 with the additional feature that the directory to be cleaned is displayed visually on the screen and the "current file" is indicated by the cursor, which can be moved **vi** style (h, j, k, and l) to any file displayed on the screen.

12. Write a program, using a mixture of C and shell commands if you wish, to provide a facility that takes a C source program as input and generates a list of correctly formatted #include statements for system header files.

13. Write a version of the **calendar** program that will do the following:
    a. Recognize the days of the week.
    b. Allow the specification of years.
    c. Understand the names and dates of customary holidays.
    d. Take phrases such as "last day of April" and "every other month."
    e. Delete entries no longer needed automatically.
    f. Remove the restriction of one entry per line.

Communications and Networking 10

A
s computer hardware becomes increasingly powerful and affordable, the need to connect computers together and have them communicate grows accordingly. There are different kinds of connections between computers. The standard RS232-type connection, which connects terminals to computers, also can connect two computers in such a way that each appears to the other as a terminal. Communication through dial-up lines with high-speed modems is another possibility, although these connections are inferior in terms of speed, quality, functionality, and reliability.

Communication between computers enables services such as file transfer, electronic mail, remote login, and distributed file systems and processes. To achieve such services, a combination of networking hardware and software must exist. To allow individual (likely different) computer systems to communicate successfully, *protocols* must be established to govern every detail in the information exchange between *foreign* computers.

In this chapter, the major UNIX facilities for communications and networking are presented. Both user-level commands and system-level mechanisms are discussed. The *interprocess communication* (*ipc*) facility of Berkeley UNIX is explained in detail. Ipc supports multiple communications domains within which communication endpoints, known as *sockets*, can be established. Processes communicate through sockets that are on the same or on different computer systems. Examples of how to use these UNIX networking facilities are given as C programs.

10.1 Connecting to a Remote System with tip

The **tip** command invokes a communications program that allows the user to connect and log in to a remote system. It can be thought of as a terminal emulation program. The local system (the system that runs **tip**) serves as a terminal to the remote system, which does not have to be a UNIX system. The general forms of the **tip** command are:

```
tip [ -v ] [ - speed ] system-name
tip [ -v ] [ - speed ] phone-number
```

The **tip** command establishes a full-duplex communications channel to the specified system, giving the appearance that your terminal is connected to the remote computer. After the communication is established, you'll see the login prompt of that remote system. From this point on, whatever you type into your terminal is transmitted directly to the remote system, and output from the remote system is displayed on your terminal. Of course, you must have an account on that system and follow its login procedure. For example:

```
tip -1200 18005551313
```

instructs **tip** to call the given number and to establish a connection at 1200 baud.

In addition to relaying characters between your terminal and the remote system, the **tip** program supports a set of useful single-character *requests*. These requests are issued using an *escape character* (default ~). The **tip** command treats a ~ at the beginning of a line in the following way:

1. The ~ is not echoed on your screen immediately as typed.

2. Whether or not the ~ is transmitted to the remote system depends on the next character you type.

3. If the next character specifies a valid **tip** request, then the entire line is taken to be a **tip** command and therefore is not transmitted to the remote system. The **tip** request is carried out, and you then are returned to the remote system.

4. If the next character is another ˜, then a single ˜, together with the rest of the line, is transmitted to the remote system. This sequence provides an escape for the escape character.

5. Otherwise, everything on the line, including the first ˜, is transmitted to the remote system.

The basic purpose of the **tip** requests is to facilitate file transfer between the local and the remote systems. The following requests are recognized:

~^D or ~.	Drops the connection and exits from **tip**. If you have not logged out on the remote system, you still may be logged in after the connection is dropped.
˜>	Transmits a file on the local system to the remote system. The > is used in the spirit of output redirection. The **tip** program prompts for the name of a local file to transmit. The effect of this request is that the content of the file will be typed to the remote system as though you had typed it in at your keyboard. This request of itself does not create a file automatically on the remote system.
~<	Stores the output of a command executed on the remote system in a local file. The **tip** program prompts first for the name of the local file to be created and then for a command to be executed on the remote computer.
~c [dir]	Changes the **tip** current working directory (on the local system, of course) to *dir* or your home directory if no argument is supplied.
~!	Invokes a subshell. Exiting the shell will return you to **tip**.
~p from [to]	Copies the local file *from* to the remote file *to*. If *to* is not specified, the same name is used. This sequence is used when the remote computer also runs a UNIX or a UNIX-like system.
~t from [to]	Instructs **tip** to copy the remote file *from* to a local file *to*. The same name is used if *to* is unspecified. Again, this sequence is used when the remote computer also runs a UNIX or a UNIX-like system.
~s	Sets a **tip** variable (more details in the next subsection).
~^Z	Suspends **tip** (by the *csh* job control mechanism).
~?	Displays a summary of the tilde escapes.

Let us now describe how to transfer files using **tip**. If you are connected to a foreign system via **tip**, and you wish to transfer a file to that foreign system, you can take the following steps:

1. Invoke a text editor on the foreign system.

2. Open the insert text mode in the editor.

3. Type in the **tip** command ~> to transfer a local file.

4. When **tip** prompts for a file name, you can give the local file name to be transmitted.

5. The **tip** program now will transmit all characters in the given file as if you were typing them. The characters are inserted in the editor buffer on the remote system.

6. After **tip** has finished transmitting the file, you are returned to the remote system.

7. Now you can edit and save the file on the foreign system.

On the other hand, if you wish to transfer a file from the foreign system to your local system, do the following:

1. Type in the **tip** command ~<.

2. You will be prompted to provide a file name on the local system. Type in a file name of your choice.

3. Now you will be prompted to provide a command to be executed on the remote system. Give a command to the remote system to display on the terminal the contents of the file you wish to transfer.

4. After the file is displayed, you may end the transaction with an interrupt.

When **tip** prompts for an argument (for example, during setup of a file transfer), the input line may be edited with the standard erase and kill characters. The line is terminated by a RETURN. A null line in response to a prompt or an interrupt will abort the dialogue and return you to the remote computer. During file transfers, **tip** displays a running count of the number of lines transferred.

The data file /etc/remote contains a description of known remote systems. It contains such information as system names, transmission speeds, parities used, and so on. The **tip** program uses this information to operate the connection to a remote system. If a speed is given on the command line (as a baud rate), then it overrides any transmission speed kept in /etc/remote. Another file /etc/phones contains a systemwide phone number database.

Variable Options of tip

Several variables are used to control the **tip** operation. For example, when using the ~< and ~> commands, the *eofread* and *eofwrite* variables are used respectively to recognize the end-of-file when reading and to specify the end-of-file when writing. File transfers normally depend on the *tandem mode* for flow control. If the remote system does not support the tandem mode (see Section 9.8), the variable *echocheck* may be set to indicate that **tip** should synchronize with the remote system on the echo of each transmitted character.

The **tip** program has four types of control variables:

- numeric
- Boolean
- character
- string

For example, a Boolean variable is set by:

~**s** echocheck   (set echocheck on)

~**s** !echocheck   (set echocheck off)

The = sign is used for assigning a value, as in:

~**s** baudrate=1200

To display values of variables use the following:

~**s** *name*?   (display the variable *name*)

~**s** all   (display all variables that the user may set)

The –v option instructs **tip** to display a variable as it is set. When the Boolean variable *script* is set to *on*, **tip** will record everything transmitted by the remote computer in the script record file specified in the variable *record* (default value tip.record). If the *beautify* variable is on, only printable ASCII characters (characters between 040 and 0177) will be recorded in the script file. The variable *exceptions* is used to indicate characters that are exceptions to the normal beautification rules.

The character variable *escape* contains the escape character (the **tip** command prefix) definition. Its default value is ˜. If this character is inconvenient, you may set the variable to some other character. Typing in two consecutive escape characters at the beginning of a line results in the transmission of one such character to the remote system. Such a sequence occasionally may be needed for an application program on the remote computer, for example, sending mail on a remote UNIX system.

10.2 UUCP

The UNIX-to-UNIX Communications Package (UUCP) is a collection of programs for file transfer, mail exchange, and remote command execution between UNIX systems through dial-up (telephone) or hardwired (RS232) connections. UUCP requests are spooled in the directory /usr/spool/uucp for execution at a later time. The purpose of the UUCP facility is to enable any two UNIX systems to communicate over a dial-up line. Therefore, an informal dial-up network of UNIX systems exists whose extent is limited only by the telephone service.

Before communication takes place, a UUCP routine (*master*) initiates a call (and a login sequence) to a target machine. The corresponding UUCP routine (*slave*) on the target machine then serves as the master's login shell. Therefore, a UUCP is treated as a user on the slave system. The time and frequency of connection between any two computers can be set individually.

File Copying: uucp

The user-level command:

uucp [*option*] ... *source-file* ... *destination-file*

is used to copy files named by the *source-file* arguments to the *destination-file* argument. Files on the local system are specified as usual. A remote file name has the form:

system-name!filename

where *system-name* is taken from a list of system names kept in the file /usr/lib/uucp/L.sys. Even local files can be given in this fashion, as long as they have the correct system name. Note: In *csh* the character ! must be quoted by a \. One useful option is −m, which asks **uucp** to send mail to the user who requested the operation when the copy operation is complete.

Although **uucp** can accept arbitrary file names from different computers, copying such files almost never works in practice: The reason is file access protection. The user UUCP must have the correct read, write, and execute permissions to access a file. These demands severely restrict the files and directories to which UUCP has access. Frequently, file copying is done through the unprotected directory /tmp or by including the file in a piece of mail sent via UUCP.

In addition to the command **uucp** that is used to copy files to systems that are linked directly to the local system, the command:

uusend [−m *mode*] *local-file* sys1!sys2! ... !*remote-file* can be used to copy a *local-file* to a *remote-file* through a sequence of UNIX systems linked by UUCP connections. The −m option specifies the file mode for the remote file. If that options is not specified, the mode of the local file is used.

UUCP Mail

Mail can be sent using the UUCP network. To perform this operation, the usual **mail** command is used, and the receiver of mail on a remote computer is specified using a sequence of system names separated by ! followed by the userid. For example:

mail kentvax\!ucbvax\!*userid*

will send the mail first to the system known as kentvax, which will forward it to the computer ucbvax. After a piece of UUCP mail arrives at the destination computer, the mail is processed by the **rmail** command and then is passed on to the **sendmail** program for delivery to the intended receiver on the destination machine.

UUCP Implementation

Some user-level commands provided by the UUCP package have been discussed. Now let us look briefly at the implementation that supports these services. The UUCP spool directory is usually /usr/spool/uucp, which contains several files and directories:

LOGFILE	records UUCP login from remote systems
SYSLOG	records UUCP transactions
C.	a directory of files representing spooled UNIX-to-UNIX copy requests
X.	a directory of files representing spooled **uux** (remote command execution) requests
D.	a directory of data files to be copied to remote systems or to be used as arguments for remote command execution

The directory /usr/lib/uucp usually contains the executable files for the UUCP package and data about remote systems:

uucico	The UNIX-to-UNIX copy-in-copy-out program. This program operates in two distinct modes: the *master* mode and the *slave* mode. When started in the master mode, it scans the spool directory for work, connects to

Figure 10.1 ▪ UUCP Connection

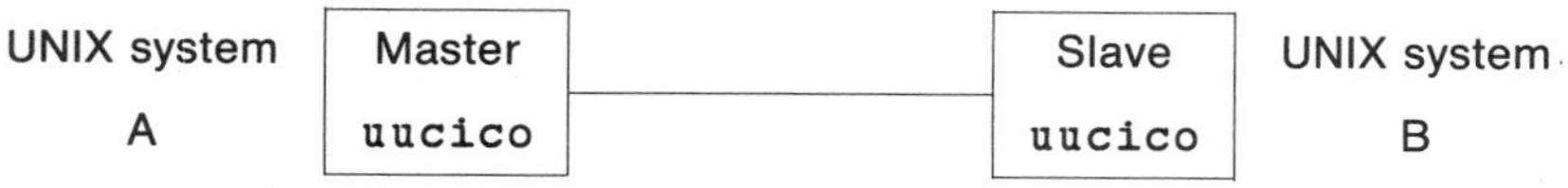

a remote system (sometimes it has to make a telephone call), negotiates a line protocol with the remote system, logs in on the remote system using a prearranged **uucp** userid, executes the copying of outstanding requests from both systems, and logs work requests and completions. The **uucico** program usually is invoked by **cron** at times specified in /usr/lib/crontab. The **uucico** program also is invoked to serve as the login shell for remote **uucp** logins; when started in this way, it is in the slave mode and cooperates with its remote counterpart (Figure 10.1).

uuxqt   This program executes remote commands requested through the **uux** command.

uulog   This program is used to update the UUCP log files.

uuclean   This program removes old files from spool directories.

L*   There are several file names with the prefix L. They keep such information as names of remote systems, userids and passwords to use, hardwired and dial-out ports to use, and telephone numbers for remote systems.

The directory /usr/spool/uucppublic serves as the home directory for remote UUCP logins. For more details, see "Implementation of a Dial-Up Network of UNIX Systems," by D. A. Nowitz & M. E. Lesk.

10.3 Networking and Interprocess Communication

Communications mechanisms like **tip** and **uucp** are based on simple and slow point-to-point connections. A *computer network*, on the other hand, is a high-speed communications medium shared by many, possibly dissimilar, computing systems (or *hosts*). A network is a combination of computer and data transmission hardware and software. Its purpose is to provide fast and reliable communications among the hosts. Typical services made possible by a network are:

- mail exchange

- file transfer

- job entry to designated host

- login on designated host

- distributed file systems

- distributed processing

In addition to host computers, the network itself may involve dedicated computers that perform network functions: For example, the DARPA (Defense Advanced Research Projects Agency) ARPANET is a nationwide network involving IMPs (interface message processors) and TIPs (terminal interface processors). Computers also are used to connect networks: For example, the NSF (National Science Foundation) CSNet is connected to the ARPANET via *relay* computers that serve as gateways between the two networks.

The preceding networks are known as *remote networks*, which are characterized by large physical distances between hosts (normally exceeding 10 km) and relatively low network transmission bit rates (normally below 0.1 megabits/sec). In contrast, a local area network (LAN) connects hosts that are located more closely together (normally much less than 10 km) and affords higher transmission rates (usually 3 to 10 megabits/sec). One LAN of interest is the Ethernet, a public-domain network supported by many computer vendors. Ethernet is becoming an industry standard, especially with UNIX systems. A LAN usually connects computers housed within one organization's facilities. Some of the computers on a LAN also may be connected to remote networks such as the ARPANET or CSNet.

To communicate on a network, a detailed set of rules and conventions must be established for each host to follow. Such rules are known as networking *protocols*. Protocols govern such details as:

- address format of hosts and processes

- data format

- manner of data transmission

- sequencing and addressing of messages

- initiating and terminating of logical connections

- establishing remote services

- accessing remote services

Thus, for one process on one host to communicate with another process on another host, both processes must follow the same protocols. The protocols usually are implemented as layers of software that come between the process and the networking hardware. The corresponding layers on different hosts perform complementary tasks to make the logical connection between the communicating processes.

10.4 Networking Commands

The remainder of this chapter deals specifically with the networking facilities provided in Berkeley UNIX. But before going into the details of the UNIX networking mechanism and its related system calls, let us discuss the user-level facilities made possible by the networking mechanism.

Remote Login: rlogin

The **rlogin** command allows a user on one computer to log in on another computer on the network. When combined with job suspension, this operation allows the user to be logged in on multiple computers at the same terminal and to switch host systems by simply resuming different **rlogin** jobs. The command:

```
rlogin host [ -ec ] [ -l remote-userid ]
```

connects your terminal to the remote UNIX system *host* by establishing a *virtual* communication circuit with a remote login *server process* on the remote host. The *remote-userid* is supplied by –l or defaults to your userid. The **rlogin** command also ensures that the remote host knows what kind of terminal you are using (as given in the environment variable TERM). All input echoing takes place at the remote site, so that (except for delays) the **rlogin** is transparent. Flow control via ^S and ^Q and flushing of input and output on interrupts are handled properly. The ~ is the escape character. A line of the form:

```
~.            (exit rlogin)
```

disconnects you from the remote host (same as **logout**), and:

```
~^Z           (suspend rlogin)
```

allows you to switch jobs.

As you may expect, you must enter the correct password before **rlogin** is successful. However, the password can be waived in certain cases. Each host has a file /etc/hosts.equiv that contains a list of *equivalent* hosts with which it shares account names. When you **rlogin** as the same user on an equivalent host, you will not be asked for a password. You also may have a private equivalence list in a file .rhosts in your home directory. This file specifies additional hosts you may log in without password. Each line in this file consists of a *host name* and a *remote-userid* separated by a space. Normally, you simply enter the host name and userid you use on each system in this .rhosts file. For example, the .rhosts file for userid pwang on host hp4 is as follows:

```
kentvax paulw
kentcs pwang
hp4 pwang
```

The .rhosts file allows user paulw on host kentvax to **rlogin** as pwang on hp4 without password checking. To avoid some security problems, the .rhosts file must be owned by either the local userid or the root and may not be a symbolic link.

If for some reason the default escape character ~ is inconvenient, you may specify a different escape character using the −e option. (Note: There is no space that separates this option flag from the argument character.) Another network-based remote login command is **telnet** that, unlike **rlogin**, does not require a UNIX environment. If a non-UNIX host does not support **rlogin**, it may offer the command **telnet** instead.

Remote Copy: rcp

The commands:

rcp *from-file to-file*
rcp [−r] *file ... directory*

copy files between UNIX hosts on a network. Each *file* or *directory* argument specifies either a remote file name of the form *host:filename*, or a local file name (with no : before the first /). If the −r option is specified and any of the source files are directories, **rcp** copies the subtree rooted at that name. In this case, the destination must be a directory. If a file name is not a full pathname, it is interpreted relative to your home directory on the remote host. A file name on a remote host may be quoted (using \, **' '**, or **'**) so that the shell metacharacters are interpreted remotely. For example:

rcp kentcs:src/*.c ~/src

copies all files src/*.c on the host kentcs to the directory ~/src on the local system. Neither source nor target files are required to be on the local machine.

The **rcp** command does not prompt for passwords, and it also uses the files /etc/hosts.equiv and $HOME/.rhosts for userid equivalence. Normally, **rcp** uses your current local userid on the remote host. The host portion of a remote file name also may take the form host.userid to specify a different userid on the remote system. Furthermore, as an equivalent user, you must have correct access permissions for the specific files on the appropriate host. Otherwise, **rcp** will fail.

On some UNIX systems, a password is required of every remote access for better security.

Remote Shell: rsh

The command:

rsh *host* [−l *userid*] [−n] *command*

executes the specified *command* using a shell on the remote *host*. The shell used is the user's default login shell. As a process, **rsh** runs on the local machine and copies its own standard input to the remote command, the standard output of the remote command to its own standard output, and the standard error of the remote command to its own standard error. Interrupt, quit, and terminate signals are propagated to the remote command. The **rsh** command normally terminates when the remote command terminates. For example:

rsh kentcs who

can be used to see who is currently logged in on the host kentcs.

The remote userid used by **rsh** is the same as your local userid, unless you specify a different remote userid with the −l option. This remote userid must have in its home directory a .rhosts file with the appropriate equivalent entry.

If you omit *command*, then instead of executing a single command, you will be logged in on the remote host using **rlogin**. It may be possible to omit **rsh** and give the command simply as:

host [−l *username*] [−n] *command*

If this works, it also means that the simple command *host* will log you in on the specified host.

Shell metacharacters that are not quoted are interpreted on the local machine, and quoted metacharacters are interpreted on the remote machine. Thus the command:

rsh *host* **cat** *remote-file* >> *local-file*

appends the file *remote-file* to the local *local-file*. Whereas:

rsh *host* **cat** *remote-file1* ">>" *remote-file2*

appends *remote-file1* to *remote-file2* on the named host.

File Transfer Program: ftp

The **ftp** command:

ftp [*options*] [*host*]

is a user interface to the ARPANET standard *file transfer protocol* (*FTP*). The **ftp** command runs an interactive program to transfer files between hosts that may or may not be under UNIX. If *host* is given on the command line, **ftp** will attempt to establish a connection to an FTP server process on that remote host before entering its command interpreter. Otherwise, **ftp** enters its command interpreter directly. Many commands are provided in **ftp** to make file manipulation on both the local and the remote computer easy. The following are the most frequently used **ftp** commands:

open *host-name*	Establishes a connection to the FTP server on the given host. By default, the remote FTP server will ask for your user name and password on the remote system.
close	Terminates the FTP session with the remote server and returns you to the command interpreter of the local **ftp** command. At this point, for example, you can issue an **open** for a different remote host.
quit (bye)	Terminates your connection with the remote FTP server and exits you from the **ftp** command (returns you to the UNIX shell level).
get (recv) *remote-file* [*local-file*]	Copies the remote file to the local host under the file name local-file or under the same name if no local file name is specified.
put (send) *local-file* [*remote-file*]	Copies the local file to the remote host under the file name remote-file or the same name if no remote file name is specified.

mget *remote-files*	Copies the named files from the current directory on the remote host to the current directory on the local host.
mput *local-files*	Copies the named files from the current directory on the local host to the current directory on the remote host.
pwd	Displays the current working directory on the remote host.
cd *dir*	Changes to the given directory on the remote host.
lcd *dir*	Changes to the given directory on the local host.
type [*type-name*]	Sets the type of file to be transferred. The default type name is ascii. Use the type name image for binary files and ebcdic for EBCDIC coded files.
help (?) [*ftp-command*]	Explains the usage of the given command or lists all the commands.

10.5 UNIX ipc Model

Now let us turn our attention to the underlying UNIX mechanisms that support networking applications. Essentially, the networking mechanism is based on an *interprocess communications* (*ipc*) scheme that allows processes on *different* hosts to exchange information. The **pipe** mechanism (see Section 9.7) used to be the only interprocess communications facility available on UNIX systems. Although **pipe** is useful, it is restrictive, because the two communicating processes must be descendants of a common ancestor. The **pipe** semantics make its application in a networking environment almost impossible. For networking, independent processes must be able to initiate and/or accept communication requests in an asynchronous manner, regardless of the location of the processes; this means that the communicating processes may be on the same computer or may be distributed on different hosts on a network. This text focuses on the ipc facility introduced in Berkeley UNIX. System V

UNIX supports ipc through a different set of facilities based on messages, shared memory, and semaphores.

The Berkeley UNIX ipc provides access to a set of communication *domains*. Two important ipc-supported domains to be discussed here are:

1. The UNIX domain for communication within the local UNIX system

2. The Internet domain for communication over the DARPA internet

Other domains can be implemented either by the system or by user-defined processes. The ipc communications domains are characterized by such properties as addressing scheme, protocols, and underlying communications facilities. The central mechanism is the *socket*. A socket is an endpoint of communication within a specific communication domain. A socket may be assigned a name (that is, an address) that allows others to refer to it. Using a socket allows a process to communicate (exchange data) with another process through its socket in the same domain. Thus, communication is conducted through a pair of cooperating sockets. Each socket of a pair of communicating sockets is known as the other's *peer*. In the UNIX domain, sockets are named with file system pathnames, for example, /dev/soc. In the Internet domain, a socket address is more complicated: It consists of a network name, a host name, and a port number. Different types of sockets are supported by different communications protocols. Processes communicate through sockets of the same type.

Client and Server

Most commonly, applications of distributed processing involve a *server* process and a *client* process. The server process provides a specific service accessible through the communications mechanism. A client process is any process that wishes to obtain such a service. A well-defined set of conventions must exist to govern how service is located, requested, accepted, and terminated. This set of conventions comprises a protocol that must be followed by both server and client. For example, the remote login command:

`rlogin` *host*

creates a client process that requires the services of the *remote login server* on a specific *host*. Together, the two processes provide the user with the capability to log in and use a remote host computer by issuing a simple command. Figure 10.2 models the communication connection between two processes in the Ethernet domain over a LAN.

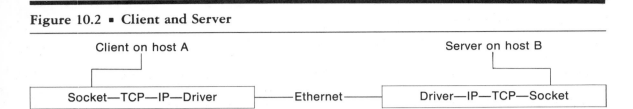

Figure 10.2 ▪ **Client and Server**

10.6 Sockets

Sockets are abstractions that serve as endpoints of communication within a domain. Each socket potentially can exchange data with any other socket within the same domain. Each socket is assigned a type property. The type defines the manner in which communication is carried out by the socket. The following types of sockets are supported:

- *stream* socket: Supports the bidirectional, reliable, sequenced, and un-duplicated flow of data without record boundaries. When put to use, a stream socket is connected to another stream socket, and the connected pair forms a two-way pipe across the network. Each socket in the pair is called the *peer* of the other. Aside from the bidirectionality of data flow, a pair of connected stream sockets provides an interface nearly identical to that of a pipe. Within the UNIX domain, a pair of connected sockets is used to implement a pipe.

- *datagram* socket: Provides bidirectional flow of data packets called *messages*. The communications channel is not promised to be sequenced, reliable, or unduplicated. That is, a process receiving messages on a datagram socket may find messages duplicated and, possibly, not in the order in which they were sent. A datagram socket does not have to be connected to a peer. A message is sent to a datagram socket by specifying its address. Datagram sockets closely model the facilities of contemporary packet-switched networks such as the Ethernet.

- *raw* socket: Gives access to the underlying communication protocols that support socket abstractions. These sockets are normally datagram-oriented, although their exact characteristics are dependent on the interface provided by the protocol. Raw sockets are not intended for the general user but for those interested in developing new communication protocols or for gaining access to esoteric facilities of an existing protocol.

The domains and standard socket types are defined in the header file <sys/socket.h>. Some defined constants for sockets are given in Figure 10.3.

Figure 10.3 ▪ Socket Constants

```
/* domains */
#define          AF_UNIX          1    /* UNIX domain, within the local
                                          host */
#define          AF_INET          2    /* Internet domain */
/* Standard socket types */
#define          SOCK_DGRAM       1    /* datagram */
#define          SOCK_STREAM      2    /* stream */
#define          SOCK RAW         3    /* raw */
```

Sockets and Protocols

An ipc communications domain implements a family of related networking protocols. Each type of socket within a domain normally is supported by a protocol of the same family. The DARPA Internet protocol family is fully supported on Berkeley UNIX through the Internet domain. In the Internet domain, the stream socket is supported by the *Transmission Control Protocol* (*TCP*), the datagram socket is supported by the *User Datagram Protocol* (*UDP*), and the raw socket is supported by the *Internet Protocol* (*IP*).

Creating Sockets

The **socket** system call:

```
#include <sys/socket.h>
```

```
s = socket( domain, type, protocol )
     int s, domain, type, protocol;
```

is used to create a socket of the indicated *type* in the given *domain*. It returns a descriptor that is used to reference the socket in other socket operations. The manifest constants in the header file are used to specify the arguments. If the protocol is left unspecified (with a 0 value), an appropriate protocol in the domain that supports the requested socket type will be selected by the system. For example:

```
s = socket(AF_UNIX, SOCK_DGRAM, 0);
```

creates a datagram socket for use within the local UNIX system. Whereas, the call:

```
s = socket(AF_INET, SOCK_STREAM, 0);
```

creates a stream socket supported by the TCP.

Socket Address

For most distributed applications, a process that provides a specific service through the ipc facility first creates a socket in an appropriate domain and of the appropriate type. Then a name (that is, an address) is assigned to the socket so that other processes can reference it. The socket name is important, because a process must specify the address of a socket to send a message or connect to it. Therefore:

1. A server process must assign its socket an address and make it known to all potential clients.

2. A client process must be able to obtain the correct socket address of any server on any host.

Internet Socket Addresses

The standard addresses for Internet services are contained in a database (usually /etc/services) that lists one line for each service. Each line has four fields:

- an official name of the service
- a unique port number
- the protocol to use
- any aliases (other names for the service)

For example, the entry:

```
ftp    21/tcp
```

specifies that the ftp (Internet file transfer) service is at port 21 and uses the TCP protocol. And the entry:

```
login    513/tcp
```

lists the remote login server to be at port 513. For a process to address a service on a remote host, a network address and a host address also must be specified in addition to the port number. The network database files /etc/hosts and /etc/networks contain such address information. Note that all hosts must have the same database files. Thus, these database files are used by networking processes just like a telphone directory is used by people.

To bind a name to a socket, the system call:

```
bind( s, name, namelen ) ;
```

is used where s is a socket descriptor, *name* is the appropriate address (usually obtained by consulting the network database files), and *namelen* is the size of the address. In the Internet domain, a socket name is an address declared

Figure 10.4 ▪ Internet Socket Address Structure

```
struct sockaddr_in {
     short    sin_family;        /* domain */
     u_short  sin_port;          /* port number */
     struct   in_addr sin_addr;  /* Internet address of host */
     char     sin_zero[8];
};
```

by the structure contained in <netinet/in.h> (Figure 10.4). The procedure to bind an Internet socket address follows the general form:

```
#include <sys/types.h>
#include <netinet/in.h>
struct sockaddr_in sin;

/* assign values to fields of sin */
     ...


bind(s, &sin, sizeof(sin));
```

UNIX Domain Socket Addresses

In the UNIX domain, a socket name is a pathname. For example:

```
s = socket(AF_UNIX, SOCK_DGRAM, 0);
bind(s, "/dev/soc", sizeof("/dev/soc")-1);
```

Note that the NULL byte at the end of a string is not counted as part of the name. On some systems under 4.2bsd, a file with the pathname is created as a side effect of **bind**. This file must be deleted (with *unlink*) by the user process if the same name is to be used again. This undesirable feature should be eliminated in future versions of Berkeley UNIX.

10.7 Making Connections

Binding a socket to a published address is only a concern of a server process. A client process does not need to **bind** a socket. However, to establish a connection, a client process does need to:

1. Find the correct address of the desired server socket.

2. Initiate a connection to the server socket.

This section discusses how a client process uses its socket to initiate a connection to a socket of a server process and how a server process arranges to listen for connection requests and accepts a connection. After a connection is made, data communication can take place using the **read** and **write** I/O system calls. Figure 10.5 illustrates server and client connections.

Initiating a Connection

The **connect** system call:

```
#include <sys/types.h>
#include <sys/socket.h>

connect(s, &name, namelen)
     int s, namelen;

     struct sockaddr name;
```

associates the socket s (in the client) to another socket (in the server) specified by the socket address *name*, which is a string in the UNIX domain and a sockaddr_in structure in the Internet domain. If s is of type SOCK_DGRAM, then this call permanently specifies the peer to which datagrams are to be sent. If s is of type SOCK_STREAM, then this call sends a connection request to the peer specified. If s is not bound to a name at the time of the **connect** call, the system will select and bind a name to it.

Accepting a Connection

A server process with a stream socket takes the following steps to get ready to accept a connection:

1. Creates a socket in the appropriate domain of the correct type.

2. Constructs the correct address and binds it to the socket.

3. Indicates a willingness to accept connection requests by executing the **listen** system call:

    listen(s, n)

    where s specifies the socket and n specifies the maximum number of pending connections (restricted to 5 or less).

4. Uses the **accept** call to wait for a connection.

For a datagram socket, only steps (1) and (2) are needed.

Figure 10.5 ▪ **Server-Client Connections**

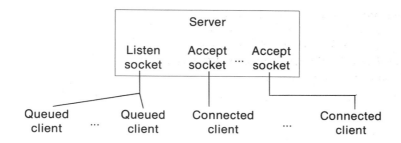

The **accept** system call:

```
#include <sys/types.h>
#include <sys/socket.h>

ns = accept( s, &addr, &addrlen ) ;
    int ns, s, addrlen;
    struc sockaddr addr;
```

accepts connections on a stream socket *s* on which a **listen** has been executed. If there are pending connections, **accept** extracts the first connection request on the queue, creates a new socket with the same properties as *s*, and returns the descriptor of this new socket. The connection listening socket *s* remains ready to receive connection requests. If no pending connections are present on the queue and the socket is not marked as nonblocking, **accept** blocks the caller until a connection is present. If the socket is marked as nonblocking and no pending connections are present on the queue, **accept** will return an error instead of blocking. The accepted socket, *ns*, is used to communicate with its peer and may not be used to accept additional connections. The argument *addr* is a result parameter that is filled with the address of the connecting peer. The *addrlen* is a value-result parameter; it initially should contain the amount of space in *addr*. On return, *addrlen* contains the actual length (in bytes) of the peer address.

10.8 Sending and Receiving Data on Sockets

For connected sockets, the basic I/O calls to send data through sockets are as follows:

```
write(s, buffer, sizeof(buffer));
read(s, buffer, sizeof(buffer));
```

Each process reads and writes its own socket, resulting in a bidirectional data flow between the connected peers. Alternatively, the socket I/O calls:

```
send(s, buffer, sizeof(buffer), opt);
recv(s, buffer, sizeof(buffer), opt);
```

can be used. These calls are the same as the **write** and **read** calls if the argument *opt* is zero. If *opt* is SOF_OOB then *out-of-band data* is sent or received. Out-of-band data can be used to communicate urgent messages such as a signal to a peer. If *opt* is SOF_PREVIEW, then **recv** returns data without removing it so a later **recv** or **read** will return the same data previously previewed.

It also is possible to send and receive messages without first making a connection. Datagram sockets can be used in this fashion. To send data on datagram sockets, the call:

```
sendto(s, buf, bufsize, opt, &to, tosize);
    int s, bufsize, tosize, opt;
    char *buf;
    struct sockaddr to;
```

is used, which returns the number of bytes sent to the socket at the address named *to*. To receive data without a connection, the call:

```
recvfrom(s, buf, bufsize, opt, &from, &fromsize);
    int s, bufsize, fromsize, opt;
    char *buf;
    struct sockaddr from;
```

is used, which returns the number of bytes received in the buffer. Again, *from* is a result parameter that holds the name of the socket that sent the data, and *fromsize* is a corresponding value-result parameter.

10.9 Examples

The best way to illustrate the complicated concepts and system calls of networking is to give a few examples. Here, complete C programs are described for a simple server process and a simple client process.

The server process first establishes a stream socket s in the UNIX domain and binds it to the name serversoc (Figure 10.6). It then uses s to listen for connection requests. The **accept** call then is used to accept a connect request and returns a new socket of the same type as s with a new descriptor ns. The

Figure 10.6 ▪ A Simple Server Process

```
#include <sys/types.h>
#include <sys/socket.h>

main()
{
    int s, ns, c, stringlen;
    char buf[256];
    char string[16];

    /* set up listening socket s */
    s = socket(AF_UNIX, SOCK_STREAM, 0);
    if (s < 0) {
            perror("server:socket");
            exit(1);
                }
    if (bind(s, "serversoc", sizeof("serversoc")-1) == -1) {
            perror("server:bind"):
            exit(1); }
    listen(s,1);

    /* accept connection request */
    stringlen=sizeof(string) -1;
    ns = accepts(s, string, &stringlen);
    if (ns < 0) {
            perror("server:accept");
            unlink("rversoc"); /* if necessary */
            exit(1);
                }

    /* data transfer on connected socket ns */
    c = read(ns, buf, sizeof(buf));
    printf("server process read: '%s'\n", buf);
    write(ns, buf, c);
    unlink("rversoc") /* if necessary */
    }
```

connected socket ns then is used in simple data transfer using **read** and **write**. Note that some 4.2bsd systems may create a file as a side effect of the **bind** call with a UNIX domain address. This file must be removed by the user process if the same socket name is to be used again.

The client process first establishes its own socket s (Figure 10.7), and then it binds the name clientsoc to it. This step is not absolutely necessary. After the **connect** call returns, a connection has been established with its peer (the serversoc socket), and data transfer can begin. The client process first writes the string "hello from client" to its own socket s, which is connected to the server's socket ns. The server reads its own accept socket ns and places the message in the buffer buf. The server then displays a message on standard output, echos what is in buf to the client by writing ns, and terminates. The client reads its socket s, receives the echoed message, displays a confirming message on the standard output, and terminates.

Figure 10.7 ▪ A Simple Client Process

```
#include <sys/types.h>
#include <sys/socket.h>

main()
{
    int s;
    char buf[256];

    s = socket(AF_UNIX, SOCK_STREAM, 0);
    bind(s, "clientsoc", sizeof("clientsoc")-1);

    /* request connection to serversoc */
    if (connect(s, "serversoc", sizeof("serversoc")-1) == -1){
        perror("client:connect");
        unlink("ientsoc"); /* if necessary */
        exit(1); };
    write(s, "hello from client", 17);

    read(s, buf, sizeof(buf));
    printf("server echoed '%s'\n", buf);
    unlink("ientsoc"); /* if necessary */
    }
```

10.10 Shutting Down Sockets

The **close** system call can, of course, be used on a socket descriptor:

```
close(s);
```

The read and write halves of a socket can be independently closed with the **shutdown** system call:

```
shutdown(s, flag);
int s, flag;
```

closes the read portion if *flag* is 0, the write portion if *flag* is 1, and both the read and the write if *flag* is 2. When **shutdown** is combined with the **socketpair** call, which creates a set of connected sockets in the UNIX domain, the **pipe** system call can be emulated exactly.

10.11 Network Databases and Address Mapping

Network Databases

As you may have discovered, there is a need to locate and construct the network address of a server socket before a client process can communicate with another process across the network. The UNIX ipc scheme supports the DARPA standard Internet protocols and address conventions. The following network database files are kept for address mapping. These files normally are created on a host computer from the official databases maintained at the ARPANET Network Information Control Center so that all hosts have local access to the same network information. Local changes to these files are made only to add hosts on a LAN or to record (unofficial) aliases.

/etc/hosts   This file contains the names and network address numbers of all Internet and local hosts accessible to the system. There is one entry for each host. Each entry is one line with several fields that are separated by white space:

address   *official-host-name*   *alias* ...

For example, the entry:

```
10.2.0.78   ucb-vax   berkeley  ucb-c70
```

says that the computer with official host name ucb-vax is alternatively known as berkeley or ucb-c70, and it has an Internet address of 10.2.0.78.

/etc/networks   This file contains information on the known networks that comprise the DARPA Internet. Each network is represented by a single line with fields separated by white space:

official-network-name   network-number   alias ...

For example:

```
ucb-ether   46
```

represents the local area network of UCB (University of California, Berkeley).

/etc/services   This file contains information regarding the known network-related services available in the DARPA Internet. Each service is represented by a single line with the following fields separated by white space:

official-service-name   port-number/protocol-name   alias ...

For example:

```
smtp    25/tcp      mail
```

represents the **sendmail** server using the Internet TCP protocol.

/etc/protocols   This file contains information regarding the known protocols used in the DARPA Internet. Each protocol is represented by a single line separated by white space with the following fields:

official-protocol-name   protocol-number   alias ...

For example, the following Internet protocols (IP) are defined:

```
icmp  1    ICMP    # Internet control message protocol
ggp   3    GGP     # gateway-gateway protocol
tcp   6    TCP     # transmission control protocol
udp   17   UDP     # user datagram protocol
```

Network Library Routines

A set of standard routines is provided in an Internet Network Library to support network address mapping. These routines consult the previously described database files and return C structures containing the needed information. Routines are provided for mapping host names to network addresses, service names to port numbers and protocols, network names to network numbers, and so on. The header file <netdb.h> must be included in any file that uses these network library routines. For instance, to obtain the host address of a host with the name ucb-vax, the library function **gethostbyname** is used:

```
#include <netdb.h>
struct hostent *hp;
hp = gethostbyname("ucb-vac");
```

This call consults /etc/hosts and returns a *hostent* structure, as follows:

```
struct      hostent {
    char    *h_name;        /* official name of host */
    char    **h_aliases;    /* alias list */
    int     h_addrtype;     /* host address type : AF_UNIX or AF_INET */
    int     h_length;       /* length of address */
    char    *h_addr;        /* address */
};
```

This structure contains information about the named host (ucb-vax). Similar sets of library functions are provided to access the network, services, and protocol databases. Examples are **gethostbyaddr**, **getnetbyname**, **getservbyname**, and **getprotobyname**.

10.12 The Remote Login Service

Server Program

To illustrate the networking material presented even further, let us study how some existing network services are implemented. Figure 10.8 shows the code segments of a remote login server program that uses sockets in the Internet domain. The Internet address variable sin is initialized on line (0). The program first consults the /etc/services database (line (1)) for an entry named login using the Internet TCP protocol. The **getservbyname** call returns a pointer to a *servent* structure:

```
struct      servent {
    char    *s_name;        /* official service name */
    char    **s_aliases;    /* alias list */
    int     s_port;         /* port number */
    char    *s_proto;       /* protocol to use */
};
```

as defined in the header file <netdb.h>. The s_port entry of this structure contains the port number assigned to the login service. This port number value is deposited in the sin variable, which is now a complete address on the local host. The remote login server creates an Internet domain stream socket on

Figure 10.8 ■ Remote Login Server Code

```
#include <sys/types.h>
#include <sys/stat.h>
#include <sys/socket.h>
#include <netinet/in.h>
#include <netdb.h>
#include <errno.h>

extern     errno;
struct     sockaddr_in sin = { AF_INET };                /* (0) */

main(argc, argv)
int argc;
char **argv;
{    int s;
     struct sockaddr_in from;
     struct servent *sp;

     sp = getservbyname("login", "tcp");                 /* (1) */
     if (sp == 0) {
          fprintf(stderr, "rlogind: tcp/login: unknown service\n");
          exit(1);
     }
#ifndef DEBUG
     /* code to disassociate from control terminal */
#endif
     sin.sin_port = sp->s_port;                           /* (2) */
     ...
     s = socket(AF_INET, SOCK_STREAM, 0);                 /* (3) */
     if (s < 0) {
          perror("rlogind: socket"); exit(1);
     }
     ...
     if (bind(s, &sin, sizeof (sin)) < 0) {               /* (4) */
          perror("rlogind: bind"); exit(1);
     }
     ...
     listen(s, 3);                                        /* (5) */
     for (;;) {                                           /* (6) */
          int ns, len = sizeof (from);
```

Figure 10.8 ▪ (*continued*)

```
            ns = accept(f, &from, &len);              /* (7) */
            if (ns < 0) {
                if (errno == EINTR) continue;
                perror("rlogind: accept");
                continue;
            }
            if (fork() == 0) {                          /* (8) */
                close(s);
                doit(ns, &from);                        /* actual service */
            }
            close(ns);
    } /* end of for */
}
```

line (3), binds the address sin to it on line (4), and begins to listen for connection requests on line (5). In the main loop of the program (starting at line (6)), the **accept** call will return when a connection request has been received from a client process. When a new socket ns, which is connected to its peer, is returned, a child process is **fork**ed to serve the client while the parent process loops back to accept other connection requests. Note how the socket s is closed in the child and the socket ns is closed in the parent. Also note that the server never exits.

Client Program

Having studied the server side of the remote login service, the client side is easier to understand. Figure 10.9 shows the relevant pieces of code for an rlogin client program. This program takes a remote host name as its first argument on the command line and establishes a full-duplex stream connection to the server process on the target host. The network library routines **getservbyname** and **gethostbyname** (line (1)) are used to obtain network address information from the database files. This information then is deposited into the sin address structure (lines (2) to (3)) to form the complete address of the server's socket. The client creates an Internet domain stream socket s, which then is connected to the server's socket specified by the address sin. Once the connection is made, a two-way communications channel with a server process and a client process at either end has been established. The main task

Figure 10.9 ▪ Remote Login Client Code

```
main(argc, argv)
int argc;
char *argv[];
{
    struct sockaddr_in sin;
    struct servent *sp;
    struct hostent *hp;
    int s;
    ...
    sp = getservbyname("login","tcp");
    if (sp == NULL) {
        fprintf(stderr, "rlogin: tcp/login: unknown service\n");
        exit(1);
    }
    hp = gethostbyname(argv[1]);                              /* (1) */
    if (hp == NULL) {
        fprintf(stderr, "rlogin: %s: unknown host\n", argv[1]);
        exit(1);
    }
    bzero((char *)&sin, sizeof (sin));                        /* (2) */
    bcopy(hp->h_addr, (char *)&sin.sin_addr, hp->h_length);
    sin.sin_family = hp->h_addrtype;
    sin.sin_port = sp->s_port;                                /* (3) */
    s = socket(AF_INET, SOCK_STREAM, 0);
    if (s < 0) {
        perror("rlogin: socket"); exit(1);
    }
    ...
    if (connect(s, (char *)&sin, sizeof (sin)) < 0) {         {/* (4) */
        perror("rlogin: connect"); exit(1);
    }
        /* now perform rlogin service */
    ...
}
```

of relaying messages between the remote host and the local user then can proceed.

Note that in lines (2) and (3) the string manipulation routines **bzero** and **bcopy** are used. They manipulate strings through byte operations:

```
bzero(s, n)
    char *s;
    int n;
```

```
bcopy(x, y, n)
    char *x, *y;
    int n;
```

The routine **bzero** assigns the value zero to *n* bytes of *s*; and **bcopy** copies
n bytes from string *x* to string *y*.

10.13 Using Datagram Sockets

As another example, let us look at mail notification via the *comsat* process.
Connectionless datagram sockets are used in this application. The comsat
server, on receipt of a datagram message of mail delivery for a user, checks
to see if the user is on-line and if so, sends a brief message about the incoming
mail to the user's terminal. The official name for this service is biff, as is
described by the /etc/services entry:

```
biff    512/udp    comsat
```

As you can see, this service resides at port 512 and uses the Internet user
datagram protocol (UDP).

Figure 10.10 contains segments of the comsat server program. An Internet
address sin is initialized (line (1)) as an external quantity. The service structure
is retrieved from the database /etc/services (line (2)). An Internet domain
datagram socket s is created on line (3). After the port number is assigned
(line (4)), the address is bound to s on line (5). The **recv** call on line (6)
blocks until a message is received on the datagram socket s. The incoming
message is returned in the character buffer msg. The task of sending the message to the user's terminal is performed in the route **mailfor**.

Figure 10.11 shows segments of a mail-delivery program that uses the
comsat service. This client program first obtains address information using the
network library functions **gethostbyname** and **getservbyname**. Then an Internet domain datagram socket f is created (line (1)). The address of the receiving datagram socket of the server process is formed by depositing the
appropriate address components in the Internet address structure biff (line
(2)). After the message is sent (line (3)), the socket f is closed. The message
in the buffer buf that is sent to the comsat server is in the form *name@offset*,
which specifies the name of the mail recipient and the position this piece of
mail is to occupy in the user's mail file. The offset is computed by the library
routine **ftell**.

Figure 10.10 ▪ Mail Notification Server Code

```
/* sections of comsat.c */

struct sockaddr_in sin = { AF_INET };                            /* (1) */
struct servent *sp;

main(argc, argv)
int argc;
char **argv;
{
    register cc;
    char buf[BUFSIZ];
    int s;
    sp = getservbyname("biff", "udp");                           /* (2) */
    if (sp == 0) {
        fprintf(stderr, "comsat: biff/udp: unknown serice\n");
        exit(1);
    }


    ...

    s = socket(AF_INET, SOCK_DGRAM, 0);                          /* (3) */
    if (s < 0) {perror("socket"); exit(1); }
    sin.sin_port = sp->s_port;                                   /* (4) */
    if (bind(s, &sin, sizeof (sin)) < 0) {                       /* (5) */
        perror("bind"); exit(1);
    }
    for ( ; ; ) {
        char msg[100];
        int cc;

        cc = recv(s, msg, sizeof (msg) -1, 0);                   /* (6) */
        if (cc <= 0) {
            if (errno != EINTR) sleep(1);
            errno = 0;
            continue;
        }
        msg[cc] = 0;
        mailfor(msg);
    }
}
```

Figure 10.11 ▪ A comsat Client

```
struct sockaddr_in biff = {AF_INET};              /*section of mail.c*/
{
    ...
    hp = gethostbyname("kentvax");
    sp = getservbyname("biff", "udp");
    if (hp && sp) {
        f = socket(AF_INET,SOCK_DGRAM,0);           /*(1)*/
        sprintf(buf, "%s@%d\n", name, ftell(malf));
    }
    ...
}

if(hp && sp){                                       /*(2)*/
    biff.sin_family = hp->h_addrtype;
    bcopy(hp->h_addr, &biff.sin_addr, hp->h_length);
    biff.sin_port = sp->s_port;

    sendto(f,buf,strlen(buf)+1,0,&biff,sizeof(biff));  /*(3)*/
    close(f);
}
```

10.14 More ipc Information

For more advanced topics covering out-of-band data, pseudoterminals, and signals related to ipc, see "A 4.2bsd Interprocess Communication Primer" by S. Leffler, R. Fabry, and W. Joy. For more information on the Berkeley UNIX implementation, see "4.2BSD Networking Implementation Notes" by S. Leffler, W. Joy, and R. Fabry.

10.15 Summary

UNIX provides both point-to-point communications commands such as **tip** and **uucp** that can work through dial-up lines and networking facilities such as **rlogin**, **rcp**, and **ftp** that are fast and more reliable.

Berkeley UNIX supports networking applications by providing a set of system-level facilities for interprocess communications (ipc) among distributed processes. Network services are set up and supported by server processes that always are ready to respond to requests for service. Client processes can access network-based services by locating the server's address and initiating a request.

The ipc hinges on the socket mechanism, which serves as endpoints for communication in a communications domain. Two important domains are the UNIX domain and the Internet domain. The former is used for communication within the local UNIX system. The latter supports the various Internet protocols that exist in the Internet protocol family, including IP (Internet protocol), TCP (transmission control protocol), and UDP (user datagram protocol).

A process communicates with another process across the network through its own sockets in the same communication domain. There are several types of sockets: Stream sockets are connected in pairs to support a bidirectional communications channel, which can be likened to a two-way pipe; datagram sockets may or may not be connected and can send/receive messages similar to data packets; and raw sockets give access to the underlying communication protocols that support socket abstractions. Raw sockets are not intended for the general programmer.

A set of network database files serves as a directory for networking services and their addresses. A library of routines exists to make it easier to use these database files in a C program.

Exercises

1. Assuming that a dial-out facility and a dial-in facility are available to a computer system, explain how a user could log in twice using one terminal. What purpose could be served by such usage?

2. Consider using **tip** to access another UNIX system and send mail on the remote system. Describe four different ways to specify a subject field. (*Hint:* Only three have to do with the escape character.)

3. Repeat Problem 2 assuming that you are on UNIX system A, **rlogin** to system B, **tip** to system C, and want to send mail on C.

4. Determine the mechanism used by **uucp** to send mail to other sites.

5. At what later times do spooled **uucp** requests get executed?

6. Can you determine who is logged in on another machine with **uucp**?

7. Can **rcp** be used with a machine where your account has a different name?

8. Discover what mechanism **tip** uses for opening modems and terminal

lines with exclusive access. Is there a chance that **tip** may not release the "lock" on these resources properly and thus cause subsequent **tip** commands to fail?

9. Experiment with the simple server and client processes given in this chapter. Establish several concurrent clients for the same server.

10. What is the major difference between **ftp** and **rcp**? Why do we need both? What about **tip**?

11. The **pipe** system call actually is implemented using the socket primitives. Find out how it is done.

12. If your computer is on a LAN and/or on a remote network, find out its network address. Which other hosts are on the LAN? What network services are being supported?

13. The command **talk** works across a network. Find out how this works.

14. Experiment with ipc by establishing a server on one host that simply echos back any messages received from a client on another host.

15. A network server usually runs as a *daemon*, a process that is disassociated from its control terminal and that never exits. What steps are needed in a C program to disassociate the process from its control terminal?

Program Maintenance

11

P

rogram maintenance is an important part of both system and application programming, and there are various tasks involved in maintaining a large software package:

- locate the bug or missing feature
- define an improvement
- modify source programs
- recompile and regenerate the system
- perform tests
- modify the documentation
- include the correction in the next software release

These activities constitute the software maintenance cycle, a simplified view of which is shown in Figure 11.1.

Figure 11.1 ▪ Software Maintenance Cycle

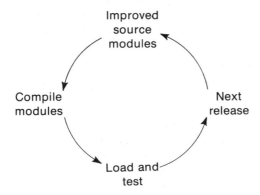

Maintenance is the predominant and most expensive phase in the overall lifespan of a large software package. The total maintenance cost of a large-scale software system can be as high as 70 percent of its lifetime cost. Thus, it is important to have efficient tools for maintaining programs.

11.1 The UNIX make **Facility**

The UNIX **make** command is a facility for maintaining computer programs. It is a useful "software engineering" tool for users, and it also is used to maintain the UNIX system itself. The **make** program follows a user-prepared description file known as a *makefile* to perform its functions. The contents of the makefile describe the dependent relationships that exist between the various program modules in a software package and specify the exact UNIX commands to update a module if such updating is necessary. Updating a program module is necessary when modifications have been made to other modules it depends on. The makefile descriptions not only direct the actions of **make** but also document the relationships between modules.

The **make** facility (or something like it) is indispensable for any software that will be maintained by a team of programmers. This situation is especially true when team members come and go or when the software is designed to be reconfigurable (customizable) after distribution. After changes are made in a software package, the command

make *target*

is used to update a given target file. The **make** command

uses the descriptions contained in the file named Makefile or makefile in the current directory to perform only those actions needed to bring the specified target file up to date. The **make** command will carry out the following operations:

1. Find the description entry for the given *target* in the makefile.

2. Recursively update all targets that the given *target* depends on.

3. Update the given *target* if necessary.

A target is usually, but not always, the name of a file in the software package. Whether or not a target requires updating is determined by comparing the last modification time stamps of the target file and of the files it depends on (as specified by the dependencies contained in the makefile). A file on which a target file depends is called a *component* of the target file. If the target file does not have the most recent time stamp, it needs updating. Figure 11.2 shows the input and functions of the **make** command.

The **make** facility often is used to automate the rather tedious process of regenerating a software system after modifications have been made to its source code modules. It also can be used to handle other procedures that relate to the maintenance of the software package, such as running *test suites* (a set of known test cases), generating cross-reference lists, and so on. The **make** facility is a UNIX utility in the sense that it relies on the UNIX file system for time information and the shell-level (*sh* only) commands to specify actions for updating targets.

Figure 11.2 ▪ Function of make

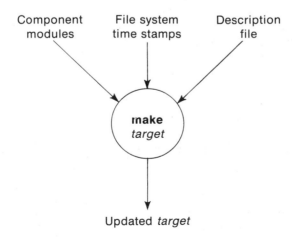

Component modules   File system time stamps   Description file

make *target*

Updated *target*

An Example Makefile

The **make** utility follows the descriptions contained in the makefile to perform its tasks. The makefile specifies two kinds of information about files contained in a software package: dependencies among files and exactly how each file is brought up to date.

A typical entry in the makefile is of the form:

target **:** *zero or more components*
TAB*command1*
TAB*command2*

...

where *target* and *components* are generally the names of files being controlled. On the first line (the dependence line), a *target* file is listed on the left-hand side of the colon (:) and is declared to be dependent on zero or more other files following the : . The sequence of commands prescribes the actions that must be taken to bring the *target* up to date in case one or more of its components have been modified. The presence of a TAB character is indicated by the word TAB. The first character of each command line must be a TAB character.

Consider a small example where the executable file myprog relies on three object files a.o, b.o, and c.o, each of which in turn depends on the corresponding source code file. The files a.o and b.o also depend on an *include* file named mydef, as illustrated by the dependence graph in Figure 11.3. Figure 11.4 shows makefile entries that describe the dependence relationships illustrated in the dependence graph.

The meaning of *dependency* as used by **make** refers only to the chain of updating activities necessary to accommodate modifications made to files in a software package. Because the file mydef is included in the files a.c and b.c, via #include, a.c and b.c do not need updating if mydef is modified. Hence, the makefile does not specify a.c or b.c as *dependent* on mydef. Instead, mydef

---

Figure 11.3 ▪ A File-Dependence Graph

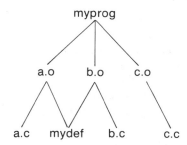

Figure 11.4 ▪ Makefile Entries

```
myprog: a.o b.o c.o
TAB     cc a.o b.o c.o -o myprog

a.o: a.c mydef
TAB     cc -c a.c

b.o: b.c mydef
TAB     cc -c b.c

c.o: c.c
TAB     cc -c c.c
```

is a component of the object files a.o and b.o, because they must be regenerated by the C compiler if either the source code or any include file changes.

Entries in Figure 11.4 are more repetitive than they need to be. The **make** utility uses certain default dependency rules to simplify frequently used entries. For example, without explicit descriptions to the contrary, any object file *name*.o is automatically dependent on the corresponding source file *name*.c. Default dependencies will be described more fully in Section 11.4. Using such default rules, the description of Figure 11.4 becomes:

```
myprog : a.o b.o c.o
TAB     cc a.o b.o c.o -o myprog

a.o b.o : mydef
```

11.2 The Description File

The description file is usually named makefile or Makefile, but it is not restricted to these names. The description file can be considered a program that **make** understands. It is in the description file of the **make** mechanism that you specify the detailed dependence relations among files under control and give the command sequences necessary to bring any file up to date. The previous example illustrates the case where targets represent files. But the description file also may contain *fake targets* that do not correspond to files. Instead of file updating, a fake target is used to trigger other actions related to the maintenance of the software package. Examples of such actions are running test cases, installing executable files in system directories, generating cross references, and removing unwanted files. Recording the command sequences for these actions in the description file not only automates the actions but also provides documentation. In fact, reading the description file is a good way to understand a software package.

There are four kinds of statements in a description file:

- macro definitions
- dependence rules
- commands
- comments

The comment convention used for **make** is similar to but not the same as that for shell scripts. A comment must begin with a # character in column one of a line. Everything from the character # until the end of the line is ignored. A statement in the **make** description file must be on one line. A long statement can be continued to the next line by quoting the NEWLINE—that is, by using a backslash (\) at the end of a line. In such a case, the \, NEWLINE, and any following TABs or blanks are replaced by a single blank.

Let us describe the other three kinds of statements in turn.

Macros

A macro is simply a parameter used in the description file. You assign or define a macro by:

NAME = value

where *NAME* is a string of letters and/or digits and *value* is any number of words terminated by a NEWLINE. White space, but no TAB, may precede a macro definition. Some sample macro definitions are as follows:

```
OBJS = a.o b.o c.o
SRCDIR = system/source
FLAGS = -c -O
ꓱ = /usr/xyz
NULL =
```

A macro can be used anywhere in the description file after it is defined. To interpolate the value of a macro in a statement, use:

$ (*NAME*)

or equivalently:

${*NAME*}

For example:

```
prog : ${OBJS}
      echo $∃
      cc ${FLAGS} $(SRCDIR)/a.c
```

Note: If a macro name contains only one character or digit, it can be invoked without the surrounding parentheses or braces.

Dependence Rules

The most important part of a **make** description file is its dependence rules. They specify which modules are dependent on which other modules in a software package and what commands should be used for updating a module. A dependence rule consists of three parts:

- one or more targets
- zero or more components
- zero or more commands for updating the targets

The general form of a dependence rule is:

target1 [*target2* ...] : [:] [*component1* ...] [; *commands*]
[TAB *commands*]
...

A *dependence line* may contain a single colon (:) or a double colon (::). A target may appear on more than one dependence line of either the single-colon or the double-colon type, but not on both:

1. *When a target is on one or more single-colon dependence lines*, only one of these dependence lines may have a sequence of commands. A command is any *sh* command within which there may be some **make** macros. If a target requires updating due to any of the dependence lines, the sequence of commands will be executed. For example:

```
prog : c.o
TAB    cc a.o b.o c.o -o prog
prog : a.o b.o
```

2. *When a target is on one or more double-colon dependence lines*, each dependence line may have its own sequence of commands. If the target is out of date on a specific dependence line, the associated commands are executed. For example:

```
prog :: a.o
TAB     command1
prog :: b.o
TAB     command2
```

Thus double-colon rules are used to specify different command sequences for different components of a target.

Specifying Commands

Each command can be given on a different line whose first character must be a TAB character (except on the dependence line). Commands can be placed on the same line if they are separated by a semicolon (;). Each command is displayed before execution. But the display can be supressed by preceding the command with a @ character (after the leading TAB). Each command line is macro-substituted by **make** before execution by an *sh* shell. A different *sh* shell is used for each line. Commands on the same line are interpreted by the same *sh* shell. A line can be continued by quoting the NEWLINE with a \. It is possible to invoke *csh* commands in a makefile through direct interpretation in the form:

TAB   **csh** *script arg1* ...

Because the **make** facility uses the character $ for macro expansion, a shell-level variable x is expressed as $x in the makefile.

11.3 Updating Target Files

The **make** description file and built-in dependency rules specify a *dependence graph* with nodes that represent targets and directed edges that indicate dependencies on component targets. Since dependence relations cannot be circular, the graph is an *acyclic-directed graph*, which means the graph contains no loops. A simple dependence graph is illustrated in Figure 11.3.

The **make** command uses this dependence graph and the "last-modified" times of target and component files to determine which targets need updating. The last-modified time is recorded automatically with a file when the file is created or modified. The following rules are used to determine whether or not a target is out of date:

1. If the target has components, first recursively update (make) each component as a target (in the given order). This procedure involves determining (using the same method) whether any component target is out of date and then performing updating actions on each out-of-date target. After the components have been updated (made), then the target's time is compared with those of its components. A target is out of date if its time precedes any of its component's times.

2. If the target has no components, it is out of date if no file exists with the same name, or it is up to date if there is such a file.

3. The time of a target or a made component is taken to be the time of a corresponding file or the current time if no such file exists.

4. If a component cannot be made as a target, it is up to date if no corresponding file exists, otherwise it is an error.

After determining that a target is out of date, **make** performs the following operations to update the target.

1. The **make** command sets the values of the special macros **$@**, **$<**, **$***, and **$?**:

   $@   is set to the name of the target (file to be made).

   $?   is set to the string of components newer than the target.

   $<   is set to the component file name generated by **make** when the action is caused by a built-in rule. See Section 11.4 for more details.

   $*   is set to the common base name of the target and the component. For example, if the target is xyz.o and the component xyz.c, then $* is set to xyz.

2. If updating commands have been supplied in the description file for the target, **make** executes them in the order given. Each updating command is displayed (on the standard output) before it is executed. However, the display is suppressed if the command is preceded by @.

3. If no updating command is specified for the target, then **make** determines if any built-in actions apply. If so, **make** performs the built-in actions.

4. If there are no explicit or built-in actions, then **make** uses the commands supplied to the default target .DEFAULT. If .DEFAULT is not given, **make** stops. It also stops if an updating command fails, unless the command is preceded by a −.

As an example, the following is a section of a description file that involves the special macro $@:

```
CFLAGS= −O
CMD= grep hostid hostname kill ld ln login\
  ls mail mkdir mt nice

${CMD} mv cp:
TAB    cc ${CFLAGS} −o $@ $@.c
```

Note that the macro CMD is continued to the next line using a \ at the end of the line. Using this description, the command:

make grep

for example, results in the updating action:

cc −O −o grep grep.c

because the macro $@ is set to grep.

11.4 Suffix Dependency and Implicit Rules

In the description file, it is possible to give dependency rules that specify how to transform a file with one suffix into a file with another suffix. All suffixes of interest must be given as components to the special target name .SUFFIXES. This feature is best explained through an example:

```
.SUFFIXES: .o .cl
.cl.o:
TAB        /usr/bin/clcompile $< >> '#errs' 2>&1
```

Here the suffixes of interest are .o (object file) and .cl (common LISP source file). The target .cl.o gives commands to transform a file with the .cl suffix into one with the .o suffix. The command invokes the common LISP compiler /usr/bin/clcompile (not a standard UNIX utility) with both standard output and standard error redirected into the file named #errs. The special macro $< is set automatically to the component file name (ending in .cl).

The **make** facility also goes one step further and provides built-in default rules for suffix dependencies and macros that are used frequently. Some of the default rules are as follows:

```
.SUFFIXES: .out .o .c .r .f .s
CC=cc
AS=as
FC=f77
RFLAGS=
FFLAGS=
LOADLIBES=
CFLAGS=
FFLAGS=

.c.o:
TAB        $(CC) $(CFLAGS) −c $<
```

```
### line A
.s.o:
TAB       $(AS) -o $@ $<

.f.out .r.out:
TAB       $(FC) $(RFLAGS) $(FFLAGS) $< $(LOADLIBES) -o $@
TAB       -rm $*.o
```

Note that the macros $@ and $< are used. For example, in the file dependency rule .s.o (line A), the macro $< stands for the component file (ending in .s), and $@ stands for the target file (ending in .o). These implicit rules make it easy to write description files for usual tasks involving C, f77, RATFOR, assembly, and object files. The default suffixes list can be appended by a .SUFFIXES entry in the user's description file. A .SUFFIXES entry with no components will reset the list to an empty list. The suffixes list is order-sensitive, and it is not easy to predict the interaction between implicit suffixes and user-supplied ones. Because of this, it is recommended that the default suffixes list be reset before any new suffixes' relations are defined.

11.5 Examples

Having learned many rules about **make** and makefiles, you are ready to apply the concepts learned to five **make** description file examples. The first example is an expanded version of the simple example contained in Figure 11.4 (Figure 11.5).

The built-in **make** macro CFLAGS is used on the **cc** line, which allows the use of

make "CFLAGS=-g" myprog

for the debugging phase of myprog. Later, to generate the production version of myprog, simply use:

make myprog

because CFLAGS is already set to -O inside the makefile.

The purpose of the fake targets named clean and all is self-evident. The command **ctags** produces a file tags that enables you to locate functions and typedefs with:

vi -t *name*

where *name* specifies a function or typedef. The target test runs test cases for the newly generated myprog and produces results in the file test.

Figure 11.5 ▪ Example One: Fake Targets

```
SRCS= a.c b.c c.c mydef
OBJS= a.o b.o c.o
CFLAGS= -O

all: myprog clean test tags

myprog: ${OBJS}
    cc ${CFLAGS} ${OBJS} myprog

a.o b.o: mydef

clean:
    rm -f ${OBJS}

test: myprog
    rm -f testresults
    myprog < testcases > test
    @echo 'test results in file: test'

tags: ${SRCS}
    ctags ${SRCS}
```

Text Formatting

The second example has to do with text formatting. In fact, it is the makefile used to manage Chapter 9 (Figure 11.6). In this example, the macro SECTS is defined as a list of file names that form the chapter. There are two sections, lowio.2 and file.3, that have tables in them and must be processed by **tbl** before **troff**. Note the use of the special macro $@ to stand for the target (for example, file.3.tbl) and $? to stand for the component (file.3). Note also that the target output depends on all $SECTS, some of which have explicit dependency lines later in the file. The file named chapter consists of a sequence of .so requests that simply *includes* the various sections of the chapter.

    With this makefile, the command:

```
make
```

issued in the same directory will print the chapter (same as **make** output). The target named preview uses **nroff** to produce a version readable on a CRT terminal. It is a good idea to preview a document before actually printing it. The target named pages works with the macro PAGES to allow printing of

Figure 11.6 ▪ Example Two: Formatting Text

```
SECTS= intro.1 lowio.2.tbl file.3.tbl example.4 \
    env.6 signal.7 pipe.8 tty.9 curses.10 chapter
PAGES=

output: $(SECTS)
    rm -f index
    troff -ms chapter 2> index

pages: $(SECTS)
    troff -ms $(PAGES) chapter 2> /dev/null

preview: $(SECTS)
    nroff -ms chapter > preview 2> index.p

lowio.2.tbl: lowio.2
    rm -f $@
    tbl $? > $@
file.3.tbl: file.3
    rm -f $@
    tbl $? > $@
```

selected pages through the invocation:

`make PAGES=-o`_list_` pages`

where _list_ is a specification of selected pages for printing. Text formatting using **troff** and other facilities is the subject of Chapter 12.

Multiple Subdirectories

The third example has to do with invoking a **make** call from within a makefile (Figure 11.7). For larger program packages, there usually are a number of subdirectories under the main directory where the package is contained. The makefile in the main directory can invoke **make** in a subdirectory, just as can any other command. In this way, the description files can reside in the sub-directories, and a **make** call invoked at the main directory's level can activate all **make** actions.

The primary target of the figure is a chess program. All source files are in C. There are two subdirectories dir1 and dir2 under the control of separate makefiles invoked by the main makefile. The /tmp is put there simply to trigger

Figure 11.7 ▪ Example Three: make in Subdirectories

```
SUBDIRS = dir1 dir2

OBJ = dir1/f1.o dir2/f2.o f3.o f4.o f5.o

CFLAGS = -O

chess: ${SUBDIRS} ${OBJ}
      cc -o chess ${OBJ}
      @echo chess done

${SUBDIRS}: /tmp
      cd $@; make ${MFLAGS}
```

the actions for the subdirectories. The MFLAGS is a **make** built-in macro that is set to any flags specified on the command line. Note also that commands to be executed in the subdirectory should be given on the same line as the **cd** command, because each new command line is executed by a different shell.

Dependence Rule Generation

In maintaining C programs that uses header files with #include lines in the source file, it is necessary to have rules in the makefile that specify the dependencies between the executable files and the header files. These rules take care of any effects to executable files caused by modifications to header files. It is possible to write the makefile in such a way that it generates most of the necessary dependence rules by searching source files for #include lines. Figure 11.8 shows a section of a description file named Makefile that performs dependence rule generation.

The macro SRC consists of a list of executable file names that correspond to their respective C source file base names. The target named depend is updated before any other actions are taken in Makefile. The actions for depend are as follows:

1. Use **grep** (Section 4.4) and **sed** (Section 4.5) to generate header file dependence rules into a temporary file named deprules. There is a space just before the TAB character in the **grep** pattern. Note the use of $$i to obtain the *sh* variable $i and the continuation of lines. Note also the use of the empty file x.c.

2. Save a backup copy of Makefile in Makefile.bak.

3. Use **ex** to delete any old dependence rules in Makefile.

Figure 11.8 ▪ Example Four: Dependence Rule Generation

```
depend:
    cat < /dev/null > x.c
    for i in ${SRC}; do \
        (echo $$i: $$i.c >>deprules; \
        /bin/grep '^#[ TAB]*include' x.c $$i.c |\
        sed -e 's,<\(.*\)>,"/usr/include\1",'\
            -e 's/:["]*"\(["]*\)".*\: \1/' \
            -e 's/\.c//' >>deprules); done
    cp Makefile Makefile.bak
    echo '/^# DO NOT DELETE THIS LINE/+2,$d|w' | ex Makefile
    cat deprules >> Makefile
    rm deprules x.c
    echo '# GENERATED DEPENDENCIES MUST BE AT EOF' >> Makefile
    echo '# IF YOU PUT STUFF HERE IT WILL GO AWAY' >> Makefile
    echo '# see make depend above' >> Makefile

# Files listed in ${NSTD} have explicit make line given below.

# DO NOT DELETE THIS LINE
# OR THIS LINE—the following rules are generated by make depend
```

4. Append the file deprules to the end of Makefile.

5. Remove any temporary files used.

Makefile for Modules Written in LISP

Franz LISP has been distributed with Berkeley UNIX. This LISP system has both an interpreter and a compiler. The compiler is called liszt and is invoked with the command **liszt**. Vaxima is a symbolic computation system that computes with mathematical formulas and has many high-level, built-in mathematical functions. For example, Vaxima can perform symbolic differentiation, integration, factoring polynomials, and so on. It is written in Franz LISP and consists of many subdirectories that contain source modules. Its maintenance is controlled by a master makefile in a main directory that also invokes makefiles residing in certain subdirectories.

In this example, a makefile is associated with ppack, a polynomial manipulation package written in LISP (Figure 11.9). A LISP object file is declared to be dependent on the corresponding source file ending in .l with the targets .SUFFIXES and .l.o. Note the use of the macro $< to denote the corresponding

Figure 11.9 ▪ Example Five: Managing LISP Modules

```
# makefile for polynomial package ppack
# macro definitions

CMPLR = liszt
OBJ = algfac.o bound.o coeff.o cxprs.o eezgcd.o \
    interface.o mulfac.o mullift.o mulsqfr.o faslc.o \
    ratcon.o special.o subst.o true.o \
    unifac.o unimod.o unipfe.o unisqfr.o util.o
LFLAGS = -m
# dependence rules
.SUFFIXES:
.SUFFIXES: .l
.l.o:
    $(CMPLR) $(LFLAGS) $< >> '#errs' 2>&1

ppack: $(OBJ)
    @echo ppack updated
```

file name ending in .l and the *sh* shell I/O redirection. Recall also that **make** echos the entire command before it is executed. If a command line is preceded by @, the line will not be echoed before it is executed.

11.6 The make **Command**

The simplest way to use the **make** command is first to move to the main directory that contains the makefile and the files (and subdirectories) of the software package. Once you are in the main directory, simply type:

make [*target ...*]

If no target is specified, the first target in the description that does not begin with a period is used. When targets are given, they are processed sequentially in the order listed.

The general form of the **make** command is:

make [*macro ...*] [−f *makefile*] [*options*] [*targets*]

A macro definition given on the command line is also in the form *string1 = string2*. Any number of macro definitions can be given on the command line.

A command line macro definition overrides any definition for the same macro in the makefile. Examples one and two in Section 11.5 illustrate this feature.

The option −f specifies the name of the makefile. As mentioned, the default file name for the makefile is makefile or Makefile (in that order) in the current working directory. A makefile named "−" denotes the standard input. The option −r instructs **make** not to use the built-in rules. Some other **make** options are as follows:

−i   instructs **make** to ignore error codes returned by invoked commands. This is equivalent to using the fake target name .IGNORE in the description file.

−s   prevents **make** from displaying command lines before executing (silent mode). This mode also is entered if the fake target .SILENT appears in the description file.

−n   instructs **make** to display commands but not to execute them. Even lines beginning with an @ sign are displayed.

−t   asks **make** to **touch** the target files (which alters their modification times to be current) rather than to issue the usual commands.

−q   asks **make** to determine whether or not the target file is up to date without performing any updating actions. The **make** command returns a zero exit status code if the target file is up to date.

−p   instructs **make** to display all the macro definitions and target descriptions. The display includes all the built-in macros and rules as well as those defined in the description file. No target is required for this option.

−d   asks **make** to enter the debug mode and display detailed information on files and times examined by **make**.

11.7 Summary

The UNIX **make** facility provides a convenient way to maintain software and document the relationships that exist between software components. It is used extensively for maintenance of UNIX system programs. The **make** command works with a user-supplied description file called a makefile. Following the dependence relations and updating commands provided in the makefile, **make** can bring the target files specified by the user up to date.

Commands in the makefile are ordinary *sh* commands with the added feature of makefile macro expansion. The **make** command also has a set of built-in macros and dependence rules, such as "*file*.o depends on *file*.c," that captures frequently used rules. You can override built-in rules with explicit rules. Preparing a makefile not only automates maintenance but also documents the relationships among the modules of a software package. Familiarity with **make** is important for any UNIX programmer.

Exercises

1. Assume that a program is written in source files prog.c, subr1.f, and subr2.c. Furthermore, assume that both prog.c and subr2.c #include the file aux.h. Design a makefile to compile this program.

2. What is the use of the @ when it precedes a command line in a makefile? Why?

3. When a file name follows the –f option, the **make** command uses that file as the makefile. Consider:

   ```
   make -f dir1/makefile
   ```

   What may be wrong with this usage?

4. Consider Example two in Section 11.5. There are several different targets with exactly the same command lines. Is there a way to avoid the repetition?

5. Consider Example three in Section 11.5. Why is the artificial component /tmp needed? How does it work?

6. Consider Example four in Section 11.5. How does the **cat** line work? Why is the empty file x.c needed?

7. Consider Example four in Section 11.5. Explain in detail how the sequence of pattern commands for **sed** works to produce the desired lines in the file deprules.

8. Consider Example four in Section 11.5. Why is the line #DO NOT DELETE . . . needed? How does it help the dependence generation?

Document Preparation

12

T he world runs on written communication, and for many professionals, the preparation of memos, letters, reports, proposals, technical papers, and other documents is a critical activity. Fortunately, the tasks involved in producing high-quality documents lend themselves to varying degrees of automation. Such tasks include:

1. Writing an initial draft document

2. Editing and revising the draft

3. Correcting errors in spelling and grammar

4. Formatting the document for printing

5. Proofreading, adjusting print format, and making final modifications

6. Printing the final document

Computerized document preparation not only makes these tasks easier and faster, but it also produces documents of very high quality. The resulting increase in productivity can be substantial.

On a computer system, interactive display text editors are used to create and revise documents (the **vi** and **emacs** editors were discussed in Chapter 2). But additional facilities are needed to perform the other tasks listed. Useful document processing utilities available on UNIX systems include:

- the **spell** spelling checker
- the **troff** text-formatting program for output on a photo typesetter or laser printer
- **nroff**, a version of **troff** for output to a letter-quality printer or a CRT terminal
- macro packages for **nroff** and **troff**
- the **tbl** preprocessor for formatting tables
- the **eqn** preprocessor for mathematical formulas in **troff**
- **neqn**, a version of **eqn** that works with **nroff**

Document Preparation Overview

Typically in UNIX, a document and its formatting instructions are entered into a file using a display editor (**vi** or **emacs**). The formatting instructions likely will involve **nroff/troff** commands and macros. There also may be **tbl** instructions for formatting tables and **eqn** instructions for typesetting mathe-

Figure 12.1 ▪ Document Preparation Overview

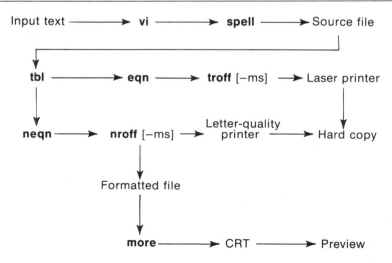

matical formulas. The document is checked for spelling errors using the **spell** program, and then it is previewed on a CRT terminal using **nroff** to uncover any formatting problems that need to be corrected. Finally, the document is printed using **troff** and a laster printer, after which it can be proofread for the last time. Figure 12.1 shows an overview of these activities.

This chapter explains in a practical way how to use the document preparation programs. Instead of presenting every detail of these programs, a task-oriented approach has been adopted: The programs are combined and used to produce letters, reports, and even books. Complete examples have been included; you may use these as templates for many applications.

12.1 Correcting Spelling Errors

UNIX keeps an on-line dictionary in the file /usr/dict/words. Several commands utilize the dictionary to help users correct spelling errors. The dictionary file is not a dictionary in the regular sense; rather, it is a list of words accumulated from many sources over time. Nor is the dictionary as complete as a large dictionary. It is, however, an effective spell-checking list that contains many commonly used words, proper names, and technical words.

Let's say you have created a file. The command:

`spell` *file*

can be used to check for spelling errors in the given *file*. The program **spell** takes the words contained in *file* as input and looks up each one in the on-line dictionary. If a word is neither in the dictionary nor derivable by applying certain inflections, prefixes, or suffixes, it is displayed one word per line on the standard output.

When using **spell**, keep in mind the following:

1. Not all misspelled words will be found, because **spell** checks words out of context. For example, no misspelling will be reported if "from" is misspelled as "form" or "message" is misspelled as "massage"; as far as **spell** is concerned, they are still correct words.

2. Not all words found by **spell** are spelled incorrectly. Some words are not included in the dictionary, and others depend on the way the words are derived.

Nevertheless, **spell** is useful for catching many errors quickly. The output from **spell** can, of course, be redirected into a file.

The **spell** program also can be used interactively to check words typed on the terminal. To invoke **spell** in this manner, simply type **spell** with no argument, followed by RETURN. Then type any number of words followed by

^^D on a separate line. In other words, when given no argument, **spell** takes input from the standard input. For example, if you enter:

```
spell
to test how the spell progarm wroks interactively
^D
```

the output result will be:

```
progarm
wroks
```

As mentioned in Section 4.3, the UNIX command **look** also helps you find a word in the on-line dictionary. To use **look**, you would use:

```
look prefix
```

to display all the words in /usr/dict/words with the same prefix. You also can use the pipeline:

```
look prefix | grep string
```

in case the *prefix* selects too many words.

12.2 nroff **and** troff

The **troff** text processing program formats text for high-resolution output devices such as laser printers or phototypesetters. A version of **troff**, known as **nroff**, is used for letter-quality printers and CRT terminals.

The input to **nroff/troff** is text interspersed with *format requests*. The output is a printable, paginated, adjusted document having a user-designed style. The **nroff/troff** programs together with associated macro packages offer unusual freedom in document styling. Their features include:

- text justification, centering, indentation, and pagination
- superscripts and subscripts
- sequence numbering for sections and pages
- arbitrary style headers and footers
- multiple-column format
- dynamic font, point size, and spacing control
- line drawing functions
- mathematical symbols and formulas
- tabulation

The **nroff** and **troff** programs are highly compatible with each other, and the same input almost always is acceptable to either. Formatting commands that are meaningful only to **troff** simply are ignored by **nroff**. Thus, a document prepared for **troff** printing also can be processed by **nroff** and vice versa. Many people find it convenient to use **nroff** to preview documents being prepared for **troff**. In this chapter, the word "troff" will stand for both **nroff** and **troff**. Commands appliable only to **troff** will be indicated.

12.3 Document Formatting with the ms Macro Package

A **nroff/troff** macro package is a library of text-formatting commands. These commands are called *macros*. A macro allows a group of formatting requests and/or text to be given a name and to be invoked by that name. A macro usually combines several primitive requests to form a higher-level request, which corresponds to a well-understood formatting function. For example, a *title macro* produces centered title lines with a larger boldface font and an appropriate amount of vertical space after the title. Such a title macro would be defined using a combination of **troff** primitive requests for line centering, size, font, and vertical spacing. Whenever **troff** encounters a macro request during document formatting, the macro is used, substituting in the primitive requests that defined it. Several macro packages are available for use with **troff**, and it also is possible to write your own macros, as is discussed in Section 12.19.

One of the most used standard macro packages is the ms macro package, which provides most of the commands you would use for day-to-day document preparation. The original manuscript of this book was prepared using ms and **troff**. The ms macros are relied on heavily in this chapter.

12.4 troff Command Basics

The **troff** processes document text and formatting commands. A command can be:

1. An *escape sequence*

2. A *primitive request*

3. A *macro*

Thus, **troff** input can be considered as a program containing commands that act on data, the text. The result of this program is a printable or, with some versions of **troff**, a printed document having the desired format.

Obviously, there must be some way to distinguish between the formatting requests and the text. An escape sequence, also referred to as a *function*, only is given in-line with text. It always begins with the **troff** escape character, the backslash (\). For example:

```
...when \fI critical mass\fP is reached ...
```

will be printed as:

```
...when critical mass is reached ...
```

This example uses two escape sequences:

\fI   (change to italic font; underline for **nroff**)

\fP   (change to previous font)

Because \ is used as an escape character, you must use the special escape \e to print \.

Neither a primitive request nor a macro can be given in-line with text. Both must begin on a new line and must begin with either a period (.) or a single quotation mark (') as the first character. For example, the **troff** request:

.ce n   (center next *n* lines)

centers the next *n* input lines of text. In our discussion, the argument *n* always stands for an integer, and it can be omitted if $n = 1$. The macro:

.PP   (begin indented paragraph)

is used at the beginning of each indented paragraph to produce a paragraph with an indented first line. The effect of introducing a request with a ' will be explained in Section 12.6.

The number of arguments to a primitive request or a macro depends on the request or the macro; some take none, some one, some several. Arguments are separated by blanks. Extra blanks between arguments or at the end of a line should be avoided. Names of primitive requests consist of two lowercase characters. Almost all ms macro names consist of two uppercase characters.

12.5 **Invoking** troff

The text of a document to be formatted, **troff** macros, and primitive requests are entered into a file and then are formatted and printed using the commands:

```
nroff -ms file > output-file
```

or

```
troff -ms file > output-file
```

The option −ms invokes the ms macro package. Other options are described in the UNIX manual pages for **troff**. The output of **nroff** also is suitable for viewing on a CRT using the **more** command. The output of **troff** usually is printed on a laser printer by another command. On most systems, this printing command is combined with **troff** to form a single command that performs both formatting and printing on a specific brand of laser printer. Depending on your local system and the printing devices used, the preceding commands may have to be modified slightly to send output to a particular printer or terminal. Your system manager can provide such information. Nevertheless, the way input files to **troff** are prepared is the same from system to system.

12.6 Text Processing

The **troff** program inputs a file and outputs a formatted document that may be printed on a laser printer. In its simplest form, **troff** absorbs input text until enough words have been assembled to fill one output line. In *filling an output line*, any white space (including a RETURN) that separates words in the input text may be replaced by the amount of space appropriate to fit the text nicely on an output line. Automatic hyphenation is used to break up long words at the ends of lines. This mode of filling lines is referred as the *fill mode*, which is the default **troff** mode. After an output line is formed, it is *flushed*; that is, it is sent to the output channel. The **troff** program repeats the process until no input remains.

If an input line begins with white space, any partially assembled line will be flushed and a new output line begun with the same number of leading spaces. The flushing of a partially formed output line is referred to as a *break*. A blank line causes a break, as do many primitive **troff** requests introduced by a period (.). The same primitive request, if introduced by a single quotation mark ('), will not cause an automatic break. This is the only difference between using a . and using a ' to introduce a request.

Filling and Adjusting Lines

When an output line is filled with enough words, **troff** inserts spaces between words to make a *flush right-hand margin*. This operation is called *adjusting* *the line*. The **troff** program normally adjusts lines. If this is undesirable, use:

`.na`   (no adjust)

to produce a ragged (nonadjusted) right margin. The command:

`.ad`   (adjust)

can be used to restore right-margin alignment. If line filling is not required, the command:

`.nf`   (no fill)

can be used to turn off the *fill* (and therefore adjust) *mode*. In the *no fill mode*, input lines are copied verbatim to the output, without regard for line length or word spacing. This mode is useful for text that is already well formatted.

Page Layout

The output line length is set by the primitive **troff** request:

`.ll N`   (set line length)

where N is a distance. A distance (denoted by N in our presentations) can be given in a number of ways, as described in Section 12.10. The ms macro package maintains the line length in a *number register*, LL, which can be set by:

`.nr LL N`   (set ms line length register)

The default value of LL is six inches. When using the ms package, a new LL setting will not take effect until the next paragraph begins. For immediate effect, use .ll. To control the left margin use:

`.po N`   (set page offset or left margin)

whose default value is zero for **nroff** and one inch for **troff**. The ms number register PO controls page offset. For example,

`.nr PO N`   (set ms page offset register)

takes effect on the next page. You could, for example, use the combination:

```
.po 1.5i
.nr PO 1.5i
```

at the beginning of a document to set the page offset to 1.5 inches.*
    The default page length is 11 inches. It can be changed using:

`.pl N`   (set page length)

Figure 12.2 ▪ **Page Layout**

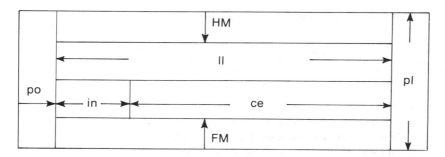

The top and bottom margins are controlled by the ms number registers:

HM   [top (head) margin register]

FM   [bottom (foot) margin register]

The default head and foot margins are one inch. These margins also can be set using .nr.

An indentation moves the beginning of lines further to the right. The following:

.in +*N*   (increase current indent by *N*)

.in −*N*   (decrease current indent by *N*)

increment and decrement indentation. Several of the previously discussed features are illustrated in Figure 12.2.

The ms package uses a set of number registers to hold such settings as left margin, line length, character size, and line spacing. These registers are used within ms-defined macros to perform various formatting functions. A change to the value of one of these registers (for example, LL and PO) takes effect only when certain ms built-in or user-requested actions take place. This presents a point of confusion. However, the user can always set *both* the ms number register and use a corresponding **troff** primitive request (for instance, .ll or .po) for immediate effect.

12.7 Formatting a Letter

Before discussing additional formats in the abstract, let's look at an example of how to format a letter using **troff** and ms (Figure 12.3). The example puts some of the commands already covered to use and provides a template for

Figure 12.3 ▪ A Letter Template

```
(1)  .nr PO 1.0i                 \" left margin 1 inch
(2)  .nr LL 6.5i                 \" line length 6.5 inches
(3)  .ND                         \" no date
(4)  .ds CH                      \" no page numbers
(5)  .LP                         \" initialize ms
(6)  .sp 5                       \" 5 blank lines
(7)  .ti +3.26i                  \" indent next line
(8)  \*(DY                       \" use register value for current date
(9)  .sp 3                       \" 3 blank lines
(10) .DS L                       \" display start, left-adjusted
     Mr. Bob Smith
     55 Avenue of the Americas
     New York, N.Y. 10249
(11) .DE                         \" display end
(12) .sp
     Dear Mr. Smith:
(13) .PP                         \" paragraph
     In reply to your letter concerning our last meeting in New York City, I am
     happy to report that our company . . .
(14) .PP
     Our division is very interested in your proposal. We wish to have a second
     meeting with you and your key staff in Palo Alto . . .
(15) .PP
     If you need more information or have any questions that I may be able to
     answer, please give me a ring. I look forward to hearing from you.
(16) .sp
(17) .in +3.26i
     Sincerely yours,
(18) .sp 3
     Charles M. Brown
(19) .in -3.26i
```

your own letters. Commands are numbered for easy reference. These numbers are not part of the example. Most commands are followed by comments that work just as do program comments; they help explain what is going on in the letter. The **troff** program ignores the \" (comment escape) and whatever follows it until the end of the line. The letter printed from Figure 12.3 is shown in Figure 12.4.

Lines 1 and 2 set the number registers PO and LL for left margin and line length, respectively. These settings conform to accepted letter formats. The ms macro package automatically prints a date at the bottom of each page and a page number (starting on page two) at the top of each page. Lines 3 and 4 disable these two functions, since they are not normally used in a letter.

Figure 12.4 ▪ Sample Letter Output

July 15, 1988

Mr. Bob Smith
55 Avenue of the Americas
New York, N.Y. 10249

Dear. Mr. Smith:
    In reply to your letter concerning our last meeting in New York
City, I am happy to report that our company . . .
    Our division is very interested in your proposal. We wish to have
a second meeting with you and your key staff in Palo Alto . .
    If you need more information or have any questions that I may
be able to answer, please give me a ring. I look forward to hearing
from you.

Sincerely yours,

Charles M. Brown

In Line 5, the macro .LP, for a left-adjusted paragraph, is used to initialize
the ms macro package. With the ms package, you cannot just begin a document
with a line of text; one of several commands must appear before the first
output line is produced to initialize the package. When in doubt, use .LP or
.PP to achieve proper initialization.

The request:

`.sp n`   (*n* blank lines)

inserts blank lines. If *n* is one, it can be omitted. Line 6 puts five blank lines
at the top of the letter. This space plus the default one-inch head margin gives
the letter enough head room. The request:

`.ti N`   (indent next line by *N*)

indents the next line of input text. It is used in Line 7 to put the date line of
the letter in the correct position (just to the right of the center).

Line 8 uses a built-in *ms string register* to form the date line. A string
register is a **troff** variable that contains a string value. Specifically, the string
register DY contains the current date in the form "*month date, year.*" The
notation *(DY instructs the value of this string register to be included in your
text. Refer to Section 12.15 for more details on defining and using registers.
Also, Appendices 6 and 7 list all built-in registers in **troff** and ms.

The example letter follows the *modified block style*, as it is called by professional typists. Three blank lines separate the date line and the left-adjusted address field. The lines of the address already are in correct format and should not be rearranged. The ms macros .DS and .DE sandwich such no-fill lines to form a *display with keep*. (*Keep* is a property that maintains selected lines on one page. Keep is discussed further in Section 12.9.) A display is not filled, and a display with keep always is kept on the same page. If there is not enough room for a display on the current page, a new page is started, and the display appears on the new page. The address in this letter appears between Lines 10 and 11, forming a left-adjusted display. The possible forms of the .DS macro are:

`.DS L`	Display lines are left-adjusted flush with the left margin.
`.DS I N`	Display lines are indented by the indicated distance *N*.
`.DS C`	Display lines are centered individually.
`.DS B`	Display lines are centered not individually but as a left-adjusted block.

A page break can occur inside a *display with no keep*, requested by the macros:

`.LD`	Left-adjusted display starts, no keep.
`.CD`	Centered display starts, no keep
`.ID N`	Indented display starts, no keep.
`.BD N`	Block-centered display starts, no keep.

All of the preceding no-fill display requests are terminated by the .DE macro.

Lines 12 through 16 are self-explanatory. Lines 17 through 19 increment and decrement the indentation to push the complimentary close and signature lines to a position aligned with the date line.

Try entering this example into a file and then type:

```
nroff -ms file >! letter
```

You can view the formatted letter by giving the command:

```
more letter
```

which should look just like the letter shown in Figure 12.4.

12.8 Formatting a Report

Let us now prepare a report using **troff** and ms. A report template suitable for reports and scientific papers is presented in Figure 12.5. In the figure, the

Figure 12.5 ▪ A Report Template

```
(1)   .nr PS 12      \" set point size register to 12
(2)   .nr VS 14      \" set vertical space register to 14
      .LP            \" initialize ms
(3)   .TL            \" title
      Software Productivity and the Computer Industry
      .sp
      An Artificial Report
(4)   .AU            \" author
(5)   Ward A. Turing\u\(dg\d
(6)   .AI            \" author institution
      Department of Computer Science
      Empire State University
      Palo Alto, California 94303
(7)   .AB            \" abstract start
      Explored are the current status and future directions in software
      production. Environments for increased productivity, reliability,
      maintainability, etc. . . .
(8)   .AE            \" abstract end
(9)   .FS            \" footnote start
      \(dg Work reported herein has been supported in part by the Columbia
      Science Foundation under Grant CBR-000001.
(10)  .FE            \" footnote end
(11)  \" if 1.5 space is needed use .nr VS 21
(12)  .NH
      Introduction
(13)  .LP
      First paragraph of the introduction section.
(14)  .LP
      Second paragraph of the introduction section.
(15)  .NH
      Software Productivity
(16)  .LP
      First paragraph of the second section.
(17)  .NH 2
      A Critical Need
(18)  .LP
      First paragraph of Section \*(SN.
(19)  .NH 2
      Major Areas for Increased Productivity
```

(continued)

Figure 12.5 ▪ (*continued*)

```
(20)  .LP
      First paragraph in Section \*(SN.
(21)  .ce
      References
(22)  .nr PS 11
(23)  .nr VS 13
(24)  .IP [1]
(25)  Chang, T. P., Smith, K., \*QThe Software Crisis,\*U The Great Empire
      Journal on Software Engineering, Vol. 13, No. 5, 1981, pp. 45-58.
(26)  .IP [2]
      More references . . .
```

macros:

.TL	title lines
.AU	author
.AI	author institution
.AB .AE	abstract start and end
.FS .FE	footnote start and end
.NH	numbered section heading
.IP	indented paragraph with hanging tag

are used and explained. Figure 12.6 shows the **troff** printing of the sample report template.

Character Size

Character size is measured by *points* in **troff**. A point is 1/72 inches. The default character size is 10 points. Depending on the capabilities of the output device, you may set the point size to larger or smaller values. Setting and changing *point size* produces different size characters in the final document. The **nroff** program cannot handle different size characters and simply ignores point size commands.

The ms macro package controls point size through the value contained in the number register PS. In the report template (Figure 12.5), Line 1 requests 12-point characters that, on many laser printers, correspond to normal, type-writer-size characters. When you specify a larger character size, the *vertical space* also must be adjusted. Vertical space is the width between the top of one line and the top of the next line. In other words, it is the character point

Figure 12.6 ▪ Output of the Report Template

Software Productivity and the Computer Industry
An Artificial Report

Ward A. Turing†

Department of Computer Science
Empire State University
Palo Alto, California 94303

ABSTRACT

Explored are the current status and future directions in software production. Environments for increased productivity, reliability, maintainability, etc. . . .

1 Introduction
First paragraph of the introduction section.
Second paragraph of the introduction section.

2 Software Productivity
First paragraph of the second section.

2.1 A Critical Need
First paragraph of Section 2.1.

2.2 Major Areas for Increased Productivity
First paragraph in Section 2.2.

References

[1] Chang, T. P., Smith, K., "The Software Crisis," The Great Empire Journal on Software Engineering, Vol. 13, No. 5, 1981, pp. 45–58.
[2] More references . . .

---

† Work reported herein has been supported in part by the Columbia Science Foundation under Grant CBR-000001.

---

size plus the size of the gap between the two lines. The default vertical space is 12. The rule of thumb is:

vertical space = character point size × 120%

Thus on Line 2, the ms number register VS, which controls vertical space, is set to 14 points. No fractional points are allowed. Line 11 contains a comment that says the vertical spacing may be increased to 21 to obtain one-and-a-half spacing for the body of the report. Just before the list of references, Lines 22 and 23, the point size and vertical spacing are reduced. A change to the registers PS or VS takes effect at the beginning of the next paragraph.

Title and Author

A paper or report usually begins with a title, an author, and an abstract, as shown in the template in Figure 12.5. On Line 3, the macro:

`.TL`   (title macro)

is followed by one or more lines for the title of the report. The title will be printed in a boldface font two points larger than the setting in the number register PS. The macros:

`.AU`   (author macro)

`.AI`   (author institution macro)

(Lines 4 and 6) center the lines that follow the title. The .TL, .AU, and .AI macros use the no-fill mode. .AU and .AI can be used repeatedly for multiple authors.

Special Symbols

Line 5 gives the author's name followed by a dagger (†), which is raised one-half of a line. The **troff** program provides many special symbols through escape sequences. Figure 12.7 lists some of these special symbols. A complete

Figure 12.7 ▪ Some troff Special Symbols

Escape sequence	Printed as
\(dg	†
\(*g	γ
\(*G	Γ
\(!=	≠
\(co	©
\(Fi	ffi
\(di	÷

listing of special symbols defined in **troff** is contained in Appendix 8. The ms macro package also defines some special symbols. The escape sequences:

*Q   (opening double quotation mark ")

*U   (closing double quotation mark ")

are used on Line 25 in the example.

Abstract

Text for the report's abstract is placed between the macros .AB and .AE, as shown in Lines 7 and 8. The abstract is formatted as a filled, centered paragraph whose line length is 5/6 of normal. The centered heading ABSTRACT is supplied automatically. If the ABSTRACT heading is not desirable, use ".AB no" to suppress it.

Footnotes

A footnote can be requested anywhere in the document. Text placed between the macros .FS and .FE will be collected, recorded, and printed on the bottom of the current page (Lines 9 and 10). By default, footnotes are 11/12 the length of the normal text, but the footnote line length can be changed by setting the number register FL.

Section Headings

The ms package provides macros for section headings that are spaced appropriately and boldfaced automatically. The macros:

.SH   (unnumbered section heading)

.NH *n*   (automatically numbered section heading)

are used for section headings (Lines 12, 15, 17, and 19). Each can be followed by one or more lines of text. Text for the heading is always followed by a .PP or .LP, indicating the end of the heading and the beginning of a paragraph (Lines 13, 14, 16, 18, and 20).

The macro .NH automatically numbers sections 1, 2, 2.1, 3.1.2, and so on. When an integer argument *n* is given, it is taken to be a *section level number*, and an appropriate subsection number is generated. Larger level numbers indicate deeper nested subsections. Current implementations support a nesting depth of five levels. Automatic section numbering allows you to add or delete sections without renumbering. An explicit:

.NH 0

resets the numbering of level 1 to one. And, the request:

```
.NH S n m ...
```

is used to obtain a specific section number *n.m* ... . From one to five integers can follow the key letter S. Subsequent .NH requests will generate section numbers based on this new setting. The string register SN is set by the .NH request and contains the current section number.

Paragraphs

The ms macro package provides a variety of macros for formatting paragraphs:

.PP	paragraph (first line indented)
.LP	block paragraph (first line not indented)
.QP	quoted paragraph
.XP	paragraph with all but first line indented
.IP	indented paragraph (with hanging label)

.PP and .LP have been discussed. A quoted paragraph, .QP, is used to include quotations from other publications. Lines in a quoted paragraph are indented on the left and right sides from the normal page. The .XP request is the opposite of the .PP request.

The indented paragraph request .IP is often used. For example, Lines 24 and 26 in Figure 12.5 use .IP for the references. The general form of .IP is:

```
.IP [ label ] [ indent ]
```

Label can be only one word. If *label* contains multiple words, the words must be enclosed in double quotation marks. *Label* is optional. If *indent* is not specified, a standard amount of indentation is used. When given, the indent

---

Figure 12.8 ▪ Formatting Indented Paragraphs

```
.IP "Step 1" 12
We explain the first step here. Use as many lines of text
as needed. These lines will be put into an indented
paragraph with the label \*QStep 1.\*U The indent is 12
characters.
.IP "Step 2"
We explain the second step here. Use as many lines of
text as needed. These lines will be put into an indented
paragraph with the label \*QStep 2.\*U Note the same
indent is in use here.
```

is specified as the number of character positions. This indent will remain in effect for subsequent .IP requests until the next .PP or .LP. For example, the source text in Figure 12.8 produces the output in Figure 12.9.

The macros:

.RS   (begin right-shift)

.RE   (end right-shift)

are used to shift the relative indentation point temporarily one TAB stop to the right. In other words, text lines between .RS and .RE are printed with an additional right-shift of one TAB stop. These macros present a convenient method to shift a section of text right by one TAB stop. For example, .RS and .RE can be combined with .IP to obtain *nested indented paragraphs*, as shown in Figure 12.10.

Figure 12.9 ▪ Formatted Indented Paragraphs

Step 1	We explain the first step here. Use as many lines of text as needed. These lines will be put into an indented paragraph with the label "Step 1." The indent is 12 characters.
Step 2	We explain the second step here. Use as many lines of text as needed. These lines will be put into an indented paragraph with the label "Step 2." Note the same indent is in use here.

Figure 12.10 ▪ Nested Indented Paragraphs

Input	Output

`.IP (1)`
`The first rule . . .`
`.RS`
`.IP (1.1)`
`.IP (1.2)`
`.RE`
`.IP (2)`
`The second rule . . .`
`.RS`
`.IP (2.1)`
`.IP (2.2)`
`.RE`
	`(1)  The first rule . . .`
	`    (1.1)`
	
	`    (1.2)`
	
	`(2)  The second rule . . .`
	`    (2.1)`
	
	`    (2.2)`

12.9 Keeping a Group of Lines Together

The **troff** program fills and provides automatic breaking of lines and pages. This feature usually is convenient, but sometimes it may separate a group of lines that should be on one page. Consider the letter template (Figure 12.3), for example. If the letter is more than one page in length, it may happen that the closing and signature lines appear alone on the second page. Worse yet, the closing may appear at the bottom of the first page and the signature line at the top of the second page. In this section, **troff** requests for keeping lines on the same page, a property referred to as *keep*, are discussed.

Lines in a no-fill display bracketed by .DS and .DE are *kept* on the same page. For filled lines, tables, and other applications, the commands:

```
.KS          (keep start)
.KE          (keep end)
```

are used to *keep* a block of lines together. .If there is not enough space for the block, a new page is started, which maintains the block on one page but may leave a large blank space at the end of the previous page.

There is also the request:

```
.KF          (keep float)
```

If the block is preceded by .KF instead of .KS and does not fit on the current page, it will be moved down through the input text until the top of the next page. Thus, .KF prevents any large blank space from being introduced into the document. Consider the letter template. To prevent the closing and signature lines from appearing on separate pages, you could insert a .KS just before the last .PP and a .KE at the end of the letter. Such a construction ensures that the last paragraph, the closing and the signature line are kept on the same page.

12.10 Units for Distance

Many **troff** and ms requests that deal with layout, position, indentation, and so on take an argument that specifies a distance. In this chapter, the symbol N has been used consistently to represent such an argument for distance. A distance argument can be given as an integer or a decimal number followed by one of the following units:

```
i          inches
c          centimeters
```

p	points (= 1/72 inch)
u	basic units (depends on the output device used)
m	ems (the width of an m)
n	ens (the width of an n)
P	pica (1/6 inch)
v	vertical line space (variable, set by .vs)

Thus, 3i, 4.5c, 5m, and 6n are all correct distance specifications. If a distance is specified with no unit, the default depends on the request. For horizontally oriented requests, an *em* is used.

For many requests that take a distance argument, an increment or decrement distance can be used instead. The increase or decrease is given by preceding the distance by a + or − sign. The effect is to increase or decrease the current setting by the given amount. For example:

```
.pl +2i
```

adds two inches to the current page length.

12.11 Vertical and Horizontal Motions

Motion requests affect the print position. Superscripts and subscripts can be positioned for printing with vertical motions. The escape sequences:

\u	(one-half line up)
\d	(one-half line down)
\v 'amt'	(move vertically by *amt*)

provide in-line vertical motion. For example, Line 5 of the report template (Figure 12.5) moves the position up one-half line, prints the dagger (†) as a superscript, and then moves back down one-half line. Always remember to insert the \d to move back down one-half line; otherwise, everything following the superscript will be affected. The vertical motion *amt* can be any valid distance, for example 2i. Positive distances such as 2i move down; negative distances, for example −2i, move up.

It also is possible to *mark* (record) an earlier vertical position on a page and then return to that vertical position later. The pair of requests:

.mk	(mark vertical position)
.rt	(return to marked vertical position)

are used for this purpose. For example:

```
.nf
.mk
Massachusetts
Ohio
Texas
.rt
.in +18
Boston
Columbus
Austin
.in -18
```

prints two columns, the first at the current indentation and the second at an additional indentation of 18 ems, as shown:

Massachusetts	Boston
Ohio	Columbus
Texas	Austin

The pair:

```
.mk A          (mark vertical position in register A)
.sp \nAu       (go to absolute vertical position given by register A)
```

is used in a similar way and allows multiple vertical positions to be recorded. The escape \nA interpolates the value of the numerical register A; u is a basic unit of distance.

For horizontal motions, the escape:

```
\h 'amt'
```

is used. The *amt* can be any valid distance. Negative distances move left, for example:

```
<\h '-.2m'=
```

prints

```
<=
```

to bring the equal sign .2m closer to the greater than sign. The escape:

```
\w 'text'
```

yields the width of *text* in basic units. For example:

```
Note\h '-\w'Note'u'Note
```

prints the word Note, moves back its horizontal width, and prints the same word again. This sequence demonstrates an alternate way to boldface a word.

It is possible to record a horizontal position in a register and return to the same horizontal position on a later line in the page using the following pair of escapes:

```
\k x                    (remember horizontal position in register x)
\h'\n xu'               (move to absolute horizontal position given by register
                         x)
```

For example:

```
.nf
Massachusetts           \kxBoston
Ohio \h'\n xu 'Columbus
Texas \h'\n xu 'Austin
.fi
```

is another way of printing two vertical columns.

Line Drawing

The escapes:

```
\l 'Nc'                 (draw horizontal line)
\L'Nc'                  (draw vertical line)
```

produce lines of length N using the optional character c. If c is omitted, a solid line is drawn. For example:

```
\kx\l'3.5i'\L'0.5i'\l'-3.5i'\h'\n xu '\L'-0.5i'\v'0.5i'
```

draws a rectangle as follows:

12.12 troff **Fonts**

One important advantage of **troff** over **nroff** is the **troff** ability to print characters in different style character sets, or *fonts*, and to print characters in different sizes in the same document. A modern laser printer or phototypesetter has several fonts immediately available, and they also provide the ability to add additional fonts or switch to different ones. The **troff** program assumes the following standard fonts:

roman

italic

bold

Exactly which and how many other fonts are available depends on your printing device and its **troff** software support.

Font Requests

For **troff**, the default font is Times Roman. The font can be changed by the request:

`.ft F`   (change to font *F*)

where the font name *F* can be:

I	(italic)
R	(roman)
B	(bold)

The **nroff** program automatically converts any italicized characters to underline characters and ignores any other fonts it cannot handle.

Often, a different font is needed only to italicize or boldface a few words. This procedure is achieved most conveniently by using the escape functions:

\fI	(switch to italic)
\fB	(switch to bold)
\fR	(switch to roman)
\fP	(return to previous font)

For example, the line:

`to show \fBbold\fP, roman, and \fIitalic\fP fonts`

is printed as

to show **bold**, roman, and *italic* fonts

A changed font does not revert to the original font unless specifically requested. Always remember to use \fP to return to the previous font.

It is also possible to *embolden* an existing font by using the request:

`.bd F n`   (embolden font *F* by $n - 1$ units)

Thus:

```
.bd I 3
This shows the effect of \fIemboldened italics.\fR
```

gives:

This shows the effect of ***emboldened italics***.

To reset an emboldened font to normal, use:

`.bd F 0`

    It also is possible to print diacritical marks such as ü and à. A complete list of such marks can be found in Appendix 6.

Varying Character Sizes

Overall character size can be controlled using the ms PS and VS number registers, as previously discussed. But for small adjustments to font sizes, the in-line escape function:

`\s ± n`   (increase/decrease font size by *n* points)

is most convenient. For example:

`get\s+2ting \s+2larger \s-2then get\s-2ting \s-2smaller\s+2`

produces the line:

getting larger then getting smaller

With the \s function, you must remember to revert to the original font size. Size changes also can be specified with the following ms requests:

`.LG`   (make larger)

`.SM`   (make smaller)

`.NL`   (return to normal size)

Each size change is two points. These requests can be repeated for increased effect. If actual underscoring, as opposed to *italicizing*, is required, use:

`.UL word`   (underscores *word*)

12.13 The .tl Request

The *three-part title* is a useful **troff** primitive request:

`.tl tl-string`

The argument *tl-string* is specified in the form:

```
xS1xS2xS3x
```

which gives three separate strings: S1, S2, and S3. The separator *x* can be any character not contained in the three strings. The .tl request prints:

S1   left-adjusted

S2   centered

S3   right-adjusted

All three strings have to be specified even if several are empty. For example:

```
.tl '''against the right margin'
```

specifies S1 and S2 as empty. This request is a convenient way of printing one or several short lines that are right-adjusted.

12.14 Page Header and Footer Lines

The **troff** ms macros, by default, will print a page heading that contains a page number starting on the second page. When used with **nroff**, ms also prints a default page footer showing the current date. The page header and footer are printed in the middle of the header and footer margin areas. The ms number registers:

HM   header margin register (default 1.0i)

FM   footer margin register (default 1.0i)

contain the widths of these margins. Number registers can be set by the .nr request, as in the request:

```
.nr HM 2i
```

which sets the header margin to two inches.

The header line consists of three parts: the left, center, and right portions, which are left-adjusted, centered, and right-adjusted, respectively. The header string registers:

LH   left header (default empty)

CH   center header (default "– page number –")

RH   right header (default empty)

contain strings that define the three header portions. Similarly, the footer line consists of the three portions defined by the following footer string registers:

LF   left footer (default empty)

CF   center footer (default date for **nroff**, empty for **troff**)

RF   right footer (default empty)

These six string registers can be redefined to tailor the appearance of the page header and footer lines. For example, you may want your page numbers centered at the bottom of the page. To do so use:

.ds CH   (define CH to be a null string)

.ds CF %   (define CF to be the current page number)

at the beginning of your document. With ms, the special character % stands for the *current page number* when used in a string or macro definition.

The ms package handles page headers and footers through two macros: .PT and .BT, which are invoked automatically at the top and bottom of each page, respectively. The macros use the six header and footer string registers to print the header and footer lines, although the actual formatting is accomplished within the .PT and .BT macros using the primitive .tl request.

The .PT and .BT macros can print different lines depending on whether the page number is even or odd. The strings are supplied through the macros:

.OH *tl-string*   defines odd-page headers

.EH *tl-string*   defines even-page headers

.OF *tl-string*   defines odd-page footers

.EF *tl-string*   defines even-page footers

These macros make it possible to put page numbers in the upper-left corner of an even page and in the upper-right corner of an odd page, as follows:

```
.EH '%'''
.OH '''%'
```

You can make minor adjustments to the page headers and footers by redefining the strings LH, CH, and RH, which are the left, center, and right portions of the page headings, respectively; and the strings LF, CF, and RF, which are the left, center and right portions of the page footer. For more complex formats, the user can redefine the macros .PT and .BT, which are invoked at the top and bottom of each page, respectively. The margins (taken from registers HM and FM, for the top and bottom margin, respectively) normally are one inch; the page header or footer is in the middle of that space. If you redefine these macros, be careful not to change parameters such as point size or font without resetting them to the original values afterward.

12.15 Using Registers

In addition to the ms internal registers such as the string register DY (the letter template) and the numeric registers PS, PO (the report template), it also is possible to define your own registers to store string or numeric values. These registers then can be *interpolated* (inserted) into your text. To define a string register use:

`.ds` *name string*

where *name* is one or two characters. A space or TAB follows *name*. *String* consists of every character thereafter, until the end of the line. A string register is interpolated with the escape:

`\*(` *name*

For example, having defined the string register Tx as follows:

`.ds Tx T\v'0.3m'E\v'-0.3m'X`

the line:

`... another popular document-formatting program is \*(Tx ...`

is printed as:

`... another popular document-formatting program is T`$_E$`X ...`

You also can define number registers in **troff**, and these, too, can be given names of one or two characters. A number register holds an integer value. The following requests are for value assignments:

`.nr` *name N* [*A*]   stores N, a number or a distance, in the named register. A distance is stored as a number of basic units. The optional A is an *auto-increment amount*, which the user may elect to associate with the named number register. This option allows the register to be incremented or decremented automatically when it is interpolated.

`.nr` *name*±*N*   increments/decrements the named register by N.

To interpolate a number register in your text, use:

`\n`*x*   or   `\n(`*xx*   interpolates the number register x or xx.

`\n`±*x*   or   `\n(`±*xx*   increments/decrements the number register x or xx (by the auto-increment) and then interpolates its value. This feature is useful in numbering a sequence of running items such as numbered references and problems in exercises.

12.16 Formatting Tables: tbl

A well-formatted table is hard to type. To help, UNIX provides the **tbl** command. This command generates the complicated sequences of **troff** commands needed to print a table, based on specifications provided by the user. The macros:

.TS	(table start)
.TE	(table end)

are used to bracket a table within a document. The document then is processed by **tbl**, whose output is subsequently piped to **troff** for formatting with the ms package. The **tbl** command is, therefore, a preprocessor for **troff** (or **nroff**). The command:

tbl *file* | **troff** −ms

is used to link **tbl** and **troff** in this manner.

The **tbl** tables are made up of columns, which may be independently centered, right-adjusted, left-adjusted, or aligned by decimal points. Headings may be placed over one or several adjacent columns. A single entry may involve multiple rows of text. Equations may be part of an entry. Optional horizontal and vertical lines may be drawn to separate table entries. Any entry can be enclosed in a box, as can the entire table. Formatting tables with primitive **troff** requests is complicated; fortunately, the same job using **tbl** is relatively straightforward.

A Simple Table

Let us first look at the source text for a simple **tbl** table:

```
(1)   .TS
(2)   center;
(3)   c s s
(4)   c c c
(5)   l n n.
(6)   Price Comparison
      .sp 2
(7)   Part→Vendor A→Vendor B
      .sp
(8)   b&w monitor→225.00→321.00
(9)   1200 modem→260.00→210.00
(10)  RS232 cable→25.50→28.00
(11)  .TE
```

The output of this table is shown in Figure 12.11. The → indicates a TAB character. The entire table is bracketed by Lines 1 and 11, using the .TS and .TE macros. The table itself is specified in three parts, exactly as follows:

```
.TS
options and overall format ;
column format by key letters .
data items for table entries
.TE
```

Each of these portions is explained in the following subsections.

Table Formats and Options

In the preceding example, the overall format is given on Line 2 of the source text. The keyword *center* means that the entire table will be centered as a block over the current line length. One or several keywords can be given, separated by commas, and terminated by a semicolon (;). The available options and formats are listed:

`center`	centers the table (default is left-adjust)
`box`	encloses the table in a box
`allbox`	encloses each item in the table in a box
`doublebox`	encloses the table in two boxes
`expand`	makes the table as wide as the current line length
`tab(x)`	uses x instead of TAB to separate data items
`linesize(n)`	sets lines or rules (for example, for box) in n point type

Figure 12.11 ▪ An Example Table

Price Comparison		
Part	Vendor A	Vendor B
b&w monitor	225.00	321.00
1200 modem	260.00	210.00
RS232 cable	25.50	28.00

Key-Letter Column Formats

Following the options listed previously are one or several rows of column format. The first format row governs the first data row; the second format row governs the second data row; and so on. The last format row governs all the remaining data rows and is terminated by a period (.). Thus, in the example, Line 3 controls the data on Line 6, and so on.

The format row is specified by *key letters*. Each row consists of as many key letters as there are columns in the table. Each key letter defines the format of one corresponding table entry. Each key letter optionally can be followed by other letters that are discussed later in this section. Entries in a format row are separated by one or more spaces. The key letters recognized by **tbl** are:

c   for centered entry

l   for left-adjusted entry

r   for right-adjusted entry

n   for numerical entry, to be aligned with other numerical entries so that the digits of numbers line up

a   for an alphabetic subcolumn; all column entries are aligned on the left with the widest entry, which is centered within the column

s   for a spanned heading, that is, to indicate that the entry from the previous column continues across this column (not allowed for the first column)

^   for a vertically spanned heading, that is, to indicate that the entry from the previous row continues down through this row (not allowed for the first row of the table)

Following these definitions, it is easy to understand the meaning of Lines 3 through 5 of the example:

line 3   c s s   centers the first column entry of Line 6 across the second and third columns, providing a heading for the table.

line 4   c c c   centers each entry given on Line 7 individually in its respective column.

line 5   l n n .   left-adjusts the first column and uses a numerical format for the second and third columns for Line 8 and the remaining data lines. The last format line is terminated by a period (.).

Data Lines of a Table

Immediately following the column format lines are the data lines for the table entries. Each data line specifies entries for one row in the table. A TAB is used to separate two data entries on the same line. The last data entry on a line is followed by a RETURN. It is all right to have fewer data entries than table columns on any given line. The remainder of the columns simply are left empty. An empty entry between other entries can be entered as \&, which is the **troff** *nonprinting zero-width* character. The **troff** or ms requests can be mixed with data lines, and data entries may contain escape sequences. The table end macro .TE is placed after the last data row.

To include a block that contains multiple lines of text as one table entry, precede the block with T{ and end the block with T} at the beginning of a new line. Therefore, the form is:

```
...→T{
block of
text
T}→...
```

If a data entry is \^, it means that the data entry in the same column above it spans downward to this entry. Vertically spanned items extending over several rows of the table normally are centered over the vertical range. If, however, the governing key letter is followed by the letter t, the vertically spanned item will begin at the top line of its range.

Horizontal and Vertical Lines

Let us take the price comparison table (Figure 12.11) and add some horizontal and vertical lines to it. The input to **tbl** then becomes:

```
(1)   .TS
(2)   center,box;
(3)   c s s
(4)   c |c |c
(5)   c |n |n.
(6)   Price Comparison
      =
(7)   Part→Vendor A→Vendor B
      _
(8)   b&w monitor→225.00→321.00
(9)   1200 modem→260.00→210.00
(10)  RS232 cable→25.50→28.00
(11)  .TE
```

The new table is shown in Figure 12.12.

Figure 12.12 ▪ A Boxed Table

Price Comparison		
Part	Vendor A	Vendor B
b&w monitor	225.00	321.00
1200 modem	260.00	210.00
RS232 cable	25.50	28.00

The additional keyword *box* on Line 2 requests that the entire table be enclosed in a box. The **tbl** command provides several ways to draw horizontal and vertical lines. A set of consistent rules is given here:

- *Vertical lines* are specified most conveniently in the format section of a table. A vertical bar (|) may be placed between column key letters, which results in a vertical line between the corresponding entries in the row. The vertical line will be extended to meet any adjoining vertical or horizontal lines, regardless of the height of the table entry. In the example, the vertical bars in Lines 4 and 5 result in the vertical lines in the table output. A vertical bar to the left of the first key letter or to the right of the last key letter produces a line at the edge of the table. Similarly, two vertical bars produce a double vertical line. Note in Figure 12.12 that the outside vertical and horizontal lines come from the overall box format.

- *Full-width horizontal lines* are requested most conveniently in the data part of a table. A data line containing only the character __ (underscore) or = (equal sign) is taken to be a single or double line, respectively, extending the full width of the table.

- *Single-column horizontal lines* are specified as follows. If a data entry is the single character __ or =, then it is printed as a single or double line extending the full width of the column. Such lines are extended to meet horizontal or vertical lines adjoining this column. To produce these characters in a column, either precede them with \& (the zero-width non-printing character) or follow them with a space before the usual TAB or NEWLINE.

- *Short horizontal lines* are specified as follows. If a data entry is the string __, then it produces a single line as wide as the contents of the column. It is not extended to meet adjoining lines.

Formulas in a Table

Another **troff** preprocessor, **eqn**, provides the ability to format mathematical formulas with relative ease. The **tbl** command allows mathematical formulas to be part of any table entry by using **eqn** commands in the data entry. The formula is *delimited* by special delimiters declared by:

```
delim(xy)
```

as a **tbl** option (given in the same line as center, box, etc.). This option specifies the use of the characters *x* and *y* as the beginning and ending **eqn** delimiters. For example, the option:

```
delim(@@)
```

allows you to use the character @ to sandwich **eqn** formulas in a table data entry. If a document contains both **tbl** and **eqn** constructs, it should be processed by **tbl** then by **eqn**. Thus, the recommended usage is:

```
tbl file | eqn | troff -ms
```

The **eqn** command is discussed in more detail in Sections 12.17 and 12.18.

Interleaving Format and Data Lines

It is possible to specify a format, provide some data lines, and then specify another format followed by some more data lines, and so on. This feature is convenient for a table with several sections (of rows), each requiring a different format. The outline of such a table is:

```
.TS
options ;
format .
data
. . .
.T&
format .
data
. . .
.T&
format .
data
. . .
.TE
```

For longer tables, this construct can bring the format closer to the data lines, which is easier to manage. For a table requiring multiple pages, it may be desirable to repeat the table heading at the top of each page, which can be done by giving the argument H to the .TS macro. If the table start macro is given as:

```
.TS H
```

then the ms request .TH must be given in the table just after the table heading data lines. All data lines before the .TH are considered table headings and are placed at the top of each page of the table.

Column Width and Separation

Column width and space between columns are produced as follows:

- *Column width:* If a key letter is followed by w(N) where N is a distance, the column will be at least that wide, even if the widest item in the column is not as wide. Equal column width is indicated by the character e following a key letter. All columns so indicated are made the same width.

- *Space between columns:* An integer may follow the key letter to indicate the amount of separation between the indicated column and the next. The number normally specifies the separation in ens. The default is 3.

Formatting a Table of Contents

As another example, consider the format for a table of contents. For this we can use the **tbl** *expand* format, as shown in Figure 12.13. The output produced from Figure 12.13 is illustrated in Figure 12.14. Note the column format r5 calls for a right-adjusted entry separated from the next column by five ens, and lw(4i) calls for a left-adjusted entry at least four inches wide.

Figure 12.13 ▪ Formatting a Table of Contents

```
.TS
expand;
r5 lw(4i) r.
Introduction→→\fB1\fP

Chapter 1→A UNIX Primer→\fB6\fP
1.1→Getting Started: Login and Logout→7
1.2→Talking to UNIX: The User Interface→8

Chapter 2→Text Editing→\fB35\fP
2.1→Getting Started with \fBvi\fP→38
2.2→Moving the Screen→39
.TE
```

Figure 12.14 ▪ A Sample Table of Contents

Creating Simple Figures

The **tbl** ability to position text in precise row-column locations makes it possible to arrange simple text patterns. Many figures contained in this book were formatted with **tbl**. For example, Figure 12.15 illustrates how Figure 7.1 was produced. The \& characters in Figure 12.15 can be omitted.

For Further Reference

Most, but certainly not all, aspects of **tbl** have been covered in this section. For more information, consult the UNIX **tbl** manual page or see the article "Tbl—A Program to Format Tables" by M. E. Lesk in the UNIX manual.

Figure 12.15 ▪ The tbl Source for Figure 7.1

```
.TS
center;
c s s s|l c r|c s s s s s s s s
|ce1 ce1 ce1 ce1 |ce1 ce1 ce1 |ce1 ce1 ce1 ce1 ce1 ce1 ce1 ce1 ce|
|l c s r|c s s|l c s s s s s s r|.
\&→\(<-→\fIrun\fP→\(->→\&
_
F→E→D→C→B→A→9→8→7→6→5→4→3→2→1→0
_
\(<-→\fItype\fP→\(->→ \& →\(<-→\fIaccess\fP→\(->
.TE
```

12.17 Formatting Mathematical Formulas: eqn

The **eqn** preprocessor provides the ability to specify mathematical formulas in a simple language that does not assume mathematical knowledge on the part of the user. The **eqn** program takes such formulas and generates **troff** requests to format the formulas in a textbook style. First, prepare a document for **troff** using ms, marking mathematical expressions and equations to be handled by **eqn** with the ms macros:

`.EQ L` *label*	(left-adjusted equation start)
`.EQ C` *label*	(centered equation start)
`.EQ I` *label*	(indented equation start)
`.EN`	(equation end)

These macros are placed at the beginning and end of formatting instructions destined for the **eqn** program. *Label* is an optional argument that, when given, will be displayed as a right-adjusted label for the equation. If neither L, C, nor I is specified for .EQ, the default is to center the equation. For example:

```
.EQ (3)
x sub 1 ^+^ y sup 2
.EN
```

is printed as:

$$x_1 + y^2 \hspace{6cm} (3)$$

Note that **eqn** prints the superscript and subscript in smaller size and that the variables are printed in italics. Sub and sup are **eqn** keywords used to control formatting of expressions. White space, one or more spaces or a RETURN, is used to separate keywords and symbols that are arguments to keywords. A document with **troff** and ms commands interspersed with **eqn** constructs is printed with the UNIX command:

eqn *file* | **troff** −ms

You can preview the document using **nroff** by issuing the UNIX command:

neqn *file* | **nroff** −ms > *file2*

The **neqn** program is the same as the **eqn** program, except it generates formatting commands suitable for **nroff**.

eqn Basics

Since **eqn** uses white space to separate keywords as well as symbols, white space contained in **eqn** input is not reflected in the output. Therefore, both:

```
.EQ                    .EQ
x + y - z = 0   and    x +
.EN                    y -    z = 0
                       .EN
```

result in the same output:

$$x+y-z$$

which looks too cramped. A printed space can be specified by the ˜ character. The character ^ represents a space that is one-half the width of ˜. It is a good idea to use ^+^ and ^=^ to ensure spaces around these operators in the output. The characters ˜ and ^ also serve to separate keywords and symbols, as does white space.

Spaces and RETURNs should be used freely in preparing **eqn** input to avoid long input lines, which may be difficult for **eqn** to work with. For formulas that are longer than the output line length, you should use consecutive .EQ/.EN constructs to break the formula explicitly into several lines. Otherwise, **eqn** will try to fit everything onto one line. Braces ({ and }) are used to group terms for **eqn** input. For example:

```
a ^+^ b  over  c ^-^ d  is
```
$$a + \frac{b}{c} - d$$

and

```
{a ^+^ b}  over  {c ^-^ d}  is
```
$$\frac{a + b}{c - d}$$

If you have any doubt, you should use braces to ensure that symbols group the way you intend them.

Greek alphabet letters often are used in mathematical formulas. The **eqn** program allows you to use Greek characters by simply typing in their English names. Therefore:

```
theta ^+^ OMEGA  over  2
```

produces

$$\theta + \frac{\Omega}{2}$$

For other special symbols used in mathematical expressions, **eqn** recognizes a set of *special sequences*, which are used in **eqn** input. Most of the **eqn** special sequences are listed in Figure 12.16.

Figure 12.16 ▪ eqn Special Sequences

Sequence	Output	Sequence	Output
>=	$\geq$	<=	$\leq$
==	$\equiv$	!=	$\neq$
+-	$\pm$	->	$\rightarrow$
<-	$\leftarrow$	<<	$<<$
>>	$>>$	inf	∞
partial	∂	half	$\frac{1}{2}$
prime	$'$	approx	$\approx$
nothing		cdot	$\cdot$
times	$\times$	del	$\triangle$
grad	∇	...	$\cdots$
,...,	$,\cdots,$	sum	$\sum$
int	$\int$	prod	$\prod$
union	$\cup$	inter	$\cap$

12.18 eqn Examples

Subscripts and Superscripts

Subscript and Superscript	
eqn Input	Printed Output
x sub j sup 3	x_j^3
cos sup 2 theta	$\cos^2 \theta$
e sup {− y sub j sup 2}	$e^{-y_j^2}$
nothing sup k A sub i	$^k A_i$
+ − ˆsqrt { x sup 2 ˆ+ˆ y sup 2 }	$\pm \sqrt{x^2 + y^2}$

Products and Quotients

A horizontal division bar is inserted with the keyword over, although a slash
(/) also can be used for quotients. The keywords left and right are used to
form large parentheses or brackets.

eqn Input	Printed Output
cos(x/3)ˆ+ˆa over b	$cos(x/3) + \dfrac{a}{b}$
1 over { 1 ˆ+ˆ 1 over x }	$\dfrac{1}{1 + \dfrac{1}{x}}$
left ({a over b} right) sup c	$\left[\dfrac{a}{b}\right]^c$
{ width ˆtimesˆ length } over 2 ˆ=ˆ area	$\dfrac{width \times length}{2} = area$
prod from i = 1 to n ˆ{x sub i}	$\displaystyle\prod_{i=1}^{n} x_i$
x ˆcdotˆ y	$x \cdot y$
alpha over beta \(diˆ gamma over delta	$\dfrac{\alpha}{\beta} \div \dfrac{\gamma}{\delta}$

Vectors and Matrices

A matrix column can be given as:

ccol   (centered column)

lcol   (left-adjusted column)

rcol   (right-adjusted column)

These sequences are meaningful only inside a matrix. For a single-column matrix, the keyword pile is easier to use. Matrix columns must have the same number of entries, and the formatting for all columns is accomplished together. In contrast, successive piles do not have to have the same length and are formatted separately.

	Vector and Matrix

eqn Input	Printed Output
grad p ˆtimesˆ v vec cdot r vec left (matrix { ccol { a above c } ccol { b above d } } right)	$\nabla p \times \vec{v}\cdot\vec{r}$ $\begin{pmatrix} a & b \\ c & d \end{pmatrix}$

eqn Input	Printed Output

left [matrix { ccol { a above c }
   ccol { b above d } } right]
  ^left [pile { x above y } right]
   ^=^ left [pile { u sub 3 above v sub 3 } right]
	$$\begin{bmatrix} a & b \\ c & d \end{bmatrix}\begin{bmatrix} x \\ y \end{bmatrix} = \begin{bmatrix} u_3 \\ v_3 \end{bmatrix}$$

A sup T B ^=^ C sup −1	$A^T B = C^{-1}$

{ left (matrix{ccol {a above b above c}
    ccol {a above b above c}
    ccol {a above b above c} }
right) } sup T
	$$\begin{pmatrix} a & a & a \\ b & b & b \\ c & c & c \end{pmatrix}^T$$

left (pile { n above n/2 } right)	$$\left(\dfrac{n}{n/2} \right)$$

Derivatives and Integrals

eqn Input	Printed Output
x dot ^=^ y dotdot ^+^ dx over dt	$\dot{x} = \ddot{y} + \dfrac{dx}{dt}$
f prime (x) ^+^ { partial z } over { partial x }	$f'(x) + \dfrac{\partial z}{\partial x}$
del U ^=^ Dv over Dt	$\Delta U = \dfrac{Dv}{Dt}$
int f(x)^dx	$\int f(x)\, dx$
int from a to b ^g(t) ^dt	$\int_a^b g(t)\, dt$

int from 0 to inf
  int from −1 to s
    alpha (r,s) ^^dr^ds
	$\int_0^\infty \int_{-1}^s \alpha(r,s)\, dr\, ds$

Sums and Limits

Sum and Limit	
eqn Input	Printed Output
sum from i=1 to n 1 over {i sup 2}	$\sum\limits_{i=1}^{n} \dfrac{1}{i^2}$
lim from {x −> inf} { left (1 ^+^ 1 over x right) } sup x	$\lim\limits_{x \to \infty} \left[1 + \dfrac{1}{x} \right]^x$
lim bar from {t −> 0} f(z,t)	$\overline{\lim\limits_{t \to 0}}\, f(z, t)$

Inequalities

Inequality	
eqn Input	Printed Output
0 ^<=^ a sup 2 + b sup 2 sum from {i != j} {x sub i y sub j} a ^==^ B ^^mod^ c beta ^>> alpha ^>= epsilon ^> 0 i ^<−^ i ^+^ 1 u ^−^ v^ ^approx^ ^0	$0 \le a^2 + b^2$ $\sum\limits_{i \ne j} x_i\, y_j$ $a \equiv B\ mod\ c$ $\beta >> \alpha \ge \epsilon > 0$ $i \leftarrow i + 1$ $u - v \approx 0$

Set Operations

Set Operation	
eqn Input	Printed Output
x^ \(mo ^S^ \(sp ^K A inter ^B \(ip^ C bar a^ union ^b^ inter ^c	$x \in S \supset \underline{K}$ $A \cap B \supseteq \overline{C}$ $a \cup b \cap c$

Large Brackets

The keywords left and right are used to create large parentheses (( )), brackets ([ ]), braces ({ }), and bars (| |) around a formula; the results are made big enough to cover the formula enclosed. Any character can be used with left and right. In particular, the *floor* and *ceiling* characters. For example:

```
left ( pile { m above n } right )
>= left ceiling { alpha over beta } right ceiling
```

produces the output:

$$\binom{m}{n} \geq \left\lceil \frac{\alpha}{\beta} \right\rceil$$

In **eqn**, braces are used to group terms and are not printed in the output unless they appear after the keywords left and right.

A left *something* need not have a corresponding right *something*, as long as the scope of the left is clear or delimited by braces. On the other hand, right cannot be given without a preceding left. However, left nothing can be used, which results in only the right portion being displayed in the output. (*Note*: nothing is an **eqn** keyword.) For example:

```
{ left nothing
      { partial y } over { partial x } right  |} sub {x = a}
```

results in

$$\frac{\partial y}{\partial x} \bigg|_{x = a}$$

In **eqn** input, anything between double quotation marks (") is printed literally. The " can be used to print **eqn** keywords and special sequences in a formula. In particular, two adjacent pairs of double quotation marks (" ") are another way to indicate nothing.

Controlling Size and Font

The **eqn** program controls its own character size, which is not coordinated with character size settings in **troff** or ms. By default, equations are set in 10-point type. Standard mathematical conventions are followed to determine which characters are roman and which are italic. Subscripts and superscripts automatically are displayed in a smaller size type than is the current character size. Keywords for changing sizes and fonts are:

`size` *n*	(display next quantity in size *n*)
`roman`	(display next quantity in roman font)
`italic`	(display next quantity in *italic* font)
`bold`	(display next quantity in **bold** font)
`fat`	(display next quantity in overstrike)

Size and font changes affect only the quantity that follows them, then they revert to their previous settings. For example:

```
siz 18 int bold { X cdot Y } ^dt
```

produces

$$\int \mathbf{X\cdot Y}\; dt$$

Size increment and decrement using + and − is allowed. The keyword fat takes the current font and widens it by overstriking. Thus:

```
fat alpha    produces   α
fat {x sub i}   produces   xᵢ
```

If an entire document is to be in a nonstandard size or font, a *global* size or font setting can be used to affect all equations thereafter:

```
.EQ
gsize 16
gfont R
.EN
```

sets the size to 16 and the font to roman. This sequence usually is inserted at the beginning of the text to control the **eqn** formulas in the entire paper.

In-Line Formulas

Not all formulas in a document are set apart from the running text. The **eqn** program uses special delimiters to insert in-line formulas. The delimiters are specified by the **eqn** request delim. For example:

```
.EQ
delim @@
.EN
```

specifies that the character @ is to be the front and back delimiter for the in-line expressions. For instance:

```
Because @alpha over {beta sub i} >= 0@, it can be shown that ...
```

produces

Because $\dfrac{\alpha}{\beta_i} \geq 0$, it can be shown that ...

Enough vertical spacing is provided automatically for such in-line expressions.

Making Small Adjustments to Spacing

The **eqn** program does a good job of displaying equations in the proper locations. Still, you may find that you need to make small adjustments to the output occasionally. Small, extra, horizontal spaces can be inserted with ~ and ^, as mentioned earlier. You also can use

back *n*   (move left *n*)

fwd *n*   (move right *n*)

to change the position of the next quantity in the formula by a small amount. The argument *n* is given in 1/100 of an em (about the width of the letter "m.") Similarly:

up *n*   (move up *n*)

down *n*   (move down *n*)

As you may expect, these four *local motions* only affect the next quantity in the input. Thus, there is no need to worry about offsetting the move after its completion.

For More Information

The **eqn** program allows you to line up several equations as well as to give a name to a long string to be used as a shorthand name. There is also the UNIX command **checkeq** that can be used to check **eqn** input for syntax errors. Additional information on **eqn** can be found in the article "Typesetting Mathematics—User's Guide" by Brain Kernighan and Lorinda Cherry in the UNIX manual. The on-line manual page on **eqn** also can be consulted.

12.19 Defining Macros

Up to now, you have been using ms-defined macros. In this section, defining your own macros is discussed. Also, some useful macros that are not available in ms are described.

Macro definitions usually are placed at the beginning of a document or are included in a document using the request:

```
.so file
```

which includes the named *file* in a **troff** input file. However, a macro can be defined anywhere, as long as it is defined before it is used. To define a macro, use:

```
.de name
one or
more lines of text
and troff requests
..
```

The macro definition begins with a .de line and terminates with a line consisting of two periods. The macro *name* is usually one or two characters in length. Since primitive **troff** requests are lowercase characters and macro packages such as ms use uppercase macro names, it is best to mix uppercase and lowercase characters in the macro names you define to avoid accidentally redefining a word already used by **troff** or ms. The request:

```
.pm           (print names of all macros)
```

lists all of the macros, so that you can be sure not to redefine a macro. It also is customary to follow the .de line with a comment that indicates the macro's usage. The end of the macro definition is marked by a line containing *only* the two periods (..).

The **troff** program ignores any intervening blanks between the leading period on a request line and the request name. This feature often is used to indent macro bodies, making it easier to see where a macro begins and ends.

Simple Examples

Consider the letter template (Figure 12.3). Say that you want to take Lines 1–6, which initialize the letter, and define them as a macro with the name Lt. Figure 12.17 shows the macro definition. Let's say you keep Lt and other macros that relate to the letter template in a file named letter-macros. Then the beginning of your letter template can become:

```
.so letter-macros
.Lt
\" < put address here >
.DE
...
```

A macro takes arguments in a manner similar to shell script positional parameters. Thus, the closing and signature lines of the letter template can be

Figure 12.17 ▪ A Macro Definition

```
.de Lt                  \" .Lt letter initialization
.       nr PO 1.0i      \" left margin 1 inch
.       nr LL 6.5i      \" line length 6.5 inches
.       ND              \" no date
.       ds CH           \" no page numbers
.       PP              \" initialize ms
.       sp 5            \" 5 blank lines
.       ti +3.26i       \" indent next line
\*(DY                   \" use register values
.       sp              \" blank line
.       DS L            \" display start, left-justified
..
```

defined into a macro Sg (Figure 12.18). With the Sg macro defined, the end
of the letter template can be simplified to, for example:

```
.Sg "John K. Smith" Director
```

The notation:

```
\\$n
```

refers to the nth argument given to the macro. Referring to an argument that
is not given simply results in a null string. Macro arguments are separated by
blanks. A group of words enclosed in double quotation marks forms a single

Figure 12.18 ▪ A Macro with Arguments

```
\" signature macro

.de Sg                  \" .Sg "John K. Smith" Director
.       sp
.       in +3.26i
Sincerely yours,
.       sp 3
\&\\$1
.       br
\&\\$2
.       in -3.26i
..
```

argument. Therefore, the preceding use of Sg gives two arguments, with \\$2 being the title Director.

In a macro definition, the zero-width nonprinting characters \& often are used at the beginning of a line to guard against the possibility that the user-supplied string (for example, \\$1 in Figure 12.18) would begin with a period or a single quotation mark. The resulting line would become a request instead of text if \& were not there. This precaution is probably redundant, however, in the Sg example.

Redefining Existing Macros

In defining your own macros, it is important to choose a name that does not conflict with an existing ms or **troff** macro; using the same name results in a redefinition of the macro, which may cause difficulties and should, in general, be avoided. Nevertheless, it is sometimes desirable to redefine an existing macro or to add to its original definition. Figure 12.19 shows several user-

Figure 12.19 ▪ Figure Caption Macros

```
.rn NH @H       \" rename the ms macro NH

.de NH          \" redefine NH to initialize
.      nr Fc 0  \" number register Fc for figure count
.      @H
..

.rm @H          \" remove @H

.de Fp          \" increment figure count
.      nr Fc +1
..

.de Fg          \" .Fg "figure caption"
.      sp
.      ce
\\fBFigure\\*(SN.\\n(Fc \\$1\\fP
.      sp 2
..

\" figure reference string register
.ds fg Figure \\*(SN.\\n(Fc
```

defined macros that work together to produce numbered figure captions and figure references. In the figure, a new ms macro NH (numbered section) is defined using three steps: (1) NH is renamed @H, (2) the new NH is defined to initialize the per-section figure count Fc to zero and then invoke the @H macro (which is the old NH macro), and (3) the temporary @H is removed. Step 3 is not required. Note that the string register SN contains the current section number maintained by the ms macro .NH.

Another application is to redefine the ms macros LP and PP to prevent automatic hyphenation of words when using ms:

```
.rn LP @P       \" rename LP as @P

.de LP          \" begin redefine LP
.    @P         \" the old LP
.    nh         \" no hyphen
..              \" end of LP

.rm @P          \" remove the temporary @P
```

Here again, removing @P is not required. PP is modified similarly.

Conditionals

The **troff** program provides a conditional request so that text and requests can be processed or not processed depending on the outcome of a *test* given to the .if request. The general form is:

`.if` *test text-or-request*

Available test forms are:

`.if` *N*	The test is satisfied if the numerical expression *N* is positive.
`.if t`	if the document is processed by **troff**
`.if n`	if the document is processed by **nroff**
`.if e`	if the current page number is even
`.if o`	if the current page number is odd
`.if` `!` *test*	The *test* is negated, that is, it is not satisfied.
`.if` `'`*s1*`'`*s2*`'`	The test is satisfied only if the two strings *s1* and *s2* are the same.

The .if request is most useful in macro definitions. Let us define a carboncopy (CC) macro for the letter template in Figure 12.3:

```
.de CC
.     if !'\\$1'' .sp2
.     if !'\\$1'' cc: \\$1
..
```

Thus, CC only displays the carbon-copy line if given an argument; otherwise, it does nothing. To include the cc feature in the letter template, put the CC macro definition in the file mymacros and put the line:

```
.CC "names"    \" fill in names or delete word names
```

at the end of the letter template. Note that double quotation marks are used to group multiple words into one argument.

12.20 Index and Table of Contents

The ms macro package provides requests to help generate a table of contents and an index for a document. In the case of a technical paper or a business report, these usually are not needed. However, for a longer document or a book, the table of contents and the index are quite important.

For a table of contents, the requests:

.XS   (table of contents entry start)

.XE   (table of contents entry end)

are used to record multiple lines of text together with the current page number. All such saved text lines are printed in the table of contents using the request:

.TC   (print table of contents)

at the end of the document. Lines bracketed by .XS and .XE are not printed in the document. A typical example of a table of contents with these requests is shown in Figure 12.20. Again, the string register SN, used and set by the .NH macro, contains the current section number. Note that in order to include a section heading in the table of contents, the same words are included twice: once for the text and once for the table of contents.

For index generation, the macro:

.IX *words*   (output *words* for index)

is used to write the given *words* (up to five) to the standard error output, together with the current page number. The words do not form part of the text. The output is formatted as one index line with each word followed by a TAB. The index line terminates in "... *page number*." When processing your document, you would redirect the **troff** standard error to a file to collect the index lines.

Figure 12.20 ▪ Generating a Table of Contents

```
.NH
Introduction
.XS
\*(SN Introduction
.XE
.PP
\" other text and requests
.NH 2
Backgrond and notations
.XS
\*(SN Background and notations
.XE
.PP
\" other text and requests
.NH
Conclusions
.XS
\*(SN Conclusions
.XE
.TC                        \" print out the table of contents
```

An Alternative Approach

As noted in the last section, generating a table of contents with the built-in ms facilities (.XS, .XE, and .TC) requires that you type section headings twice: once to include the heading in the document itself and then again, bracketed by .XS and .XE, to include the heading in the table of contents. Such repetition also is needed for index generation. This procedure can mean a lot of extra typing and a longer source document. Also, if you subsequently modify a heading or index entry, you must make the change in two places, increasing the chance for discrepancy between what appears in the text and what is listed in the table of contents or the index. The .TC request presents an additional problem, because it causes the table of contents to be printed at the end of a document instead of the beginning. Further, the table of contents is printed with the format supplied by .TC. You may not want the table of contents formatted in this way and you *certainly* do not want the table of contents at the end of your document! This section presents a more efficient and practical way to prepare the table of contents and the index. Characteristics of this approach are as follows:

1. Table of contents data is sent to standard error together with index data to be collected in a file (*index file*).

2. Unnecessary repetition of text in the **troff** source file is eliminated by macros that send the same text both to the index file and to the output text.

3. Lines belonging to the table of contents are flagged to be easily distinguishable from index data.

This approach to index and table of contents generation is based on the following group of four user-defined macros, which use the primitive **troff** request:

```
.tm string          (output string to standard error)
```

1. Indexed Numbered Header Macro

```
.de IH      \" header into index for table of contents
.     tm TC \\*(SN→\\$1 →\\n%
\\$1
..
```

Note that → stands for TAB. This macro is used after a .NH or .SH line for section headings. For example:

```
.NH 2
.IH "Macro Definitions"
```

results in the section heading "Macro Definitions" with its automatically-generated section number being placed both in the document and in the index file. The index entry produced by the preceding requests looks like the following:

```
TC 12.19→Macro Definitions→425
```

The leading TC flags the line as a table of contents line and sets it apart from index lines in the index file. The → characters are for subsequent **tbl** formatting of the table of contents (see Figure 12.13).

2. Indexed Italic Macro

```
.de II      \" in-line indexed italic
.     tm \\$1→\\n%
\\fI\\$1\\fP
..
```

Since a high percentage of index words are to be italicized, the preceding macro performs both functions—it italicizes and it indexes. For example:

```
.LP
A major magazine has predicted that sales of
.II"desktop publishing"
systems using high-performance personal computers will grow
to over 5 billion dollars by 1990.
```

produces the text:

A major magazine has predicted that sales of *desktop publishing* systems using high-performance personal computers will grow to over 5 billion dollars by 1990.

and the index entry:

desktop publishing→460

3. In-Line Index Macro

```
.de IR \" in-line index
.       tm \\$1→\\n%
\\$1
..
```

This macro works the same as .II, but it does not italicize. It is more convenient to use than the .IX macro, because the argument to .IR is part of the running text.

4. End-of-File Macro

```
.em ep

.de ep
.       tm LAST \\n%
..
```

The macro .em defines the user-selected name, .ep, as the *end-of-file* macro, which is automatically invoked by **troff** when the end of the input file is reached. This definition of .ep causes the page number of the last page to be written out into the index file and to be flagged by the word LAST. This sequence records in the index file for a chapter the number of the chapter's last page—which is important for the correct pagination of books and large documents whose chapters are processed separately.

Using the four macros described, the table of contents and index of a book can be prepared in the following way:

1. While printing each chapter separately, you can collect and store index and table of contents information for each chapter in its respective index file.

2. You can use the shell-level command "**fgrep** TC" to separate out from each index file all lines flagged as table of contents entries.

3. You can format and print the resulting table of contents (using **tbl**, **eqn**, and **troff** as appropriate). (See Figure 12.13.)

4. You can use the techniques discussed in Section 4.6 to produce the index.

12.21 nroff/troff **Command Line Options**

As mentioned, text formatting under UNIX is accomplished by preparing a file that contains text and formatting requests. This file then is processed by **troff** or **nroff** to produce a printed or printable version of the file in the specified format. The shell-level commands:

```
troff [ option ] ... [ file ] ...
nroff [ option ] ... [ file ] ...
```

are used to invoke **nroff/troff** on the specified *files*. If no file argument is given, the standard input is used, which occurs when **troff/nroff** is part of a pipe.

Depending on the equipment your UNIX system uses, the **troff** output may be printed on a laser printer or displayed on a high-resolution bit-mapped screen. The convention is to use a variation of the word **troff** as the command name to produce output on a specific brand of printer. For example, the command **itroff** is used to send **troff** output to an Imagen Corporation laser printer. Documentation for your local UNIX system will provide such information.

The **nroff** program does not produce output directly on a special printing device. Instead, it formats the input file into an ASCII file, which can be sent to a letter-quality, hard-copy printer or a CRT. For an installation with output devices for **troff**, the command **nroff** is used most frequently as a quick way to view the document before it is sent through **troff**.

Standard **troff** macro packages are kept in a system directory, usually:

```
/usr/lib/tmac
```

with file names of the form

```
tmac.name
```

The option

```
-mname
```

is used to insert the definitions contained in the macro package at the beginning of the input file before it is processed by **nroff/troff**. For example, the ms macro package is kept in the file

`/usr/lib/tmac/tmac.s`

and the option

`-ms`

is used to process a file that requires macros defined by the ms package.

Other important options are as follows:

`-o`*list* print only pages whose page numbers appear in the comma-separated *list* of numbers and ranges. Possible ranges are:

N–M	pages *N* through *M*
–N	at the beginning of the list means from the beginning to page *N*
N–	at the end of the list means from *N* to the end of the document

For example:

`troff -o-7,13,17,60-71,89-` *file*

`-T`*name* specifies *name* as the output terminal. The given *name* actually specifies a *character driving table* used with a specific terminal or typing element on a terminal. The table used is /usr/lib/term/tab*name*. The directory /usr/lib/term usually contains all the supported driving .tables on your system.

The manual pages for **nroff/troff** list all possible options. Other important references are *Nroff/Troff User's Manual* by J. F. Ossanna, which is a complete reference manual, and *A Troff Tutorial* by B. W. Kernighan. These articles can be found in the UNIX manuals.

12.22 A Letter-Formatting Program

In this section, text formatting is combined with shell script writing to construct a program that enables the user to enter the contents of a letter interactively and to produce the **nroff/troff** source file for formatting the letter. This program has been constructed for, tested, and used by secretaries.

A file named letter-macros that contains the macro given in Figure 12.17 is required. The same program is shown both as a *sh* and *csh* script. Comparing the two scripts is a good way to enhance your understanding of the differences and similarities between the two shells. The letter-formatting *sh* script is as follows:

```
: ## sh script lett for formatting a business letter

if test $1
then
      echo Hello... creating letter $1
      echo do not begin any line with a period '.'
      echo terminate input with a Ctrl-D as 1st char of line
      echo to abort this letter, just type Ctrl-C
      echo ''
else
echo Usage: $0 newfile
exit 1
fi
echo type address :
(echo '.so letter-macros'; echo'.Lt'; cat) > $1
echo type name \(e.g. Dear Bob, or Dear Mr. Smith:\) :
read name
(echo '.DE' ; echo '.sp' ; echo $name; echo '.sp') >> $1
echo type all paragraphs, end with a lone Ctrl-D on the last line.
cat >> $1
echo type complimentary close '(e.g. Sincerely yours,)' :
read sa
echo type signature '(e.g. Paul S. Wang)' :
read sg
echo type title '(e.g. Professor)' :
read tl
(echo '.sp 2' ; echo '.in +3.26i' ; echo '.nf' ; echo $sa
echo '.sp 3' ; echo $sg; echo $tl
echo '.in -3.26i' ; echo '.sp 2') >> $1
echo type any p.s., enclosure, cc lines :
cat >> $1
echo O.K. Letter is in $1. To print out letter type:
echo troff \(or equivalent\) -ms $1
```

The letter-formatting *csh* script is as follows:

```
## csh script lett for formatting a business letter

if ($#argv == 1) then
        echo Hello... creating letter $1
        echo do not begin any line with a period '.'
```

```
        echo terminate input with a ^D as 1st char of line
        echo to abort this letter, just type ^C
        echo
    else
        echo Usage: $0 newfile
        exit (1)
endif

echo type address:
(echo '.so letter-macros' ; echo '.Lt' ; cat) > $1
echo type name \(e.g. Dear Bob, or Dear Mr. Smith:\) :
set name = $<
(echo '.DE' ; echo '.sp' ; echo $name; echo '.sp') >> $1
echo type all paragraphs, end with lone ^D on last line.
cat >> $1
echo type complimentary close '(e.g. Sincerely yours,)' :
set sa = $<
echo type signature '(e.g. Paul S. Wang)' :
set sg = $<
echo type title '(e.g. Professor)' :
set tl = $<
(echo '.sp 2' ; echo '.in +3.26i' ; echo '.nf' ; echo $sa; \
echo '.sp 3' ; echo $sg ; echo $tl ; echo '.in -3.26i' ; \
echo '.sp 2') >> $1
echo type any p.s., enclosure, cc lines :
cat >> $1
echo
echo O.K. Letter is in $1. To print out letter type:
echo troff \(or equivalent\) -ms $1
```

12.23 Summary

UNIX includes the document preparation facilities **spell**, **nroff/troff**, ms, **eqn**, and **tbl**. The **troff** program formats output for a high-resolution device such as a laser printer. The **nroff** program works the same as the **troff** program, but it produces output for terminals and letter-quality printers. The **nroff** program can be used to preview a document prepared for **troff**.

The ms package contains a collection of useful macros for **nroff/troff** that meet frequent formatting needs: page layouts, title and author placement, abstract formatting, footnotes, paragraphing, indenting of paragraphs with hanging labels, automatic numbering of section headings, and so on.

Equations and tables can be formatted using the preprocessors **neqn/eqn** and **tbl**, respectively.

To prepare a document for processing by **nroff/troff**, you insert formatting requests in the text of your document. Most requests are keyed by a period (.) or a single quotation mark (') in column one. In-text requests are introduced by the \ escape. A multitude of formatting requests range from switching print fonts to drawing lines.

A macro is defined by giving a name to a sequence of requests. The ms macro package consists of many frequently used macros, which are defined using the basic **nroff** and **troff** requests. You may define your own macros and redefine existing macros. There are also registers that are used as variables to store numeric or string values.

A letter and a report template are given to help you get started with document formatting. Many example tables and equations are supplied as well. Letter-writing *sh* and *csh* scripts are given at the end of the chapter. They combine shell-level programming with skills in document formatting.

Complete listings of **troff** and ms requests together with other useful information are provided in the appendices.

Exercises

1. What is the difference between the primitive commands .ps and .vs and the ms number registers PS and VS, respectively?

2. It is not easy to create a large empty space at the top of a page with **nroff/troff**. Can you find a way?

3. What combination of ms requests should be used to produce a block-centered display with keep that is enclosed in a box? Many figures in this book were created in this way. (Hint: Use .B1 and .B2).

4. The **tbl** program can be handy in producing figures of all sorts. For example, the text portion of Figure 1.1 was produced using **tbl**. The **tbl** program also produced Figure 7.3. Can you explain how Figure 1.1 (except the curved lines) was accomplished?

5. How can you use Greek letters in a table?

6. How many ways do you know to right-adjust a few words on a page?

7. By increasing the font size, it is easy to produce handsome overhead slides using **troff**. Experiment with this and produce an overhead slide for yourself.

8. Find out how to make a page number skip a few pages. You don't want to waste paper by using a repeated .bp.

9. Modify the letter template (Figure 12.3) to use the macros Lt, Sg, and CC.

10. Explain how a series of items such as exercise problems can be numbered automatically using number registers.

11. Print a table with **eqn** formulas.

12. Figure out how to make page numbers appear on the upper or lower corners of each page.

13. Modify either of the letter-formatting scripts given at the end of the chapter to append an address to an address file automatically.

14. What other improvements would you make to the letter-formatting script?

Appendix 1
Command Index

Regular UNIX commands and shell built-in commands mentioned in this book
are listed here with section numbers.

Command	Description and Sections
adb	Debugger 1.11
alias	Defines/displays command aliases (*csh*) 5.5, 5.7, 6.9
ar	Archive maintainer 8.5
as	Assembler 8.2
at	Schedules commands for later execution 4.10, 4.13, 6.6
awk	A pattern processing program 4.6, 4.7, 4.13
basename	Gives the basename part a file name 7.9
bg	Puts job in the background (*csh*) 1.9, 5.4
biff	Enables immediate mail notification 1.8, 5.8
break	Flow control (*csh*) 6.3
breaksw	Flow control (*csh*) 6.3, 6.5
calendar	Reminders service 4.0, 4.10, 4.13
cat	Catenates and displays files 1.2, 1.6, 1.7, 1.10, 4.9, 5.3, 5.8, 7.1
cc	C compiler 1.7, 1.9, 1.10, 8.2, 8.3, 8.7
cd	Changes working directory (*csh* and *sh*) 1.4, 5.7, 5.8, 7.2
chdir	Changes working directory, same as *cd* (*csh* and *sh*) 5.7, 5.8, 6.7, 6.9
chgrp	Changes file groupid 7.3
chmod	Changes file mode 1.3, 1.5, 4.12, 6.1, 7.3, 9.1, 9.2
chown	Changes file ownerid 7.3, 9.2
chsh	Changes default shell 5.9

432

Command	Description and Sections
clear	Clears terminal screen 5.7
cmp	Compares two files 7.9
comm	Selects/rejects lines common to two sorted files 4.3, 7.9
continue	Flow control (*csh*) 6.3, 6.7
cp	File copy 1.4, 1.10
crypt	Encrypts/decodes file 4.8, 4.13
csh	C shell 1.2, 1.6, 1.9, 1.10, 1.12, 5.0, 6.0, 6.8
ctags	Creates tags file 7.9
date	Displays current date and time 1.2, 1.10, 6.6
dbx	Source-level symbolic debugger 1.11, 8.2, 8.8
df	Displays information on available free disk space 7.4, 7.9
diff	Indicates differences between two files 5.7, 7.9
du	Displays total disk space used (in KB) under a directory 6.7, 7.9
dump	File system backup 7.5
echo	Outputs command line arguments to standard output (also *csh*) 1.2, 1.3, 6.5, 6.8
ed	Line editor 1.11, 4.5
edquota	File quota editor 7.6
egrep	Extended **grep** 4.4, 4.6, 4.13
emacs	Display editor 1.11, 2.18
eqn	Equation-formatting program (a **troff** preprocessor) 1.11, 12.0, 12.13, 12.14, 12.15
eval	Evaluates as command 6.5, 6.7
ex	Text editor 4.5
exit	Terminates shell and sets exit status (*sh* and *csh*) 6.3
expand	Replaces tabs by spaces 4.2, 4.13
export	Puts variable in the environment (*sh*) 6.14, 9.5
finger	(or **f**) Consults on-line user information database 1.8
fg	Brings job into foreground (*csh*) 1.9, 5.1
fgrep	Fast string **grep** 4.4, 4.13
find	File tree traversal 4.11, 4.12, 4.13, 6.7, 7.3
foreach	Iteration control (*csh*) 6.3, 6.6, 6.7
fsck	File system check 7.5
ftp	File transfer program 10.4
goto	Unconditional branch (*csh*) 6.3
grep	Regular expression pattern searcher 4.4, 4.5, 4.7

Command	Description and Sections
head	Displays first few lines of a file 4.1, 6.7, 7.9
hostname	Displays system name 1.2, 6.6
if	Conditional branch (*csh* and *sh*) 6.3, 6.9, 6.10
itroff	Laser printing 12.21
jobs	Displays information on jobs (*csh*) 1.9, 5.5
kill	Sends interrupt signal to a process (also *csh*) 1.9, 5.5, 6.10, 9.6
ld	Linking loader 7.3, 8.2, 8.4
learn	A program to help learn UNIX 1.10
leave	Sets alarm clock 4.10
lint	C program verifier 8.0, 8.6, 8.8
lisp	List processing language 1.7, 1.10, 5.3
ln	Links files 7.1
login	Logs in again or as another user 1.10
logout	Terminates login shell 1.1, 1.10, 5.5
look	Displays lines with given prefix in a sorted file 1.2, 4.3, 4.7, 12.1
lpq	Examines printer queue 1.10, 4.9
lpr	Requests spooled printing 1.10, 4.0, 4.9
lprm	Removes from printer queue 1.10, 4.9
ls	Lists file status information 1.2, 1.4, 1.5, 1.6, 7.1, 7.2, 7.3, 7.4
mail	Sends/receives mail 1.8, 1.9, 3.1, 4.10, 5.7, 5.10, 6.6, 7.3, 10.2
make	Software maintenance program 1.11, 11.1, 11.6
man	Consults on-line manual pages 1.2, 1.10, 1.12
mesg	Permits/denies messages 1.8
mkdir	Creates a new directory 1.4, 1.10
mknod	Creates a special file 7.7
more	File perusal filter for CRT 1.6, 1.10, 4.1, 6.7, 12.0, 12.7
mount	Attaches a file system 7.4, 7.9
mv	Renames files 1.4, 1.7, 1.10, 4.7
neqn	Equation preprocessing for **nroff** 12.0, 12.18
nroff	Document formattor for letter-quality printer 1.11, 12.0, 12.2, 12.21
onintr	Sets interrupt trap (*csh*) 6.10
passwd	Changes login password 1.2, 1.10
pc	Pascal compiler 1.7, 1.10
pix	Pascal interpreter 1.7, 1.10

Command	Description and Sections
print	Prints hard copy 4.12, 5.1
printenv	Displays environment variables and values (*csh*) 6.11
ps	Displays process information 5.5, 8.1, 9.4
pwd	Displays current working directory 1.4, 1.10, 5.7, 5.8, 6.1, 10.4
quota	Displays disk space usage and limits 7.6
quotaoff	Disables file system quota 7.6
quotaon	Enables file system quota 7.6
ranlib	Converts archive file for random access 8.5
rcp	Remote **cp** 10.4
rehash	Establishes new command hash table (*csh*) 5.2, 5.7, 6.1, 6.11
rlogin	Remote login 10.4, 10.5
rm	Removes directory entry/deletes file 1.4, 1.10, 4.8, 5.2, 5.7, 6.10, 7.1, 7.8
rmail	Processes **uucp** mail 10.2
rmdir	Deletes empty directory 1.4, 1.10, 7.9
rsh	Remote shell command execution 10.4
script	Records terminal session in a file 1.7, 1.10
sed	Stream editor 4.5, 4.6, 4.7, 4.13
set	Makes/displays variable assignment (*csh*) 5.2, 6.4
setenv	Sets environment variable (*csh*) 5.7, 6.4, 6.11, 6.14
sh	Bourne shell 1.2, 5.5, 6.1, 6.13, 6.14, 6.15, 6.16, 6.17
shift	Shortens a multivalued variable (*csh*) 6.3
size	Gives size of an object file 7.9
sort	Orders lines of files 4.3, 4.6, 4.7, 5.3, 7.9
source	Takes commands from file (*csh*) 6.9
spell	Spelling checker 12.1
split	Splits up a larger file 7.9
stat	Displays file status information 7.3
stop	Suspends a job (*csh*) 5.5
sum	Displays a checksum and the number of blocks of a file 7.9
switch	Flow control (*csh*) 6.3, 6.5, 6.7
tail	Displays last lines of a file 4.1, 5.5, 6.7, 7.9
talk	On-line two-way communication between users 1.8, 1.10, 9.9, 9.10
tar	Packs/unpacks files into/from a single file 4.11, 4.13
tbl	Table-formatting preprocessor for **nroff/troff** 12.0, 12.13

Command	Description and Sections
telnet	Login across network 10.4
test	Tests conditions 7.3
tip	Remote system access and terminal emulation 10.1, 10.3
touch	Updates file modification time 6.10, 7.9
tr	Character translator filter 4.2, 4.5, 4.7
troff	Document formattor for high-resolution output device 7.8, 12.0, 12.2, 12.5, 12.21
tset	Initializes terminal 5.8
umask	Sets file creation mask 7.2, 9.2
umount	Detaches a file system 7.4
unalias	Removes aliases 5.7
unexpand	Converts spaces into tabs 4.2, 4.13
uniq	Reports repeated lines 7.9
unset	Unsets variables (*csh*) 5.7, 6.8
unsetenv	Unsets environment variables (*csh*) 6.11
uucp	UNIX-UNIX copy 7.8, 10.2
uudecode	Decodes binary file encoded by **uuencode** 7.9
uuencode	Encodes binary file for **mail** 7.9
vi	Visual text editor 1.3, 2.0, 4.8
w	Displays activities of on-line users 1.3, 1.8, 1.10
wc	Counts characters, words, lines in files 7.9
while	Iteration control (*csh*) 6.3, 6.7
who	Displays current users on the system 1.0, 1.2, 1.8, 1.10
write	Writes to another user's terminal 1.8, 1.10

Appendix 2
vi Character Functions

This appendix describes the **vi** character functions. The uppercase, lowercase, and control letters (a–z) are presented followed by other control characters, special characters, and digits in the ASCII collating sequence.

For each character, both its meaning as a command and any meaning it may have in the insert mode or during command input are listed.

A	Appends at the end of the current line, a synonym for **$a**.
a	Enters the insert mode and appends the text after the cursor. The insertion terminates with an ESC. A count (an integer preceding the command) *n* inserts *n* copies of the text, provided that the inserted text is all on one line.
^A	Unused
B	The cursor is moved backward over a *sequence,* which is a series of nonblank characters, and is placed at the beginning of the sequence. A count repeats the effect.
b	Backs up to the beginning of a *word,* which is a series of alphanumeric characters or a series of special characters, in the current line. A count repeats the effect.
^B	Moves the window backward. A count specifies repetition. Two lines of continuity are kept if possible.
C	Changes the rest of the text on the current line; a synonym for **c$**.
c	An operator that changes the specified object, replacing it with the supplied input text up to an ESC. If more than a portion of a single line is affected, the text that is changed away is saved in the numeric buffers. If only a portion of the current line is affected, then the last character to be changed away is marked with a $. A count causes that many objects to be affected, thus both **3c)** and **c3)** change the next three sentences.
^C	Unused
D	Deletes the rest of the text on the current line; a synonym for **d$**.

d	An operator that deletes the specified object. If more than a portion of a line is affected, the text is saved in the numeric buffers. A count causes that many objects to be affected; thus **3dw** is the same as **d3w**.
^D	As a command, scrolls down one-half window of text. A count gives the number of (logical) lines to scroll, and the count is recorded for future **^D** and **^U** commands. During an insert, **^D** backtabs over white space supplied by autoindent, which cannot be erased using the erase character.
E	Moves the cursor forward to the end of a sequence. A count repeats the effect.
e	Advances the cursor to the end of the next word. A count repeats the effect.
^E	Exposes one more line below the current screen in the file, leaving the cursor where it is if possible.
F	The command **F**c searches backward in the current line for a single given character c. A count repeats the search that many times.
f	The command fc finds the first instance of the character c following the cursor on the current line. A count repeats the find.
^F	Forward window. A count specifies repetition. Two lines of continuity are kept if possible.
G	The command nG moves the cursor to the first nonblank character of line n, or the last line if n is not given. The screen is redrawn with the new current line in the center if necessary.
g	Unused
^G	Displays the current file name, whether it has been modified, the current line number, the number of lines in the file, and the percentage of the way through the file based on the current position. (Equivalent to the command **:f.**)
H	The command nH moves the cursor to the first nonblank character of line n on the screen, or the first line on the screen if n is not given.
h	Moves the cursor left one character on the current line (same as LEFT ARROW).
^H	(BACKSPACE) same as LEFT ARROW (see **h**). During an insert, eliminates the last input character, backing over it but not erasing it; it remains so you can see what you typed if you wish to type something only slightly different.
I	Inserts at the beginning of a line; a synonym for ^ followed by **i**.
i	Same as **a** except that it inserts text before the cursor.
^I	(TAB) not a command character. When inserted it displays as some number of spaces. When the cursor is at a TAB character, it rests at the last of the spaces that represent the TAB. The spacing of TAB stops is controlled by the tabstop option.
J	Joins the current line and the next line into one line, supplying appropriate white space between the lines: one space between words, two spaces after a ., and no spaces if the first character of the second line is). A count joins that many lines.
j	Moves the cursor down one line in the same column. If the position does not exist, **vi** comes as close as possible to the same column (same as DOWN ARROW).
^J	(LF) same as DOWN ARROW (see **j**).

K	Unused
k	Works the same as **j** except the cursor is moved up one line (same as UP ARROW).
^K	Unused
L	Moves the cursor to the first nonwhite character of the last line on the screen. The command *n***L** moves the cursor to the first nonwhite character of the *n*th line from the bottom. Operators affect whole lines when used with **L**.
l	Moves the cursor right one character on the current line (same as RIGHT ARROW or SPACEBAR).
^L	Represents the ASCII formfeed character, it clears and redraws the screen. It is useful after a transmission error, if characters typed by a program other than the editor scramble the screen, or after output is stopped by an interrupt.
M	Moves the cursor to the first nonwhite character of the line in the middle of the screen.
m	The command **m***x* marks the current position of the cursor in the mark register *x* (a–z). The mark register then can be used with the command ` or '.
^M	A RETURN advances to the next line, leaving the cursor at the first nonwhite position in the line. Given a count, it advances that many lines. During an insert, a RETURN continues the insert text onto another line.
N	Scans for the next match of the previous search pattern, but in the reverse direction; this is the reverse of **n**.
n	Repeats the last / or ? search command.
^N	Same as DOWN ARROW (see **j**).
O	Opens a new line above the current line and enters the insert mode. A count can be used on dumb terminals to specify a number of lines to be opened; this is generally obsolete, as the slowopen option works better.
o	Same as **O** except it opens new lines below the current line.
^O	Unused
P	Places the last deleted text back before the cursor or above the current line. The text returns as whole lines above the cursor if it was deleted as whole lines. Otherwise, the text is inserted just before the cursor. The command **"***x***P** retrieves the contents of the buffer *x*. Buffers 1–9 contain deleted material; buffers a–z are available for general use.
p	Same as **P**, except it places text after the cursor or below the current line.
^P	Same as UP ARROW (see **k**).
Q	Enters the **ex** command mode from **vi**. In this mode, whole lines form commands, ending with a RETURN. You can give all the : commands; the editor supplies the : as a prompt.
q	Unused
^Q	Not a command character. In the input mode, **^Q** quotes the next character, the same as **^V**. It is better to use **^V**.
R	Replaces characters on the screen with characters you type (overlay fashion). Terminates with an ESC.

r	Replaces the single character at the cursor with a single character you type. The new character may be a RETURN. This is the easiest way to split lines. The command *n*r replaces each of the following *n* characters with the single character given.
^R	Redraws the current screen, eliminating display lines not corresponding to physical lines (lines with only a single @ character on them). On hard-copy terminals in the *open* mode, retypes the current line.
S	Changes whole lines, a synonym for **cc**. A count substitutes for that many lines. The lines are saved in the numeric buffers and are erased on the screen before the substitution begins.
s	Changes the single character under the cursor to the text that follows up to an ESC. The command *n*s changes *n* characters from the current line. The last character to be changed is marked with $ as in **c**.
^S	Unused
T	The command **T***x* moves the cursor toward the beginning of the current line and places it just after the character *x*.
t	The command **t***x* advances the cursor to just before the next character *x* in the current line. It is most useful with operators such as **d** and **c** to delete the characters up to a character. You can use **.** to delete addditional characters if **t** does not delete enough characters the first time.
^T	Not a command character. During an insert, with autoindent set and at the beginning of the line, inserts shiftwidth white space. A count repeats the effect. Most useful with operators such as **d**.
U	Restores the current line to its original state (cancels any modifications). This works only before you leave the current line.
u	Undoes the last modification made to the current buffer. A consecutive **u** will cancel the effect of the previous **u**. When **u** is used after an insert of more than one line, the lines are saved in the numeric named buffers.
^U	Scrolls the screen up, inverting ^D, which scrolls down. Counts work as they do for ^D, and the previous scroll amount is common to both. On a dumb terminal, ^U often necessitates clearing and redrawing the screen further back in the file.
V	Unused
v	Unused
^V	Not a command character. In the input mode, quotes the next character so that it is possible to insert nondisplaying and special characters into the file.
W	Moves the cursor forward to the beginning of a sequence in the current line. A count repeats the effect.
w	Advances the cursor to the beginning of the next word in the current line.
^W	Not a command character. During an insert, backs up as **b** would in the command mode; the deleted characters remain on the display.
X	Deletes the character before the cursor. A count repeats the effect, but only characters on the current line are deleted.

x	Deletes the single character under the cursor. With a count, deletes that many characters forward from the cursor position, but only on the current line.
^X	Unused
Y	Saves (yanks) a copy of the current line into the unnamed buffer (the dtb), to be pasted in a different location by a later **p** or **P**; a very useful synonym for **yy**. A count yanks that many lines. May be preceded by a buffer name to yank lines into that buffer.
y	The operator **y** yanks a given object into the dtb (deleted text) buffer. If preceded by a buffer name, the text also is placed in that buffer. Text can be recovered by a later **p** or **P**.
^Y	Exposes one more line above the current screen, leaving the cursor where it is if possible.
ZZ	Saves the file on disk and exits **vi**. (Same as **:x**RETURN.) If any changes have been made to the buffer, the buffer is written out to the current file. Then the editor terminates.
z	Redisplays text around the current line (**z.**, **z−**, and **z**RETURN).
^Z	Suspends the **vi** editor, returns to the shell level. Same as the command **:stop**.
^@	Not a command character. If typed as the first character of an insertion, it is replaced with the last text inserted, and the insert terminates. Only 128 characters are saved from the last insert; if more characters were inserted, the mechanism is not available. **^@** cannot be part of the file due to the editor implementation.
^[	(ESC) cancels a partially formed command and terminates most commands. If an ESC is given when quiescent in the command mode, the editor rings the bell or flashes the screen. You thus can press ESC to return to the command mode (when the editor rings the bell).
^	Unused
^]	Searches for the word that is after the cursor as a tag defined in a tags file. Equivalent to typing **:ta**, the word, and then pressing RETURN. Mnemonically, this command is "go right to."
^^	Returns to the previous position in the last edited file. (Equivalent to the command **:e #**.)
^_	Unused
SPACE	Same as RIGHT ARROW (see **l**).
!	An operator that processes lines from the buffer with shell-level reformatting commands. Follow **!** with the object to be processed and then the command name terminated by RETURN. The command *n***!!** causes *n* lines to be filtered; otherwise a count is passed on to the object after the **!**. Thus **2!}fmt**RETURN reformats the next two paragraphs by running them through the program **fmt**. To read a file or the output of a shell-level command into the buffer use **:r**. To execute a shell-level command use **:!**.
"	The double quotation mark is a buffer name prefix. The buffers **1–9** are used for saving deleted text, and the buffers **a–z** can hold text.
#	The macro character that, when followed by a number, substitutes for a function key on terminals without function keys.
$	Moves to the end of the current line. Use *n*$ to go to the end of the *n*th following line. (**2$** goes to the end of the next line.) If you use **:se list**, then the end of each line will be shown by displaying a $ after the end of the displayed text in the line.

%	Moves the cursor to the parenthesis or brace that balances the parenthesis or brace at the current cursor position.
&	Repeats the previous :s substitute command (a synonym for the command :&).
'	When ' is followed by another ', the cursor is returned to the previous context at the beginning of a line. The previous context is set whenever the current line is moved in a nonrelative way. When ' is followed by a letter a–z, the cursor returns to the line that was marked with this letter with a m (or :k) command, at the first nonwhite character in the line. When ' is used with an operator such as d, the operation takes place over complete lines; if you use ` instead, the operation takes place from the exact marked place to the current cursor position within the line.
(	Retreats to the beginning of a sentence or to the beginning of a LISP s-expression if the lisp option is set. A sentence ends with a ., !, or ?, which is followed by either the end of a line or by two spaces. Any number of closing),], ", and ' characters may appear after the ., !, or ? and before the spaces or end of line. Sentences also begin at paragraph and section boundaries (see { and [[). A count advances that many sentences.
)	Advances to the beginning of a sentence. A count repeats the effect.
*	Unused
+	Same as RETURN when used as a command.
,	Reverse of the last f, F, t, or T command, looking the other way in the current line. Especially useful after typing too many ; characters. A count repeats the search.
−	Retreats to the previous line at the first nonwhite character. This is the inverse of + and RETURN. If the line moved to is not on the screen, the screen is scrolled or cleared and redrawn if scrolling is not possible. If a large amount of scrolling would be required, the screen also is cleared and redrawn, with the current line at the center.
.	Repeats the last command that changed the buffer. Especially useful when deleting words or lines; you can delete some words or lines and then press . to delete additional ones. Given a count, it passes the count on to the command being repeated. Thus after a 2dw, 3. deletes three words.
/	The search command. The search begins when you press RETURN or ESC to terminate the pattern; the cursor moves to the beginning of the last line to indicate that the search is in progress; the search then may be aborted with a DEL or RUBOUT, or by backspacing when at the beginning of the bottom line, returning the cursor to its initial position. Searches normally wrap endaround to find a string anywhere in the buffer.
	When used with an operator, the enclosed region normally is affected. By specifying an offset from the line matched by the pattern, you can force whole lines to be affected. To do so, give a pattern with a closing / and then an offset $+n$ or $-n$. To include the character / in the search string, you must escape it with a preceding \.
0	As a command, moves the cursor to the first column on the current line. Also used in forming numbers after an initial 1–9.
1–9	Used to form counts and numeric arguments to commands.

:	A prefix to a set of commands for file and option manipulation and escapes to the system. Input is given on the bottom line and terminated with a RETURN, and the command then is executed. You can return to where you were pressing DEL if you press : accidentally.
;	Repeats the last single character find that used **f, F, t,** or **T.** A count iterates the basic scan.
<	An operator that shifts lines left one shiftwidth, normally eight spaces. Like all operators, affects lines when repeated, as in <<. Counts are passed through to the basic object, thus 3<< shifts three lines.
=	Reindents line for LISP, as though it was typed in with the lisp and autoindent options set.
>	Same as <, but shifts to the right.
?	A search command, same as / except that it scans backward.
@	Invokes a macro in a named buffer. For example, **@**x invokes a macro defined in the buffer x.
[[	Moves the cursor backward to the previous section boundary. A section begins at each macro contained in the option sections, normally a .NH or .SH. A section also begins at any line whose first character is a formfeed or a {. The latter makes it easy to peruse backward, a function at a time, in C programs. If the lisp option is set, a section also begins with a (in column one, which is useful for moving backward over top-level LISP expressions.
****	Unused
]]	Moves the cursor forward to a section boundary.
^	Moves the cursor to the first nonwhite position on the current line.
_	(Underscore) unused
`	The two-character combination ` ` returns the cursor to the previous context. The previous context is recorded whenever the current line is moved in a nonrelative way. The ` followed by a letter **a–z** returns the cursor to the position marked by the letter (see **m**). When ` is used with an operator such as **d,** the operation takes place from the exact marked place to the current position within the line; the operation takes place over complete lines if ` is used.
{	Moves the cursor backward to the beginning of the preceding paragraph. A paragraph begins at each macro in the paragraphs option, normally .IP, .LP, .PP, .QP, and .bp. A paragraph also begins after a completely empty line and at each section boundary (see **[[**).
|	The command n| places the cursor on the character in column n on the current line.
}	Moves the cursor forward to the beginning of the next paragraph. See { for the definition of paragraph.
~	Changes the case of the character under the cursor.
DELETE	The delete key interrupts the editor, returning **vi** to the command mode.

Appendix 3
Frequent **emacs** Commands

Listed here are the key sequences and their usual command names for the most frequently used **emacs** commands.

Cursor Motion			
ESC-<	beginning-of-file	ESC->	end-of-file
ˆN	next-line	ˆP	previous-line
ˆA	beginning-of-line	ˆE	end-of-line
ˆF	forward-character	ˆB	backward-character
ˆT	scroll-one-line-up	ESC-z	scroll-one-line-down
ˆV	next-page	ESC-v	previous-page
ˆX-l	goto-line	ESC-]	forward-paragraph
ˆS	search-forward	ˆR	search-reverse

Deletion			
ˆI	insert TAB	ˆQ	quote-character
ˆJ	newline-and-indent	ˆO	newline-and-backup
ˆD	delete-next-character	ˆ?	delete-previous-character
ESC-d	delete-next-word	ESC-ˆ?	delete-previous-word

Cut and Paste			
ˆY	yank-from-killbuffer	ˆW	delete-to-killbuffer
ˆ@	set-mark		(from mark to point)
ˆK	kill-to-end-of-line	ESC-w	copy-region-as-kill

Window Operations			
ˆX-n	next-window	ˆX-p	previous-window
ˆX-1	delete-other-windows	ˆX-2	split-current-window
ˆX-z	enlarge-window	ˆX-ˆZ	shrink-window

File I/O			
ˆX-ˆR	read-file	ˆX-ˆI	insert-file
ˆX-ˆF	write-file-exit	ˆX-ˆM	write-modified-files
ˆX-ˆS	write-current-file	ˆX-ˆV	visit-file
ˆX-ˆW	write-named-file		

Miscellaneous			
ˆL	redraw-display	ˆG	abort-command
ESC-x	full-command-name	ˆX-ˆU	undo
ESC-?	apropos	ˆZ	pause-emacs
ˆU	argument-prefix	ESC-*number*	repeat-command

Appendix 4
csh Special Characters

Characters	Use
>, <, &, !	I/O redirection
|	pipe
!, ˜, *, $, :	history substitution
$, {, }	variable substitution
`	command substitution
[,], *, ?, {, }	file name expansion
', ", \	quote characters
&, ;	command termination
(,)	command grouping
#	comment character inside scripts
SPACE, TAB	blank characters
NEWLINE	command line termination
^C or DELETE	interrupt character*
^H	character erase*
^W	word erase*
^U	line erase*

Characters	Use
^O	flush output*
^S, ^Q	output flow control*
<<	here document
&&, ||	conditional execution of commands

* User-settable entries

Appendix 5
csh and *sh* Shell Constructs

csh	sh
foreach *var* (*wordlist*) *commandlist* **end**	**for** *var* in *word1 word2* . . . **do** *commandlist* **done**

if (*expr1*) **then**
 commandlist
 [**else if** (*expr2*) **then**
 commandlist] . . .
 [**else**
 commandlist]
 endif
	if *commandlist*
	 then *commandlist*
	 [**else** *commandlist*]
	 fi

switch (*str*)
 case *pattern*:
     breaksw
    . . .
 [default:
     commandlist]
 endsw
	case *var* in
	 pattern) *commandlist* ;;
	 commandlist . . .
	 [*) *commandlist* ;;]
	 esac

while (*expr*) *commandlist* **end**	**while** *commandlist* **do** *commandlist* **done**
goto *label*	(not available)
break	**break** [*n*]
continue	**continue** [*n*]

csh	sh
set *var* = *string*	*var* = *string*
set *var* = (*s1, s2*. . .)	(not available)
set *var*[*n*] = *string*	(not available)
@ *var* = *expression*	no built-in counterpart, use: *var* = ` expr `
@ *var*[*n*] = *expression*	(not available)
(not available)	**until** (similar to **while**)
built-in logical expressions	no built-in logical expressions
built-in tests for file status	none, use UNIX **test** command (/bin/test)

Appendix 6
The ms Macro Package

Requests

Most requests defined in the ms macro package are listed here. Optional arguments are enclosed in square brackets. The argument N is a distance, and n is an integer. Any initial value related to a request is indicated. The initial value "if t" ("if n") indicates a default request if processed by **troff**(**nroff**). If two initial values are indicated, the first applies to **nroff** and the second to **troff**. Whether a request breaks out a line is also indicated by a y (yes) or an n (no). A second y indicates a request that resets values based on the current setting of ms built-in number registers.

Requests to Be Placed at the Beginning of a Document

Macro Name	Initial Value	Break? Reset?	Explanation
.AB [x]	—	y	Begins abstract; if x = no, do not label abstract.
.AE	—	y	Ends abstract.
.AI	—	y	Author's institution.
.AM	—	n	Better accent mark definitions.
.AU	—	y	Author's name.
.BT	date	n	Bottom title, printed at foot of page.
.DA [x]	if n	n	Forces date x at bottom of page; today if no x.
.EF x	—	n	Even-page footer x (three-part footer as for .tl).
.EH x	—	n	Even-page header x (three-part header as for .tl).
.HD	undef	n	Optional page header below header margin.

Macro Name	Initial Value	Break? Reset?	Explanation
.ND [x]	if t	n	No date in page footer; x is optional date on cover.
.OF x	—	n	Odd-page footer x (three-part footer as for .tl).
.OH x	—	n	Odd-page header x (three-part header as for .tl).
.PT	– % –	n	Default page title, printed automatically at head of page.
.RP [x]	—	n	Requests the released paper format that is used with .TL, .AU, .AI, and optionally .AB. A cover page is generated with information supplied by these requests. The title also is printed on the first page. If x = no, the author and affiliation duplication on the first page is eliminated.
.TL	—	y	Title printed in boldface and two points larger.

Indentations, Exdentations, and Paragraphs

Macro Name	Initial Value	Break? Reset?	Explanation
.IP x N	—	y,y	Indented paragraph, with hanging tag x; N = indent.
.LP	—	y,y	Left-adjusted (block) paragraph.
.PP	—	y,y	Paragraph with first line indented.
.QP	—	y,y	Quotes paragraph (indented and shorter).
.RE	5n	y,y	Retreats: moves position of relative indentation left.
.RS	5n	y,y	Right-shifts: moves position of relative indentation right.
.XP	—	y,y	Paragraph with all but the first line indented.

Requests Related to Footnotes and References

Macro Name	Initial Value	Break? Reset?	Explanation
.FE	—	n	Ends footnote to be placed at bottom of page.
.FP	—	n	Numbered footnote paragraph; may be redefined.
.FS [x]	—	n	Starts footnote; x is optional footnote label.
.]—	—	n	Beginning of refer reference.
.[0	—	n	Ends unclassifiable type of reference.
.[n	—	n	Ends classified reference n = 1:journal-article, 2:book, 3:book-article, 4:report.

Requests Related to the Index

Macro Name	Initial Value	Break? Reset?	Explanation
.IX a b	—	y	Index words a, b, and so on (up to five levels).
.PX [x]	—	y	Prints index (table of contents); x = no, suppresses title.
.XA x N	—	y	Another index entry; x = page or no for none; N = indent.
.XE	—	y	Ends index entry (or series of .IX entries).
.XS x N	—	y	Begins index entry; x = page or no for none; N = indent.

Requests Related to Fonts

Macro Name	Initial Value	Break? Reset?	Explanation
.B [x]	—	n	Emboldens the word x; if no x, switches to boldface.
.I [x]	—	n	Italicizes the word x; if no x, switches to italics.
.R	on	n	Returns to roman font.
.UL x	—	n	Underscores the word x, even in **troff**.
.LG	—	n	Larger; increases point size by two points.
.NL	10p	n	Sets point size back to normal.
.SM	—	n	Smaller; decreases point size by two points.

Requests Related to Section Headers

Macro Name	Initial Value	Break? Reset?	Explanation
.NH [x [n]]	—	y,y	Numbered header; x is header level (top-level if not given), x = 0 resets header counts, x = S sets top-level header count to n.
.SH	—	y,y	Unnumbered section header, in boldface.

Requests Related to Equations and Tables

Macro Name	Initial Value	Break? Reset?	Explanation
.EN	—	y	Ends displayed equation produced by **eqn**.
.EQ [x [y]]	—	y	Begins equation; x = L (left-adjusted), I (indented), or C (centered, the default); y is optional equation label.
.TE	—	y	Ends table processed by **tbl**.
.TH	—	y	Ends multipage header of table.
.TS [H]	—	y,y	Begins table; table has multipage header if H is given.

Requests Related to Boxes, Displays, and Keeps

Macro Name	Initial Value	Break? Reset?	Explanation
.B1	—	y	Begins text to be enclosed in a box.
.B2	—	y	Ends boxed text and displays it.
.BX x	—	n	Displays word x in a box.
.DE	—	y	Ends display (unfilled text) of any kind.
.DS x N	I	y	Begins display with keep; x = I, L, C, B (block centered); N is optional indent.
.ID N	8n, .5i	y	Indented display with no keep; N = indent.
.LD	—	y	Left-adjusted display with no keep.
.CD	—	y	Centered display with no keep.
.BD	—	y	Block centered display with no keep.
.KE	—	n	Ends keep of any kind.
.KF	—	n	Begins floating keep.
.KS	—	y	Begins keep; unit kept together on a single page.

Other Requests

Macro Name	Initial Value	Break? Reset?	Explanation
.CM	if t	n	Displays cut marks between pages.
.MC N	—	y,y	Multiple columns; N is column width.
.TA	8n,5n	n	Set tabs to 8n, 16n, . . . (**nroff**); 5n, 10n, . . . (**troff**).
.TC [x]	—	y	Displays table of contents at end; x = no, suppresses title.
.UX [x]	—	n	UNIX; trademark message first time; x appended.
.1C	on	y,y	One-column format, on a new page.
.2C	—	y,y	Begins two-column format.

Registers

Formatting distances can be controlled in *ms* by means of built-in number registers. For example:

.nr LL 6.5i

sets the line length to 6.5 inches. The following is a table of number registers and their default values.

Name	Register Controls	Takes Effect	Default
PS	Point size	Paragraph	10
VS	Vertical spacing	Paragraph	12
LL	Line length	Paragraph	6i
LT	Title length	Next page	Same as LL
FL	Footnote length	Next .FS	5.5i
PD	Paragraph distance	Paragraph	1v (if n), .3v (if t)
DD	Display distance	Displays	1v (if n), .5v (if t)
PI	Paragraph indent	Paragraph	5n
PN	Page number	Next use	
QI	Quote indent	Next .QP	5n
FI	Footnote indent	Next .FS	2n
PO	Page offset	Next page	0 (if n), ~1i (if t)

Name	Register Controls	Takes Effect	Default
HM	Header margin	Next page	1i
FM	Footer margin	Next page	1i
FF	Footnote format	Next .FS	0 (1, 2, 3 available)
CW	Column width	Next 2C	7/15 LL
GW	Gap between columns		Next 2C 1/15 LL

When resetting these values, make sure to specify the appropriate units. Setting the line length to 7, for example, will result in output with one character per line. Setting FF to 1 suppresses footnote superscripting; setting FF to 2 also suppresses indentation of the first line; and setting FF to 3 produces an .IP-like footnote paragraph.

The following is a list of string registers available in ms; they may be used anywhere in the text.

Name	String's Function
*Q	Quote (")
*U	Unquote (")
#*–	Dash (–)
*(MO	Month (month of the year)
*(DY	Day (current date)
*(SN	Current section number
**	Automatically numbered footnote
*´	Acute accent (before letter)
*`	Grave accent (before letter)
*^	Circumflex (before letter)
*,	Cedilla (before letter)
*:	Umlaut (before letter)
*~	Tilde (before letter)

When using the extended diacritical marks available with .AM, these strings should come after, rather than before, the letter to be accented.

Internal ms Register Names

The following register names are used internally by ms. Independent use of these names in your own macros may produce incorrect output. Note that no lowercase letters are used in any ms internal name.

Number Registers Used in ms										
:	DW	GW	HM	IQ	LL	NA	OJ	PO	T.	TV
#T	EF	H1	HT	IR	LT	NC	PD	PQ	TB	VS
1T	FL	H3	IK	KI	MM	NF	PF	PX	TD	YE
AV	FM	H4	IM	L1	MN	NS	PI	RO	TN	YY
CW	FP	H5	IP	LE	MO	OI	PN	ST	TQ	ZN

String Registers Used in ms										
'	A5	CB	DW	EZ	I	KF	MR	R1	RT	TL
`	AB	CC	DY	FA	I1	KQ	ND	R2	S0	TM
^	AE	CD	E1	FE	I2	KS	NH	R3	S1	TQ
~	AI	CF	E2	FJ	I3	LB	NL	R4	S2	TS
:	AU	CH	E3	FK	I4	LD	NP	R5	SG	TT
,	B	CM	E4	FN	I5	LG	OD	RC	SH	UL
1C	BG	CS	E5	FO	ID	LP	OK	RE	SM	WB
2C	BT	CT	EE	FQ	IE	ME	PP	RF	SN	WH
A1	C	D	EL	FS	IM	MF	PT	RH	SY	WT
A2	C1	DA	EM	FV	IP	MH	PY	RP	TA	XD
A3	C2	DE	EN	FY	IZ	MN	QF	RQ	TE	XF
A4	CA	DS	EQ	HO	KE	MO	R	RS	TH	XK

Appendix 7
nroff/troff Requests

Text Filling and Adjusting

.br	Breaks (begins a new output line).
.fi	Fills output lines.
.nf	No filling or adjusting of output lines.
.ad *c*	Adjusts output lines with mode *c, c* = l, r, b, c, for left margin, right margin, both, and centering, respectively.
.na	No output line adjusting.

Line Length, Indenting, and Centering

.ll $\pm N$	Line length is set to N, increased ($+N$), or decreased ($-N$).
.in $\pm N$	Sets indent.
.ce N	Centers following N input text lines.
.ti $\pm N$	Indents the next output line.

Font and Character Size Control

.ps $\pm N$	Sets point size.
\s$\pm N$	Sets point size (escape sequence).
.ss N	SPACE character size set to $N/36$ em.
.cs $F\ N\ M$	Constant character-width mode, width N for font F. The optional M defines the width of em in points.
.bd $F\ N$	Emboldens font F by $N-1$ units.

.ft F	Changes to font $F = x, xx,$ or 1–4. (same as \f$x$, \f(xx, \f$N$).
.fp N F	Font F mounted on physical position $1 \leq N \leq 4$.

Page Control

.pl ± N	Page length.
.bp ± N	Ejects current page; next page number N if given.
.pn ± N	Next page number N.
.po ± N	Page offset.
.ne N	Needs vertical space N for next output line (default is vertical spacing V).

Vertical Spacing

.vs N	Vertical baseline spacing (V).
.ls N	Outputs $N - 1$ Vs after each text output line.
.sp N	Spaces vertical distance N in either direction.
.sv N	Saves vertical distance N.
.os	Outputs saved vertical distance.
.ns	Turns no-space mode on.
.rs	Restores spacing; turns no-space mode off.

Horizontal and Vertical Motions

\h'N'	Local horizontal motion; moves right N (negative left).
\v'N'	Local vertical motion; moves down N (negative up).
\k$x$	Marks current horizontal position in register x.
\h' | \n$x$u'	Returns to marked horizontal position in register x.
.mk R	Marks current vertical position in register R.
.rt ±N	Returns (upward only) to marked vertical position.
\l'Nc'	Draws horizontal line N (optionally with char c).
\L'Nc'	Draws vertical line N (optionally with char c).
\d	Forward (down) 1/2 em vertical motion (1/2 line in **nroff**).
\u	Reverse (up) 1/2 em vertical motion (1/2 line in **nroff**).

Macros, Diversion, and Position Traps

.de *xx yy*   Defines or redefines macro *xx*; end at a line containing . . or, optionally, a request .*yy*.

.am *xx yy*   Appends to a macro.

.rm *xx*   Removes request, macro, or string register.

.rn *xx yy*   Renames request, macro, or string register *xx* to *yy*.

.di *xx*   Diverts output to macro *xx*.

.da *xx*   Diverts and appends to *xx*.

.wh *N xx*   Sets location trap; negative is with respect to page bottom.

.ch *xx N*   Changes trap location.

.dt *N xx*   Sets a diversion trap.

.it *N xx*   Sets an input line count trap.

.em *xx*   End macro is *xx*.

Number and String Registers

.nr *R ±N M*   Defines and sets number register *R*. Auto-increment amount *M* is optional.

.af *R c*   Assigns output format to number register *R* (*c* = 1, i, I, a, A).

.rr *R*   Removes number register *R*.

.ds *xx string*   Defines a string register *xx* containing *string*.

.as *xx string*   Appends *string* to the string register *xx*.

Tabs, Leaders, and Fields

.ta *Nt* . . .   Sets TAB stops. The optional *t* specifies a TAB type: R (right), C (centered), L (left, the default).

.tc *c*   TAB repetition character.

.lc *c*   Leader repetition character.

.fc *a b*   Sets field delimiter *a* and pad character *b*.

Input and Output Conventions and Character Translations

.ec *c*	Sets escape character to *c* (default \).
.eo	Turns off escape character mechanism (restored by .ec).
.lg *N*	Ligature mode on if $N > 0$.
.ul *N*	Underscores (italicizes in **troff**) the next *N* input lines.
.cu *N*	Continuous underscore in **nroff**; like .ul in **troff**.
.uf *F*	Sets underscore font to *F* (to be switched to by .ul).
.cc *c*	Sets control character to *c* (default .).
.c2 *c*	Sets nobreak control character to *c* (default ´).
.tr *abcd.* . .	Translates *a* to *b*, and so on for output.

Hyphenation

.nh	No hyphenation.
.hy *N*	Enables hyphenation; $N =$ mode.
.hc *c*	Hyphenation indicator character *c*.
.hw *word1* . . .	Exception words for hyphenation.

Three-Part Titles

.tl *'left'center'right'*	Three-part title.
.pc *c*	Page number character.
.lt $\pm N$	Length of title.

Output Line Numbering

.nm $\pm N\ M\ S\ I$	Turns output line number mode on or off, sets parameters.
.nn *N*	Turns output line number mode off for the next *N* lines.

Conditional Acceptance of Input

.if *c text*	If condition *c* is true, then accepts *text* as input, for multiline use \{*text*\}.

.if !c *text*	If condition *c* is false, then accepts *text*.
.if *N text*	If expression $N > 0$, accepts *text*.
.if !*N text*	If expression $N \leq 0$, accepts *text*.
.if ´*string1*´*string2*´ *text*	If *string1* identical to *string2*, accepts *text*.
.if ! ´*string1*´*string2*´ *text*	If *string1* not identical to *string2*, accepts *text*.
.ie *c text*	If portion of if-else (with all the preceding if forms).
.el *text*	Else portion of if-else.

Input/Output File Switching

.so *filename*	Includes given source file (may be nested).
.nx *filename*	Next file.
.pi *program*	Pipes output to *program* (**nroff** only).

Miscellaneous

.ev *N*	Switches to environment $N = 0, 1, 2$ (push down). Use .ev to pop up and restore a previous environment.
.rd *prompt*	Reads interactive insertion.
.ex	Exits from **nroff/troff**.
.mc *c N*	Sets margin character *c* and separation *N*.
.tm *string*	Displays *string* on terminal (UNIX standard error output).
.ig *yy*	Ignores until . . or *yy* request.
.pm *t*	Displays macro names and sizes; if *t* is given, displays only total sizes.
.fl	Flushes output buffer.

Escape Sequences

Sequence	Meaning
\\	Prevents or delays the interpretation of \.
\e	Printable version of the current escape character.
\´	´ (acute accent); equivalent to \(aa.
\`	` (grave accent); equivalent to \(ga.

Sequence	Meaning
\\-	Minus sign in the current font.
\\.	Period; to prevent or delay the interpretation of ., in .de, for example.
\\(SPACE)	Unpaddable space-size SPACE character.
\\0	Digit width SPACE.
\\|	1/6 em narrow SPACE character (zero width in **nroff**).
\\^	1/12 em half-narrow SPACE character (zero width in **nroff**).
\\&	Nondisplaying, zero-width character.
\\!	Transparent line indicator.
\\"	Beginning of comment.
\\$N	Interpolates argument $1 \leq N \leq 9$.
\\%	Default optional hyphenation character.
\\(xx	Special character xx.
*x, *(xx	Interpolates string x or xx.
\\a	Noninterpreted leader character.
\\b´abc . . .´	Bracket building function.
\\c	Interrupts text processing.
\\fx, \\f(xx, \\fN	Changes to font named x or xx, or at position N.
\\nx, \\n(xx	Interpolates number register x or xx.
\\o´abc . . .´	Overstrikes characters a, b, c, . . .
\\p	Breaks and spreads output line.
\\r	Reverses (up) 1 em vertical motion (reverses LINEFEED in **nroff**).
\\sN, \\s±N	Point-size change function.
\\t	Noninterpreted horizontal TAB.
\\w´string´	Interpolates width of *string*.
\\x´N´	Extra line space function (negative before, positive after).
\\zc	Prints c with zero width (without spacing).
\\{	Begins conditional input.
\\}	Ends conditional input.
\\NEWLINE	Concealed (ignored) NEWLINE.
\\X	Same as X for any character X not listed in this table.

Predefined General Number Registers

Name	Description
%	Current page number.
ct	Character type (set by width function).
dl	Width (maximum) of last completed diversion.
dn	Height (vertical size) of last completed diversion.
dw	Current day of the week (1–7).
dy	Current day of the month (1–31).
hp	Current horizontal place on input line.
ln	Output line number.
mo	Current month (1–12).
nl	Vertical position of last printed text baseline.
sb	Depth of string below baseline (generated by width function).
st	Height of string above baseline (generated by width function).
yr	Last two digits of current year.

Predefined Read-Only Number Registers

Name	Description
.$	Number of arguments available at the current macro level.
.A	Sets to 1 in **troff**, if −a option used; always 1 in **nroff**.
.H	Available horizontal resolution in basic units.
.T	Sets to 1 in **nroff**, if −T option used; always 0 in **troff**.
.V	Available vertical resolution in basic units.
.a	Postline extra line space most recently utilized using \x′N′.
.c	Number of lines read from current input file.
.d	Current vertical place in current diversion; equal to nl, if no diversion.
.f	Current font as physical quadrant (1–4).
.h	Text baseline high-water mark on current page or diversion.
.i	Current indent.

Name	Description
.l	Current line length.
.n	Length of text portion on previous output line.
.o	Current page offset.
.p	Current page length.
.s	Current point size.
.t	Distance to the next trap.
.u	Equal to 1 in the fill mode and 0 in the no-fill mode.
.v	Current vertical line spacing.
.w	Width of previous character.
.x	Reserved version-dependent register.
.y	Reserved version-dependent register.
.z	Name of current diversion.

Appendix 8
troff Special Characters

'	´	close quotation mark	`	`	open quotation mark
—	\(em	3/4 em-dash	–	–	hyphen
–	\(hy	hyphen	–	\\–	current font minus
•	\(bu	bullet		\(sq	square
—	\(ru	rule	¼	\(14	1/4
	\(12	1/2		\(34	3/4
fi	\(fi	fi	fl	\(fl	fl
ff	\(ff	ff	ffi	\(Fi	ffi
ffl	\(Fl	ffl	°	\(de	degree
†	\(dg	dagger	'	\(fm	foot mark
¢	\(ct	cent sign	®	\(rg	**registered**
©	\(co	copyright	+	\(pl	math plus
–	\(mi	math minus	=	\(eq	math equals
*	\(**	math star	§	\(sc	section
´	\(aa	acute accent	`	\(ga	grave accent
—	\(ul	underscore	/	\(sl	slash (matching backslash)
α	\(*a	alpha (lowercase)	β	\(*b	beta (lowercase)
γ	\(*g	gamma (lowercase)	δ	\(*d	delta (lowercase)
ε	\(*e	epsilon (lowercase)	ζ	\(*z	zeta (lowercase)
η	\(*y	eta (lowercase)	θ	\(*h	theta (lowercase)
ι	\(*i	iota (lowercase)	κ	\(*k	kappa (lowercase)
λ	\(*l	lambda (lowercase)	μ	\(*m	mu (lowercase)
ν	\(*n	nu (lowercase)	ξ	\(*c	xi (lowercase)
o	\(*o	omicron (lowercase)	π	\(*p	pi (lowercase)

ρ	\(*r	rho (lowercase)	σ	\(*s	sigma (lowercase)
φ	\(ts	terminal sigma (lowercase)	τ	\(*t	tau (lowercase)
υ	\(*u	upsilon (lowercase)	φ	\(*f	phi (lowercase)
χ	\(*x	chi (lowercase)	ψ	\(*q	psi (lowercase)
ω	\(*w	omega (lowercase)	A	\(*A	alpha (uppercase)
B	\(*B	beta (uppercase)	Γ	\(*G	gamma (uppercase)
Δ	\(*D	delta (uppercase)	E	\(*E	epsilon (uppercase)
Z	\(*Z	zeta (uppercase)	H	\(*Y	eta (uppercase)
Θ	\(*H	theta (uppercase)	I	\(*I	iota (uppercase)
K	\(*K	kappa (uppercase)	Λ	\(*L	lambda (uppercase)
M	\(*M	mu (uppercase)	N	\(*N	nu (uppercase)
Ξ	\(*C	xi (uppercase)	O	\(*O	omicron (uppercase)
Π	\(*P	pi (uppercase)	P	\(*R	rho (uppercase)
Σ	\(*S	sigma (uppercase)	T	\(*T	tau (uppercase)
Υ	\(*U	upsilon (uppercase)	Φ	\(*F	phi (uppercase)
X	\(*X	chi (uppercase)	Ψ	\(*Q	psi (uppercase)
Ω	\(*W	omega (uppercase)	√	\(sr	square root
—	\(rn	root en extender	≥	\(>=	>=
≤	\(<=	<=	≡	\(==	identically equal
≃	\(~=	approx =	~	\(ap	approximates
≠	\(!=	not equal	→	\(->	right arrow
←	\(<-	left arrow	↑	\(ua	up arrow
↓	\(da	down arrow	×	\(mu	multiply
÷	\(di	divide	±	\(+-	plus/minus
∪	\(cu	cup (union)	∩	\(ca	cap (intersection)
⊂	\(sb	subset of	⊃	\(sp	superset of
⊆	\(ib	improper subset	⊇	\(ip	improper superset
∞	\(if	infinity	∂	\(pd	partial derivative
∇	\(gr	gradient	¬	\(no	not
∫	\(is	integral sign	≈	\(pt	proportional to
∅	\(es	empty set	∈	\(mo	member of
|	\(br	box vertical rule	‡	\(dd	double dagger
⇒	\(rh	right hand	⇐	\(lh	left hand
○	\(ci	circle	|	\(or	or
⎩	\(lb	left bottom of curly bracket	⎰	\(lt	left top of curly bracket
⎭	\(rb	right bottom of curly bracket	⎱	\(rt	right top of curly bracket

⎬	\(rk	center of right curly bracket	⎨	\(lk	center of left curly bracket
⎣	\(lf	left floor	⎪	\(bv	bold vertical
⎡	\(lc	left ceiling	⎦	\(rf	right floor
			⎤	\(rc	right ceiling

Appendix 9
UNIX System Calls

accept: Accepts a connection on a socket.

```
#include <sys/types.h>
#include <sys/socket.h>

ns = accept(s, addr, addrlen)
int ns, s;
struct sockaddr *addr;
int *addrlen;
```

access: Determines accessibility of a file.

```
#include <sys/file.h>

#define R_OK      4
/* test for read permission */
#define W_OK      2
/* test for write permission */
#define X_OK      1
/* test for execute (search) permission */
#define F_OK      0
/* test for presence of file */

accessible = access(path, mode)
int accessible;
char *path;
int mode;
```

acct: Turns accounting on or off.

```
acct(file)
char *file;
```

bind: Binds a name to a socket.

```
#include <sys/types.h>
#include <sys/socket.h>

bind(s, name, namelen)
int s;
struct sockaddr *name;
int namelen;
```

brk, sbrk: Changes data segment size.

```
caddr_t brk(addr)
caddr_ addr;

caddr_t sbrk(incr)
int incr;
```

chdir: Changes current working directory.

chdir(path)
char *path;

chmod: Changes mode of file.

chmod(path, mode)
char *path;
int mode;

fchmod(fd, mode)
int fd, mode;

chown: Changes owner and group of a file.

chown(path, owner, group)
char *path;
int owner, group;

fchown(fd, owner, group)
int fd, owner, group;

chroot: Changes root directory.

chroot(dirname)
char *dirname;

close: Deletes a descriptor.

close(d)
int d;

connect: Initiates a connection on a socket.

#include <sys/types.h>
#include <sys/socket.h>

connect(s, name, namelen)
int s;
struct sockaddr *name;
int namelen;

creat: Creates a new file.

creat(name, mode)
char *name;

dup, dup2: Duplicates a descriptor.

newd = **dup**(oldd)
int newd, oldd;

dup2(oldd, newd)
int oldd; newd;

execve: Executes a file.

execve(name, argv, envp)
char *name, *argv[], *envp[];

_exit: Terminates a process.

_exit(status)
int status;

fcntl: File control.

#include <fcntl.h>

res = **fcntl**(fd, cmd, arg)
int res;
int fd, cmd, arg;

flock: Applies or removes an advisory lock on an open file.

#include <sys/file.h>

#define LOCK__SH 1
/* shared lock */
#define LOCK__EX 2
/* exclusive lock */

```
#define LOCK_NB 4
/* don't block when locking */
#define LOCK_UN 8
/* unlock */

flock(fd, operation)
int fd, operation;
```

fork: Creates a new process.

```
pid = fork()
int pid;
```

fsync: Synchronizes a file's in-core state with that on disk.

```
fsync(fd)
int fd;
```

getdtablesize: Gets descriptor table size.

```
nds = getdtablesize()
int nds;
```

getgid, getegid: Gets group identity.

```
gid = getgid()
int gid;

egid = getegid()
int egid;
```

getgroups: Gets group access list.

```
#include <sys/param.h>

getgroups(ngroups, gidset)
int *ngroups, *gidset;
```

gethostid, sethostid: Gets/sets a unique identifier of current host.

```
hostid = gethostid()
int hostid;

sethostid (hostid)
int hostid;
```

gethostname, sethostname: Gets/sets name of current host.

```
gethostname(name, namelen)
char *name;
int namelen;

sethostname(name, namelen)
char *name;
int namelen;
```

getitimer, setitimer: Gets/sets value of an interval timer.

```
#include <sys/time.h>

#define ITIMER_REAL 0
/* real time intervals */
#define ITIMER_VIRTUAL 1
/* virtual time intervals */
#define ITIMER_PROF 2
/* user and system virtual time */

getitimer(which, value)
int which;
struct itimerval *value;

setitimer(which, value, ovalue)
int which;
struct itimerval *value, *ovalue;
```

getpagesize: Gets system page size.

pagesize = **getpagesize**()
int pagesize;

getpeername: Gets name of connected peer.

getpeername(s, name, namelen)
int s;
struct sockaddr *name;
int *namelen;

getpgrp: Gets process group.

pgrp = **getpgrp**(pid)
int prgp;
int pid;

getpid, getppid: Gets process identification.

pid = **getpid**()
long pid;

ppid = **getppid**()
long ppid;

getpriority, setpriority: Gets/sets program scheduling priority.

#include <sys/resource.h>

#define PRIO_PROCESS 0
/* process */
#define PRIO_PGRP 1
/* process group */
#define PRIO_USER 2
/* userid */

prio = **getpriority**(which, who)
int prio, which, who;

setpriority(which, who, prio)
int which, who, prio;

getrlimit, setrlimit: Controls maximum system resource consumption.

#include <sys/time.h>
#include <sys/resource.h>

getrlimit(resource, rlp)
int resource;
struct rlimit *rlp;

setrlimit(resource, rlp)
int resource;
struct rlimit *rlp;

getrusage: Gets information about resource utilization.

#include <sys/time.h>
#include <sys/resource.h>

#define RUSAGE_SELF 0
/* calling process */
#define RUSAGE_CHILDREN −1
/* terminated child processes */

getrusage(who, rusage)
int who;
struct rusage *rusage;

getsockname: Gets socket name.

getsockname(s, name, namelen)
int s;
struct sockaddr *name;
int *namelen;

getsockopt, setsockopt: Gets/sets options on sockets.

```
#include <sys/types.h>
#include <sys/socket.h>

getsockopt(s,level,optname,optval,optlen)
int s, level, optname;
char *optval;
int *optlen;

setsockopt(s,level,optname,optval,optlen)
int s, level, optname;
char *optval;
int optlen;
```

gettimeofday, settimeofday: Gets/sets date and time.

```
#include <sys/time.h>

gettimeofday(tp, tzp)
struct timeval *tp;
struct timezone *tzp;

settimeofday(tp, tzp)
struct timeval *tp;
struct timezone *tzp;
```

getuid, geteuid: Gets user identity.

```
uid = getuid()
int uid;

euid = geteuid()
int euid;
```

ioctl: Control device.

```
#include <sys/ioctl.h>

ioctl(d, request, argp)
int d, request;
char *argp;
```

kill: Sends signal to a process.

```
kill(pid, sig)
int pid; sig;
```

killpg: Sends signal to a process group.

```
killpg(pgrp, sig)
int pgrp, sig;
```

link: Creates a hard link to a file.

```
link(name1, name2)
char *name1, *name2;
```

listen: Listens for connections on a socket.

```
listen(s, backlog)
int s, backlog;
```

lseek: Moves read/write pointer.

```
#define L_SET 0
/* set the seek pointer */
#define L_INCR 1
/* increment the seek pointer */
#define L_XTND 2
/* extend the file size */

pos = lseek(d, offset, whence)
int pos;
int d, offset, whence;
```

mkdir: Creates a directory file.

```
mkdir(path, mode)
char *path;
int mode;
```

mknod: Creates a special file.

mknod(path, mode, dev)
char *path;
int mode, dev;

mount, umount: Mounts or removes a file system.

mount(special, name, rwflag)
char *special, *name;
int rwflag;

umount(special)
char *special;

open: Opens a file for reading or writing, or creates a new file.

#include <sys/file.h>

open(path, flags, mode)
char *path;
int flags, mode;

pipe: Creates an interprocess communication channel.

pipe(fildes)
int fildes[2];

profil: Execution time profile.

profil(buff, bufsiz, offset, scale)
char *buff;
int bufsiz, offset, scale;

ptrace: Process trace.

#include <signal.h>

ptrace(request, pid, addr, data)
int request, pid, *addr, data;

quota: Manipulates disk quotas.

#include <sys/quota.h>

quota(cmd, uid, arg, addr)
int cmd, uid, arg;
caddr_t addr;

read, readv: Reads input.

cc = **read**(d, buf, nbytes)
int cc, d;
char *buf;
int nbytes;

#include <sys/types.h>
#include <sys/uio.h>

cc = **readv**(d, iov, iovcnt)
int cc, d;
struct iovec *iov;
int iovcnt;

readlink: Reads value of a symbolic link.

cc = **readlink**(path, buf, bufsiz)
int cc;
char *path, *buf;
int bufsiz;

reboot: Reboots system or halts processor.

#include <sys/reboot.h>

reboot(howto)
int howto;

recv, recvfrom, recvmsg: Receives a message from a socket.

```
#include <sys/types.h>
#include <sys/socket.h>

cc = recv(s, buf, len, flags)
int cc, s;
char *buf;
int len, flags;

cc = recvfrom(s,buf,len,flags,from,fromlen)
int cc, s;
char *buf;
int len, flags;
struct sockaddr *from;
int *fromlen;

cc = recvmsg(s, msg, flags)
int cc, s;
struct msghdr msg[];
int flags;
```

rename: Changes the name of a file.

```
rename(from, to)
char *from, *to;
```

rmdir: Removes a directory file.

```
rmdir(path)
char *path;
```

select: Synchronous I/O multiplexing.

```
#include <sys/time.h>

int select(nfds, readfds, writefds, execptfds,
       timeout)
int nfds, *readfds, *writefds, *execptfds;
struct timeval *timeout;
```

send, sendto, sendmsg: Sends a message from a socket.

```
#include <sys/types.h>
#include <sys/socket.h>

cc = send(s, msg, len, flags)
int cc, s;
char *msg;
int len, flags;

cc = sendto(s, msg, len, flags, to, tolen)
int cc, s;
char *msg;
int len, flags;
struct sockaddr *to;
int tolen;

cc = sendmsg(s, msg, flags)
int cc, s;
struct msghdr msg[];
int flags;
```

setgroups: Sets group access list.

```
#include <sys/param.h>

setgroups(ngroups, gidset)
int ngroups, *gidset;
```

setpgrp: Sets process group.

```
setpgrp(pid, pgrp)
int pid, pgrp;
```

setquota: Enables/disables quotas on a file system.

```
setquota(special, file)
char *special, *file;
```

setregid: Sets real and effective groupid.

setregid(rgid, egid)
int rgid, egid;

setreuid: Sets real and effective userids

setreuid(ruid, euid)
int ruid, euid;

shutdown: Shuts down part of a full-duplex connection.

shutdown(s, how)
int s, how;

sigblock: Blocks signals.

sigblock(mask);
int mask;

sigpause: Automatically releases blocked signals and waits for an interrupt.

sigpause(sigmask)
int sigmask;

sigsetmask: Sets current signal mask.

sigsetmask(mask);
int mask;

sigstack: Sets and/or gets signal stack context.

#include <signal.h>

```
struct sigstack {
        caddr_t         ss_sp;
        int             ss_onstack;
};
```

sigstack(ss, oss);
struct sigstack *ss, *oss;

sigvec: Software signal facilities.

#include <signal.h>

```
struct sigvec {
        int             (*sv_handler)();
        int             sv_mask;
        int             sv_onstack;
};
```

sigvec(sig, vec, ovec)
int sig;
struct sigvec *vec, *ovec;

socket: Creates an endpoint for communication.

#include <sys/types.h>
#include <sys/socket.h>

s = **socket**(af, type, protocol)
int s, af, type, protocol;

socketpair: Creates a pair of connected sockets.

#include <sys/types.h>
#include <sys/socket.h>

socketpair(d, type, protocol, sv)
int d, type, protocol;
int sv[2];

stat, lstat, fstat: Gets file status.

```
#include <sys/types.h>
#include <sys/stat.h>

stat(path, buf)
char *path;
struct stat *buf;

lstat(path, buf)
char *path;
struct stat *buf;

fstat(fd, buf)
int fd;
struct stat *buf;
```

swapon: Adds a swap device for interleaved paging/swapping.

```
swapon(special)
char *special;
```

symlink: Creates a symbolic link to a file.

```
symlink(name1, name2)
char *name1, *name2;
```

sync: Updates super block.

```
sync()
```

syscall: Indirect system call.

```
syscall(number, arg, . . .) (VAX-11)
```

truncate: Truncates a file to a specified length.

```
truncate(path, length)
char *path;
int length;

ftruncate(fd, length)
int fd, length;
```

umask: Sets a file creation mode mask.

```
oumask = umask(numask)
int oumask, numask;
```

unlink: Removes a directory entry.

```
unlink(path)
char *path;
```

utimes: Sets file times.

```
#include <sys/time.h>

utimes(file, tvp)
char *file;
struct timeval *tvp[2];
```

vfork: Spawns a new process in a virtual-memory efficient way.

```
pid = vfork()
int pid;
```

vhangup: Virtually "hangs up" the current control terminal.

```
vhangup()
```

wait, wait3: Waits for a process to terminate.

```
#include <sys/wait.h>
```

```
pid = wait(status)
int pid;
union wait *status;

pid = wait(0)
int pid;

#include <sys/time.h>
#include <sys/resource.h>

pid = wait3(status, options, rusage)
int pid;
union wait *status;
int options;
struct rusage *rusage;
```

write, writev: Writes on a file.

```
write(d, buf, nbytes)
int d;
char *buf;
int nbytes;

#include <sys/types.h>
#include <sys/uio.h>

writev(d, iov, ioveclen)
int d;
struct iovec *iov;
int ioveclen;
```

Appendix 10
UNIX Signals

Signals			
Symbol	Number	Default Action	Meaning
SIGHUP	1	exit	hangs up
SIGINT	2	exit	interrupts
SIGQUIT	3	core dump	quits
SIGILL	4	core dump	illegal instruction
SIGTRAP	5	core dump	trace trap
SIGIOT	6	core dump	IOT instruction
SIGEMT	7	core dump	EMT instruction
SIGFPE	8	core dump	floating point exception
SIGKILL	9	exit	kills (cannot be caught or ignored)
SIGBUS	10	core dump	bus error
SIGSEGV	11	core dump	segmentation violation
SIGSYS	12	core dump	bad argument to system call
SIGPIPE	13	exit	writes on a pipe with no one to read it
SIGALRM	14	exit	alarm clock
SIGTERM	15	exit	software termination signal
SIGURG	16	discard	urgent condition present on socket
SIGSTOP	17	suspend	stops (cannot be caught or ignored)
SIGTSTP	18	suspend	stop signal generated from keyboard
SIGCONT	19	discard	continues after stop
SIGCHLD	20	discard	child status has changed

Signals			
Symbol	Number	Default Action	Meaning
SIGTTIN	21	suspend	background read attempted from control terminal
SIGTTOU	22	suspend	background write attempted to control terminal
SIGIO	23	discard	I/O is possible on a descriptor
SIGXCPU	24	exit	CPU time limit exceeded
SIGXFSZ	25	exit	file size limit exceeded
SIGVTALRM	26	exit	virtual time alarm
SIGPROF	27	exit	profiling timer alarm

Appendix 11
Standard C Library Routines

abort: Generates a fault to terminate.

abs: Integer absolute value.

abs(i)
int i;

atof, atoi, atol: Converts ASCII to numbers.

double **atof**(nptr)
char *nptr;

atoi(nptr)
char *nptr;

long **atol**(nptr)
char *nptr;

bcopy, bcmp, bzero, ffs: Bit and byte string operations

bcopy(b1, b2, length)
char *b1, *b2;
int length;

bcmp(b1, b2, length)
char *b1, *b2;
int length;

bzero(b, length)
char *b;
int length;

ffs(i)
int i;

crypt, setkey, encrypt: DES encryption.

char ***crypt**(key, salt)
char *key, *salt;

setkey(key)
char *key;

encrypt(block, edflag)
char *block;

ctime, localtime, gmtime, asctime, timezone: Converts date and time to ASCII.

char ***ctime**(clock)
long *clock;

#include <sys/time.h>

struct tm ***localtime**(clock)
long *clock;

struct tm ***gmtime**(clock)
long *clock;

char ***asctime**(tm)
struct tm *tm;

char ***timezone**(zone, dst)

ecvt, fcvt, gcvt: Output conversion.

char ***ecvt**(value, ndigit, decpt, sign)
double value;
int ndigit, *decpt, *sign;

char ***fcvt**(value, ndigit, decpt, sign)
double value;
int ndigit, *decpt, *sign;

char ***gcvt**(value, ndigit, buf)
double value;
char *buf;

end, etext, edata: Last locations in program.

extern **end**;
extern **etext**;
extern **edata**;

execl, execv, execle, execlp, execvp, exec, exece, exect, environ: Executes a file.

execl(name, arg0, arg1, . . . , argn, 0)
char *name, *arg0, *arg1, . . . , *argn;

execv(name, argv)
char *name, *argv[];

execle(name, arg0, arg1, . . . , argn, 0, envp)
char *name, *arg0, *arg1, . . . , *argn, *envp[];

exect(name, argv, envp)
char *name, *argv[], *envp[];

extern **char** **environ**;

exit: Terminates a process after flushing any pending output.

exit(status)
int status;

frexp, ldexp, modf: Splits into mantissa and exponent.

double **frexp**(value, eptr)
double value;
int *eptr;

double **ldexp**(value, exp)
double value;

double **modf**(value, iptr)
double value, *iptr;

getenv: Value for an environment name.

char ***getenv**(name)
char *name;

getgrent, getgrgid, getgrnam, setgrent, endgrent: Gets group file entry.

#include <grp.h>

struct group ***getgrent**()

struct group *getgrgid(gid)
int gid;

struct group *getgrnam(name)
char *name;

setgrent()

endgrent()

getlogin: Gets login name.

char *getlogin()

getpass: Reads a password.

char *getpass(prompt)
char *prompt;

getpwent, getpwuid, getpwnam, setpwent, endpwent: Gets password file entry.

#include <pwd.h>

struct passwd *getpwent()

struct passwd *getpwuid(uid)
int uid;

struct passwd *getpwnam(name)
char *name;

int setpwent()

int endpwent()

getwd: Gets current working directory pathname.

char *getwd(pathname)
char *pathname;

insque, remque: Inserts/removes an element from a queue.

struct qelem {struct   qelem *q—forw;
        struct   qelem *q—back;
        char q—data[]; };

insque(elem, pred)
struct qelem *elem, *pred;
remque(elem)
struct qelem *elem;

isalpha, isupper, islower, isdigit, isalnum, isspace, ispunct, isprint, iscntrl, isascii: Character classification macros.

#include <ctype.h>

isalpha(c)

. . .

malloc, free, realloc, calloc, alloca: Memory allocator.

char *malloc(size)
unsigned size;

free(ptr)
char *ptr;

char *realloc(ptr, size)
char *ptr;
unsigned size;

char *calloc(nelem, elsize)
unsigned nelem, elsize;

char *alloca(size)
int size;

mktemp: Creates a unique file name.

```
char *mktemp(template)
char *template;


monitor, monstartup, moncontrol: Prepares an
execution profile.

monitor(lowpc, highpc, buffer, bufsize, nfunc)
int (*lowpc)(), (*highpc)();
short buffer[];

monstartup(lowpc, highpc)
int (*lowpc)(), (*highpc)();

moncontrol(mode)


nlist: Gets entries from a name list.

#include <nlist.h>

nlist(filename, nl)
char *filename;
struct nlist nl[];


opendir, readdir, telldir, seekdir, rewinddir,
closedir: Directory operations.

#include <sys/dir.h>

DIR *opendir(filename)
char *filename;

struct direct
*readdir(dirp)
DIR *dirp;

long telldir(dirp)
DIR *dirp;

seekdir(dirp, loc)
DIR *dirp;
long loc;
```

```
rewinddir(dirp)
DIR *dirp;

closedir(dirp)
DIR *dirp;


perror, sys_errlist, sys_nerr: System error
messages.

perror(s)
char *s;

int sys_nerr;
char *sys_errlist[];


popen, pclose: Initiates I/O to/from a process.

#include <stdio.h>

FILE *popen(command, type)
char *command, *type;

pclose(stream)
FILE *stream;


psignal, sys_siglist: System signal messages.

psignal(sig, s)
unsigned sig;
char *s;

char *sys_siglist[];


qsort: Quicker sort.

qsort(base, nel, width, compar)
char *base;
int (*compar)();   /* a comparison routine */
```

random, srandom, initstate, setstate: Better random number generator; routines for changing generators.

long **random**()

srandom(seed)
int seed;

char ***initstate**(seed, state, n)
unsigned seed;
char *state;
int n;

char ***setstate**(state)
char *state;

re__comp, re__exec: Regular expression handler.

char ***re__comp**(s)
char *s;

re__exec(s)
char *s;

scandir: Scans a directory.

#include <sys/types.h>
#include <sys/dir.h>

scandir(dirname, namelist, select, compar)
char *dirname;
struct direct *(*namelist[]);
int (*select)();
int (*compar)();   /* a sorting routine */

alphasort(d1, d2)   /* compares d1 and d2 alphabetically */
struct direct **d1, **d2;

setjmp, longjmp: Nonlocal goto.

#include <setjmp.h>

setjmp(env)
jmp__buf env;

longjmp(env, val)
jmp__buf env;

__setjmp(env)
jmp__buf env;

__longjmp(env, val)
jmp__buf env;

setuid, seteuid, setruid, setgid, setegid, setrgid: Sets userid and groupid.

setuid(uid)
seteuid(euid)
setruid(ruid)

setgid(gid)
setegid(egid)
setrgid(rgid)

sleep: Suspends execution for an interval.

sleep(seconds)
unsigned seconds;

strcat, strncat, strcmp, strncmp, strcpy, strncpy, strlen, index, rindex: String operations.

#include <strings.h>

char ***strcat**(s1, s2)
char *s1, *s2;

char ***strncat**(s1, s2, n)
char *s1, *s2;

strcmp(s1, s2)
char *s1, *s2;

strncmp(s1, s2, n)
char *s1, *s2;

char ***strcpy**(s1, s2)
char *s1, *s2;

char ***strncpy**(s1, s2, n)
char *s1, *s2;

strlen(s)
char *s;

char ***index**(s, c)
char *s, c;

char ***rindex**(s, c)
char *s, c;

swab: Swaps bytes.

swab(from, to, nbytes)
char *from, *to;

syslog, openlog, closelog: Controls system log.

#include <syslog.h>

openlog(ident, logstat)
char *ident;

syslog(priority, message, parameters . . .)
char *message;

closelog()

system: Issues a shell command.

system(string)
char *string;

ttyname, isatty, ttyslot: Finds the name of a terminal.

char ***ttyname**(filedes)

isatty(filedes)

ttyslot()

valloc: Aligned memory allocator.

char ***valloc**(size)
unsigned size;

varargs: Variable argument list macros.

#include <varargs.h>

function(**va_alist**)
va_dcl
va_list pvar;
va_start(pvar);

f = **va_arg**(pvar, type);

va_end(pvar);

Appendix 12
Standard I/O Library Routines

fclose, fflush: Closes or flushes a stream.

#include <stdio.h>

fclose(stream)
FILE *stream;

fflush(stream)
FILE *stream;

ferror, feof, clearerr, fileno: Stream status queries.

#include <stdio.h>

feof(stream)
FILE *stream;

ferror(stream)
FILE *stream

clearerr(stream)
FILE *stream

fileno(stream)
FILE *stream;

fopen, freopen, fdopen: Opens a stream.

#include <stdio.h>

FILE ***fopen**(filename, type)
char *filename, *type;

FILE ***freopen**(filename, type, stream)
char *filename, *type;
FILE *stream;

FILE ***fdopen**(fildes, type)
char *type;

fread, fwrite: Buffered binary I/O.

#include <stdio.h>

fread(ptr, sizeof(*ptr), nitems, stream)
FILE *stream;

fwrite(ptr, sizeof(*ptr), nitems, stream)
FILE *stream;

fseek, ftell, rewind: Repositions a stream.

#include <stdio.h>

```
fseek(stream, offset, ptrname)
FILE *stream;
long offset;

long ftell(stream)
FILE *stream;

rewind(stream)
```

getc, getchar, fgetc, getw: Gets character or word from stream.

```
#include <stdio.h>

int getc(stream)
FILE *stream;

int getchar()

int fgetc(stream)
FILE *stream;

int getw(stream)
FILE *stream;
```

gets, fgets: Gets a string from a stream.

```
#include <stdio.h>

char *gets(s)
char *s;

char *fgets(s, n, stream)
char *s;
FILE *stream;
```

printf, fprintf, sprintf: Formatted output conversion.

```
#include <stdio.h>
```

```
printf(format [ , arg ] . . .)
char *format;

fprintf(stream, format [ , arg ] . . .)
FILE *stream;
char *format;

sprintf(s, format [ , arg ] . . .)
char *s, format;

#include <varargs.h>
_doprnt(format, args, stream)
char *format;
va_list *args;
FILE *stream;
```

putc, putchar, fputc, putw: Puts character or word on a stream.

```
#include <stdio.h>

int putc(c, stream)
char c;
FILE *stream;

putchar(c)

fputc(c, stream)
FILE *stream;

putw(w, stream)
FILE *stream;
```

puts, fputs: Puts a string on a stream.

```
#include <stdio.h>

puts(s)
char *s;

fputs(s, stream)
char *s;
FILE *stream;
```

scanf, fscanf, sscanf: Formatted input conversion.

#include <stdio.h>

scanf(format [, pointer] . . .)
char *format;

fscanf(stream, format [, pointer] . . .)
FILE *stream;
char *format;

sscanf(s, format [, pointer] . . .)
char *s, *format;

setbuf, setbuffer, setlinebuf: Assigns buffering to a stream.

#include <stdio.h>

setbuf(stream, buf)
FILE *stream;
char *buf;

setbuffer(stream, buf, size)
FILE *stream;
char *buf;
int size;

setlinebuf(stream)
FILE *stream;

stdio: Standard buffered I/O package.

#include <stdio.h>

FILE *stdin;
FILE *stdout;
FILE *stderr;

ungetc: Pushes character back into the input stream.

#include <stdio.h>
ungetc(c, stream)
FILE *stream;

Appendix 13
Internet Network Library Routines

gethostent, gethostbyaddr, gethostbyname, sethostent, endhostent: Gets network host entry.

#include <netdb.h>

struct hostent ***gethostent**()

struct hostent ***gethostbyname**(name)
char *name;

struct hostent ***gethostbyaddr**(addr, len, type)
char *addr; int len, type;

sethostent(stayopen)
int stayopen

endhostent()

getnetent, getnetbyaddr, getnetbyname, setnetent, endnetent: Gets network entry.

#include <netdb.h>

struct netent ***getnetent**()

struct netent ***getnetbyname**(name)
char *name;

struct netent ***getnetbyaddr**(net)
long net;

setnetent(stayopen)
int stayopen

endnetent()

getprotoent, getprotobynumber, getprotobyname, setprotoent, endprotoent: Gets protocol entry.

#include <netdb.h>

struct protoent ***getprotoent**()

struct protoent ***getprotobyname**(name)
char *name;

struct protoent ***getprotobynumber**(proto)
int proto;

setprotoent(stayopen)
int stayopen

endprotoent()

getservent, getservbyport, getservbyname, setservent, endservent: Gets service entry.

#include <netdb.h>

struct servent ***getservent**()

struct servent ***getservbyname**(name, proto)
char *name, *proto;

struct servent ***getservbyport**(port, proto)
int port; char *proto;

setservent(stayopen)
int stayopen

endservent()

htonl, htons, ntohl, ntohs: Converts values between the host and network byte order.

#include <sys/types.h>
#include <netinet/in.h>

netlong = **htonl**(hostlong);
u__long netlong, hostlong;

netshort = **htons**(hostshort);
u__short netshort, hostshort;

hostlong = **ntohl**(netlong);
u__long hostlong, netlong;

hostshort = **ntohs**(netshort);
u__short hostshort, netshort;

inet__addr, inet__network, inet__ntoa, inet__makeaddr, inet__lnaof, inet__netof: Internet address manipulation routines.

#include <sys/socket.h>
#include <netinet/in.h>
#include <arpa/inet.h>

struct in__addr **inet__addr**(cp)
char *cp;

int **inet__network**(cp)
char *cp;

char ***inet__ntoa**(in)
struct inet__addr in;

struct in__addr **inet__makeaddr**(net, lna)
int net, lna;

int **inet__lnaof**(in)
struct in__addr in;

int **inet__netof**(in)
struct in__addr in;

Appendix 14
vi Quick Reference*

Entering and Exiting vi

vi *file*	Edits *file*.
vi +*n file*	Edits *file,* cursor at line *n*.
vi + *file*	Edits *file,* cursor at end.
vi –r	Lists system saved files.
vi –r *file*	Edits system saved *file*.
vi *file* . . .	Edits first *file*; rest via **:n**.
vi –t *tag*	Edits file through *tag* in tags file.
vi +/*pattern file*	Edits file, cursor at *pattern*.
view *file*	**vi** *file,* no modification.
ZZ	Exits from **vi**, saving changes.
^Z	Stops **vi** for later resumption.

The Display

Last line	Error messages, echoing input to **:**, **/**, **?**, and **!**, feedback about I/O and large changes.
@ lines	On screen only, not in file.
~ lines	Lines past end of file.
^x	Control characters, **^?** is delete.
TABs	Expands to spaces, cursor on last space.

---

*Appendix 14 and Appendix 15 are from the *UNIX Programmer's Manual,* published by the University of California, Berkeley, copyright 1979, 1980 Regents of the University of California.

vi States

Command
: Executes commands; the normal and initial state. Other modes return to command mode. ESC cancels a partial command.

Insert
: Entered by **a**, **i**, **A**, **I**, **o**, **O**, **c**, **C**, **s**, **S**, **R**, followed by arbitrary text terminated by ESC. An interrupt aborts an insertion.

Last line
: Reads user input for commands **:**, **/**, **?**, or **!**, which terminates in ESC or RETURN. An interrupt aborts.

Counts Before vi Commands

Line/column number	**z**, **G**, |
Scroll amount	**^D**, **^U**
Replicate insert	**A**, **i**, **A**, **I**
Repeat effect	Most rest

Simple Commands

dw	Deletes a word.
de	Deletes a word leaving punctuation.
dd	Deletes a line.
3dd	Deletes three lines.
i*text*ESC	Inserts *text*.
cw*text*ESC	Changes word to *text*.
ea*s*ESC	Pluralizes word.
xp	Transposes characters.

Interrupting, Cancelling

ESC	Ends insert, input, or incomplete command.
^?	(DELETE) interrupts **vi**.
^L	Redisplays screen.

File Manipulation

:w	Writes back changes.
:wq	Writes and quits.

:q	Quits.
:q!	Quits, discards changes.
:e *file*	Edits *file*.
:e!	Reedits, discards changes.
:e + *file*	Edits *file,* starting at the end.
:e +*n file*	Edits *file,* starting at line *n*.
:e #	Edits an alternate file.
ˆ↑	Synonym for **:e #**.
:w *file*	Writes to *file*.
:w! *file*	Overwrites *file*.
:sh	Runs default shell, then returns.
:!*cmd*	Runs shell-level *cmd*, then returns.
:n	Edits next file in argument list.
:n *args*	Specifies new argument list.
:f	Displays current file and line.
ˆG	Synonym for **:f**.
:ta *tag*	Goes to tags file entry *tag*.
ˆ]	Same as **:ta**, but current word is *tag*.

Positioning Within File

ˆF	Moves forward a screen.
ˆB	Moves backward a screen.
ˆD	Scrolls down one-half screen.
ˆU	Scrolls up one-half screen.
G	Goto line (end default).
/pattern	Searches forward for *pattern*.
?pattern	Searches backward for *pattern*.
n	Repeats last / or ?.
N	Reverses last / or ?.
/pattern/ +*n*	Goto *n*th line after *pattern*.
?pattern?−*n*	Goto *n*th line before *pattern*.
]]	Next section or function.
[[	Previous section or function.
%	Finds matching (,), {, or }.

Adjusting the Screen

^L	Clears and redisplays
^R	Redisplays, eliminates @ lines.
zRETURN	Current line at window top.
z–	Current line at window bottom.
z.	Current line at window center.
/pattern/z–	Line with *pattern* at bottom.
z*n*	Uses *n*-line window.
^E	Scrolls window down one line.
^Y	Scrolls window up one line.

Marking and Returning

``	Returns to previous context.
''	Returns to previous context at first nonblank character of the line.
m*x*	Marks position with letter *x*.
`*x*	Returns to marked position *x*.
'*x*	Returns to *x* at first nonblank character in line.

Line Positioning

H	Moves to the first window line.
L	Moves to the last window line.
M	Moves to the middle window line.
+	Next line.
–	Previous line.
RETURN	Same as +.
↓ or j	Next line, same column.
↑ or k	Previous line, same column.

Character Positioning

^	First nonblank character.
0	Beginning of line (column one).
$	End of line (last character).

h or ←	Previous character.
l or →	Next character.
ˆ**H**	Same as ←.
SPACE	Same as →.
f*x*	Finds *x* forward in current line.
F*x*	Finds *x* backward in current line.
t*x*	Moves forward to *x* in current line.
T*x*	Moves backward to *x* in current line.
;	Repeats last **f**, **F**, **t**, or **T**.
,	; in the reverse direction.
|	Moves to specified column.
%	Moves to matching (, {,), or }.

Words, Sentences, Paragraphs

w	Next word.
b	Moves backward to the beginning of a word.
e	End of word.
)	Next sentence.
}	Next paragraph.
(	Moves backward to the beginning of a sentence.
{	Moves backward to the beginning of a paragraph.
W	Next blank delimited word.
B	Moves backward to the beginning of a blank delimited word.
E	End of blank delimited word.

Commands for LISP

)	Forward s-expression.
}	Forward s-expression but does not stop at atoms.
(	Backward s-expression.
{	Backward s-expression but does not stop at atoms.

Corrections During Insert

ˆ**H**	Deletes last input character.
ˆ**W**	Deletes last input word.

erase	Character erase, same as ^H.
kill	Line kill, deletes entire input line.
\	Escapes character erase and line kill.
ESC	Ends insertion, returns to command mode.
interrupt	Aborts insert.
^D	Backtabs over blanks supplied by autoindent.
^^D	Kills autoindent; autoindent remains effective for next line.
O^D	Kills autoindent; until next indent.
^V	Quotes any special character.

Insert and Replace

a	Inserts after cursor.
i	Inserts before cursor.
A	Inserts at end of current line.
I	Inserts before first nonblank character of current line.
o	Opens a line for insertion below current line.
O	Opens a line for insertion above current line.
r*x*	Replaces current character with *x*.
R	Overwrites characters.
~	Changes case of current character.

Operators (Double to Affect Lines)

d	Deletes text object.
c	Changes text object.
<	Left-shifts text object.
>	Right-shifts text object.
!	Filters text object through command.
=	Indents s-expression for LISP.
y	Yanks text object to buffer.

Miscellaneous Operations

C	Changes rest of line.
D	Deletes rest of line.

s	Substitutes characters.
S	Substitutes lines.
J	Joins lines.
x	Deletes characters.
X	Deletes characters before cursor.
Y	Yanks lines.

Yank and Put

p or "*x*p	Places deleted or buffer *x* text after current position/line.
P or "*x*P	Places deleted or buffer *x* text before current position/line.
"*x*y	Yanks text object to buffer *x*.
"*x*d	Deletes text object into buffer *x*.

Undo, Redo, and Retrieve

u	Undoes last change.
U	Restores current line.
.	Repeats last change
"*n*P	Retrieves *n*th last delete.

Appendix 15
ex Quick Reference

Entering/Exiting ex

ex *file*	Edits *file,* starts at end.
ex **+***n file*	Edits *file,* at line *n.*
ex **−t** *tag*	Edits through *tag* in tags file.
ex **−r**	Lists saved files.
ex **−r** *file*	Recovers *file.*
ex *file* . . .	Edits first *file*; rest via **:n**.
ex **−R** *file*	Reads *file,* no modifications.
x	Exits, saving changes.
q!	Exits, discarding changes.

ex States

Command	Normal and initial state. Input prompted for by **:**. Your kill character cancels any partial command.
Insert	Entered by **a**, **i**, and **c** followed by arbitrary text terminated by a line with only **.** in it. An interrupt aborts the insertion.
Open/visual	Entered by **open** or **vi**, terminated by **Q** or ⌐\.

ex Commands (in Boldface)

Name	Short	Name	Short	Name	Short
abbreviate	**ab**	**next**	**n**	**unabbreviate**	**una**
append	**a**	**number**	**nu**	**undo**	**u**
args	**ar**	**open**	**o**	**unmap**	**unm**
change	**c**	**preserve**	**pre**	version	ve
copy	**co**	**print**	**p**	visual	vi
delete	**d**	**put**	**pu**	write	w
edit	**e**	**quit**	**q**	xit	x
file	**f**	**read**	**re**	yank	ya
global	**g**	**recover**	**rec**	window	z
insert	**i**	**rewind**	**rew**	shell escape	!
join	**j**	**set**	**se**	left-shift	<
list	**l**	**shell**	**sh**	display next	RETURN
define macro	**map**	**source**	**so**	resubstitute	**&**
mark	**ma**	**stop**	**st**	right-shift	>
move	**m**	**substitute**	**s**	scroll	^D

ex Command Addresses

n	Line *n*	/*pattern*		Next *pattern*	
.	Current line	?*pattern*		Previous *pattern*	
$	*Last line*	*m−n*		*n* before *m*	
+	Next line	*m,n*		*m* through *n*	
−	Previous line	´*x*		Marked by *x*	
+*n*	*n* forward	´´		Previous context	
%	Same as 1,$				

Initializing Options

EXINIT	Shell environment variable with **ex** option settings.
set *x*	Enables option.
set no*x*	Disables option.
set *x* = *val*	Assigns value *val*.

set	Displays changed options.	
set all	Displays all options.	
set *x?*	Displays value of option *x*.	

Useful Options

Name	Short	Meaning
autoindent	ai	Automatically supplies indent.
autowrite	aw	Outputs file before changing files.
ignorecase	ic	Ignores case in searching.
lisp		(,), {, and } are for s-expressions.
list		Displays TAB as ^I and end of line as $.
magic		Enables ., [, * special in patterns.
number	nu	Numbers lines.
paragraphs	para	Paragraph definitions.
redraw		Simulates a smart terminal.
scroll		Number of lines to scroll.
sections	sect	Section definitions.
shiftwidth	sw	For <, >, and ^D while inserting.
showmatch	sm	Indicates matching character as) and } are typed.
slowopen	slow	No updates during an insert.
window		Number of lines for visual mode window.
wrapscan	ws	Enables search around end of buffer.
wrapmargin	wm	Automatic line splitting.

Search Pattern Formation

^	Matches beginning of line.
$	Matches end of line.
.	Matches any character.
\<	Matches beginning of word.
\>	Matches end of word.
[*str*]	Matches any character in *string*.
[^*str*]	Matches any character not in *string*.
[*x–y*]	Matches any character between *x* and *y*.
*c**	Matches a sequence of zero or more *c*.

Bibliography

Babaoglu, O., and W. Joy. "Converting a Swap-Based System to Do Paging in an Architecture Lacking Page-Referenced Bits." *Proceedings of the 8th Symposium on Operating Systems Principles, ACM Operating Systems Review* 15(5) (December 1981): 78–86.

Bourne, S. R. "The UNIX Shell." *The Bell System Technical Journal* 57, no. 6, part 2 (July–August 1978): 1971–90.

Bourne, S. R. *The UNIX System*. Reading, Mass.: Addison-Wesley, 1983.

Comer, D. *Operating System Design: The XINU Approach*. Englewood Cliffs, N.J.: Prentice-Hall, 1984.

Fiedler, D., and B. H. Hunter. *UNIX System Administration*. Hasbrouck Heights, N.J.: Hayden Books, 1986.

Fritz, T. E., J. E. Hefner, and T. M. Raleigh. "A Network of Computers Running the UNIX System." *The AT&T Bell Laboratories Technical Journal* 63, no. 6, part 2 (October 1984): 1877–96.

Grampp, F. T., and R. H. Morris. "UNIX Operating System Security." *The AT&T Bell Laboratories Technical Journal* 63, no. 6, part 2 (October 1984): 1649–72.

Johnson, S. C., and D. M. Ritchie. "Portability of C Programs and the UNIX System." *The Bell System Technical Journal* 57, no. 6, part 2 (July–August 1978): 2021–48.

Kavaler, P., and A. Greenspan. "Extending UNIX to Local Area Networks." *Mini-Micro Systems* (September 1983): 197–202.

Kernighan, B. W., and L. L. Cherry. "Typesetting Mathematics—User's Guide." *User's Supplementary Manual*, 4.3bsd UNIX, University of California at Berkeley.

Kernighan, B. W., and R. Pike. *The UNIX Programming Environment*. Englewood Cliffs, N.J.: Prentice-Hall, 1984.

Kernighan, B. W., and D. M. Ritchie. *The C Programming Language*. Englewood Cliffs, N.J.: Prentice-Hall, 1978.

Leffler, S. J., R. S. Fabry, and N. W. Joy. "A 4.2bsd Interprocess Communication Primer." *Programmer's Supplementary Manual*, 4.3bsd UNIX, University of California at Berkeley.

Lesk, M. E. "Tbl—A Program to Format Tables." *User's Supplementary Manual*, 4.3bsd UNIX, University of California at Berkeley.

McKusick, M. K., W. N. Joy, S. J. Leffler, and R. S. Fabry. "A Fast File System for UNIX." *ACM Transactions on Computer Systems* 2(3) (August 1984): 181–97.

Nowitz, D. A., and M. E. Lesk. "Implementation of a Dial-Up Network of UNIX Systems." *IEEE Proceedings of Fall 1980 COMPCON* (Fall 1980): 483–86.

Organick, E. I. *The Multics System: An Examination of Its Structure*. Cambridge, Mass.: MIT Press, 1972.

Ossanna, J. F. "Nroff/Troff User's Manual." *User's Supplementary Manual*, 4.3bsd UNIX, University of California at Berkeley.

Pike, R., and B. W. Kernighan. "Program Design in the UNIX System Environment." *The AT&T Bell Laboratories Technical Journal* 63, no. 6, part 2 (October 1984): 1595–1606.

Postel, J., ed. "DOD Standard Transmission Control Protocol." *ACM Computer Communication Review* 10, no. 4, (October 1980): 52–132.

Postel, J., C. A. Sunshine, and D. Cohen. "The ARPA Internet Protocol." *Computer Networks* 5, no. 4 (July 1981): 261–71.

Ritchie, D. M. "The Evolution of the UNIX Time-Sharing System." *The AT&T Bell Laboratories Technical Journal* 63, no. 6, part 2 (October 1984): 1577–94.

Ritchie, D. M., and K. Thompson. "The UNIX Time-Sharing System." *The Bell System Technical Journal* 57, no. 6, part 2 (July–August 1978): 1905–30.

Rosler, L. "The Evolution of C—Past and Future." *The AT&T Bell Laboratories Technical Journal* 63, no. 6, part 2 (October 1984): 1685–1700.

Sandberg, R., D. Goldberg, S. Kleiman, D. Walsh, and B. Lyon. "Design and Implementation of the Sun Network File System." *Proceedings of the USENIX Conference* (Summer 1985): 119–31.

Stroustrup, B. *The C++ Programming Language*. Reading, Mass.: Addison-Wesley, 1985.

Thomas, R., L. R. Gogers, and J. L. Yates. *Advanced Programmer's Guide to UNIX SYSTEM V*. Berkeley: Osborne/McGraw-Hill, 1985.

Thompson, K. "UNIX Implementation." *The Bell System Technical Journal* 57, no. 6, part 2 (July–August 1978): 1931–46.

Todino, G., and T. O'Reilly. *Managing UUCP and Usenet*. Newton, Mass.: O'-Reilly and Associates, 1986.

Waite, M., D. Martin, and S. Prata. *UNIX SYSTEM V Primer*. Indianapolis, Ind.: Howard W. Sams, 1985.

Index

$ (dollar sign):
  prompt, 9
  in search patterns, 66–67
  makefile macro prefix, 360
  shell variable prefix, 12
% (per cent):
  in *csh* shell, 144
  prompt, 9
( ) (ellipses), 44
  in commands, 11
  commands enclosed in, 147
. (period) command, 58
.exrc, 73
.login, 51, 57
  csh initialization file, 1
.profile, 12, 51
.tl (title) **troff** request, 397–98
— (dash), 44
  in options, 12
/ (forward search **vi** command),
  66
:g (global) **vi** command, 65
:m (move) **vi** command, 62
:map **vi** command, 70–71
:q! **vi** command, 15, 52
:r (read) **vi** command, 63
:s (substitute) **vi** command, 64–
  66
:set **vi** command, 69–70
:w (write) **vi** command, 63
:w! **vi** command, 52
> (chevron, right) prompt, 9
? (backward search **vi** command),
  66

@ (at sign), 14
  as **vi** deleted line marker, 58
  csh command, 188
  vi macro invocation, 71
[ ] (brackets), 44, 415
  in commands, 11
\ (backslash)
  escape character in **troff**, 378
  quote character in *csh*, 167
  quote character in **vi**, 67
˜ (tilde), 16
  mail command prefix, 91
  tip command prefix, 321
  vi command, 59
ˆ (control character), 10
  in search patterns, 66–67
ˆ@ (set mark) **emacs** command,
  77
ˆC, 34, 37
  interrupt character, 14, 203
  in **vi**, 18
ˆD, 10
  exit command, 90–91
  to logout, 10
  for sending mail, 87–88
ˆG (abort) **emacs** command, 79,
  81
ˆH, 14
ˆK **emacs** command, 78. *See also*
  cut and paste
ˆO (interrupt character), 15
ˆQ (interrupt character), 15
ˆS (interrupt character), 15
ˆU, 14

ˆV quote character in **vi**, 57
ˆW, 14
ˆY **vi** command, 78. *See also* **y**
  (yank) command in **vi**
ˆZ, 36–37, 90, 149, 209
  in Berkeley UNIX, 81
  job suspension, 169

a (append) **vi** command, 56
aborting:
  commands, 8, 14–15
  in **emacs**, 76
  mail, 90–91
access control, 23–25, 45, 222–24
  enforcement, 227
  of files, 2–3, 4, 8, 130
adb debugging program, 42
adjusting lines, 379–80
Advanced Research Projects
  Agency
  Network (ARPANET), 86, 98,
  327
AIX (IBM) operating system, 2, 5
alias:
  in *csh* shell, 201–2, 209
  definition, 163
  substitution, 155–57
  in *sh* shell, 209
American Telephone and
  Telegraph (AT&T), 1–2
application programs, 1
apropos function, 81
archives, 252–53
ar command, 252

processes: (*continued*)
  running states, 282
  termination, 292
process table, 283–84
products and quotients, 411–12
program maintenance, 355–72
programming languages, 42
prompt, 9
  in *sh* and *csh* shells, 209
protection (for files):
  bits, 23–25
  mode, 24, 224
protocols, 327
ps command, 284–86
public-key cryptosystem, 103
put. *See* cut and paste
pwd command, 20

q command in **mail**, 97
quit. *See also* exiting
  from mail, 90, 97–98
quotas, 232–33
quoting:
  in *csh* shell, 167–69
  in search patterns, 67–68

R command in **mail**, 95–96
r command in **mail**, 96
RATFOR, 42
raw socket, 334
rcp command, 42, 329–30
read:
  command, 63
  system call, 270–71
receive mode in **mail**, 92–94
redirection. *See also* shell scripts
  of I/O, 25–27, 45, 147–49,
    211–12
  of output, 3, 134
  region, 77, 78
registers, 400
regular expression, 67–68, 122
rehash command, 146
relational operations, 211
remote login service, 345–49
remote network, 86, 98, 327. *See*
  also local area network
    (LAN)
removable file system, 229–31

removing directories, 274
repeat count for **vi** commands,
  52
requests, 321
RETURN:
  on command line, 11
  in **vi**, 56
Ritchie, Dennis, 4, 5
rlogin command, 42, 328
rm command, 21
rmdir command, 21
rmdir system call, 274
root, 23
  directory, 2
  file system, 229
rsh command, 330

save, 100–101
scratch file, 21
screen:
  positioning, 53
  updating, 313–14
script. *See* redirection
script command, 29
scrolling, 53–54
sdb debugging program, 42
search, 53, 66–68. *See also*
  substitution
  with find, 138–40
search patterns:
  grep, 117–18
  in **sed**, 119
  vi, 66
secret mail, 103
section headings, 389–90
sed, 118–20. *See also* **awk** filter;
    grep commands; stream
    editor
select system call, 315
send mode, 91–92
  process, 333–34
  program, 345–47
set operations, 414
set/unset commands, 100–102
set-userid mode, 227–28
shell, 6, 7, 9, 10–15. *See also csh*
    shell; *sh* shell
  commands, 44–45
  escape, 90

initialization of, 165–66
  scripts, 17, 172–218
    csh shell scripts, 178–87
  variable, 12
  use of, 143–71
shift command, 181
sh shell, 10, 44, 144, 208–16. *See*
    also Bourne shell; .profile
  versus *csh* shell, 208–10
  in I/O redirection, 26
  TERM, 51
  writing procedures, 212–13
shutdown system call, 343
signals, 295–300
  trapping, 297
signal system call, 297
single-colon dependence lines,
  361
sockets, 320, 334–37
  addresses, 336–39
  creation of, 335
  sending and receiving data,
    339–40
  shutting down, 343
sort command, 110–13
source code, 5, 27
spacing, 417
special characters, 167–69
  in search patterns, 66–67
  special files, 220–21
  creation of, 233
spell command, 42, 375
split windows in **emacs**, 79–80
standard error output, 25
standard input, 25
standard input/output, 147
standard output, 25
status:
  of files, 224–25
  line of **vi**, 52, 53
stream editor, 118–20. *See also*
    grep commands; **sed**
stream socket, 334
string:
  options, 68–69
  register, 383
  variable, 323
subject field, 87
subscripts and superscripts, 411